3 1510 00023 9229

D1161869

"We're going in," the blond young officer at the left seat controls of the C-47 advised his co-pilot on the intercom. The co-pilot gulped, flicked the button on his microphone, and repeated the order to the three battered twin-engine transports following behind in the darkness of the night. Below, a T formation of bonfires flickered, splashing the darkness with light from the line of flames.

. . . the bonfires mark the landing zone for another hazardous midnight rendezvous . . . a rendezvous with partisan fighters, far behind the enemy lines . . . The OSS is at work again.

This book details the formation of the OSS—forerunner of the CIA—from its beginnings, when it was described by Radio Berlin as "fifty professors, twenty monkeys, ten goats, twelve guinea pigs and a staff of Jewish scribblers," through its development into an organization which made decisive contributions to the Allied victory.

ALSO BY EDWARD HYMOFF

REVISED & UPDATED

The OSS In World War II

Edward Hymoff

RICHARDSON & STEIRMAN
NEW YORK
1986

DEDICATION

For Mother, Pauline and Aunt Ida . . .
who recall those anxious days, months and
years on the home front—waiting.

Contents

Preface

In July 1971 my old friend, fellow author, and sometime collaborator, Martin Caidin, suggested that I contact George Young, the editor in chief of Ballantine Books, about a history of the OSS. "You were associated with OSS, and you've done some magazine pieces about the organization," said Marty. "I'll tell George that you will ring him."

I did, and my fourteen-chapter outline has expanded into this book, double the size of what I had expected to produce.

I began the research for this book in London in September 1971, and I wish to thank Mrs. Meryl Eady, Librarian of the International Institute of Strategic Studies (of which I am a member), for canvassing various libraries, including the War Office Library, for much background data. And my thanks, too, to my good friend, Rep. Robert H. Steele of Connecticut, and his Assistant, Steve Berg, for aid at the Library of Congress. I never knew that so much had been written about OSS, although the greater part of this material is of little consequence. Of course, there's thanks to Ballantine Books production editor, David Frederickson, who accepted my manuscript two and three chapters at a time and spent the short summer nights reading about an episode in American history of which was before his time.

Thanks, too, must go to all those former members of OSS who agreed to recent interviews and to those interviewed in the past who were unaware, as I was at the time, that their recollections of past experiences would later become part of a book.

Finally, my thanks to my typist, Sara Wiederschall, who managed to type some 500 pages while working full-time and caring for her young family. Therefore, I must also offer commendation to the Wiederschalls, who allowed their wife and mother to type late at home a few nights, and to her employers, Bixler-Eaton Associates, Inc., of Bedford Village, New York, who permitted some typing on their premises—and who in the process also became World War II history buffs, even though it all had occurred before their time.

Yonkers, N.Y.
August 15, 1972

Prologue

It was late April 1944, a warm spring day in Brindisi, an Adriatic port city on the heel of the Italian boot. I had completed loading a C–47 with "packages"—supplies for Marshal Tito's partisans in Yugoslavia. In fact, the loading had been done by partisans from the large camp the Yugoslavs maintained on the outskirts of Brindisi near the airbase. The airbase operated by the Fifteenth Air Force Special Group was strictly an Off Limits area, for it was from this base that all secret air missions and spy missions were flown to the Balkans, northern Italy, and Central European points beyond, including Poland.

I had been put in charge of packaging weapons, ammunition, and demolitions and this was my second week on the job. The airmen were an easy bunch to get along with, as Air Force people I've since met in other wartime situations have been. When they knew they were carrying explosives along with weapons and ammo, they'd invariably ask the same question in the same way: "You're sure this stuff won't go up? Dammit, if it does . . ."

"Don't worry, you won't even hear the bang," I quipped in reply.

The sun was hot on the airstrip when we had finished loading, and the crew was making last-minute checks of the aircraft when the pilot dropped out of the back cargo hatch to relieve himself in the grass some feet away before he took off. As he walked back to the aircraft buttoning his coveralls, he stopped beside me to inhale the last of a cigarette.

"Are you with this OSS outfit?" he asked me. I replied that I was, in a way, and that I was on detached service from the Engineer Depot in Bari which, along with being the largest

1

Italian port city on the Adriatic, was also headquarters for Fifteenth Air Force and the OSS element in Brindisi.

"Ever fly one of these supply missions?" he asked. I shook my head. "Want to come along? This should be a milk run." My credo then, as it is today, is that I'll go anywhere, anytime.

He asked me if I had to get permission from anybody to make the flight. "Negative," I replied. For more than a year—ever since I was drafted in early 1943 like everybody else a few months after they had turned 18—I had had to obtain permission from superiors. As in any military organization, you don't make a move unless somebody with more stripes or bars or oak leaves of gold or silver, or even the eagles of a colonel, gives his permission to eat, to sleep, to work—and on occasion, even to seek relief in a latrine. Only this time I didn't have to ask anybody for permission. In fact, I had no immediate superior in Brindisi. I had received a special assignment to OSS to collect, coordinate, and supervise delivery of supplies, and the only time questions would be raised was if the equipment or weapons or demolitions didn't arrive on time to be sent off to destinations behind enemy lines.

And I was just a lowly Private First Class, about the last person who would carry any clout in an organization chock full of stripes and brass like OSS. Which was one of the things I liked about OSS. It was so *un-military*.

The C–47 pilot finished his cigarette and dropped the smoking butt on the grass, heeling it into the ground. "Let's go," he said; ten minutes later we were airborne and over the Adriatic. Destination: an airstrip somewhere in Yugoslavia. It was a daylight flight and the airstrip—carved from the terrain, or so it appeared from above—soon was visible through the cockpit window from my vantage point standing behind the pilot and co-pilot. Minutes later we were on the ground, after a bumpy landing and an even more rattling taxi to the side of the strip.

The rear cargo hatch was opened, and men in heavy woolen British-cut uniforms climbed aboard. Cargo belts were quickly loosened by experienced hands and the packages were swiftly removed by the brawny men—all speaking the strange language which I was slowly getting accustomed to hearing and haltingly learning to speak while working with the Yugoslav partisans at Brindisi. I took in this strange tableau behind enemy lines. There were a few British soldiers among the people clustered around the tent which served as the airstrip operations center. Among the four or five jeeps parked alongside the tent were three men clad in U.S. Army paratrooper uniforms. They displayed neither rank nor insignia, only a small American flag sewn on the right shoulder and a black strip with faded yellow letters on the left shoulder reading U.S. CONTINGENT. Two of the Americans climbed out of the jeep and pulled out backpacks and Sten guns, waved good-bye to the man at the wheel, and slowly walked toward me.

"You with this plane?" one of them asked. I nodded. "Bari or Brindisi?" the second American inquired. I told him that we were out of Brindisi and that I was just along for the ride. I asked them if they were from SO or OG—terms I had learned during the past two weeks—and one of them, his voice laced with suspicion, shot back: "Say, what outfit are you with?"

"Yours," I replied, adding, "SBS [Strategic Balkan Services] in Bari. Colonel Huntington's group."

"You must be new," one of them nodded; the ice was broken. No more suspicion, no longer on their guard, even though they were not yet safely back in Italy. They said they had parachuted into Yugoslavia nearly eight weeks before, had joined some partisans, blown up some bridges, ambushed a few convoys, and, mission completed, they were returning to headquarters in Bari to make their reports. "Look us up if you get up that way," they added.

My first contact with OSS had occurred the previous summer at Camp Claiborne, Louisiana. I was young, eager, and full of piss and vinegar; I was in the Corps of Engineers assigned to a Depot Company and was attending a Demolitions School to learn all about explosives and how to handle them—and use them destructively. One day the commanding officer of the school summoned Pvt. Edward Hymoff, ASN 31299460, to his office and introduced me to a major who was thin and as nervous as I was. I didn't know it at the time, but he was probably nervous because he was trying to meet his quota of recruits for OSS and if he didn't, well, perhaps he'd be fired. Of course, I had never heard of OSS in June 1943, so I stood there at attention and wondered why the CO of the Demolitions Section of the Combat Engineers School had summoned me. I had a reputation for infractions against established order—hijinks, more than serious delinquency—and I wondered what I had done to warrant a summons to the major's inner sanctum. Men wearing four or more stripes on their arms or any kind of officer's insignia were to be feared, scorned, or respected, depending upon the attitude of the individual soldier of lower rank. My attitude toward the military even then could be measured as something between scorn and respect for the majority of my superiors; for I had quickly learned after entering the service that not only *is* there a better way to do things, including the ones I was ordered to do, but that there always *was* a better way and why didn't these clowns who gave the orders know it? So much for the arrogance and irreverence of youth.

Only this time I was pleasantly surprised as I stood at attention (the CO forgot to order me to stand at ease) and listened to the major extol my attributes as a student who learned quickly and well—the best demolitions man that the school had come across in a long time and a natural for this kind of work. Furthermore, I had scored high on what passed for an IQ test, was in excellent physical shape (at that point in time), and I had even applied for Officer Candidate School. The OCS Interview Board, meeting four weeks later, had selected me as one of the applicants to be interviewed and considered. The nervous visitor's boredom began to show at the overlong build-up I was receiving—and I was privately wondering: Was the CO trying to get rid of me? All that I heard were attributes, and accolades, minus virtues; even then it appeared obvious that my CO was trying to con his visitor.

"Well, Major," my CO said when he was finished, "I'll leave you two alone." He got up from behind his desk and walked out of the office, deliberately closing the door behind him. And I still remained at attention. Well, almost but not quite. The visiting officer quickly got to his feet, bumped himself as he skirted around the desk and sat down in the CO's chair. Then he motioned me to sit down, dug into his briefcase, and pulled out a folder marked with a red tab. Squinting hard, I could make out my name inscribed on it; peeking out from within his briefcase on the desk were other folders, some with red tabs and others with green and yellow tabs.

He still hadn't said anything. He opened the folder, quickly scanned some papers, and then looked up at me. "Why do you want to volunteer for dangerous and hazardous duty?" he suddenly asked, without even introducing himself or saying where he was from. I thought he was an advance scout from the OCS Interview Board! I had seen a notice on the bulletin board that offered assignments to GIs who were fluent in languages, had university degrees, had traveled, and had majored in history, government, or political science. (I hadn't even graduated high school, quitting because it was a bore, what with the war on and the commonplace disrupted by wartime.) Buried in the heavy military jargon of the memorandum was something about an assignment that *might* expose the candidate to "dangerous and hazardous duty."

Never slow to respond, I replied that I'd go anywhere to get out of Camp Claiborne and its mud and heat and rain and damned mosquitos. I didn't tell him that the newly formed Engineer Depot Company (to which I had been assigned after basic training earlier in the year in the more comfortable—for me anyway—snow and subzero temperatures at Fort Snelling, Minnesota) was a collection of cast-offs, including the officers. Originally, the adjutant had assigned me to a clerical school so that I could become a clerk-typist; but I wasn't in the Army to be a clerk-typist. My schoolboy friends were in the Navy, or they were training in the Army Air Force as navigators, bombardiers, and gunners (with basic training in Miami Beach hotels while I cavorted in the Minnesota winter wonderland).

The interviewer allowed as how I didn't come up to the requirements of a college degree and language fluency ("But I was damned good in high school French") or political science and travel background ("Sir, I read a lot, and history and geography have made me aware of what the world is really like"). "On the other hand," he thought aloud, "you do have a high AGCT, and OCS is considering you and . . .

hmmm . . . you're also very good at demolitions." The questions that followed concerned my family background and where my parents were born, and whether I had any outdoorsmanship. I told him that I had been very active in the Boy Scouts and scouting, had been an Explorer Scout right up to induction, and was a few merit badges short of Eagle Scout (I'd lost interest in *that* kind of bird-watching after my teen-age genes switched my interest to more shapely birds).

Finally, he asked me one more time if I was in any way concerned about "dangerous and hazardous duty," if I were to receive a new assignment based on this interview. I emphasized again that there was a war on and I would like to see some action (if I didn't, how could I explain to my father, a World War I veteran who served with Eddie Rickenbacker and Billy Mitchell in the Army Air Corps on the Western Front, that I was stuck in a rear-echelon outfit and never heard a shot fired in anger?). Such was the arrogance of youth.

"Sir," I finally asked the interviewing officer, "what's all this for?"

He shook his head, closing the red-tab folder marked "Hymoff, E. ASN 31299460 CE [Corps of Engineers] Demolitions." I asked him what kind of a unit he came from. "Classified!" he replied abruptly. Where was he from? "Washington," he answered, rising to his feet and indicating that the interview was over. I never learned his name and I never saw him again, but I did find out that I was the only person interviewed at the Demolitions School. Whether or not he had interviewed others at Camp Claiborne, I know not—although Mel Richter, a neighborhood friend from Boston, who had been drafted the same day and had gone through basic training with me, later parachuted into China with OSS. He was a Harvard graduate, and despite extremely thick lenses, he had made the grade with OSS.

Letters from my parents shortly after the interview with the mysterious major advised me that the FBI had been around asking questions of neighbors—about my character, whether I ever got into any trouble (they might have been told by some of the people on Wilcock Street that at times I was considered the next thing to a wild juvenile delinquent *circa* 1939), and whether I could be trusted with money or secret information (neither I nor the FBI had any inkling that I'd later wind up as an inquisitive journalist). But for months there was still no word from the man from Washington.

Meantime, the Army launched maneuvers in the Camp Claiborne area, and, having completed Demolitions School, I returned to my Engineer Depot Company, which had been preparing for the military exercises. These maneuvers would include moving through a gassed area of forest. It was supposed to make the war games realistic, although neither the Allies nor the Axis had used gas up to that point (June 1943) and never did throughout the war. Every man in the company had been issued a gas mask and, during my absence at Demolitions School, each person had been through a test chamber to check out his mask and have it adjusted. All except me. I returned in time for the maneuvers, found myself with full pack, rifle, and gas mask strapped to my head, charging through a wooded area that had been gassed by whatever combination of chemicals the Chemical Warfare Corps had mixed in with the smoke.

Whatever it was, it got to me through what turned out to be a defective gas mask. Choking and coughing and gagging, I pulled my helmet off my head, and fumbling, ripped off my gas mask. Then I ran back the way I had come still carrying my M-1. The excuses and explanations and investigation that followed bore out my contention that I had a defective gas mask to begin with, and the matter was quickly forgotten. Meantime, Army CIC (Counterintelligence) agents had been at work secretly asking questions about Pvt. E. Hymoff, who couldn't help but learn that CIC had been secretly engaged in ferreting out the many personal secrets of his nineteen and a half years.

In September 1943 my Engineer Depot Company had been transferred to Marion, Ohio, smack in the middle of the hay-fever and asthma season. I ended up in an Army hospital in Columbus, Ohio, with a bad case of asthma in lungs seared by a touch of mustard gas during maneuvers the previous June. This hospitalization almost got me a medical discharge, which I turned down because the Army had offered to send me to college under the ASTP (Army Scholastic Training Program). I preferred and requested pre-med schooling and then medical school under this accelerated program. Unfortunately, I was selected instead for the engineering program—which would give me an assignment to either Massachusetts Institute of Technology or Northeastern University, both at home. Stubbornly, I demanded the medical course; equally adamant, the Army told me to take the engineering course or leave it. A year later, virtually the entire ASTP engineering program closed down, and students ended up in the infantry as replacements for casualties suffered in the invasions of Normandy and southern France and during the Battle of the Bulge in December 1944.

Still bothered by my Camp Claiborne injury, I was assigned to the newly opened Newton D. Baker Army Hospital at Martinsburg, West Virginia, and shortly thereafter—still a private—I received a visitor from Washington.

This one identified himself; he was from OSS and asked me if I was still interested in that possibly "dangerous and hazardous duty" assignment. If so, I could visit his organization's Personnel Section in Washington as I was only an hour away by train. And I did, but we agreed that I had better put off any transfer to an OSS S&T (Schools and Training) detachment until the doctors gave me a clean bill of health. I never did officially join OSS in the United States, nor undertake special training. In retrospect, it appears, if they were considering a nineteen-year-old for possible training and duty in mid-1943, that OSS must have had serious recruiting problems and was forced to scrape the bottom of the barrel. Or was the mysterious major at Camp Claiborne faced with meeting his quota or being fired from his traveling and expense-account assignment? Was this how I happened to slip into the OSS recruit file?

In February 1944 I received overseas orders. I rushed to OSS headquarters in Washington and touched base with Personnel Section, explained that I had orders to I knew not where as a Corps of Engineers replacement, and would rather join an organization which appeared to be involved in interesting work, the details of which I was still unaware. A young lieutenant, handling me like the private soldier that I was, passed me on to a grandmotherly type who patiently heard me out before escorting me to a grandfatherly type who listened to my request before introducing me to a major.

The upshot of it was that the OSS Personnel Division had lost my red-tabbed folder marked "Hymoff, E. ASN 31299460 CE Demolitions." In fact, they didn't have any record of me that anybody could lay his hands on, and the major politely said there was nothing he could do and don't call us, we'll call you. If only I had known the likes of General "Wild Bill" Donovan way back then.

By the time I arrived in Italy, via some weeks in North Africa which included hiking across the Atlas Mountains and other assorted adventures, and another ocean voyage from Casablanca to Bari that included an enemy air attack on our convoy, I had all but forgotten about OSS. Shortly after I arrived in Bari and was assigned to a Corps of Engineers unit, another summons came for Pvt. E. Hymoff to appear before his CO—and I had not been with this unit long enough to get into trouble. There was another officer present. He was from the Strategic Balkan Services and they were in temporary need of somebody who knew how to handle explosives and demolition accessories—fuses, timers, caps, primacord, and other items required to detonate everything from dynamite to half-pound blocks of TNT and the new gelatin explosive now known as "plastic."

"Sir, why have I been selected?" I asked my CO, not knowing exactly what I might be in for. I was wary about anybody else "volunteering" my services, and every GI learns right away that usually it's unwise to volunteer. Privates don't question lieutenant colonels who direct large logistics operations. He announced that he had more experienced people, among them three master sergeants, who really know what the supply business is all about and had been handling demolitions for years.

"But Hymoff," he directed his comments at me and his visitor from SBS, "the major's operation also requires somebody with a security clearance; and you're the only person out of 467 here—including myself—who has a SECRET clearance. It would take about eight weeks to get a security clearance for one of our more *experienced* people." Again he underscored the word *experience*—for both my benefit and the major's, in the event I came a cropper and SBS tried to lay the blame on the Engineer Depot commander. It was one of my earliest experiences with the "cover my ass" procedure.

It also was my first indication that I had received a security clearance. At least the Army had not lost this record as OSS headquarters in Washington had misplaced my folder. The major told my CO that he'd arrange for orders temporarily transferring me to SBS, and as I walked him to his jeep I was full of questions. What is SBS and what does it do? I'd be briefed in a day or two. Exactly what am I supposed to do? Again, in a day or two. And then I had a bright thought and in my best inside-information whisper, I asked softly from the side of my mouth, "Sir, you wouldn't by chance be with OSS?" That got a response!

How did I know about OSS? It's a Top Secret organization! Somebody from his headquarters was talking too much and word was getting around town. "Who do you know from our organization?" he asked me indignantly. "I'll nail his hide for discussing our unit."

I told him that it was just a surmise on my part, since I had probably received my security clearance while undergoing investigation for possible assignment to OSS. And then I explained how I had first heard about OSS and the final indignity of the Personnel Division losing my red-tabbed folder. With this explanation, I was welcomed by the major like a long-lost relative who had suddenly appeared on the scene from the old country.

I never again met the major who was the G–1 of 2677th Regiment (Provisional) OSS. However, several days later I met Colonel Ellery C. Huntington, Jr.,* for whom I went to work coordinating supplies for his American Military Mission (AMM) to Marshal Tito. It was a high-pressure assignment and a very high-priority supply classification, which meant that anybody representing OSS who appeared at any supply point would receive immediate service and woe unto the officer or sergeant or GI who questioned this OSS authority and priority. (It was known as the "mysterious SBS"

---

*Just before going into his office a sergeant at 2677 HQ informed me that Huntington was a football star and All-American from Colgate in his day. As I later learned, gridiron greats and college football players in general were given first crack at OSS. Many was the time that somebody would be pointed out to me with the explanation that he had played football for one college or another.

to U.S. military forces in the Bari area, whose personnel were unaware of the very existence of OSS as a Top Secret intelligence organization.)

My meeting with the colonel was brief. "I hope you know something about explosives?" he began our conversation, after we were introduced. "The last 'expert' we had is gone. Accident. I don't think he knew much about TNT."

I assured him that I did, that I'd be careful. Actually, Colonel Huntington's question about my knowledge of explosives turned out later to be connected with several bad shipments from the United States. Under certain climatic and temperature conditions, explosives are very unstable. A bad shipment could be worthless and dangerous or both, and there were several instances when OG and SO teams in the field were unable to carry out their missions because explosives failed to detonate or did so prematurely. The casualties were serious.

Once on official detached service from the Engineer Depot, I was sent to Brindisi. There I was assigned my own jeep to facilitate commuting between OSS Bari and OSS Brindisi and other military establishments in between, and armed with my priority orders (or letters of credit, if you will) I began to meet the demands of OSS in the field.

My first flight to Yugoslavia was followed by others, and to Greece, too. I heard shots fired in anger (something I couldn't write home about because OSS was classified) and I later learned several packages mailed to me by relatives and friends had been returned stamped "Missing in Action." Somebody had erred, and the anguish it caused at home ran deep for some weeks. That was the result of a three-day trip—since my status was detached, I hadn't reported my trip to anyone— to the island of Vis, a midpoint in the Adriatic used as a jumping-off point for Maritime Unit (MU) penetrations of the long and heavily indented Yugoslav, Albanian, and Greek coastlines.

I also visited several of my boyhood friends in the AAF to discover that we boys had fast become men. I had to turn down Eddie Dunn's offer to fly on a mission with his B–24 Liberator crew; he was a ball-turret gunner.

On an earlier visit to Ed Wolfe, a B–17 Flying Fort radar

officer or navigator—or was it Morris Rosenbloom, a B–24 co-pilot?—I had flown a hairy mission and watched with awe, and no little concern, the carpet of black smoke, and felt the flak concussion that rocked the aircraft. The preflight briefing included a short statement that in the event we were forced to bail out the chances were that we would run into American "intelligence people" in Northern Italy and Yugoslavia. Of course, the A–2 officer commenting on escape and evasion (E&E) attempted to set our minds at ease by relating how, just the day before, a crew had bailed out over Yugoslavia, was picked up within hours, and late that night the airmen were back at their base and preparing to fly another mission the following day. I knew that, with the exception of the morale-building item about repatriation the same day, the story was true, and that OSS and Air Crew Rescue Unit (ACRU) teams working with them had rescued hundreds of airmen who had been shot down and bailed out. I couldn't tell my old friends at that time exactly what I was doing; they would introduce me to their crewmates as a guy with a soft desk job in Bari.

Upon my return to Brindisi I had mentioned the bombing mission; I was ordered not to fly any others. I was privy to too much secret information to risk capture, although it was okay to fly a special-operations delivery mission. The reasoning: In the company of OSS and the partisans, even behind enemy lines, there was less chance of capture than in parachuting from a disabled bomber—possibly into enemy hands.

On another occasion visiting one of my boyhood pals, the brakes of my jeep failed and I skidded into a parked staff car in front of a bomb-wing headquarters. I looked about nervously before backing away and retreating, when an MP came bounding down the steps of the school which was the wing headquarters. A large window was shoved open and a voice of authority and doom bellowed to the MP to "arrest that man!" He did. The voice from the third floor ordered the MP to escort me upstairs, and he did—at gunpoint. I was ushered into the office of Brigadier General Davenport Johnson, who blistered my ass, calling me a reckless driver. Didn't I know that staff cars were hard to come by and difficult to repair?

"Soldier, what's your name and where are you from?" he

demanded from behind his desk, pencil in hand, as I stood at attention wondering how I was going to explain this in Bari or Brindisi. Do I tell a general officer what organization I'm attached to or the one I'm detached from? My thoughts were of MP reports catching up with my personal 201 file records and, although I wasn't worried about any reaction from OSS headquarters, the information and paper work wouldn't sit too well with the Engineer Depot's CO, to whom I was still linked by virtue of my detached status. And until I could burn that bridge . . .

"Well, soldier . . ." the general prodded ominously. I announced my rank (now a less lowly PFC) and name—and I was wondering if I should carry on like a prisoner of war and give him my serial number, too, because at that very moment I felt that I was a captive in enemy territory.

"Hymoff . . . Hymoff," the general repeated. "Say, are you related to Gus Hymoff of Boston?"

"Yes, sir," I replied still at attention. "My dad." Quickly, the general's tone changed from angry (put on) to warm and friendly. He told me how he and my father had served together in the Ninety-fifth Pursuit Squadron in World War I and had seen each other about twice over the years; and I ended up having dinner with the general and staying the night in his quarters as his personal guest.

Thanks to the general, I later managed to obtain a transfer to Fifteenth Air Force when OSS headquarters in Bari curtailed operations in Greece and Yugoslavia at the end of 1944. My stint with OSS had ended, along with a few adventures, but as the years passed I seemed to follow in the wake of the OSS or, in my many subsequent foreign travels, to cross the paths of OSS alumni.

In the summer of 1951 I was working on the city desk of the New York *World-Telegram & Sun* when a story broke on the wire about an OSS officer who was killed because he refused to arm Communist partisans in northern Italy and for the huge amount of gold he carried, rumored at upwards of $150,000. I turned to my boss, growling Bert McDonald—a grizzled city editor right out of the movie *Front Page*—and said that inasmuch as I had been associated with OSS during the war I might be able to get some more information.

"Who do you know?" he asked.

"Well, there's General Donovan, who headed OSS," I continued. "I don't know him personally. In fact, I never even met him, but if I can get through and introduce myself as one of his former guys—sort of—maybe he'll open up and we might be able to score."

The city editor told me to go ahead. I didn't even know where General Donovan could be found in New York City, but a newspaper morgue, or library, is a great source of information. There were a number of thick envelopes with clips about General Donovan going back a number of years and, of course, in the most recent clips the mention of his law firm. I rang up his law office. It brought back memories of the OSS Personnel Division in Washington, especially all those people to whom I had to repeat the same story. I spoke to five people at least, and they all volunteered the information that they, too, had served with OSS. But they didn't put me through to the General. As lawyers and masters at the art of saying nothing while speaking volumes, they couldn't be pinned down as to whether or not General Donovan was at hand, on a business trip, or on vacation.

Apparently, Donovan and Company couldn't afford to ignore the story that was fast building up about the murder of Major William V. Holohan, who headed the "Mangosteen" Mission to northern Italy. Specifically, Holohan mysteriously disappeared almost two and a half months after he had parachuted near Lake Como with his group, composed of Lieutenants Victor Giannino and Aldo Icardi and Sergeants (T/Sgt) Arthur Ciarmicola and (S/Sgt) Carl LoDolce. They parachuted in on September 26, 1944, and Major Holohan disappeared on December 6. Lieutenant Giannino and Sgt. Ciarmicola were away at the time, which left Holohan, Icardi, and LoDolce, the Mangosteen radio operator, and two Italian partisans working for the OSS team in the area when it came under attack on the night of December 6. The group broke and scattered. Holohan disappeared completely until June 1950, when a body, said to be his, was recovered from Lake Orta—which was in the Mangosteen Mission's AO.

Two former Italian partisans were said to have confessed, about two months prior to the recovery of the body from the lake, to being implicated in the murder of Major Holohan.[1]

They also had accused Icardi and LoDolce of masterminding the murder of the missing OSS major. The story broke in mid-August 1951 in the September issue of *True* Magazine. The Pentagon immediately issued a lengthy press release supporting the charges made by the two former Italian partisans, although in 1947 Army investigators had contacted Icardi and, as he later wrote, he received a clean bill after submitting to a series of lie-detector tests. LoDolce also had been contacted by the CID (Army Corps of Military Police Criminal Investigation Division) during this same period. Later, under pressure from interrogation from the Army, he broke down and confessed to killing Holohan. However, his experience with OSS behind enemy lines had caused a nervous breakdown that later required a hair-raising escape from Italy which didn't add to his delicate emotional and nervous condition. At the time he confessed under hard questioning, he also had suffered the loss of a younger brother who was killed in action two weeks earlier in Korea.[2]

Of course, newspaper reporters covering the story had been unaware of these developments, and, as the story and its element of cloak-and-dagger murder mystery continued to unravel, the press was scurrying around in an effort to pick up any small item that would make a new headline. On the night of August 15, a Wednesday, General Donovan held a meeting with a group of reporters, and I attended as one of the two from my paper. I was full of questions, and one of them revolved around the $100,000 in gold that Holohan reportedly was carrying on his person or had in his possession.

"Sir, isn't that a lot of weight in gold for one man to be carrying?" I asked. He agreed. He also admitted that he knew Holohan personally and had personally selected him for the mission, although the OSS officer couldn't speak Italian and knew little French. At the time the story appeared in print, to me it appeared full of holes, and the florid-faced, grey-haired man who faced the press, speaking very low, was disappointingly vague. He was actually unacquainted with details; he had been directing a loose and unusual wartime organization that at times resembled a fumbling bureaucracy. The General allowed as how toward the end of the war OSS heard that Holohan was dead, and "later came rumors that he had been murdered."

"I ordered an investigation," added General Donovan, "but we (OSS) were going out of business, and we had no chance to press it. I didn't know then and I don't know now whether he was murdered by his own people or by some of the partisans."[3]

After the interrogation I brushed past two of his young law-firm aides who were fending off additional questions from reporters, trying to grab an additional moment and an exclusive additional quote. I introduced myself to the legendary head of OSS and explained that I had worked with 2677 Regiment in Bari on detached service.

"Oh," he said and smiled. "Welcome. Always glad to meet one of our OSS veterans. Where did you say you served?" He had other things on his mind, obviously. And by the time the following Monday had come around the story had all but disappeared from the newspapers. Nor did I ever score that exclusive I had hoped to get from the director of the OSS; I never met him again. But then, this was only one of many minor stories that I covered over the years.

As a correspondent in Korea in late 1952 I managed to land surreptitiously on an offshore island in a boat hired from a fisherman and, to the surprise and consternation of a number of Americans—military and otherwise—I uncovered a small segment of the secret operations of United Nations Partisan Forces Korea. It was an OSS-type operation and, I thought to myself, one would think that these people involved with UNPFK had learned something from the OSS experience of World War II. But it was not to be and, as I learned subsequently, there had been less than ten OSS people assigned to this behind-the-lines operation during the Korean conflict.

In Hanoi in early 1954, I met with a group of Viet Minh officials and was asked why the United States had turned away from these nationalists and their cause. They mentioned the OSS people they had met during the closing days of World War II and how American medical care and medicines provided by OSS had saved Ho Chi Minh's life. Driving from

Hanoi beyond French checkpoints was not dangerous for American journalists in early 1954. I had obtained some small American flags in Hong Kong on my way to Indochina, and displaying the Stars and Stripes on my rented vehicle was the best password for driving safely past Viet Minh roadblocks. They'd even warn of danger ahead. As disclosed in the Pentagon papers seventeen years later, a CIA team composed of former OSS men arrived in Indochina later that year bent on fighting a war in the shadows in support of what to some, including myself way back then, was a questionable American foreign policy in Southeast Asia.

And there were the Algerians and Corsicans I met during the rebellion in Algeria in 1956, some of whom had served with OSS. In Cyprus and Greece the following year there were veterans of the *Andarte* who remembered their Greek-American OSS, SO, OG, and SI friends. Later there was a collaborative writing effort with "Mac"—Brigadier General Monro MacCloskey, USAF (Ret.). And in Vietnam in 1968, while I was writing a history of the Fourth Infantry Division commanded by Major General William R. Peers, the former commander of OSS Detachment 101 in Burma, he occasionally reminisced about that era and compared it to Vietnam. Later we exchanged autographed books; his was *Behind the Burma Road,* co-authored in 1963 with Dean Brelis, who in 1968 covered the Vietnam conflict for NBC News.

If I have told more humorous anecdotes than specific personal behind-the-lines adventures in this Prologue, it is only because memories and names and places do fade after more than a quarter of a century, and my own exciting experiences with OSS were repetitious to the point of boredom, especially for one who has added thousands of additional names and places to an equally adventurous itinerary across this span of years.

Nor have I tried to analyze to any great extent the successes or failures of OSS during World War II. This is meant to be a popular history of America's first intelligence service and nothing more. Perhaps one day the real story of OSS will be told in detail, including all of its successes, mishaps, errors, and other assorted misdeeds, and the adventures of civilians in and out of uniform who were rank amateurs in a delicate business. Suffice it to say that the Office of Strategic Services was a happening during World War II that will not soon be forgotten.

1

And the Lord spake unto Moses saying,
Send thou men, that they may search the land
of Canaan. . . .
And Moses sent them to spy out the land of
Canaan, and said unto them, . . . Go up into
the mountain:
And see the land, what it is; and the people
that dwelleth therein, whether they be strong
or weak, few or many;
And what the land is that they dwell in,
whether it be good or bad; and what cities
they be that they dwell in, whether in tents or
in strongholds.

—Numbers, xiii

MYSTERY MAN SIGNS U.S. YOUTHS AS WAR FLIERS

The tall, hawk-faced man glanced at the newspaper headline and chuckled. "So now I'm a 'mystery man,'" he chortled, handing the New York *Journal-American* back to his visitor seated in the parlor of a plush suite in Manhattan's Sherry-Netherlands Hotel.

"Yes," the visitor replied, grinning somewhat impishly, "and from what this story says, you've also got the FBI on your tail."

"Then I'm going to need a lawyer, Bill. You're hired!"

The two men laughed together at their attempt at wry humor. Actually, what they had been discussing was no laughing matter in late February 1940. Once again Europe was engulfed in war, and the armies of traditional enemies were marching side by side as allies. Germany already had gobbled up Austria and Czechoslovakia; then with Soviet

Russia she had devoured Poland during the months of September and October 1939. The Red Army had also swept across the tiny Baltic countries of Estonia, Latvia, and Lithuania, to become bogged down later in Finland.

Along the western redoubt of the European continent, Belgium, the Netherlands, and Denmark braced for the holocaust that was to come, while a self-deluded France huddled behind the Maginot Line. At the same time British determination was first displayed in the flak-spotted skies over London and the factory cities in the heartland of a fast-fading empire.

Inside the luxurious hotel suite, Colonel William J. "Wild Bill" Donovan, sometime intelligence agent without portfolio, White House confidant, legendary World War I hero, and holder of the Congressional Medal of Honor, and Colonel Charles M. Sweeny (not Sweeney, as his name was often misspelled), a soldier of fortune born to wealth and also a legend in his own time, were analyzing the global military situation and a few specific political points in particular. While these two warriors of yesteryear were discussing the general international situation, Donovan, now a ruddy-faced Wall Street lawyer, was trying to glean information from the soldier of fortune that he could pass on to President Franklin D. Roosevelt.

Specifically, Donovan was interested in Sweeny's assessment of the state of England's defenses, the strength of the Royal Air Force, the attitude of the British people toward a potential invasion of England and Scotland, and whether, as Winston Churchill would declare the following July 14, they would "defend every village, every town and every city."

Sweeny was the father of the Eagle Squadron of American fighter pilots, who would acquit themselves bravely throughout the Battle of Britain—which had begun only three short weeks earlier on February 3. He was back in his own country now on a not-so-secret recruiting mission on behalf of the RAF and England. Potential pilots were relatively easy to come by; a week earlier he had found ten young Americans who wanted to fight in the air, split them into groups of five, and given them train fare and expense money for a secret trip to Canada where they would be able to enlist in the

RAF. Sweeny's biggest problem in early 1940 was scouring the U.S. for qualified airplane mechanics. When he visited some of the hangars at major municipal airports and tried to enlist mechanics with the promise of a bonus—half paid on signing up in Canada and the remainder in U.S. greenbacks upon arrival in England—airline officials got wind of his mission. Formal complaints were made to the Justice Department.

In one case that made headlines, an appeal was made to the FBI by the parents of nineteen-year-old Clyde Hodges, Jr., who was among the volunteers for flight training who had crossed into Canada. Moreover, the isolationists in Congress had picked up the scent of "warmonger" Sweeny, and the Justice Department warned that recruiting activities on behalf of a foreign government engaged in war constituted a violation of American neutrality laws.

The G-men, as FBI agents were affectionately known to Americans of that era, had lost Sweeny's trail in Chicago. The lanky soldier of fortune, who had lived by the gun most of his adult life, had a sixth sense when it came to retreating under fire. He had quickly left Chicago, and his hotel was left with the stock answer that "Colonel Sweeny has checked out and has left no forwarding address."

Using another name, he had checked into the Sherry-Netherlands, but was spotted by a globe-trotting acquaintance who had passed a remark to a friend which, in turn, had found its way to Donovan's sensitive ears.[1]

The lawyer had become a walking collection agency and repository of information and, by virtue of his curiosity about people and events, he had begun to play the role of a self-appointed, unofficial intelligence agent working in the clear rather than in the "black," as the original professionals under his wartime command would later call it. He had read about Sweeny's activities in newspapers; this was an opportunity to obtain some up-to-date intelligence about the situation in England. As a presidential confidant with regular access to the White House, Donovan and his informal and unofficial reports were always welcomed by FDR.

Donovan was one of the few private citizens close to the Washington establishment in the late 1930s who were well aware that it would be only a matter of time before the

United States would become involved in World War II. But now, in late February 1940, he had telephoned Sweeny and introduced himself. After all, their paths had crossed several times, as far back as World War I in France and also during the intervening years; they were two "old" warriors of the same generation and cast in the same mold, and each admired the other's past exploits.

Sweeny was not given to explaining or apologizing for his actions. As far as he was concerned, the U.S. would soon be involved in the war, and he would later be commended for his efforts. However, he wanted the FBI off his back. He had a serious mission to complete.

"Look, Bill," he said to Donovan in parting, "see what you can do in Washington to get the G-men to leave me alone. All I need is another month. But you're going to have to move fast to make up for lost time."[2]

And time had indeed been lost. America had lived in innocence until it was jolted out of its complacency by World War I—the war that was fought "to end all wars." But it was the ashes of World War I and its aftermath that fertilized the seeds of World War II. Few Americans were aware of what was happening.

Political ideologies in the wake of World War I had replaced the rule of imperial prerogatives in Germany, the Austro-Hungarian Empire of Vienna waltzes and *gemütlichkeit*, and tyrannical Romanov Russia. On the heels of those who heavy-handedly shaped the nations which spawned both Communist and Fascist ideologies followed the leaders who had come to power during this massive change in the social and political upheaval that followed the first World War. These technocrats were the policemen of the new order, and they brooked no interference from their fellow citizens. Where opposition arose, it was quickly demolished; and if those who spoke out against these leaders and their governments were unfortunate enough to escape the firing squad, they ended their lives tragically in isolated prison camps.

In the new police states the authorities charged with preventing opposition created special intelligence organizations for just this purpose. These totalitarian "law-enforcement" agencies soon were transformed into secret police organizations, and within the police states of the 1920s and 1930s, the first of the modern totalitarian intelligence organizations were born. Initially, it was counterintelligence on a police level: the protection of the state and its leaders from the activities of dissidents within the country's borders. As the totalitarian states grew in political and military strength, their respective counterintelligence agencies became the nuclei of external intelligence forces. Their duty was to dispatch spies abroad to collect information about potential enemies and, as history has since recorded, to spy upon those nations which were to become their victims.

One of the first uses of organized modern intelligence by the United States was launched shortly after America's entry into World War I. Herbert O. Yardley, a young code clerk in the State Department, sold the War Department on the idea that the enemy used codes as a method of transmitting vital information, and that he could crack these codes. The Army set up Yardley in the secret cryptologic Military Intelligence Division section called MI-8. Soon, MI-8 duties encompassed reading suspect international mail for messages written in invisible ink, and in the course of these intelligence activities many codes were cracked and several German spies were caught.

But intelligence operations as part of national policy ran against the American ethic. After World War I ended, Yardley again sold both the War and State Departments on the idea of a "permanent organization for code and cipher investigation and attack." Perhaps it was even more fitting that this official postwar code-breaking organization, later referred to in whispered conversations by Washington insiders as the "Black Chamber," originally was established in New York, the same city which also became home base to the unofficial one-man intelligence activities of William J. Donovan.

The Black Chamber's first major intelligence coup of the postwar era was the cracking of the Japanese diplomatic code prior to the 1920 conference for naval disarmament. Japanese translators were hard to come by, and one, a former missionary, quit after a few months when he realized the espionage nature of the secret work in which he was engaged. Clearly this was just one indication that the national attitude on espionage was that it was snooping. By the mid-twenties the Black Chamber had managed to crack the diplomatic codes of Argentina, Brazil, Chile, Costa Rica, and other small countries as well as the secret messages sent by England, France, Germany, and the Soviet Union to their diplomats and military attachés in the United States, or wherever the men in cutaway coats and striped pants congregated for international conferences.[3]

But a few months after Herbert Hoover became president in 1929, the Black Chamber's activities suddenly ceased. The new administration's Secretary of State, Henry L. Stimson, unlike his predecessors who supported the Black Chamber, was shocked to learn of the cryptologic group's existence. So far as he, a statesman of the old school, was concerned, the Black Chamber was a dirty business and a violation of the principle of mutual trust by which he conducted his personal affairs and his foreign policy.[4] Stimson might have been shocked to learn that at that time the major European diplomats of his generation, like their predecessors before them, conducted the affairs of their respective nations with the code-breaking and espionage assistance of their national intelligence agencies.

However, outraged by the existence of the Black Chamber, Stimson ordered this small group disbanded with the admonition, "Gentlemen don't read each other's mail!"[5]

Paradoxically, the two decades preceding World War II glorified espionage and the activities of spies. The novels of E. Phillips Oppenheim, describing the adventures of mysterious beauties on the Orient Express between Paris and Istanbul and the fictitious mayhem on this international train, caught the public's fancy. Meanwhile, America's greatest code-breaker and head of the Black Chamber, who had been fired by the Secretary of State, was unable to find suitable employment. Yardley could not tell prospective employers that he had directed a very sensitive intelligence operation. Also, dismissal from the State Department at that time carried the same stigma as being fired by the federal government as a security risk was to become twenty years later. Strapped for funds during the first years of the Depression, Yardley wrote a book, *The American Black Chamber*, which became an overnight sensation. A best seller of its day, it was even more popular after the State Department in diplomatic double-

talk was "disposed to discredit" the book and Yardley's version of events in the nation's first official intelligence project.
The War Department, managed in 1931 by stiff-necked generals with even less imagination or flair for language, lied
about the very existence of the Black Chamber.[6]

It goes without saying that, of the information gleaned
from nearly fifty thousand major coded messages, little was
used by American policy planners other than to rebut an
adversary at an occasional diplomatic conference. The War
Department generals concerned themselves with developing
weapons to fight the previous war based upon reports from
America's military attachés overseas. Intelligence operations
were left to officers assigned to G–2 duties because of poor
fitness reports, rather than for specialized knowledge and
talents.

Moreover, among the civilian population there were few
Americans with the intellectual curiosity of a Colonel Donovan, or with his inclination to visit the great capitals of
Europe and other hot spots more in keeping with the work of
adventurous foreign correspondents. It was on one such business visit to Germany in 1932 that he first became alarmed
at the rapid growth of the National Socialist movement and
what it stood for. In the mid-thirties Donovan's travels took
him to Rome where he met Mussolini, thence to Libya and
Abyssinia where Ethiopian natives were using spears against
Italian bombers, artillery, and poison gas. His visit to Marshal
Badoglio's headquarters would prove invaluable nearly a
decade later when the first attempt was made during World
War II to lure Italy away from the Axis.

Later during the turbulent decade of the thirties, Donovan
visited Spain during that country's tragic civil war, which had
become a testing ground for German, Italian, and Russian
troops, tactics, aircraft, and other weapons.

Although he traveled as a private citizen, Donovan's
itinerary was known to his personal friend, President
Roosevelt, and other international-minded members of the
White House staff. Following each of his visits abroad, Donovan would lunch with FDR and brief the President on what
he had observed, the conversations he had had with states-
men, military commanders, and public figures, and his assessment of events. Both FDR and Donovan were in agree-

ment: War clouds were gathering fast. On April 7, 1939, ten
divisions of Italian troops were landed on the Adriatic coast of
Albania, and the land of mountain tribes was annexed by the
Fascist government of Benito Mussolini.

Donovan, who had been an assistant attorney general with
the Justice Department in the mid-twenties, was as much
at home in Washington as he was in New York. Although a
Republican, he was highly regarded by the men supporting
President Roosevelt's third-term bid in 1940. This group included the internationalists in his own party. At one time
FDR had considered Donovan for the important post of
Secretary of War, but other advisers prevailed, and the
portfolio went to Henry L. Stimson, who had held the same
office under President William H. Taft three decades earlier.
Paradoxically, Stimson accepted the intelligence later gleaned
by the U.S. Navy's cracking the Japanese code after his appointment as Secretary of War in late 1940. Evidently Stimson's entire attitude had changed on the subject of gentlemen
reading the mail of others.[7]

The origins of the modern American intelligence community—and later the Central Intelligence Agency with its
many-sided operations—can be traced to the personal efforts
of William J. Donovan. Although Donovan was not the only
source of information tapped by President Roosevelt, the
grey-haired lawyer was considered by the White House to be
a prime source of "intelligence data." His bits of information
collected from people "in the know" during his world-wide
travels added to the greater picture of the late thirties and
first years of the wartime forties.

By early spring of 1940 the big question in Washington
was whether England could hold out against a possible invasion if the Maginot Line collapsed and France fell before
the German invaders. The prelude to the French defeat occurred on April 9, when the Wehrmacht's armored panzer
divisions swept across Denmark in a matter of hours and, at
the same time, attacked Norway with a combined airborne
and amphibious invasion. Oslo fell on April 10. The subsequent two months were marked by British and French landings in Norway, with unsuccessful battles for port cities.
Finland was then fighting a losing but telling campaign

against the Red Army. Only 300,000 Finns, 80 percent of whom were mobilized reservists, were arrayed against nearly a million invaders.

By early May the Wehrmacht was ready for phase two of its western campaign to conquer the European continent. Some 2.5 million men—104 infantry divisions, 9 motorized divisions, and 10 panzer divisions—were assembled along Nazi Germany's western borders from northern Holland to Switzerland. Organized in three army groups—Group B in the north, Group A in the center, and Group C in the south—the Wehrmacht faced the small Dutch and Belgian forces and the larger French and British armies. The latter had been landed on the Continent during the preceding months of the "phony war" or *"Sitzkrieg,"* as it was called by those western Europeans who mistakenly believed that the World War I allies would once again defeat the common enemy—*les boches.*

In Washington there was confusion. Some generals in the War Department insisted that the Allies would hold fast behind the Maginot Line. The State Department was a nonentity. Diplomatic cables were garbled with facts garnered at cocktail parties. The White House didn't even have a war room; confusion and misreading of fast-breaking events was the rule rather than the exception.

The prime question on May 1, 1940, was: Will France hold? There were three Allied army groups composed of some thirty-eight poorly trained Belgian and Dutch divisions hurriedly mobilized for the emergency and totaling a million men. Ninety French divisions, of which thirteen were entrenched Maginot Line troops incapable of deployment, nine British divisions representing that nation's expeditionary force, and one Polish division of expatriates and those who had escaped the holocaust the year before, faced the formidable and confident Wehrmacht.

Accurate German intelligence indicated that in general the western coalition lacked modern weapons and equipment—and aircraft. Allied intelligence was unaware that its forces outnumbered the Nazi panzer divisions—3,600 tanks to the Wehrmacht's 2,574—or that the Allies, in turn, were outnumbered by the Luftwaffe's two air fleets of 3,500 combat planes deployed against nearly 2,000 outdated and modern aircraft of the west.

In Washington there was no regular flow of information that could in any way be described as "intelligence."

The Germans assaulted Belgian and Dutch airfields on May 10; Belgium and the Netherlands fell five days later. By the end of the month the British Expeditionary Force was assembled on the beaches at Dunkirk for evacuation back to England, while the battered French forces were chewed up in the relentless march westward and southward by the Wehrmacht.

German intelligence agencies pulled out all the tricks of the trade. The Fifth Column, the carefully placed agents and sympathizers and their new method of warfare, honed to a fine edge by Germany, was pressed into service. Although the massive Nazi military force was capable of winning the final battle on its own, the intelligence service created by the Germans was of immeasurable value. And this intelligence service stretched its tentacles all the way to the United States. In fact, the intelligence activities of the German Abwehr within the borders of the U.S. were for quite some time as incomprehensible to the American leaders as they were to the American people.

The Federal Bureau of Investigation became the counter-intelligence arm of the U.S. government, but the narrow vision of J. Edgar Hoover and his associates perceived only the clear and present danger to the United States. Intelligence, as the G-men saw it, was collecting information about the enemy within rather than the enemy without. Later, the FBI would become embroiled in a political battle for control of the nation's wartime and postwar intelligence establishment.

Meantime, the U.S. geared for the war to come. The first draft of Americans into the armed forces faced serious political opposition in Congress during the summer of 1940, but was ultimately passed by a single vote in mid-September. That same summer Secretary of the Navy Frank Knox proposed to FDR that Donovan be dispatched overseas to England to find out whether the British could hold out now that France had fallen along with Belgium and Holland.

The Wehrmacht was poised on the Channel beaches of France—facing England.

The American envoy to London, Ambassador Joseph P. Kennedy, had been burning up the diplomatic wires advising Secretary of State Cordell Hull that England could never hold out against a German invasion. Kennedy also advised that it would be in the best interests of the United States to seek an accommodation with Germany, that something could be worked out. FDR preferred independent assessments of events to official versions from diplomats or military commanders.[8]

Before Donovan departed, he was contacted by an old acquaintance who had recently established himself in New York City as chief of British intelligence in the United States. He was William Stephenson, Canadian industrialist and World War I flying ace, who first fought in the trenches of Flanders Fields. Later he had joined the Royal Flying Corps, had shot down twenty German aircraft and two observation balloons, was in turn shot down twice by the enemy, crash-landing once on the Allied side of the trenches and later on the German side. He was taken prisoner, and subsequently escaped from a prison camp. Stephenson's wartime career complemented that of the American lawyer with whom he was to establish a close working relation and a warm friendship.

"Big Bill" Stephenson and "Little Bill" Donovan met shortly after the fall of France. Like Donovan, Stephenson had his own coterie of close friends and valuable acquaintances who could be called upon to provide the type of intelligence required by the Foreign Office in London or the War Ministry for both short- and long-range planning. Aware that Donovan was a confidant of FDR, Stephenson prevailed on high-ranking British military and civilian officials to roll out the red carpet. "The procurement of certain supplies for Britain was high on the list," Stephenson recalled some years later, "and it was the burning urgency of the attempt to fulfill this requirement that made me instinctively . . . concentrate on a single individual who, despite all my contacts in high places, might achieve more than any widespread effort on the official or sub-official levels which had so far been unproductive. My assessment was proved correct in the event. Donovan, by virtue of his very independence of thought and action, inevitably had his critics, but there were few among them who would deny the credit due to him for having reached a correct appraisal of the international situation in the summer of 1940."[9]

The United States, added Stephenson, was debating two courses of action: One was to give Britain all-out aid by supplying fifty obsolete destroyers and other material support in the form of aircraft, vehicles, gasoline, and weapons. The other alternative was to give Britain up for lost and concentrate on rearming America.

> That the former course was eventually pursued was due in large measure to Donovan's tireless advocacy of it. Immediately after the fall of France not even the President himself could feel assured that aid to Britain was not to be wasted in the circumstances. Dispatches from the Ambassadors in London and Paris stress[ed] that Britain's cause was hopeless, and the majority of the Cabinet here was inclined to the same conclusion, all of which found vigorous expression in organized isolationism.... Donovan, on the other hand, was convinced that granted sufficient aid from the United States, Britain could and would survive. It was my task first to inform him of Britain's foremost requirements so that he could make them known in appropriate quarters, and secondly, to furnish him with concrete evidence in support of his contention that American materiel assistance would not be improvident charity but a sound investment.[10]

Armed with two letters, one signed by Secretary of State Hull to all American diplomatic and consular officers in countries through which Donovan would pass ordering "such courtesies and assistance as you may be able to render," and the other addressed to British publisher Lord Beaverbrook from Secretary of the Navy Frank Knox, also a newspaper publisher, advising that the bearer was on "an official mission for me, with the full approval of the President of the United States," America's intelligence agent without portfolio on July 14 took Pan American's multi-engine "Clipper" flying boat to Lisbon.[11]

Throughout the wartime years, Lisbon was a hotbed of intrigue, with the spies of many nations and their informants stumbling over one another in their search for information, especially of important news such as the arrival of William J. Donovan and others who were private citizens, but close to FDR. Any good intelligence service thrives on just such bits of information.

Unaware of Donovan's mission or arrival until he later learned of the visit from an American news correspondent, Ambassador Kennedy became enraged at this deliberate oversight by Washington. Thanks to Stephenson, whose efforts persuaded "my friends in high places to bare their breasts," Donovan was received in audience by King George VI and met with Prime Minister Winston S. Churchill and members of the wartime cabinet. Nothing in the way of defense plans was held back by the men who directed Britain's destiny.[12]

Even more important than learning about the secrets of Britain's early warning radar system, coastal defenses, and the newest Spitfire and Hurricane fighter planes, Donovan was introduced to the greatest of all the Empire's traditional and modern secrets—England's most secret intelligence service, the basis of organized espionage planned and tightly controlled by a handful of grey men engaged in what Rudyard Kipling, himself once a spy in Her Majesty's service, had once described as "the great game." For the first time in the history of England's very private espionage operation, a non-Englishman, one not even a subject of the King, was accorded an introduction into the mysteries of the Secret Intelligence Service (SIS).[13]

It was at this point in time that what had been the faint glimmer of an idea in the back of Donovan's mind began to take shape. There were other more pressing problems, but the constant reminder that the United States lacked an organized intelligence-gathering organization continued to nag Donovan.

It was the big picture that concerned the sometime adviser to the White House. Time and again little bits and pieces began to fall into place, and what had been a murky situation for Donovan took on a clear aura of forthcoming events of great moment.

Shortly before the presidential election of 1940, Donovan accompanied the Secretary of the Navy on an inspection tour of the Hawaiian Islands, America's major bastion in the

Pacific. About a hundred miles from Pearl Harbor, the SEC/NAV and his VIP guest, strapped side by side in a small COD transport plane, were launched from the carrier USS *Enterprise* and flew the remaining short distance to their destination.

Observed Donovan to his host: "If we can do this, the Japs can do it too."[14]

2

The great thing is to get the true picture,
whatever it is.
—WINSTON CHURCHILL, in a note to the chief
of the Imperial General Staff, November 24,
1940

The United States always has been an open country, too
much so in the opinion of many officials entrusted with keeping secret the nation's diplomatic and military affairs. In
fact, if these officials could have had their way, there would
long ago have been a tight clampdown on the publishing of
information considered vital to national defense. However,
many feel that the withholding of information previously
available to the public inevitably would result in still another
loss of civil rights guaranteed by the Constitution. Thus, the
democracy which Americans take for granted would soon take
on a new pattern.

As subsequent disclosures of events since the wartime
years of the forties have proved, few official secrets in these
United States remain secrets for too long—especially the
movements of men of note. So it was that in early 1941
FDR asked Donovan to visit London again and then proceed
to the Middle East for an up-dated assessment of the diplomatic and military situation as it affected Britain. At issue
was the deployment of the U.S. Navy to protect British shipping in the Atlantic from German undersea raiders, pocket
battleships, and heavily armed ships disguised as freighters.
Additional information was required by White House advisers.
Donovan's "cover" this time was to be an "official" representative of the Navy Department.[1]

Again, the chief of British intelligence in the United States

33

would clear the way for the American envoy's visit; only this time, because the situation required it, Stephenson accompanied Donovan to London. But this time Donovan lost his "cover" because of a small oversight that made the headlines and undoubtedly evoked a few choice expletives from men in the White House, the State Department, the Foreign Office in Whitehall, and, more importantly, from the faceless men who directed British intelligence.

Traveling under an assumed name with passport to match, Donovan was spotted in Baltimore, where the Pan American clipper started on the first leg of the lengthy transatlantic flight. Although he answered to the name of Donald Williams, Donovan's luggage bore the initials WJD. His travels during the latter years of the thirties had aroused the curiosity of the press, and soon headlines described him as a MAN OF MYSTERY and AMERICA'S SECRET ENVOY. The senior columnist of *The New York Times* and chief of its Washington news bureau complained that "mysterious emissaries" could do no more than cause difficulties for the State Department's foreign service officers who by all rights should conduct the type of affairs entrusted to Donovan. The caustic commentary of the Hearst newspapers' Westbrook Pegler, who disliked the Roosevelt clan with a passion, described how "Our Colonel Wild Bill Donovan . . . seems to have a 50-trip ticket on the clippers, which he must use up in a certain time or forfeit the remainder."[2]

With his cover shattered by one headline—DONOVAN SECRETLY FLIES TO EUROPE ON ANOTHER 'MYSTERY MISSION'—he was spotted by reporters in London, and the N.Y. *Herald Tribune* on December 17 quoted him: "I can't say anything about why I am here, but please don't make me mysterious or important." Meanwhile, Stephenson had been able to maintain his own cover and slipped easily into London at the same time, insisting again, as he had in his earlier coded messages to his superiors, that Donovan "can play a great role, perhaps a vital one, but it may not be consistent with orthodox diplomacy nor confined to its channels."[3]

In the eyes of the professionals who directed British SIS, anything that was not consistent with orthodox diplomacy fell into the realm of intelligence operations and, as they were disposed to evaluate Donovan's "cover" *faux pas*, he had compromised himself in what could only be regarded as a major *gaffe*.

As suddenly as he had surfaced in Baltimore in early December and in London two weeks later, Donovan just as quickly disappeared as Britian's SIS professionals arranged his itinerary. In his earlier visit to SIS headquarters Donovan had, by virtue of a tight schedule, covered only the bare rudiments of total wartime intelligence operations. This time he was given a thorough briefing in many of the techniques the British were using to support agents and other clandestine operations in enemy-occupied territory on the Continent. He was introduced to Colonel Stewart Menzies, the legendary "M" who headed up British intelligence, and his deputy, Lt. Col. Laurence Douglas Grand who directed the super-secret activities of SIS and its small army of agents around the world. He was shown the plans for SOE operations in Europe and the Middle East and how SO–1 would handle all propaganda and SO–2 the hit-and-run sabotage of the enemy's war machine.

British staff officers, speaking in clipped tones that betrayed their upper-class backgrounds, opened up an entire new world to Donovan—the world of espionage which often required cheating, stealing, lying, torture, and even killing. He learned how the British infiltrated agents into occupied Europe by sea from fast boats or submarines, by air in small Lysander single-engine aircraft that touched down on remote meadows or, when this was not possible, by parachute. Finally, he was shown some of the training facilities for spies.[4]

This second VIP course in how espionage works had decided Donovan. The United States would have to consider establishing its own national intelligence organization. Clearly, this would be one of the items to discuss with the President after he returned to Washington.

A week later he was flown secretly in an RAF bomber to Britain's Middle East military headquarters for discussions with the commanders of the Mediterranean fleet and the army's land forces. But his disappearance from the scene prompted wild speculation in American newspapers about his European mission. Little would American columnists and editors be aware of his additional travels after he completed his primary mission to London and the Middle East. A message from Churchill to FDR on January 28, 1941, thanked the President for Donovan's "fine work," with the added request that America's "mystery man" extend his overseas visit and hasten on to Bulgaria and Yugoslavia.[5]

British intelligence had learned that the Germans had a timetable for the conquest of the Balkans, to precede the planned invasion of the Soviet Union—despite the Nazi-Soviet Non-Aggression Treaty of August 27, 1939, signed four days before the Wehrmacht invasion of Poland. This pact also had contained a secret clause dividing Poland between the two temporary allies. Churchill's information, which he had passed on to Donovan and to FDR, underscored Nazi plans to invade the Soviet Union with a large-scale offensive set for May 15. Bulgaria had fallen under the sway of pro-Nazi members of the government of King Boris. Hungary and Rumania had become Nazi satellites, and in early 1941 Berlin was putting heavy pressure on Paul, Prince Regent of Yugoslavia, with the direct threat of military force, to knuckle under and join the Italian-German Axis.

Donovan's role was clear: As *agent provocateur* he was to implant seeds of doubt in the minds of the men who directed the affairs of Bulgaria and Yugoslavia. Churchill's reasoning was simple: As an American whose nation had no axe to grind in Europe or the Balkans, Donovan easily was the best person to handle so delicate a mission to Sofia and Belgrade. The European chessboard was complex to say the least, and Churchill, a chessmaster without par, used every pawn he could muster in the big-power political game, including the unlikeliest of all—America's Wild Bill Donovan. However, like Churchill, Donovan was under no delusions. He may not have understood the full impact he might have in an area about which he knew very little. But, on the other hand, he was well aware that the United States would soon be involved in a global conflict that might require an American role in unlikely places.

Churchill also was attempting to buy time—even a day or two would help—in order to provide the Soviets with fullest details of the impending Nazi double cross and invasion of

Russia. Thanks to Donovan, Churchill had time to advise Moscow of Berlin's aggressive intentions, but his intelligence fell on Josef Stalin's deaf ears.

Donovan's first stop, in Sofia, enraged the Germans. He met with King Boris and other officials and, with carefully chosen words, managed to plant the seeds of doubt that Churchill desired. Bulgaria was on the verge of agreeing to permit Nazi troops unrestricted passage through this Balkan heartland from which Germany would be able to launch its attack against the USSR. Donovan's discussions prompted the Bulgarian king and his officials to delay their decision for eight days.

During his stay in Sofia, Donovan observed firsthand how the Nazi intelligence apparatus worked. He was shadowed constantly by German agents who followed him even into the royal palace. At one point, German agents searched his overcoat, which had been taken from Donovan by one of the palace butlers. They removed his passport which, by virtue of his connections in Washington, bore the color and identifying markings of the official credentials issued to Americans on official business. Before leaving London he had been issued a diplomatic passport to facilitate his movement through the sensitive Balkan region.

His next stop after Sofia was Belgrade, and the Orient Express, setting for many novels of espionage huggermugger, was delayed for half an hour so that frantic American diplomats could arrange for him to cross the frontier into Yugoslavia, where another diplomatic passport awaited him. For Donovan it was no longer fun and games; the Germans had started playing dirty pool. The Nazi propaganda machine, ever alert to win a point by any means, tried to discredit Donovan by engaging in one of the Big Lie techniques refined by Dr. Joseph P. Goebbels. The Nazi press and radio announced that the U.S. Government had ordered Donovan's immediate recall for actions embarrassing to the diplomat's calling—"because he dishonored his military uniform and sullied his diplomatic status by getting himself into a state of complete drunkenness in a Sofia cabaret."[6]

It didn't take too much imagination on Donovan's part to realize that an entire espionage organization was arrayed against him in Sofia, and that he could expect similar treatment in Belgrade. The political analysts in the American legation in Sofia, with a strong assist from their British colleagues, had briefed their VIP visitor about the situation. Donovan, with a flair for getting directly to the core of a complex problem, had been given additional clout by the time he arrived in Belgrade. The White House, via State Department coded cables, had forwarded a memo from FDR to Donovan advising the private envoy to point out to Yugoslavia's Regent that the United States would not look too kindly on any nation that would knuckle under to the Nazis. ". . . any nation which tamely submits on the grounds of being quickly overrun, would receive less sympathy from the world than a nation which resists," FDR declared, "even if this resistance can be continued for only a few weeks."[7]

But Donovan arrived too late. Adolf Hitler had summoned Yugoslavia's pro-Nazi prime minister and foreign minister to Berchtesgaden where they officially committed their country to the Axis. With an eye toward even the most fleeting opportunity, Donovan was told by the American diplomats on the scene that the general commanding the Yugoslav air force and a group of Serbian nationalist officers had formed a secret organization to resist Nazi infiltration of their country. Donovan visited the opposition group at their headquarters outside Belgrade, where he was asked point-blank if Britain could hold out against the Nazis and whether the United States would enter the war. Speaking as a private citizen and emphasizing that these were his personal views, Donovan answered affirmatively to both questions.

Three weeks later, Donovan was back in Washington, after stopping in Istanbul for private talks with Turkish leaders and other stops in Iraq, Palestine, North Africa, Spain, and Portugal. On March 19, the morning after his late-evening return to Washington, Donovan reported his observations at breakfast with FDR and other White House aides. During his absence the isolationists in Congress had managed to throw one roadblock after another into the President's own international wheeling and dealing on behalf of Britain and a still unaware American public. Meanwhile, in an effort to checkmate the Nazis, Churchill on March 7 began to deploy 57,000 of his best Middle East command troops to Greece in anticipation of German intervention in the Balkans. On March 27 the dissident Yugoslav air force officers launched a successful *coup d'état* that overthrew the Prince Regent's collaborationist government.

Donovan had carried out his mission well, and Churchill later credited him with delaying the Nazi invasion of the Soviet Union by five weeks. The delay ultimately set back the Wehrmacht timetable for conquering all of western Russia before the harsh winter set in, duplicating the severe climatic conditions that led to Napoleon's disastrous retreat from Moscow. The Wehrmacht would invade Russia on June 22 along a 2,000-mile front, thirty-eight days off schedule, finally failing when initial gains turned into costly defeats.

On April 6 the Wehrmacht marched simultaneously against Yugoslavia and Greece. The Yugoslavs, crushed by the Nazi iron fist, surrendered unconditionally eleven days later. The Greek army surrendered on April 23; their British ally evacuated 43,000 troops to Malta and other Middle East ports in Egypt and Palestine, minus their equipment, which they were forced to leave on the beaches. A strong British force on the island of Crete was finally overcome on May 31, and nearly 12,000 English, Australian, and New Zealand troops surrendered following a series of battles in the island's mountains. Two attempts to reinforce the British forces by sea had been repulsed by the Germans with heavy losses.

By this time it was quite obvious to the men in the White House and the State Department that events in Europe were fast coming to a head. In an effort to alert the public to the danger that faced the United States, FDR asked Donovan, regarded by the American public as a national hero, to speak to the nation following his return in mid-March. On a three-network national radio hookup, Donovan described Germany as a "formidable, a resourceful and a ruthless foe . . . aiming at absolute domination of the world." Then he warned that America's "only choice is to decide whether or not we will resist. And to decide in time: while resistance is still possible, while others are still alive to stand beside us."[8]

Nazi propaganda had called him an *agent provocateur* because of his interference in the sovereign affairs of Bulgaria and Yugoslavia, and his activities there were embellished by the German propaganda machine. The Italian press was no less vituperative; one Fascist newspaper called him "Washington's No. 2 *Agent Provocateur.*" Donovan's characteristic sense of humor prevailed: "Who's number one?" he asked.[9]

Donovan's adventures in Bulgaria and Yugoslavia, coming right after his exposure to the departments of British intelligence concerned with secret intelligence activities and special operations behind enemy lines, had crystallized ideas that heretofore had been only fleeting thoughts. He was now convinced that the United States was in dire need of a national intelligence agency. The complexity of coalition warfare and global military operations in the fourth decade of the twentieth century demanded its creation.

Upon his return to Washington in March 1941, Donovan proposed the same type of intelligence service as that of his British friends. It was now quite obvious to him that America needed a hard-hitting psychological warfare organization and a sabotage and subversion branch similar to the British Special Operations Executive (SOE) and its sister Psychological Warfare Executive (PWE).

At the same time that battles were raging in the Balkans and the occupation troops of the Wehrmacht were goose-stepping across Western Europe, a gaggle of U.S. Government agencies in Washington were, in typical bureaucratic fashion, at odds with each other. Individually, they collected the bits and pieces of a complex mosaic without understanding exactly what they had within their grasp. The Office of Naval Intelligence had managed to crack the Japanese diplomatic code with the assistance of the U.S. Army's Signal (Corps) Intelligence Service; and intercepts of the most important advices from Tokyo to Japanese diplomats in Washington and abroad had become regular reading for important American military and civilian officials.[10] Despite this reading of "the mail of others," however, the Japanese attack against Pearl Harbor still occurred as planned by Nippon's Imperial General Staff.

The intelligence was available but clearly there was a lack of coordination and, more specifically, an organization that could assess, display, and communicate many bits of information simultaneously to those agencies which would be required to act individually or in concert upon its receipt.

Of the eight Federal agencies involved in gathering intelligence of importance to their respective organizations in the spring of 1941, the Army's G-2, by the nature of inter-service rivalry, was constantly at odds with the naval personnel who worked for ONI. The State Department's diplomatic corps overseas reported only to their immediate superiors who were part of a small, tightly knit group of elitists who, until the U.S. went to war, lived for the most part in an outdated world of tradition and protocol. Then there was the Treasury Department's Secret Service responsible for tracking down counterfeiters and people who were a threat to the safety of the President. The Labor Department's Immigration and Naturalization Service attempted to keep track of the tens of thousands of immigrants and refugees from totalitarianism who had managed to reach the U.S. The Federal Communications Commission monitored all foreign short-wave radio broadcasts from which little was gleaned because of the bulk of words laboriously recorded each day—to be translated at a later time. And the FBI did its best under impossible circumstances to guard the nation's thousands of miles of relatively open frontiers against the infiltration of enemies foreign, and to keep tabs on the anti-American activities of enemies domestic.

Clearly, the many uncoordinated intelligence activities of the Federal Government were in a state of complete disarray. On June 18, 1941, FDR summoned Donovan to the White House to discuss the formation of a national intelligence agency whose mission would include the planning of espionage operations and other behind-the-lines activities. The new organization which FDR asked Donovan to direct was given the all-inclusive title of Coordinator of Information (COI). A formal announcement was made on July 11, 1941, in a Presidential Executive Order stating vaguely that COI was to "collect and analyze all information and data which may bear upon national security, to correlate such information and data, and make the same available to the President and such departments and officials of the Government as the President may determine, and to carry out when requested by the President such supplementary activities as may facilitate the securing of information important for national security and not now available to the Government."[11]

Behind the appointment of Donovan as director of COI

and the establishing of the organization was the fine hand of
William Stephenson's intelligence operation in the U.S.—
British Security Co-ordination—directed out of Room 3603
of the RCA Building in Rockefeller Center. A favorite of
Churchill, Donovan was also the Prime Minister's unqualified
choice to head the American intelligence agency. Moreover,
several other men in London of stature and foresight always
saw eye-to-eye with Stephenson on all matters relating to
British-American exchanges, including the disclosure of
Britain's most secret intelligence service to Donovan. Stephenson later recalled the PM's "orders in relation to our friend
Donovan." But human frailties abound even in the most
disciplined of professions, nor was Britain's SIS any exception. There were those at SIS who recalled Donovan's earlier
fumblings. Out of a sense of class-conscious pride concocted
from old school ties and tradition, there was strong opposition
to helping an ally build a rival intelligence service.

"Nonetheless," added Stephenson, "had it been comprehended . . . to what extent I was supplying our friend with
secret information to build up his candidacy for the position
I wanted to see him achieve here, there would have been such
a cold blast of horror sweep through that on your first visit
to it [SIS headquarters] you would have had to find your way
over one corpse after another."12

Donovan had voiced his desire to command an infantry
division when the U.S. went to war. Desk work and administration were anathema to him but he finally accepted FDR's
offer to head COI with rank of major general and reporting
responsibility only to the President. Stephenson was relieved
to learn of Donovan's decision to accept the newly created
post. Donovan, in turn, confronted the head of BSC and
with mock seriousness accused him of having "intrigued and
driven me into the job." Stephenson's coded message to
London informing SIS headquarters of the birth of COI bore
the additional comment: "You can imagine how relieved I
am after three months of battle and jockeying for position in
Washington that our man is in a position of such importance
to our efforts."13

Those government departments whose officials moved in
the corridors of power were quick to learn about the establish-

ment of COI and the appointment of its first director. The
FBI's J. Edgar Hoover protested loudly enough to elicit a
promise from FDR that COI would be expressly forbidden to
conduct espionage activities within the U.S. After all, hadn't
the FBI unmasked the pro-Nazi German-American Bund?
Another government agency under State Department auspices
obtained a concession that COI would engage in no espionage
activities south of the border or elsewhere in Latin America.
The FBI later, in cooperation with BSC, would assume all
counterintelligence functions in Latin America and Mexico,
where Nazi intelligence operatives moved with impunity. And
in the Army's G–2, Major General George V. Strong considered that the establishment of COI was in conflict with the
intelligence role of his service. Specifically, he was unable to
understand the difference between tactical or battlefield intelligence and strategic intelligence that would be gathered by
COI, and he would carry this animosity to COI's successor
organization—the Office of Strategic Services.

Meanwhile, isolationist senators on Capitol Hill took up
the cudgel against Donovan and COI. First they warned that
there was a danger of White House control of intelligence
and investigative agencies, reading into the purposely vague
Executive Order the possible threats to civil liberties that a
score of years later would have evoked a hue and cry from
more sophisticated Americans. When this tactic failed, Senators Robert A. Taft and Burton K. Wheeler opposed Donovan's promotion from colonel to two-star general. This particular ploy worked, and Donovan assumed command of
COI as a civilian who would be called "Mister" instead of
"General."

A national strategy was developing in Washington as the
pressure of events brought the threat of war ever closer with
each passing month. For all practical purposes, FDR and
his advisers planned in the summer of '41 as if the U.S. was,
indeed, already at war with the Axis. In the privacy of the
White House, presidential advisers worked round the clock
to create a national strategy—specifically the art and science
of developing and using the political, economic, and psychological powers of the U.S., together with armed forces yet
to be mobilized, to secure national objectives. Little thought

was given to postwar objectives. Primary concern was how to defeat the common enemy in what ultimately would become coalition warfare.

The basis of America's national strategy rested on the success or failure of COI. A strong strategic intelligence organization had to be created from whole cloth. The key word: knowledge—knowledge of the capabilities and vulnerabilities of both friendly and enemy nations which national planners would require to build up strong defenses.

Within COI a new language and terminology was created. The building-block process required the collection of factual data which COI's handful of staffers began to call "raw intelligence." The next step was the development of the "intelligence collection plan" for gathering information from all available sources to meet "intelligence requirements." If "intelligence" was the product of a careful "intelligence process," there would be little room for error in the basic collection, evaluation, analysis, integration, and interpretation of all the available information about the enemy. Errors could cost lives.

The primary repository of much basic knowledge about the world beyond American borders was then, as it is now, the Library of Congress. However, COI also required a number of "experts" whose experience and knowledge also could be utilized to tap the valuable information buried in the stacks of the grey marble and granite building behind the Capitol. Donovan's COI, by necessity, was organized quietly if not secretly. He asked an old World War I buddy, Edward Buxton, to join COI as his deputy director. James Murphy, who was Donovan's law clerk when he was an assistant attorney general, was recruited as his special assistant. Donovan, an idea man and planner who intensely disliked the details of administrative work, preferred to leave the routine management problems to colleagues he could trust.

What passed for an organizational flow chart, changing virtually from day to day, displayed two complementary departments: a Research and Analysis division and a Foreign Information Service. Donovan's personal experiences with the Axis propaganda machine, which had on occasion directly attacked him by name, required a coordinated reply. The Big Lie was to be rebutted within a matter of hours by way of

American short-wave radio. Although the creation of COI
had been announced in a deliberately vague Executive Order,
Nazi Germany's corps of spies in Washington was quick to
report back to Berlin that the new executive agency was to
become the center for all U.S. intelligence operations and
that Colonel Donovan would be America's first spymaster.
"America's secret service," announced Radio Berlin to the
world, "is under a renegade Irishman named Wild Bill, who
prepared for his job by visiting a chain of Balkan nightclubs
and brothels."

Donovan's reply to the Goebbels brand of propaganda was
to plan a coordinated counterpropaganda campaign. Washington was aware that the Nazi Big Lie technique had telling
effect. "Subtle, damnable, designing programs destroy liberty
and undermine democracy," declared an outraged congressman on the floor of the House of Representatives. "The
strongest point for this skullduggery is South America. . . .
Facist nations are growing bolder. The world is poisoned by
propaganda." At the time that Representative Emanuel Celler
(D.–N.Y.) castigated his own government for not countering
the mass of radio propaganda aimed around the world from
powerful short-wave transmitters in Germany and Italy,
American short-wave broadcasts to Europe in French, German, Italian, and English prior to the outbreak of World
War II were often criticized on the basis of poor technical
quality and program content. Nor would these programs be
received as well abroad as anti-American broadcasts that were
beamed to the Americans. In the late thirties international
broadcasting operations in the U.S. were conducted by
American commercial networks, and many European listeners
felt that the foreign-language announcers were not always
qualified for the work demanded of them. One European radio
official referred to the use of "schoolboy German" in the
summer of 1938.[14]

The growing staff working in the office of the Coordinator
of Information was under the bureaucratic gun, and the
experts, brought in from the academic world, were asked to
do for the U.S. in weeks what the research facilities of the
Germans and Japanese had accomplished for the Axis over
a period of years. The inflow of material was tremendous and
the gearing of scholarship to the prewar mobilization effort

produced large quantities of political, sociological, geographic, economic, and other data, most of it carefully classified SECRET, even when copied out of books in the Library of Congress. But it was a beginning.[15]

Donovan's next move was to marshal a psychological warfare operation to counter the Axis propaganda broadcasts; the Foreign Information Service was created in August 1944, directed by the prominent playwright and White House speechwriter Robert Sherwood. Like Donovan an FDR confidant, Sherwood immediately launched FIS broadcasting operations after but little consultation with Donovan, also nominally FIS director. Since all broadcasting facilities were in New York City, Sherwood decided to move his operation out of Washington, and liaison between FIS in New York and COI in the nation's capital was virtually nonexistent. The commercial networks received the radio scripts provided by FIS, and America's overseas voice began to be heard. But the radio scripts were poorly checked and often the wrong emphasis was aired. A coherent policy was lacking.

The policy coordination problem was solved the following summer when COI became OSS and FIS became a division of the Office of War Information. The root of the problem: an intense mutual dislike, never resolved, between Donovan and Sherwood.

Meantime, the COI pattern of growth exceeded all bounds. Donovan managed to recruit Dr. James Phinney Baxter, president of Williams College, to head up R&A, the heart of COI. Among other prominent academics who accepted the call to the nation's first intelligence agency was Professor William L. Langer, distinguished Harvard historian who would later become chief of R&A and direct its huge staff through the end of the war. Others who left their campuses were Dr. Edward Mason, economist; Dean Calvin Hooper of Duke University; Dr. Edward Meade of Princeton's Institute for Advanced Studies; Dr. Henry Field, curator of physical anthropology at Chicago's Field Museum; Carl Kaysen, John Sawyer, Fred Burkhard, John K. Fairbank, Ralph Bunche, Franklin Ford, Henry L. Roberts, and Charles Kindleberger. Also among the early recruits to COI and later to OSS were Lyman B. Kirkpatrick, Jr., Sherman Kent, Ray Cline, Allen

Dulles, and Richard Helms, all of whom would remain in the postwar intelligence community.[16]

Donovan selected well; the original COI staff would hold together through traumatic growing pains while dodging snipers from other government agencies in competition with the nation's first "spooks." If the soft-spoken lawyer felt the weight of his responsibilities and myriad problems, he rarely showed the effects of these pressures. One obstacle after another he ultimately tore down, deftly outflanked, or simply ignored. Working on the premise that the best defense against bureaucratic obstacles was an imaginative offense, Donovan brought in David K. E. Bruce and introduced him to Stephenson of SIS. Bruce was requested to learn everything he could from the head of BSC about Britain's secret intelligence service and organize its American equivalent (which was given the designation SAB for Special Activities Bruce). The COI's sabotage branch, patterned after Britain's SOE, was placed in the hands of former newspaperman M. P. Goodfellow and designated SAG for Special Activities Goodfellow. Bruce and Goodfellow were directed to visit an intelligence training school at a secret site near Toronto which SIS had set up in late 1941. America's fledgling intelligence officials had a lot to learn about "the great game."[17]

Stephenson observed a number of obstacles that COI faced from the moment it was created until the Japanese attack against Pearl Harbor nearly five months later. It represented more the promise than the fact of American participation in secret operations abroad, and essentially was a long-term investment requiring more assistance than it could give in return. It was a pioneer organization lacking the four hundred years of experience of the British intelligence service. As long as America was not at war, COI's director had responsibility without the clout to command and demand.

COI's attempt to launch propaganda broadcasting operations failed because private industry controlled short-wave broadcasting facilities, and private management time and again refused to follow COI directives or use FIS material. Nor was the State Department of any help in its constant refusal to cooperate with COI, whose covert activities it saw as endangering U.S. neutrality. Although Cordell Hull had promised cooperation initially, his subordinates continued to withhold the necessary help needed to provide "cover" for its agents abroad. The collaboration of other Government agencies—required if COI was to function in its primary mission of correlating all intelligence—was lacking because of blatant hostility laced with skepticism of an organization staffed by amateurs. The FBI and the military services feared the infringement of COI in their respective spheres of influence.

The military services were particularly at fault. In mid-1941, Japanese diplomatic cables and short-wave radio messages were intercepted and decoded by the Army and Navy, whose senior officers, selected only those messages they determined would interest the President. They were never passed on to COI for evaluation. Donovan was not on the list of senior officials privy to this TOP SECRET intelligence.[18]

On Sunday afternoon, December 7, 1941, Donovan, an ardent football fan since his college quarterbacking at Columbia, was attending a professional game between the Dodgers and the Giants at New York's Polo Grounds. Many years later, Corey Ford, who served in OSS wrote in Donovan's biography:

> To the annoyance of the spectators, the loudspeaker account of the game was interrupted for an announcement: "Colonel William Donovan, come to the box office at once. There is an important phone message."
>
> Donovan paused at the exit a moment to watch the next play. [Pug] Manders plunged across the goal line for the Dodgers' second touchdown, and as the crowd cheered, he made his way downstairs to the office, where a telephone lay uncradled on the desk. An awed attendant said: "The White House calling, Colonel." Donovan picked up the phone.
>
> James Roosevelt answered: "The President wants to see you at once. It's an emergency."*

---

*James Roosevelt, FDR's eldest son and a Marine Corps captain on the White House military staff in October 1941, had been assigned by his father as military aide to Donovan and liaison officer between COI and other government agencies. Obviously aware of the problems faced by Donovan and COI, the President believed he could keep the fledgling intelligence organization out of trouble if he had somebody in the organization with primary loyalty to the White House.

The Dodgers won the game, and the crowd filed slowly out of the stands. It was not until they reached the street that they learned of the Japanese attack on Pearl Harbor.[19]

World War II had finally caught up with the United States, shattering what has since been described as an "era of innocence." And when war finally did come, Stephenson noted some years later, Donovan was expected by the Joint Chiefs of Staff, "as justification for the continuance of his organization, to produce immediate results despite the fact that he had insufficient time and authority to make adequate preparations." Stephenson added, in a pointed reference to his own service, which saved America's wartime intelligence organization from an early demise:

> . . . if Donovan had not been able to rely upon BSC assistance, his organization could not have survived. Indeed, it is a fact that, before he had his own operational machinery in working order, which was not until several months after Pearl Harbor, he was entirely dependent upon it.[20]

3

We came unto the land whither thou sentest us, and surely it floweth with milk and honey; and this is the fruit of it.

Nevertheless the people be strong that dwell in the land, and the cities are walled, and very great: and moreover we saw the children of Anak there. . . .

And there we saw the giants, the sons of Anak, which come of the giants: and we were in our own sight as grasshoppers, and so we were in their sight.

—Numbers, xiii

Washington, D.C., December 8, 1941. Monday morning. Helmeted marines in greatcoats moved swiftly to assigned positions on and about Capitol Hill, double-timing, heels thudding against the cold pavement, bayonets gleaming brightly at the end of rifles held at port arms—at the ready. Other men took up positions of guard on the Hill and elsewhere in the nation's capital. Some were Army troops who dropped from the backs of trucks at street corners. Others wore civilian clothes—Secret Service men with riot guns poised and members of the District of Columbia Police Department.

On the Hill the United States officially and formally prepared to go to war. Several thousand miles to the west, Pearl Harbor lay in shambles. On the previous morning some crude leaflets had fluttered down on the flaming island of Oahu. They read: GODDAMN AMERICANS ALL GO TO HELL. This ludicrous attempt at psychological warfare that fell to the ground at fortress Pearl came to rest in the midst of shock-

50

ing reality. More than 4,000 Americans were dead or wounded by Japanese bombs and by explosions aboard stricken ships. The U.S. Navy alone lost more men during the two-hour attack on December 7 than it had yielded to its enemies in two previous wars. Before the first day of America's active involvement in World War II had ended, the U.S. had lost two-thirds of all its aircraft in the Pacific and its air superiority. The mighty Pacific fleet, the pride of the U.S. Navy, had been all but smashed in one fell swoop, in an attack made possible by the enemy's own naval force.

The successfully bombed targets had been plotted and identified by a Japanese espionage ring that had been carefully infiltrated into Pearl Harbor over a long period of time.

At precisely 12:23 P.M. on the day after the attack, the Doorkeeper of the House of Representatives announced to the packed House chamber and gallery: "Ladies and Gentlemen, the President of the United States!" Immediately, like a breaking wave, the assembled throng rose noisily to its feet—members of the Senate and House, justices of the Supreme Court in their flowing black robes, officials of the government including the highest ranking admirals and generals, and in the crowded gallery the diplomatic corps and a few privileged visitors and guests.

For a moment there hung a thick and heavy silence; abruptly it vanished in a roar of applause. Not even Sam Rayburn, the politically powerful House Speaker, could stem with his gavel the ovation that burst forth. Franklin Delano Roosevelt waited well over a minute for the cheering and shouting and applause to die down. Nothing in FDR's two terms as Chief Executive rivaled the spirited, tumultuous roar. After the chaplain's brief prayer, the President spoke for six and one-half minutes. His sentences, ringing and clearly enunciated, were punctuated repeatedly by outbreaks of wild applause. His voice lashed out; it drilled into the ears of all present, to those Americans across the land glued to their radios and to the besieged and conquered peoples of the world—and to the common enemies—the names of the lands suffering from the blows of Japanese steel. One by one, in staccato fashion, they came: the Philippines, Midway, Wake, Guam, Pearl Harbor, Hong Kong, Malaya, and others. The phrase that all Americans and much of the world would come to know so well rang out in clarion tones: "We will gain the inevitable triumph, so help us God."

And then came the culmination of the brief, emotional address, the request of the President to the Congress: "I ask that the Congress declare that since the unprovoked and dastardly attack by Japan on Sunday, December 7, a state of war has existed between the United States and the Japanese Empire."*

But it was on the day five months earlier when the President had signed the Executive Order formally establishing the office of Coordinator of Information, that Colonel William J. Donovan, U.S. Army (Ret.), had gone to war against the future enemies of the United States. After the President's speech ended, Donovan switched off the radio in his office in the old National Health Institute building, a few blocks west of the Lincoln Memorial in a run-down section of Washington at the corner of 25th and E Streets. The driveway entrance to the complex of drab brick and limestone buildings was unmarked, but inside there was much activity, mostly on the part of researchers who carried briefcases full of books from the Library of Congress, marked pages to be copied, and then handed them to batteries of typists.

As COI grew, Donovan's headquarters was forced to move five times between July 11 and the debacle at Pearl Harbor. The final address, the complex at 25th and E Street, with its Q Building inner sanctum, would remain his headquarters until the end of the war.[1] But no matter what the inconveniences of moving an expanding headquarters so many times during the first months of COI's existence, Donovan had time to offer some ideas and plans to be worked out. During his visit to London and the Middle East earlier in the year, he had discussed long-range British military strategy with a number of high-ranking Brtish officers. The Wehrmacht's Afrika Korps, and Germany's Italian allies were build-

---

*Germany and Italy declared war on the U.S. on December 11, and and on the same day the Congress voted affirmatively on FDR's request to "recognize a state of war between the United States and Germany, and between the United States and Italy."

ing up their forces in North Africa. Britain's SOE desert raiders were wreaking havoc on the enemy.

Since the defeat of France the previous year and the formation of the collaborationist Vichy government nominally headed by aging World War I hero Marshal Henri Philippe Pétain, the bulk of the French fleet lay bottled up in the French North African ports of Algiers, Oran, Casablanca, and in the Atlantic port of Dakar in French West Africa. A French squadron of one battleship, four cruisers, and three destroyers also lay at anchor in the Egyptian port of Alexandria, then also a major British naval base. Although the French Navy's allegiance was to Vichy, then under the political domination of Germany, the French fleet was a prize coveted by Berlin. If Hitler could take possession of these warships, the German navy would gain immeasurable superiority over the British navy. Germany, then, would rule the waves. The threat of such a powerful naval force added to the danger of the invasion of England. Even more important, in terms of long-range strategy, a more powerful German navy might in the future threaten the shores of the United States.

In an effort to scratch the potential threat to England of French warships in German hands, British naval units on July 3, 1940, appeared off Oran, Algiers, and Casablanca and signaled the French naval commanders either to join England and fight against Germany or to sail their warships to English ports for internment. The French naval commanders refused. The British then shelled the French ships; some of the smaller warships were sunk or seriously damaged. The French squadron at Alexandria surrendered.

In 1940 German submarines and surface sea raiders were regularly sinking British freighters carrying war supplies to England. Again, the Admiralty's strategists in London decided to take action, and a force of Free French ships filled with amphibious troops, joined by British naval units, atter pted on September 22 to invade the port of Dakar and wrest this vital Atlantic base from its Vichy defenders. The Admiralty feared that Dakar might be used by the Germans as a submarine base.

This view of the global military picture was not lost on

Donovan in 1941. Although these attempts by the British to checkmate the Germans had occurred the previous year, it was obvious that North Africa would become an active military theater. His friends in London had informed him that they expected to invade North Africa with American assistance—when the United States actively joined the Allies.

Although not quite ready for the kind of clandestine intelligence operations the British were conducting, during the six weeks preceding Pearl Harbor COI began to work with the first American agents who had been secretly recruited overseas—for service in North Africa. Nor had Donovan forgotten about Charlie Sweeny, now Group Captain in the Royal Air Force Reserve who, once the United States went to war, wished to serve his own country.

By mid-1941 Sweeny was back in the United States supervising aircraft procurement for the RAF. The official climate had changed since the previous year. The FBI was no longer concerned with his activities; Nazi espionage was taking up the time of the G-men. The Battle of Britain had filled the months of August through October 1940, and Sweeny had been involved with his beloved Eagle Squadron of American volunteers, participating in ground operations while watching many of the young pilots he had recruited take off in their single-engine fighter planes to battle the Luftwaffe, some never to return. The planned German invasion of Britain, Operation SEA LION, had been crushed by the RAF. Churchill's ringing words, "Never in the field of human conflict, was so much owed by so many to so few," included the Eagle Squadron and the men who helped make possible this group of volunteer pilots. The Luftwaffe lost 1,733 aircraft, compared to 915 British craft lost in aerial combat.

Donovan's ever-sensitive antennae had picked up news of Sweeny's return, and COI's director, still an avid collector of information, again met with the aging soldier of fortune. Sweeny answered all of Donovan's questions about the strength of the RAF and how the bombing campaign was going against Germany, whether night bombing or day bombing was more effective, and how well the latest German fighters performed against the RAF. This was the type of information that Donovan needed.

"What are your plans, Charlie?"

The old soldier shrugged.

"We're going to be in this war soon enough, y'know," Donovan added, pausing for a moment as an idea came to mind. "If you come to work for us, I think I have a job for you."

The COI director knew Sweeny's history: For three years at the turn of the century he had attended West Point, where he learned the rudiments of soldiering before resigning. In Mexico and Latin America he had fought on the side of several underdog revolutionary armies as a guerrilla leader and, once the revolutions were successful, had served as a colonel or general in the armies of the new governments. He had trained in North Africa with the French Foreign Legion during World War I, then had fought in the trenches, winning a commission, medals, and the adulation of the French people. After his experience with the Foreign Legion (he learned Arabic, French, and Polish), and service in the U.S. Army in France as an infantry battalion commander and later a staff officer at AEF headquarters, he accepted his discharge overseas and joined the fledgling Polish Army of Premier Ignace Paderewski as a colonel in charge of officer training. He fought against the Bolshevik forces of Marshal Mikhail N. Tukhachevski, receiving medals for heroism and a promotion to brigadier general for utilizing the army's cavalry and aircraft that pushed the enemy back into Russia.

After leaving Poland in 1923 he recruited fifteen American pilots, some of whom had fought for France in the Lafayette Escadrille, and organized a squadron of rickety World War I biplanes which he hired out to the Sultan of Morocco. The Sultan was then engaged in a war with the fierce Berber chief, Abd-el-Krim, who had come out of the Riff Mountains in an effort to carve out a kindgom and oust the French administration and the ruling sultanate.

After Morocco, Sweeny's travels took him to Asia until the mid-thirties, when he returned to Europe to join the Spanish Loyalist forces as a staff officer and planner. Multilingual and obviously at home both in the bush and at chic soirees, Sweeny was the ideal secret agent to carry out Donovan's plan to organize the Arabs of North Africa against the Vichy French and their Nazi masters. The plan was to send Sweeny to the region of French West Africa around Dakar where, as an American version of Lawrence of Arabia, he would organize the Arabs into a guerrilla army that might conceivably take the port city. Far-fetched? The COI director's mind was already functioning in the realm of strategic intelligence. The strategically located city would be a welcome naval and air base, as events would later prove.

Sweeny could then work his way north into French North Africa, perhaps with an organization of agents and partisans, Donovan reasoned. After all, if T. E. Lawrence could organize the Bedouins for the British in World War I, there was no reason why Sweeny couldn't accomplish a similar mission with the Berbers in World War II. Sweeny was agreeable to the assignment, which called for guile instead of battlefield gallantry. He had summed it up himself: "Dammit, at my age I'm just too old to fight!" At sixty, he was still in excellent health, and more important to COI, sound of mind and spirit.

But once again a suspicious bureaucracy intervened. Technically, the U.S. maintained diplomatic relations with Vichy France after the German conquest in 1940. State Department analysts viewed any clandestine operations in French territory by the U.S. with disfavor. Secretary of State Hull exploded indignantly when he discovered COI's plan to dispatch Sweeny to French West Africa and thence to the North African littoral. He summoned Donovan to his office in the ornate mass of late nineteenth-century architecture adjacent to the White House.

"You're attempting to interfere in diplomatic relations with a friendly country; this is unacceptable," Hull lectured. "We don't need trigger-happy buccaneers handling our diplomatic affairs."[2]

The State Department still wielded major influence in matters of intelligence-gathering during the critical months before Pearl Harbor. Hull was able to block COI's plans for Sweeny by ordering that his passport be revoked and any future passport be denied. But Hull didn't stop Sweeny from leaving the country. Wearing his RAF uniform, the old warrior flew back to England in March 1942 to rejoin Britain's air arm as an operational liaison officer between the Royal Air Force and the U.S. Army Air Force, whose advance units had begun to arrive in England. He wouldn't return home until the war ended.

But Donovan had other plans afoot. GYMNAST and SUPER-GYMNAST basically were British plans for military operations in North Africa to be implemented with the assistance of the United States once it became a belligerent. Although this was expected by FDR and his closest advisers to happen soon, little long-range strategic planning was going on in the War Department; its problems were more immediate.

In September 1940 Selective Service had been instituted, and the first draftees were taken into the Army, many of them harboring bitterness, antiwar sentiment, and a strong aversion to all things military.

A year later, September 1941, Selective Service was continued by a single vote in the House of Representatives. During this period, just a few months before Pearl Harbor, the Army represented a huge national investment. It had been built up from less than half a million men in the fall of 1940 to 1,638,086 men, in both the land forces and the Air Corps, by the time the 1941 maneuvers were taking place. And while debate about the draft had split the parties on Capitol Hill virtually down the middle, nearly 850,000 of these draftees and their regular Army officers and senior sergeants were on field maneuvers where the password amongst the troops was OHIO—"Over the Hill in October" if the men were not released from service after their one-year tours were up. The vote to renew Selective Service extended these early draftees and the Japanese attack further extended their military service "for the duration plus six months."

The requirements of twentieth-century warfare had not yet reached the ears of tradition-bound professional officers directing the maneuvers that fall of '41. An incident during the war games illustrates COI's problems with the War Department since its inception the previous July. One of the men who had written the master plan for the maneuvers was Colonel Dwight D. Eisenhower. Even he had overlooked the value of behind-the-lines guerrilla warfare. Paramilitary operations when planned in concert with conventional military strategy could be of immeasurable value to any field commander, but only a very small number of Army intelligence officers comprehended guerrilla warfare. They also mistakenly equated the use of guerrilla forces with the Nazi Fifth Column supported by the traitorous quislings of that era—named after Vidkun Quisling, who collaborated with the Nazis after his native Norway was invaded.

A little-reported incident of behind-the-lines guerrilla operations during the maneuvers came as a shock to both senior Army officers and to the 20,000 citizens of the friendly little city of Monroe, Louisiana, where residents loved to play host to tourists. In the midst of the military exercises, the city was full of visitors, including handsome, suntanned young men who patted babies, smiled at girls, drank nothing stronger than beer, and in other ways generally made themselves agreeable. Then, early one evening, this peaceful picture changed. Suddenly, in different parts of the city hundreds of the pleasant tourists whipped out pistols and hidden submachine guns. They quickly commandeered buses and other private vehicles and, identified by the military caps and cartridge belts they wore, burst into the homes of municipal officials and arrested them. They took over the waterworks, the electric utility plant, and the city's main telephone exchange and telephone office, and marched into the local radio station and newspaper. At the same time, a small single-engine Piper Cub circled low overhead and dropped leaflets advising the populace that an army was marching on the city and that resistance would be futile.

Before the majority of Monroe's citizens could comprehend what was happening, trucks began to rumble into the city to the accompaniment of screaming sirens, bursting smoke bombs, and firecrackers. Machine guns were set up at strategic intersections and on rooftops overlooking the downtown streets. Mortars and 37mm antitank guns were placed at other strategic points. The following day a special newspaper edition appeared announcing the prohibition of church meetings and other public gatherings, the rationing of food, and the requisitioning of automobiles, gasoline, and food stuffs. Meanwhile, a small band of Fifth Columnists, young men who had lived in Monroe all their lives, passed out pennants welcoming the invaders. This surprise invasion and conquest was climaxed by the appearance of "General Squarehead." Wearing a World War I German helmet and speaking with a thick accent, the conqueror, flanked by storm troopers, rode into the city.

General Squarehead was Cadet Ed Glusman of Louisiana State University's Reserve Officer Training Corps. The eight hundred invaders and four hundred advance Fifth Columnists, including local quislings, also were students from LSU. Slowly Monroe's citizens began to understand, and they quickly entered into the spirit of the field exercise. Wasn't the U.S. Army all around in the area? This must be part of the maneuvers. Or was it?

The Red and Blue Army lines were well defined on the terrain maps. Monroe was deep within Blue Army lines when an operations officer handed a dispatch to Colonel Eisenhower, architect of the Blue Army "battle" plan.

"Impossible!" exclaimed Ike. "There can't be any Red forces this far north." The Blue Army command post was thrown into an uproar. A mechanized infantry unit supported by tanks was sent to recapture the city.

Confusion also reigned in the Red Army headquarters. The commanding general wanted to know, "Who's the damned fool who moved that far into enemy territory?" Nobody on the staff could identify the unit holding Monroe. In fact, all Red Army units were accounted for. However, intelligence sections of both war games armies reported that the city was still under military control, and the commanders of each army requested that umpires drive into Monroe and get to the bottom of the situation. A vehicle with a white flag fluttering from its radio antenna drove to the city's outskirts and was met by the guerrillas. The inspection team demanded to be taken to the commanding officer of the unit holding the city. The umpires, a lieutenant colonel and a captain, were asked to walk with an escort of guerrillas. The captain pulled the white flag from the vehicle and held it with one outstretched hand as they walked down the main street of Monroe. The city was silent, as in a shoot-out scene in a Western.

As the umpires came into view, General Squarehead turned to one of his officers. "I wonder if they want us to surrender?"

"I dunno," replied one of his guerrilla aides, hurriedly

leafing through an ROTC manual. "Say, General Square—, I mean, Ed. There's nothing in here that tells us how to surrender. All it says is that a white flag means a temporary truce, to talk."

The student soldiers playing the part of guerrillas were perplexed by the formal attitude of the umpires. The captain methodically took notes as his superior asked the commander of the guerrillas exactly what Blue Army unit had taken the city.

"Why?" the guerrilla leader asked.

"So we can keep the records straight at our command post," the lieutenant colonel replied. His jaw dropped in surprise when he was told the guerrillas were no more than college students. When word reached the headquarters of both armies, there was anger on the part of the generals and colonels whose war games had been halted. "College hijinks!" exploded Ike, his face turning a telltale red. "Send out an order that we want no more ROTC units involved in the maneuvers. I want them to stay the hell out of this operation. We have enough college officers causing us problems."

Unappreciated and duly censured, the ROTC cadets pulled out of Monroe after bringing the maneuvers of '41 to a grinding halt for forty-eight hours. They were ahead of their time, but a year later General Dwight D. Eisenhower, planner and commander of the invasion of North Africa, would be thankful for agents in place and guerrilla forces behind enemy lines. He would, before war's end, call on his special operations units behind enemy lines to play their intelligence and guerrilla roles to the fullest.[8]

The incident in Monroe, Louisiana, had not gone unnoticed by Donovan and his colleagues in COI. It was a lesson he took to heart. COI would have a department dedicated to training men to fight behind enemy lines—with local anti-Nazi partisans. At that time, Donovan was receiving regular reports from SIS in London about the partisan warfare of the anti-Nazi Chetniks of Yugoslavia's General Draza Mihailovic. The resistance movement was beginning to show its head ever so slowly. British intelligence was nurturing this growing anti-Nazi movement in many occupied countries. But it was apparent to the British that it would be a few years before English troops would fight the Germans on the Continent. It was equally apparent to Donovan that the United States would have to develop COI's capabilities in the field of guerrilla warfare. His attempt to use Sweeny had been shot down by the State Department for what Cordell Hull and his associates considered good reason. State Department officials wanted to control intelligence gathering, and in the bureaucratic in-fighting then occurring in Washington, the men of State had come up with what they considered the opportunity to make their point with the President and his advisers.

After the fall of France and the establishment of the Vichy regime of Marshal Pétain and Premier Pierre Laval, the U.S. counselor at the American embassy in Vichy signed an agreement with the new government whereby the U.S. would ship vital raw materials to French North Africa. However, there was the added stipulation by the United States that American consular attachés would be permitted to supervise the arrival and distribution of the shipments to make certain that none of the cargoes fell into German hands. "Maintaining U.S. neutrality" was the official reason for these terms. Unofficially, State, with strong support from the White House, looked upon this as the perfect opportunity to infiltrate Vichy and North Africa with men whose primary missions would be to collect any and all types of information.

This diverse group of thirteen men, who later referred to themselves as "the plotters," were as amateur a group of spies as any nation could field. Unknown to Admiral William D. Leahy, the U.S. Ambassador in Vichy, his unorthodox counselor, Robert A. Murphy, had organized the secret agents who reported directly to him. He, in turn, reported directly to the Secretary of State and, as ordered, to COI. There were, of course, other U.S. intelligence operations going on at the same time. The Office of Naval Intelligence used the services of Lieutenant Commander Thomas C. Cassady, a World War I flying ace, who made four secret visits in mufti into German-occupied France during his tenure in Vichy as a U.S. Navy military attaché.[4] Army intelligence, headed by Major General George V. Strong, refused to cooperate at all with COI or the State Department, and definitely not with the U.S. Navy.

The plotters took up their duties in August 1941, shortly after COI came to life. By mid-October Donovan had presented a plan to the President for covert intelligence operations and, with Africa and other backwater areas in mind, he suggested "that the aid of native chiefs be obtained, the loyalty of the inhabitants cultivated, fifth columnists organized and placed, demolition materials cached, and guerrilla bands of bold and daring men organized and installed."

Meanwhile, working for their State Department boss, the thirteen newcomers to the espionage business established a radio network across North Africa. Although carried on the official diplomatic rosters as commercial consular attachés, far down in the embassy pecking order, they used their covers to best advantage. Prior to joining the State Department's North African intelligence project, Stafford Reid had been in the construction business. Sidney Bartlett made his mark in the California oil fields, Leland Rounds had been a businessman, John Knox had graduated from St. Cyr (the French Military Academy), John Boyd had been a Coca-Cola branch manager in Marseilles, Harry Woodruff and John Utter had been associated in banking in Paris. Franklin Canfield was a young lawyer, Donald Q. Coster an advertising man, Kenneth Pendar a Harvard librarian, Carleton Coon a Harvard anthropologist, Ridgeway Knight a wine merchant, and Gordon Browne had traveled extensively in North Africa in times past. However, they all had one common capability—they all spoke French fluently.[5]

The clandestine radio stations code-named *Midway* at Tangiers, *Lincoln* at Casablanca, *Yankee* at Algiers, *Pilgrim* at Tunis and *Franklin* at Oran were soon sending reports— about military movements of French army and naval units; about events; about Arab and French sentiment toward the Vichy regime; and information about the Germans who were everywhere. The plotters also collected maps and charted possible landing fields and, as they became more experienced in the great game of espionage, they began thinking dirty. Moving about as they did, even though French North Africa was supposed to be "neutral" territory, they knew they were beginning to come under surveillance of the skilled professionals of the German Army's own intelligence organization, the Abwehr.

As soon as war was declared on December 8, 1941, the President's orders were explicit to all Federal agencies in the intelligence-gathering business, and especially to the War and State departments. They all were to direct their collected information to COI. Only a few weeks before, Donovan, thanks to his own personal methods of collecting information, had learned about the State Department operation in North Africa. Assisted by his friends in the White House, he received from the State Department a piece of the action—State, despite its own reluctance, would forward information to COI.

Donovan delegated William A. Eddy, a former college president and World War I Marine hero, to represent COI in dealing with State's North African intelligence project. Eddy was the perfect choice. Born in Syria of missionary parents, he spoke Arabic fluently and knew the 2,500-mile stretch of the Fertile Crescent and North Africa intimately. Donovan's own long-range plans for Eddy he kept to himself, but the time would soon come when he would send Eddy to North Africa to supervise U.S. intelligence operations. A month after Pearl Harbor, Eddy was on his way to North Africa by way of Vichy France, wearing the uniform of a colonel in the Marine Corps. His official title: Naval Attaché.

Meanwhile, the plotters were learning what the spy business was all about. Pendar even suggested that when the Allies invaded North Africa, he be "authorized to arrange for the assassination of the German Armistice Commission at Casablanca." John Boyd and Stafford Reid soon found themselves in trouble with their superiors in the embassy. Inasmuch as Murphy was the only member of the American diplomatic staff who knew of the espionage mission shared by his thirteen agents, he had to go to the assistance of Boyd, Reid and others, because they were accused of "not doing their jobs" and "not performing their work consistent with the high standards of the Department of State." On several occasions, some of the plotters were on the verge of being fired and were saved only by Murphy's intercession. That all-important "cover" came first. On yet another occasion the *Midway* transmitter was in danger of exposure by the wife of the

U.S. consul. The transmitter was hidden atop the roof of the consulate and Madame Consul complained to her husband that "tapping noises on the roof" were keeping her awake at night. Radio *Midway* was quickly and quietly dismantled and moved.

Nor was Abwehr fooled by the plotters. A German message, intercepted by the U.S. short-wave radio monitoring service and decoded, warned, "There are ten United States citizens in Casablanca who are there for the purpose of forming a fifth column to pave the way for intended Allied disembarkations next spring."

By early 1942 Operations GYMNAST and SUPER-GYMNAST had been retitled Operation TORCH—the Allied invasion of North Africa.[6] Donovan's COI organization was on the firing line. The scheduled North African invasion had quickly become the first major test for America's fledging intelligence organization. Now that the United States was at war, there was, finally, one organization to coordinate, evaluate, and interpret vital information that once refined would be classified as intelligence. Now there was an agency in Washington charged with putting the jigsaw pieces together to see what pictures would develop or what pieces of the puzzle were missing—and direct the acquisition of those missing pieces.

Although previously there had been uncoordinated intelligence organizations in the Army, Navy, State Department and FBI, the COI was now given the responsibility for gathering together all the U.S. intelligence and presenting this information to the Chiefs of Staff and to General Dwight D. Eisenhower, commander of Operation TORCH.

The success or failure of the invasion of North Africa fell on the shoulders of the men and women of COI—and the thirteen plotters, spy chief Colonel Eddy, and diplomat Robert Murphy. Yet many skeptics in official Washington would continue to believe that an intelligence-gathering organization of rank amateurs should not be entrusted with such responsibilities, especially as they trespassed into the areas that had long been serviced by the established military and civil bureaucracies.

The staff of the Co-ordinator of Information—all two

thousand of them in early 1942 and fewer in number than the regiment their director had commanded in World War I— had been committed and dedicated to the success of Operation TORCH.

4

> Knowledge of the country is to a general
> what a musket is to an infantryman and what
> the rules of arithmetic are to a geometrician.
> If he does not know the country he will do
> nothing but make gross mistakes. . . . Therefore,
> study the country where you are going to act.
> —FREDERICK THE GREAT: *Instructions
> for His Generals*, 1747.

December 22, 1941. Gloom prevailed at a meeting of President Roosevelt and senior American military leaders with Prime Minister Churchill and British generals and admirals, who had secretly come to Washington, D. C. For the Americans at the Arcadia Conference, the depression following the attack against Pearl Harbor had not yet lifted. The British, on the other hand, were of greater spirit. After all, the United States—and the as yet untapped military power that it represented—was now directly involved in World War II, committed until the end.

Britain's professional soldiers and the Empire's effusive Prime Minister were relieved of tremendous anxiety when Japan attacked Pearl Harbor. No matter that within a period of weeks Hong Kong and Singapore would fall to the Japanese juggernaut. With the United States and its vast resources on the side of the Allies, it was only a matter of time—time based on long-range planning, not immediate results or early victories against the Axis.

At the Arcadia meeting decisions were made, subject to later change, to give first priority to the defeat of the Germans and the Italians—the Western Axis. Japan was to be checked until the Western Axis was defeated. Then, the full weight of the Allies, the Soviets included, would fall upon the Land of the Rising Sun. During that twenty-three-day meeting that ended on January 14, 1942, Churchill and FDR designated the top military leaders of both countries as Combined Chiefs of Staff and directed them to plan their first major military operation against the Western Axis—the invasion of North Africa. But this strategic decision evoked the first serious strain in the Allied coalition, between British and American military leaders. An invasion of North Africa was considered a relatively cheap means of seizing the initiative from the Nazis. It would bring the "neutral" French military forces under nominal command of the Vichy government back into the war against Germany. Finally, as Churchill noted time and again, control of North Africa would give the Allies yet another jumping-off point for the final assault of the Nazi-occupied Continent, or, as he often referred to the Balkan invasion corridor, the place from which to strike "at the soft underbelly of Europe."

As for FDR, he too preferred an invasion of North Africa as soon as possible, because it promised an early commitment of U.S. military force against the common enemy. But the men who managed the War Department continued to fight their own bureaucratic battle in an effort to change the mind of the White House and No. 10 Downing Street. The United States, distant from the air raids, the desert battles, and the fighting in the Russian Motherland, was necessary to any Allied victory. The War Department's Chiefs of Staff actually prevailed for a while. Operation BOLERO, a build-up of men and supplies and other assets for the invasion of the Continent from England, supplanted the Mediterranean operation aimed against North Africa. British generals questioned the Allies' ability to successfully carry out an invasion in 1943, and for four months the controversy raged between senior American officers and their British counterparts. Meanwhile, the Germans had begun a massive sealift of men to North Africa, and in short order, while American and British generals argued their respective cases, Hitler had built up his vaunted Afrika Korps, commanded by Field Marshal Erwin Rommel, the "Desert Fox." The Afrika Korps ranged across Egypt and Libya, putting the British to flight at Tobruk. And back in Washington, the generals in the War Department, chagrined because their British counterparts appeared to have more leverage through Churchill with their President, at one stage considered switching the major U.S. effort to the Pacific.[1]

Finally, President Roosevelt would have no more bickering from the Chiefs of Staff, killing any hopes for a 1943 invasion of France, and BOLERO resources were diverted to Operation TORCH. The director of COI, on the fringes of the controversy between U.S. and British military leaders, plumped for his friends in London. They had *the* intelligence direct from France, the occupied Low Countries, and elsewhere in occupied Europe, and even from within Nazi Germany. The German war machine was powerfully efficient. An Allied invasion in 1943 would be sheer folly, and any premature defeat would only slow down the momentum of the Allies.

The full resources of COI were directed at North Africa and Operation TORCH. A number of important questions had to be answered if the invasion was to be successful. Some were political but the majority were of a military nature; a few fell into that grey realm of politico-military affairs. Of the latter questions, paramount importance rested on the French Army and Navy. Would they turn against the Germans and fight on the Allied side? Or would they fight for the Germans against the Allies? Could they be provoked either way? Finally, could any of the French generals or admirals be bought? This last question offended the sensibilities of some top American military leaders who equated the code of conduct of Allied officers with their own West Point and Annapolis ethics. It was left to the subterranean machinations of COI to discover what price, if any, could buy the senior French commanders.

Colonel Eddy and Robert Murphy were in personal touch with senior French Army officers and also discovered that the admirals of the French Navy were not disposed to cooperate with the United States, because of America's very close alliance with England. They could not forgive the British for bombarding the French fleet in 1941, although some of COI's historians thought this animosity was centuries old. Moreover, the French Army general staff in North Africa, a group of ultraconservatives, owed their allegiance to aging Marshal Pétain and the France he represented, although they indicated to Eddy and Murphy on occasion that if the Americans did invade they would come to the aid of the Allied forces. This was the only type of potential resistance that they could discover. The Arab population was neutral to a fault: the Arabs had been conquered by France, and if they, in turn, were to be ruled by the Germans, so be it. It was the will of Allah.

Eddy requested that tons of military supplies be shipped secretly to North Africa, and Donovan replied that the huge amounts amazed him. Eddy thought that if the French were willing to risk their lives to receive and unload these supplies, they should be sent. Donovan retorted that supplies were needed in Australia, and a fleet was already on its way to the Southwest Pacific.

Eddy: "It is my conviction that failure on our part to give this support will be fatal to our plans to keep Morocco and North Africa strong enough to resist enemy aggression. We will not find such leaders elsewhere, and we dare not lose them now. . . ."[2]

The secret cables between COI Washington and COI Casablanca continued through the spring. Donovan, under extreme pressure, was deliberately evasive with his senior agent in the field because of War Department politics at home and the push for BOLERO. Nor was the enemy standing still. When Pierre Laval grasped the reins of government in Vichy, he began to replace senior Army and Navy officers with his own followers. The Afrika Korps was heavily engaged with the British Eighth Army, and the German plan was to receive from their collaborator in Vichy the surrender of the French Army and Navy and, of course, the tanks and artillery and warships as a formidable prize.

Working closely in tandem, Eddy and Murphy were unaware of the seriousness of the supply situation in the United States. America really began to gear up for the war the day after Pearl Harbor, but it would be nearly a year before the massive outpouring of war materiel began. It was during the first six months of 1942 that the War Department's Chiefs of Staff, now known as the Joint Chiefs of Staff, or

JCS, came to the conclusion that there was nothing that the United States or the Allies could do militarily to prevent the Axis from taking all of North Africa. It was their considered judgment that COI should organize guerrilla forces which could take to the hills and strike the Axis from mountain redoubts, coordinating their operations with the future Allied landing in North Africa. Some of the Joint Chiefs and their subordinates were the men who, along with then Colonel Eisenhower, had roundly condemned the unplanned ROTC guerrilla operation in Monroe, Louisiana, less than ten months earlier. They had not believed in guerrilla warfare in 1941. By mid-1942 the realities of World War II had made some of them firm believers in guerrilla supporting operations, as COI presented a continuing flow of information about growing resistance activities in occupied Europe.

In Africa the thirteen plotters continued their spying, collecting information about French troop movements, the arrival and departure of freighters and tankers (some of which were waylaid by British submarines in the Mediterranean and sunk as a result of radio reports by these COI–State Department agents), the seasonal tidal changes, dock and harbor facilities, the location of coastal artillery, and any other intelligence on request. In Washington, COI had begun to put together the massive jigsaw puzzle.

The office of Coordinator of Information had become unwieldy, and President Roosevelt decided that it would be best to divorce the nation's wartime propaganda arm from COI. It made sense. The efforts of COI would be most effective directed at strategic intelligence of a military nature. Any of COI's propaganda work should be in the field and concern itself with "black" or covert activities aimed at breaking the morale of the enemy. While Donovan, who was referred to by his COI staff as the "Colonel" after Pearl Harbor, was visiting in London with the Combined Chiefs of Staff and meeting with the chief of SIS to arrange even further collaboration with British intelligence, he was advised that FDR had signed a Military Order as Commander-in-Chief, renaming COI the Office of Strategic Services. In executive order No. 9182 that same day, June 13, 1942, FDR transferred all "white" or overt propaganda activities to the new Office of War Information, headed by former newspaperman and radio commentator Elmer Davis. COI's Foreign Information Service headed by Robert Sherwood became the Overseas Branch of OWI.

It was during this critical period that Donovan's centralized intelligence service struggled for its very survival. For the President had directed that OSS operate under "the jurisdiction of the United States Joint Chiefs of Staff . . . to collect and to analyze such strategic information as may be required by the USJCS; and to plan and operate such special services as may be directed by the Joint Chiefs of Staff." In October 1941, FDR had quietly authorized Donovan to begin on a small scale to recruit and train spies and saboteurs and plan guerrilla operations against a future enemy.[8]

As the invasion of North Africa approached, OSS was involved in jurisdictional problems with the JCS. Army intelligence and ONI wanted to dispense with the many civilian experts whom Donovan had recruited. The Army's G–2, General Strong, "hated the OSS . . . and vowed that he would not rely upon its intelligence collection system but established his own in 1942. . . . Undaunted by the opposition . . . Donovan moved ahead with the development of his organization."[4]

He had planned well. Nothing stood in the way of OSS participation in Operation TORCH and, thanks to his friends in British intelligence, Donovan time and again was able to provide the JCS with information which the service intelligence organizations could not provide. He, too, knew how to play the game of one-upsmanship.

The thirteen plotters smuggled a French harbor pilot from France back to North Africa to guide American warships into the harbors they might invade. They also spread false rumors about the invasion occurring at Dakar, on the coast one-third of the way south between Casablanca and Capetown, and elements of the Nazi Atlantic Fleet actually steamed for the Atlantic port on the coast of Africa.

Early in October General Eisenhower, commanding Operation TORCH and wearing the three stars of a lieutenant general, summoned his second in command, General Mark Clark, who had also participated in the Louisiana maneuvers a year earlier. The invasion of North Africa was scheduled for early November. Only the latest intelligence information to be assessed by a high-ranking officer and members of his staff was needed. At the same time both COI and SIS had picked up bits and pieces and, with confirmation from pro-Allied French officers, learned of an impending Axis invasion of French North Africa. The French officers requested a meeting with high-ranking Allied officers. Specifically, they wanted to know what kind of military assistance they could expect if they sided with the Allies.

Operation TORCH had become a race against time. General Eisenhower reasoned that a secret meeting with the French could provide information that would save many lives. On the other hand, a tremendous risk was involved, and the mission could be blown. Discovery might warn Vichy and the Nazis that an Allied landing was imminent, stepping up any plans that Hitler had to take over French North Africa.

"Will you go to North Africa?" Ike asked his deputy, General Clark. "The French will speak to an American military man only. And it's dangerous, especially if you're caught."

The six-foot-three-inch general nodded assent. He asked to select the men he felt could contribute most to the mission, and picked from the American military staff Navy Captain Jerauld Wright, a crack shot with a pistol; Colonel Julius Holmes, a diplomat in uniform with prior experience in North Africa and fluent in French; Brigadier General Lyman Lemnitzer, one of the senior operations officers in G–3, and Colonel Arch Hamblen, a logistics expert who specialized in transportation problems. They secretly left London headquarters and flew to Gibraltar, where they boarded a British submarine and met their escorts, three commando officers who would take them ashore in kayaks, lightweight wood and canvas boats that required expert handling. The submarine headed east into the Mediterranean, and on the night of October 20 surfaced seventy-five miles west of Algiers.[5]

A light blinked from the shore. The coast was clear. The Americans piled into the tiny boats and then waited as one kayak was rowed ashore with Colonel Holmes. There was no room for error. When the kayak grated against the beach, Holmes and his commando escort stepped out, pulling the craft out of the water. Then, carbines held ready, they waited. There was movement in the night, and a voice called out softly in English, "Who's there?" No coded password. Just a simple question which received an equally terse query from Holmes, "Who're you?"

Ridgeway Knight introduced himself; Holmes did likewise and asked for Bob Murphy. He was told that Murphy would be along at any moment. The commando officer, listening to the conversation, decided all was clear and signaled the submarine to send in the other boats with Clark, Lemnitzer, and Wright. By the time they landed Murphy had arrived, and the Americans, the British commandos, and their greeters trudged through the sand to a nearby house owned by Jacques Tessier, an anti-Fascist French farmer. There they were greeted by OSS's Colonel Eddy, who had met the senior members of Eisenhower's staff the previous July during a special visit to London to receive a briefing about Operation TORCH.

On the morning of the twenty-second, General Charles Mast and Colonel d'Astier de la Vigerie arrived and immediately went into conference with the visiting delegation from London. General Mast asked if the invasion could be delayed about six weeks. Clark came bluntly to the point. Plans could not be changed. He couldn't inform the French general, for security reasons, that the Western Task Force filled with troops had already sailed from the United States and that the Central Task Force had embarked from England along with the Eastern Task Force, a combined American-British fleet. What Clark and his staff wanted to know was the assistance they could expect from the French Army and Navy. Mast was equally blunt. No help from the Navy; possibly resistance.

From the Army? Token resistance in the Algiers area. Elsewhere? Mast shrugged his Gallic shoulders. Then the technical military questions of an intelligence nature. How much ship tonnage could the port of Oran accommodate during a twenty-four-hour period? How much cargo could be unloaded during a similar period? Algiers? The same questions. Casablanca? Port Lyautey?

The airfields? How long are the runways? What condition? What kind of military aircraft are parked? The railroad system? Power generators? Food stocks to feed the populace?

And so it went. By the time the Americans and the French officers had completed their conference early that evening, all of the available last-minute intelligence that was required had been obtained. Outside the weather began to whip up heavy seas, and the French general and his staff assistant agreed to join the Americans at dinner to answer any final questions.

But security had been broken. Two servants employed by French *colon* Tessier had been summarily dismissed the day before the meeting. Angry and suspicious, they vented their anger by reporting to the local police that something was afoot at the seashore house, once a smugglers' haven. That night a police patrol drove to the cottage, but a young French Army officer on guard spotted their approach and ran into the cottage shouting, *"Les gendarmes arrivent!"* The visitors jumped to their feet and were hustled into the cellar while Murphy and Knight quickly removed evidence that more than just two Americans were present with "friends." He told the French officer who had been on guard to go back outside and advise the police that two American diplomats were having a party, had selected the cottage as an out-of-the-way spot to entertain their girl friends with black-market wine and dinner, and, emphasized Murphy in fluent French, "if they break it up it will create an international incident—and repercussions for the police officials."[6]

The police patrol bought the story. Shortly after they departed, Murphy clambered into the cellar and suggested that the visitors wait out the night. But Clark would have none of it. The police could return at any time. Too much was at stake. They had to try to return to the submarine, and if they waited outside they could make a break into the night if the police did return, or shoot it out if they had to. Later, they managed to launch their flimsy boats and return to the submarine. But General Clark lost his pants weighted with $2,000 in gold coins, and the kayaks drifted away and were surfed ashore. Murphy and Knight spent the rest of the early morning hours patrolling the beach, picking up the battered pieces of the kayaks, and burying the remains along with other bits of evidence that strangers had been present.

Several hours after the submarine had gotten under way,

a flying boat landed alongside, and the American officers were transferred aboard and flown to Gibraltar to brief the invasion staff.

In North Africa, meanwhile, OSS had its work cut out. A handful of anti-Vichy Frenchmen had been recruited and armed. Some were to coordinate the landings on the beaches. Others were to blow up vital installations if necessary and, at the same time, pass on last-minute information to the secret radio stations.* Colonel Eddy received information that the French Army at Oran would resist the Allied invasion, and he broadcast this warning to Gibraltar, where all wave bands used by the OSS station radios were being monitored.

At 0030 hours, November 8, 1942, the OSS secret radio stations began picking up a coded message addressed directly to the plotters and other American agents in North Africa. The message was in French: *"Écoute, écoute, Yankee, Franklin, Pilgrim, Midway, Lincoln. Robert arrive! Robert arrive!"*

The invasion of North Africa had begun.

---

*At the time of the Allied invasion of North Africa, nineteen Frenchmen joined the OSS-backed resistance movement after President Roosevelt's appeal to all French citizens in the invasion area for assistance in what was the first step in the liberation of France. These nineteen men assisted in cutting communications and sabotaging coast artillery, which was rendered ineffective against invading American troops.

Shortly afterward, they were arrested by the remnants of the Vichy regime and court-martialed for treason by a French general who later switched his allegiance. After U.S. forces consolidated positions in North Africa, OSS representatives tried to persuade General George S. Patton to intercede with French military officials and have the men freed.

Patton refused, claiming: "They got what they deserved; it was treason, wasn't it?" However, when General Charles DeGaulle assumed the reins of government in North Africa on behalf of the Free French forces, he set right this miscarriage of justice and ordered the nineteen Frenchmen pardoned, decorated and as many of them as were veterans of the French Army, promoted.

5

> As living spies we must recruit men who
> are intelligent but appear to be stupid; who
> seem to be dull but are strong in heart; men
> who are agile, vigorous, hardy and brave; well-
> versed in lowly matters and able to endure
> hunger, cold, filth, and humiliation.
>
> —SUN TZU (400–320 B.C.):
> *The Art of War*

Whether it was COI or OSS, America's wartime intelligence
agency was a catchall organization which, during its early
COI era, had been described by Radio Berlin as "fifty professors, twenty monkeys, ten goats, twelve guinea pigs and a
staff of Jewish scribblers." The animals were on the top floor
of the former National Health Institute building, where an
experimental laboratory was the last remaining NHI department after COI headquarters was set up.

At the beginning, however, the vital core of American
intelligence was the group of middle-aged specialists in the
social sciences who proved that libraries and dated and near-
crumbling German publications could reveal more important
facts than a battalion of Mata Haris. By the time OSS was
formed, Donovan's intelligence organization was receiving
its share of derision in wartime alphabetized Washington. Although it was supposed to be a secret service, the OSS was
called by detractors "Oh, So Social" because of the prominent Social Register names who had joined up; or "Oh, So
Secret" since people could only guess what was going on
down by the gas works at 25th and E Streets, N.W. Others
referred to the organization as "Oh, Shush Shush" or "Oh,
So Stupid." As there were no professionals in this field in the

76

United States, offense was not taken by the rapidly growing OSS staff. They were much too busy working round the clock on Operation TORCH and training people to operate in uniform or behind enemy lines as spies.

Donovan, no great shakes as an administrator, tapped his law firm for the assistance of people he could trust implicitly—men like Otto C. Doering, Jr., and Ned Putzell, who followed him to Washington. What angered old-line Washington bureaucrats most was Donovan's recruiting other administrators from the private sector who had made their mark in their respective professions. Financiers Junius P. Morgan, Charles Cheston, and Russell Forgan were joined by international lawyer Allen Dulles; ex-Governor William Vanderbilt of Rhode Island; Louis Ream of U.S. Steel; Atherton Richards of the Hawaiian Pineapple Company; pollster Elmo Roper; movie star Sterling Hayden, who later sailed small boats across the Adriatic between Italy and German-occupied Balkans; Notre Dame halfback Joe Savoldi, who parachuted behind enemy lines in Italy; Prince of Imperial Russia Serge Obolensky, labor lawyer Arthur Goldberg; and Minnesota legislator John A. Blatnik.* Soldiers of fortune like Charlie Sweeny were few and far between.

How were men and women recruited into OSS? There were no application forms and no formal announcement. People were recruited if they had the expertise that COI originally needed—academic specialties or other knowledge of distant lands and their people, climate, terrain, politics, and industries. They were recruited as administrators who could keep secret the most private affairs of OSS, such as the movement of millions of dollars in currency from the U.S. to Europe to pay the resistance movements of many nations. By late 1942 they were being recruited in greater numbers for "dangerous and hazardous duty" behind enemy lines.

There were, according to Congressman John E. Rankin, "Communists in the OSS." And he was right. There was a

---

*Blatnik, a congressman since 1946, was accused by his opponent in the 1946 Congressional campaign of "collaborating with Communists," because he had spent nine months in Yugoslavia with an OSS mission to Marshal Tito.

cross-section of first generation Americans and Mayflower Americans, Republicans and Democrats, Socialists and Communists, mechanics and artists, second-story men and ex-cops, and many who had little or no aversion to danger and adventure. There were scholars, and there were suave smooth-talkers who had managed to sell their expertise at nothing to a friend of a friend who happened to be in OSS. Donovan could seldom say "no" to an applicant recommended by a friend of a friend. When approached he'd wriggle out by advising the applicant to write him a memorandum about how "you could be of service to this organization, and if I agree with you, you're hired." Some applicants, without much to offer or knowledge of OSS, managed to slip through the door during the first year, and some, with connections in high places, were granted commissions and then did nothing but travel around the world with Class A priority at Government expense.[1]

OSS was that kind of outfit—the good with the bad. By mid-1943 complaints about incompetence in the field began arriving at OSS headquarters in Washington. There were even a few dramatic mental crack-ups, and the urgent need for more careful screening of OSS recruits became clear. It was also clear to the OSS top command that the agency required more administrative and operational cohesion. Nine major OSS branches were created and committed to the organizational chart:

> *Research and Analysis* (R&A)—The original core of academics around whose activities the entire organization revolved. This branch became responsible for the production of economic, military, social, and political studies, and estimates for every strategic area from Europe to the Far East.
>
> *Secret Intelligence* (SI)—To gather on-the-spot information from within neutral and enemy territory.
>
> *Special Operations* (SO)—To conduct sabotage and work with resistance forces in enemy-occupied territory.
>
> *Counterintelligence* (X-2)—The protection of American and Allied intelligence operations and the identification of enemy agents overseas.
>
> *Morale Operations* (MO)—The creation and dissemination of "black" or covert propaganda.

Operational Groups (OG)—To train, supply, and lead guerrilla forces in enemy territory.

Maritime Unit (MU)—To conduct maritime sabotage, deliver supplies, and land agents and guerrilla forces in enemy territory from the sea.

Schools and Training (S&T)—Responsible for the assessment and training of recruits in the United States and overseas.

Foreign Nationalities (FN)—A major unit with activities centered in the U.S. where its staff obtained all manner of information about enemy nations or enemy-occupied areas from refugees, political escapees, or exiles.[2]

To solve the assessment and training problem in the United States, OSS later took over the 118-acre estate of a prominent Washington hotel family and turned it into a screening center known as Area S. But one of the earlier training centers, set up in the summer of 1942, is best described by Lyman B. Kirkpatrick, Jr., who at an early date was advised by no less a personage than Secretary of the Navy Frank Knox against joining OSS. "Look, young man," Knox warned Kirkpatrick, "I know Bill Donovan well and consider him a good friend. But don't go into that crazy outfit!"[3] Kirkpatrick's first exposure to an early training center continues:

> I was instructed to pack enough clothes and toilet articles to last a week; dress would be informal and should include clothing for outside activity. I was to advise my family that I would be gone until Friday afternoon, but to give no indication where I was going. (I did not know myself, so how could I?) And I was to leave a telephone number in Washington to be used only in an emergency. Finally, I was to be on the 11th Street side of the Raleigh Hotel in downtown Washington at 3 P.M. on Sunday. A black Chevrolet with District of Columbia plates would drive up, and I should ask the driver if he was "Alex." If the answer was affirmative, I should get in. I should never use any name but my first one (which always impressed me as ridiculous, since mine is rather distinctive) and I should not reveal to anyone what my assignment was to be. There would be additional instructions upon arrival.

I followed instructions to the letter. . . .

At some distance into the countryside the car arrived at a locked gate that was quickly opened for us, and a half-mile farther up the driveway we arrived at a large, pleasant country house. At the door one of the staff checked us in, told us where to find our rooms, cautioned us against using other than our first names, and advised us that there would be a meeting before dinner. . . .

For four weeks we were introduced into the intricacies of intelligence operations. Our instructors were frank in acknowledging their own inadequate backgrounds and experience in intelligence work, many of them having had only a few weeks of training themselves, and one having spent some time in England being trained by the British. We learned such things as simple coding and decoding methods for sending messages. We were given some books on intelligence to read, in many instances more fiction than fact. We received extensive training in fieldcraft, including the handling of guns, silent killing, and all of the other aptitudes that secret agents are supposed to possess.[4]

Extreme secrecy was demanded of recruits into COI and later into OSS. But flaws in the haphazard build-up of COI and OSS began to show in mid-1943, during which time the nation's intelligence organization "was busily and somewhat hazardously recruiting personnel without benefit of any professional or uniform screening process. Then came the exciting stimulus: the suggestion by an official from OSS in London who had recently visited a WOSB (War Office Selection Board which tested candidates for commissions in the British Army) unit in Britain that a psychological-psychiatric assessment unit be established in the United States. This idea was presented in October 1943, at one of the morning executive staff meetings. . . . It was well received by those of the recruiting branch who were present and especially by Colonels John A. Hoag and Henson L. Robinson of the Schools and Training Branch, whose training programs had carried the brunt of too many cases of bad recruitment."[5] The problem was summed up in an early 1943 classified memorandum:

The organization has been recruiting too many men, civilian or military, who have the intelligence and

sometimes the necessary mechanical training but who
lack common sense, know nothing about working with
men or how to look after the welfare and the morale
of the men under them. We simply must have men who
can shoulder responsibility and use initiative with
common sense. Simply because a man has intelligence
does not qualify him for this type of work. In some
instances we also have had men who fall into the class
of the high-strung or emotional type. We simply cannot
use men of that type in the field when they have to live
with Chinese, eat Chinese food, and be under pressure
at times. In most cases these men have suffered nervous
breakdowns and other nervous ailments. Whether men
are recruited in the States or here in the field they
must be checked by a doctor and a psychiatrist before
being pronounced fit for the field. . . . For us it is
more important since our men spend from three to
six months in the field without seeing American installations. We have had at least eight men, who for
various quirks in their make-up, have had to be pulled
from the field . . . [who] should never have been sent
to the field. . . . Others simply wouldn't fit anywhere.
One was definitely a psychiatric case.[6]

The OSS had come of age with the establishment of Stations S, W, and F in the greater Washington area and WS in
California; and later similar assessment and training facilities
in Algiers, using British SIS and SOE Parachute and Intelligence School at Oujda near Oran, and centers in India,
Ceylon, and China. Originally, COI had used the British
training station in Canada, and during the build-up of American forces in England, British intelligence training centers
in England and Scotland were utilized to school the U.S.
military personnel recruited from among the troops in the
British Isles. The original staff of Station S (for "Secret") had
no criteria for the screening-out process other than information obtained from the British. In fact, no member of this
original assessment staff possessed any intimate knowledge
of OSS. The men and women who launched the program,
later adopted by many of the nation's largest corporations
as an executive recruiting tool, had no idea what the qualifications were for a spy, saboteur, resistance group leader, section leader, liaison pilot, paratrooper, base station operator,

communications operator, demolitions instructor, field representative, or even a pigeoneer.[7]

Although a few operations were underway in mid-1943 and others were being secretly planned, those that had been launched were happening in remote areas behind enemy lines and outside the range of witnesses. At some bases, OSS commanding officers for months at a time were unaware of what their agents and operational groups were doing. The rules of the intelligence game were changing from week to week and month to month, and for the majority of OSS personnel in the field their successes—and their failures—were the result of on-the-job training: learning the intelligence business the hard way.

From sparse reports but mostly by osmosis, the S&T assessment staffs laboriously developed the programs which, beginning in December 1943 until the war ended in August 1945, screened 5,391 recruits in the United States. They were above average in intelligence, thanks to the original screening procedure which ruled out a good many candidates during basic interviews. Those selected for the primary test at the assessment stations were a cosmopolitan group compared to their fellow citizens. About half had visited foreign countries: a fifth had traveled in Europe, one-twentieth had visited Africa or Asia, one-tenth had journeyed to Latin America, one-eighth had visited two or more continents, and one-fifth had spent five years or more abroad. Of course, many of the candidates were foreign-born or political refugees.

One in four spoke a foreign language fluently, and one in twelve spoke two or more. More than fifty languages were spoken by the candidates who had gone through the assessment course. Many had college degrees; some where PhDs—compared to 59.5 percent of the American population who had only elementary-school education.[8] That this category of the upper socioeconomic strata of the nation predominated in OSS explains why many of the early recruits to COI and OSS were names commonly associated with the Social Register. Who else among the American population would have had the benefits of a university education and travel then associated with social status?

At Station S, for example, 2,372 volunteer recruits were screened, and of every four assessed, one failed outright, two were passed with reservations, and one was immediately accepted after the arduous tests and offered the more dangerous behind-the-lines missions. The two who passed with reservations were assigned to intelligence duties overseas which involved little danger. Fifty-two emotional breakdowns occurred among OSS personnel during the war, and of these, two men had managed to pass the Station S screening procedure.

Recruits arrived at Station S in small groups, some of them officers with rank as high as colonel. There were privates, sergeants, and civilians, including some women. And they arrived in uniforms devoid of rank or in mufti and, of course, incognito. At S they were again cautioned not to reveal their true names, ranks, or backgrounds. On the first day, the assessment program included maximum stress conditions for the new arrivals. They were presented physical problems to solve such as moving a group of men and a hundred-pound rock across a brook without falling in, all the while under deliberate verbal harassment by members of the assessment staff. Their only equipment to complete the maneuver consisted of wooden planks too short to span the creek. There were terrain tests, obstacle courses, and other physical endurance contests, all sparked by psychological pressures imposed on the recruits.

On the second day, the testing tended more toward the intelligence and military side, such as the mining of vital enemy bridges, assassination of collaborator officials, interrogation of prisoners, and reporting enemy strengths and movements. The third day was concerned with filling out questionnaires "of a sociometric nature" in which the recruits made value judgments about events and contrived situations, and about their colleagues among the candidates. The fourth day wound up the assessment program. Those who had passed easily relaxed while the assessment staff conferred about questionable candidates, whether to pass them with reservations or fail them outright.[8]

Clearly, by early 1944, OSS had come of age. Donovan, who had been placed on active duty by FDR shortly after Pearl Harbor, was promoted to brigadier general in April 1943 in order to deal more effectively with Allied intelligence officials; he would be promoted to major general in November 1944. He had become the father figure; the affable but not complete executive who rarely said "no" to applicants for jobs with OSS or to ideas, however farfetched. Some have described him as a visionary, however impractical. On the other hand, as director of a federal agency—albeit a part of the vast military bureaucracy—he had by late 1943 become a globe-trotting symbol, referred to as "the chief" or Code Number 109—and was the idol of OSS men in the field. He had compensated for his own administrative ineffectiveness by using loyal deputies whom he could trust to carry out his ideas and maintain tight control of the organization, acting in his name. Donovan knew that success for OSS might be credited to others, but any failures would reflect on him personally. There were many in the Pentagon—which had become War Department headquarters in 1943—and on Capitol Hill who had their long knives ready and waiting for any slip made by the commanding general of OSS or his secret agency.

It was also that kind of war.

6

Nothing is more worthy of the attention of a good general than the endeavor to penetrate the designs of the enemy.

—NICCOLÒ MACHIAVELLI:
Discorsi, 1531

Although there were admirals and generals on the JCS who would have preferred their version of conventional military intelligence operations, they had been made aware of Donovan's White House connections. The President was *the* Commander-in-Chief and Donovan was a very close friend of the CinC. But in the Southwest Pacific, General Douglas MacArthur would have none of OSS or its predecessor COI, despite strong suggestions from FDR. Of all America's generals and admirals, the square-jawed military leader who commanded GHQ—and virtually all forces in the western Pacific—was the only theater commander with stature enough to ignore directives from the White House or the Pentagon during World War II. Instead, MacArthur set up his own cloak-and-dagger organization, including the Allied Intelligence Bureau, which directed all behind-the-lines activities. MacArthur's later rebuttal to queries about his reluctance to accept OSS was that he couldn't afford to wait for the nation's first intelligence organization to get under way. He was faced with an immediate military situation that required intelligence on the spot.[1]

The Navy, meantime, channeled some of its intelligence activities into competition in the far Pacific with anything that COI then had in mind. On the morning of December 9, 1941, Rear Admiral Willis A. Lee, director of ONI, proposed that his agency organize a secret force in China that was used

85

initially to radio vital weather information to Pacific Fleet units. An old China hand, Lee believed that he could marshal the resources of China's own intelligence service which was under the command of Lieutenant General Tai Li, later referred to as Fu Manchu by the OSS detachments that were posted to China in late 1943. The result of ONI's initial effort to set up its own intelligence apparatus in the Far East was the Sino-American Cooperative Organization, or SACO. Called "Socko" by the sailors and marines who were assigned to the Chinese hinterlands, the organization was led by Commander Milton E. Miles who, in order to obtain the cooperation of the Chinese, became second in command under General Tai Li. Miles launched SACO in May 1942, and for eighteen months his operation deep inside China was no more than a whisper in Washington. As with other government agencies, the Navy attempted to play one-upsmanship in the event that OSS might fail and be absorbed by one of the military services. General Donovan visited Chungking in December 1943 to enlist the aid of General Claire Chennault, who commanded the 14th Air Force, for a better-coordinated intelligence operation. It was only then that OSS was able to overcome the objections of General Tai Li.

Chennault, who was a favorite of Madame Chiang, was able to override the Chinese intelligence chief's objections to his retaining full control of all intelligence activities. General Tai Li at one point appealed to General MacArthur's GHQ in Australia to keep OSS out of the Pacific Theater entirely; and throughout the war he regularly forwarded all manner of reports to GHQ in an effort to provoke MacArthur into halting the OSS build-up in Asia. The Chinese intelligence chief continued to play his own game throughout the war and continually tried to intrude himself into OSS operations, delaying in 1943 the insertion of the first American team into Thailand.

But R&A's scholars, even prior to Pearl Harbor, had begun to organize a huge file of basic intelligence data about the Far East that would be used by the staff at the proper time. The prime intelligence target by necessity was occupied Europe, and organizing OSS to tackle this problem had taken first priority.

Operating out of Cairo and London, OSS staffs began to organize their resources and still maintain secrecy. But the Abwehr was everywhere, including Cairo, and in 1943 only a few Americans spoke any of several Arabic dialects. Relying on the British to provide basic counterintelligence, the X–2 people reported to OSS chief in Cairo, Colonel John Tuhlman, that a group of merchants with business ties in Turkey and Palestine were suspected of being enemy agents. Even more frustrating, they spoke in dialects that were unintelligible to the CI people of X–2.

One night in the home of Britain's Desert Air Force chief, Air Marshal Arthur Tedder, Tuhlman was engaged in small-talk around the dinner table when his ears perked up. Mrs. Tedder casually mentioned the linguistic abilities of their twelve-year-old son, who had learned a number of dialects during the family's extended residence in the Middle East. After dinner, Colonel Tuhlman took the Tedders aside and quickly advised them of the serious problem with enemy agents.

"Can we borrow your son for a short period?" Tuhlman asked the Tedders. "He might be able to pick up the information we want."

"A counterspy?" the Air Marshal's wife asked. Tuhlman, holding his breath, nodded silently.

Mrs. Tedder looked at her husband. He agreed. "Is there any danger?" she asked Tuhlman. He replied that all would be asked of the youngster would be to play in the lobby of a hotel frequented by the merchants. That is, if Mrs. Tedder wouldn't mind visiting the hotel's patio for a spot of tea with her son when she received a phone call from an X–2 agent or his British partner advising of the merchants' arrival. Mrs. Tedder's appearance in the hotel would raise no suspicions: it was a place she visited frequently.

She agreed. Every Englishman was expected to do his duty, including her young son. It was a great adventure for young Tedder, and he carried out his role as directed. Playing near the merchants, he overheard them discuss a sabotage project they were about to begin. This confirmed the suspicions of X–2 agents, who reported to the OSS chief that the merchants definitely were spies. He ordered their arrest, and the ring of Abwehr agents was broken up, thanks to the help of the youngest counterspy ever "hired" by OSS. Tuhlman offered young Tedder anything he would like as payment for his part in cracking the spy ring. He requested a stamp album. The eight-dollar item was flown priority air freight from Washington.

But the cost of operating a secret intelligence service soared in short time. Agents were paid various amounts, but those who were recruited in their native countries, in Europe, or the United States signed employment contracts for which they were paid $100 to $150 a month, plus a $5,000 life insurance policy to be awarded to anyone they designated. It was a simple contract reading: "The employer shall pay the employe the sum of _____ dollars in the currency of the United States of America each month while said contract is in force. . . . This contract is a voluntary act of the employe undertaken without duress."* Even spies require gainful employment.

Obtaining cash from the U.S. government proved difficult, even in wartime with less supervision expected under the circumstances. It takes a lot of cold, hard cash to conduct the business of intelligence-gathering. It takes cash in various currencies and, on occasion, intelligence work requires the use of gold in exchange for information. Also, OSS was not managed according to the latest federal administrative manuals or regulations. The first requests for cash came in late 1941 from COI's thirteen State Department plotters in North Africa for use as expense and travel money, and

---

*Since all OSS operational records are in the custody of the CIA, the secret lists of World War II agents employed by the OSS and copies of their signed contracts have been used time and again by the U.S. postwar intelligence agency. Many former OSS agents of foreign nationality, or "indigenous personnel" as they were referred to, have since become wealthy or prominent or politically powerful in their respective countries.

The threat of exposure by the U.S. agency holding copies of these "contracts" has been used on occasion to obtain information. This secret file of former OSS agents was one of the bonuses inherited by CIA.

later to purchase small tidbits of information. By late 1942 OSS in London began forwarding requests back to head-quarters in Washington for large amounts of cash. The first major request was for $3 million, immediately required by British SIS agents in occupied Europe.

There was consternation in OSS Washington, to say the least. In the administrative side of the organization, officials wondered how they could go about explaining their request for such a huge amount of money. There were certain procedures demanded by the Treasury Department which didn't take into consideration that one government agency, for security reasons, just couldn't account for the money item by item nor list how it would be used. The expenditure of public monies also could come under the sharp scrutiny of enemy intelligence; clever analysts in Berlin might be able to discover where this money was going and what it might be used for.

Another problem was how to move this amount of cash after it had been obtained. How much weight and space, for example, does two, three, or five million dollars in $50 and $100 bills take up on an aircraft? Should it be moved in locked canvas mail sacks, or heavy strongboxes or in ordinary suitcases? How should the money be protected against the danger of possible capture? By destructive con-tainers of acid shipped along with the currency or thermite fire grenades packed among the stacks of money? There were many official avenues for the transfer of huge amounts of money between the U.S. Treasury and the Bank of England. But too many people would have been involved in this on-going transfer of funds, and security might have been en-dangered. Nor did the OSS commanding general himself agonize over money, as he could rarely be pinned down in one place long enough to submit his personal expense accounts. In fact, during the early months of COI his ex-penditures came from his own pocket. He had made it clear that he didn't want to be bothered by financial problems. After all, that's why he had brought in top financial experts, not only to analyze the economy of Nazi Germany and the Axis and the flow of money in wartime Europe, but who could bring some sense of fiscal management into a growing agency.

Finally, how does one issue currency for secret activities in enemy-occupied countries? It can't be newly printed currency, for if an agent or members of the underground resistance were caught with crinkly fresh greenbacks, they would find it difficult to explain that it was something they had either earned conducting a little black-market business on the side, or had hoarded against another Depression. In wartime Europe, the American dollar was considered a very hard currency—as good as gold. And then, of course, there was gold—louis d'or coins and gold sovereigns which were more than worth their weight.*

During a two-year period beginning in early 1942, OSS secretly transferred $18 million in cash to British intelligence. After Donovan obtained FDR's personal intercession with the Secretary of the Treasury, the OSS finance officer, Lane Rehm, was able to withdraw large-denomination notes without answering too many questions. The Treasury, however, demanded repayment within ninety days. The first withdrawal of $3 million was flown to England. This new currency was exchanged in England for small-denomination bills that had been collected by the Bank of England. This well-used currency, mostly from the first American forces to arrive in England in the spring of 1942, was flown back to OSS in Washington and returned back to the Treasury.

But the X–2 security staff, saddled with the responsibility of riding shotgun on the currency deliveries, soon learned that if four mail sacks were required for $50 and $100 denomination bills totaling $3 million, upwards of forty mail sacks were required to transport the same amount of currency in smaller denominations. This meant that more shotgun guards were needed on the return flight to the U.S.—an assignment for which the X–2 staff in London eagerly bid.

Most of the original withdrawal of $3 million was delivered to Poland by SIS which, throughout the war, maintained a closer contact with the Polish underground than OSS. On another occasion the Treasury refused to turn over currency

---

*There was very little accounting in the field for this money and gold other than barely legible signatures on tattered pieces of paper. As a result, many millions of dollars escaped audit.

to OSS because repayment had been slow. Although some $34 million of OSS funds in gold and U.S. currency had been transported to Poland for use by the anti-Nazi resistance forces, no trace of this money existed at war's end.

Meanwhile, the OSS office in Berne, headed by Allen Dulles, known as Number 110 in the OSS message codebook, was saddled with the additional responsibility of collecting small-denomination U.S. currency from the Swiss banking community for later use to pay for secret services rendered in occupied Europe. In one report made by OSS London to headquarters in Washington, an opinion was expressed that much of the new $50 and $100 U.S. currency sent to Poland by the British had been paid to high-ranking members of the German occupation forces who, in turn, managed to deposit this money in Swiss bank accounts.*

Although well-used small-denomination bills were preferred by agents for operations at their level, new bills in denominations of $50 and $100 were sent to the underground in Poland for other uses. The large bills, along with gold, bought the services of the enemy, collaborators, and those Poles who set a price on their help. Also, the large-denomination bills in amounts of five, ten, or twenty thousand dollars represented "official" Polish government-in-exile funds used by officials in Poland to conduct wartime business. Just as in Poland, American dollars elsewhere in Europe served an important purpose in the intelligence business. And OSS was the goose that laid the golden eggs—perhaps as much as $135 million worth.

If the intricacies of the money game in intelligence operations were difficult for OSS officials to grasp, so too were the political games to which many Americans were exposed on

---

*Postwar investigations by war-crimes agencies of many nations came to naught concerning the question of Nazi ownership of safe-deposit boxes or numbered bank accounts. Swiss banking officials, despite acquiescence of their government, to this day have declined to address this question.

Some of the accounts established by Nazi officials have gone unclaimed since the end of World War II. It is assumed that the men who had established secret numbered accounts perished during the final months of the Third Reich.

missions behind enemy lines. By late 1943 the British expressed admiration for the alacrity with which Americans in
OSS learned how to develop and conduct special operations:
hit-and-run guerrilla raids, sabotage, ambushes, etc. No one
ever could fault the American as a fighter. But when it came
to understanding the politics of a particular country or region,
suddenly he was at a loss to understand the strong animosity
between resistance forces dedicated to destroying their common enemy.

In Yugoslavia OSS operational groups attached to Marshal
Tito had been forewarned to beware of the Chetnik partisans
of Yugoslav Army General Draza Mihailovic. In Greece,
OSS teams later found themselves caught in a crossfire between royalist and Communist factions who, while fighting
their common enemy, also found time to engage in shoot-outs
with each other. Nor was there much difference to the pattern
in France where pro-Communist guerrillas competed with
their fellow anti-Nazi *citoyens* for political control of the
underground, and of France *après la guerre.*

The problem faced by OSS people assigned to operate
behind enemy lines was summed up by one American, who
explained that those who

> hailed from nations where freedom was deeply ingrained
> found it hard to fathom the political passions and rival-
> ries unleashed by totalitarianism. Many did not readily
> understand why the patriots were not content merely to
> carry out sabotage assignments and report intelligence.
> The political goals of leftist parties transcended strictly
> military operations, of course, but sometimes these re-
> mained a riddle to Allied personnel, who understandably
> could be confused by the intricacies of Italian multiparty
> politics. And even if they grasped the political ramifica-
> tions of the underground, liaison officers might well be
> tempted to reflect either the prejudices of the group
> with which they worked most closely or of the group
> whose program most nearly coincided with their own
> politico-economic predilections.[2]

Politics would be equally complex for those OSS agents
assigned to Thailand, Indochina, and China. Unaware of the
implications of their actions, they would help create, by
virtue of their secret assignments to organize and on occasion

to fight with underground resistance forces, a future political environment that would pose problems of diplomatic policy. In the cases of Indochina and Greece, for example, OSS wartime operations would affect the future course of American foreign policy.

England, France, Belgium, Holland, Germany, Italy, Austria, Czechoslovakia, Switzerland, the Balkans, North Africa, India, Burma, Ceylon, China—by late 1943 these had become the friendly, neutral, and enemy-occupied stamping grounds for the global operations of OSS. A year after Pearl Harbor, the United States was deep in the intelligence business; indeed, so involved that what had been created by OSS would, after the war, survive, continue, and by Presidential Executive Order ultimately become the U.S. Central Intelligence Agency. But America's intelligence experience in World War II would become both legend at home and folklore abroad, featured on the covers of paperback thrillers, in the pages of periodicals and books, and committed to films starring Gary Cooper, Alan Ladd, James Cagney and a host of other cinema idols.

7

The life of spies is to know, not to be known.
—GEORGE HERBERT:
Outlandish Proverbs, 1640

As the war progressed and the Army and Navy built up their reconnaissance of the enemy-occupied areas of the world, the R&A branch in Washington continued to do the drudging work that was the main contribution of OSS to final victory. The government's civilian and military policy-makers depended on the thousands of R&A background studies, and the OSS map division, specializing in topographical charts of amazing accuracy and detail, turned out eight thousand titles by war's end. Churchill preferred OSS maps to all others; at one conference when FDR visited the Prime Minister's room, Churchill pointed to the wall with his ever-present cigar and said, "See, I've got them, too."

The R&A specialists became more venturesome with experience in this new field of intelligence analysis. An economic-objectives unit at OSS headquarters in Washington assisted the Army Air Force in working out an "optimum maturity" schedule for the strategic bombing of enemy ball-bearing fighter-planes, and oil production targets, estimating how long it would take to rebuild the shattered industries before they should be scheduled for a second targeting. In the field OSS agents pieced together enough information from captured enemy units to arrive at extremely accurate analyses of Nazi weapons production. Those engaged in more or less open intelligence collection were often hard put to determine whether they were involved in R&A work or were actually closer to activities of a military nature.

Peter Karlow originally had been hired as a field staff man in New York City—which meant that he handled everything from recruiting, to discussing with German political refugees what it was like in the old days living in Wiesbaden, and then collecting the names of those who lived at certain addresses on a particular street. The R&A branch was very thorough. Although Karlow never knew why he was asked to collect such odd bits of information, he assumed that it was part of an operation which might involve an American spy who had to know these minute details. Karlow, also an engineer, later found himself inspecting burned-out Wehrmacht Tiger tanks in Italy shortly after the Allied invasion at Salerno, September 9, 1943. The withdrawing Nazis had left booby traps in their destroyed armor, making his "civilian" status doubly dangerous.

As a result of his technical background, Karlow became one of the first military-operations analysts in OSS and at one point found himself assisting OSS guerrillas in Corsica to organize a Maritime Unit operation aimed at behind-the-lines activities in southern France. Later, he established an observation post atop an 837-foot peak on Gorgona Island from where OSS agents could peer through a telescope into Leghorn Harbor, which was occupied by the Wehrmacht. Similar OPs were established on the islands of Capraia and Elba, further to the south, and later OSS-led Italian partisans spied on enemy ship movements or radioed information to Allied aircraft attacking German vessels or oil-storage installations along the western coast of the Italian boot.

Karlow was wounded when his PT boat struck a mine during a run to shore to land a party of guerrillas. He recuperated from his wounds back in the U.S. and wound up his wartime career in R&A in Washington.

And then there were the usual wartime snafus concerning America's first intelligence agency—"snafu" for Situation Normal, All Fouled Up, or the stronger four-letter term used by GIs in place of "fouled up." Although the men who headed up OSS tried to impress on their subordinates the absolute need for secrecy, including byzantine methods of recruiting by name request, Ralph W. Donnelly in the summer of 1943 held the distinction of having been one of the handful of employees who had come through the front door. A teacher in the Washington, D.C., public school system during the war years, Donnelly was on vacation when he decided to seek summer employment with the federal government.

"We've got just the job for you," he was told by an interviewer at the Civil Service Commission office. Among his specializations, he had listed geography as one of his major studies in college.

"The job is with some agency called the Office of Strategic Services," the interviewer disclosed. Donnelly said that he had never heard of the agency and asked for more information about OSS.

The interviewer leaned closer and whispered: "It's secret work, and I never heard of this agency before. We just heard about it today."

He was told to go to an address on 24th Street, N.W., a converted apartment building with Army military policemen on duty inside the entrance. He was hired on the spot. Assigned to the Africa-Europe Division's Utilities Section headed up by Dr. Preston James, then one of the nation's leading geographers, Donnelly was introduced to his colleagues.

"Who introduced you?" one of his associates asked at lunch a few days later. Donnelly described his visit to the Civil Service Commission, and within a matter of hours he was pointed out as the only man in the division who held the distinction of having been "officially" recruited through the front door.

Later, as OSS continued its rapid expansion, the Civil Service Commission was relied on to find many of the specialists who later joined the agency. The Utilities Section to which Donnelly had been assigned was responsible for collecting data about various cities and towns in occupied Europe, collating information about water supplies, telephone systems, electricity, sewer, and natural gas utilities, and even the names of civil servants in the various countries who worked in these facilities—and their political attitudes and affiliations. In Germany, this information would prove valuable to American troops who would later occupy many of the municipalities.[1]

Much of the information was obtained from ten- and fifteen-year-old German technical journals or from American manufacturers who might have sold the equipment that had been installed. One young Army corporal, a refugee from Austria who worked in the section, was delighted to meet Professor Eric Fischer, a well-known geographer under whom he had studied at the University of Vienna a few years before the Nazi invasion and annexation of Austria in 1938. Professor Fischer, who had hiked through much of his native land and neighboring Germany, provided much of the information that was later used by the commanding generals of American infantry divisions spearheading drives into the Fatherland.

Some of the important intelligence provided by the Utilities Section pinpointed the overhead clearances and the size of the gates of some of the ancient, formerly walled Rhineland cities and towns. Thus American tanks and trucks could avoid becoming lodged in the entrances during battle and possibly holding up an advance. In battle, forewarned is forearmed; and OSS's aim was to help win battles through superior knowledge of the enemy and the terrain.

Nor was R&A concerned only with Europe. Attention was focused on Asia, and specifically Burma, which was a key link in the Allied supply chain from India to China. Before Japan invaded Burma on January 12, 1942, Britain supplied Singapore by sea and land from India. But the Japanese marched two divisions into Burma from Thailand and also used Burmese revolutionary Aung San and his "Thirty Comrades." These Fifth Columnists incited some of the population to rebellion against the British and supported sabotage behind Allied lines in exchange for a promise to free Burma from British control after World War II. The old Burma Road, originally nothing more than a truck-width muddy trail that stretched from Rangoon to China, had been captured by the invading Japanese thus forcing resupply by air over the Himalayan "Hump." After Pearl Harbor the Allies agreed that a land supply route had to be created from India across northern Burma into China to enable Chiang Kai-shek's armies to continue the fight against the Japanese.

The Japanese had dug in quickly after taking Burma. They, too, realized its strategic potential and quickly began improving shipbuilding facilities in Rangoon. Early OSS reports disclosed that by mid-1942 the enemy had begun building at least six vessels, each about one hundred feet long, to be launched the following year and used as "coasters." One report said:

> This period from laying down to launching at Rangoon was some 9 to 11 months for the first ship to be begun . . . at the Dawbon yard. . . . So far as the development of standard wooden shipbuilding in Burma is concerned, it would appear that the Japanese are confining themselves for the time being to vessels of 100' long. Possible sites for building vessels of this length are plentiful, but facilities for vessels over 100' would appear more limited. Supplies of timber appear to be readily available. The extension of the Government Dockyard at Rangoon tends to indicate that this yard is likely to be the main center of the building of standard wooden vessels.[2]

It was in early 1942 that War Department planners realized that if the Japanese were not blocked in Southeast Asia, they would become a greater threat to future operations in the Far East. That the Japanese were capable of marshaling anti-British segments of the population and using the various industrial facilities could not be ignored. In fact, R&A geographers suggested the possibility of alternative supply routes across the roof of the world—from India into Tibet and then into China. Exotic names were outlined in R&A reports that were issued by COI in early 1942—Lhasa, Mt. Kanchenjunga, Gopa Pass, Bay of Bengal, Irawaddy River, and Myitkyina.

The British forces in Burma were fast crumbling under the relentless advance of the Japanese Fifteenth Army commanded by Lieutenant General Shojiro Iida, when Lieutenant General Joseph "Vinegar Joe" Stilwell was dispatched with two Chinese armies down the Burma Road to assist the battered ally. These two Chinese armies, the Fifth and Sixth, also ran into the enemy meatgrinder, and by year's end the Japanese controlled all of Burma.

The only positive action that the United States was in a position to take in Southeast Asia by early 1942 fell to COI. While battered American troops and their Philippine allies were withdrawing on the Bataan peninsula toward the island fortress of Corregidor in Manila Bay, COI had come up with an audacious plan: A force of specially trained jungle fighters, mainly guerrillas, could wreak havoc against the Japanese who themselves were considered by the War Department to be excellent jungle fighters. Hadn't the enemy moved through the jungles of Malaya to attack and conquer Singapore from the rear? And Burma, too, by way of jungle marches from Thailand?

In an exchange of messages between Stilwell and Donovan, the peppery deputy to Chiang Kai-shek agreed to accept an American guerrilla team. At the same time, Donovan also ordered his staff to set up a plan for sending another small American group to visit the Dalai Lama at his temple fortress in Tibet's "Forbidden City" of Lhasa. Nothing would be left to chance; during the dark days of early 1942 every possible opportunity, no matter how remote, had to be explored or, if possible, ventured. Stilwell was asked by Donovan to recommend somebody to organize the Burma project while COI provided the operations plan for the mission to Tibet.

As the experts in Far Eastern affairs continued to pull additional data out of the Library of Congress and from their own experience in Southeast Asia, plans to infiltrate the Kingdom of Thailand and the French colony of Indochina, both under strong Japanese political and military domination, also began to take shape.

Stilwell's only recommendation was husky Captain Carl Eifler, a former policeman, border patrol ranger in the American Southwest, and Deputy Collector of Customs in Honolulu until Pearl Harbor had ended his civilian career. A reserve officer, he was recalled to active duty and assigned an infantry company in the Thirty-fifth Infantry Regiment then in training in the Hawaiian Islands. By mid-March he had been reassigned to COI headquarters in Washington on a "name request" order issued by Donovan. By the time he met with the COI director, the situation on Bataan was serious. Eifler was told to assist in setting up a plan for a small unit of jungle warriors to be flown to any one of several areas in Southeast Asia or even North Asia.

"We and the British are falling apart at the seams," Eifler was told by Donovan. "You might be sent anywhere—Dutch East Indies, Burma, Thailand, Indochina, or even to China.

Anywhere. And soon. Your mission is intelligence gathering, bridge blowing, assassination, and anything else that will stop the Japs."

Eifler, a hulking 250-pounder who towered six feet two inches, was told to select anybody he wanted from the COI staff or to recommend for name transfers anybody he knew in the Army or Navy who might make good guerrilla fighters. During his brief Washington tour, he was introduced to terms like espionage, sabotage, propaganda, escape and evasion, intelligence collection, and other secret subjects. At his introductory meeting with Donovan, he was also told that as the United States was new to this kind of warfare, he'd have to start from scratch and learn it all from books and classified instruction manuals that COI had received from British SIS and SOE.

"The people you select will determine the success or failure of your mission," Donovan also advised his latest recruit from Honolulu.

Among the men in the first group that Eifler selected for what on April 14, 1942, became Detachment 101 of COI, were Captain John G. Coughlin, a West Pointer and even taller at six feet five inches, and diminutive Captain Archie Chun Ming, to give the original group of five an Oriental flavor. Coughlin then recommended a close friend, Captain William R. "Ray" Peers, who would later command Detachment 101, the nation's first wartime guerrilla force.[3]

By early 1943 America's OSS guerrillas were in action behind enemy lines in Burma and in North Africa, and by the end of the year they had been infiltrated into Italy and the Balkans, with additional intelligence probes in France and the Low Countries.

In January 1943, FDR and Churchill met at Casablanca to discuss what would come next after the Germans and Italians had been defeated in North Africa and the Middle East. At the same time Major Jerry Sage, code name "Dagger," was conducting hit-and-run attacks against the Afrika Korps with an OSS guerrilla unit from Experimental Detachment G–3 (Provisional). This unit was made up of Arabs and anti-Fascist Spanish refugees who had fled their homeland after the bloody Spanish Civil War had ended in

1939. Major Sage was captured in March, and his operations behind enemy lines ceased. Escaping once from his original captors, he was recaptured along with an American and a South African and successfully passed himself off as a downed airman. Flown to Italy and then transported to Stalag III in Germany, a prison camp for Allied airmen, Sage continued to maintain his fictional Army Air Force cover. His assignment to Experimental Detachment G-3 (Prov.), the cover name for OSS operations in North Africa following Operation TORCH, would remain as secret as this special unit. Finally, he managed to escape into the Soviet Union and in early 1945 was repatriated back to the U.S., his OSS career as a behind-the-lines guerrilla somewhat abbreviated, although partially successful during the early 1943 Allied drive for Tunis.

Detachment 101 was on its way to Southeast Asia. Early in 1942, before it became OSS, COI had set up an important station in Berne, Switzerland, headed by Allen W. Dulles, and another listening post in Istanbul about the same time. Both were vital posts, and the OSS contingent was spied upon by the same enemy agents the Americans spied upon in return. In Istanbul, for example, there were not only Abwehr spies but secret agents from Italy, Japan, the Soviet Union, and, of course, from Britain's SIS. At times the confluence of secret agents from Allied and Axis camps resembled a Marx brothers comedy—if for no other reason than the resemblance of some of the spies to moustachioed Groucho, curly-haired Harpo, and heavily accented and quick-witted Chico.

Turhan Celik, then a sophomore at Robert College, one of the oldest American colleges outside the United States, recalls that all foreigners in Istanbul during World War II were regarded by the Turkish citizenry as spies. During the 1942 summer vacation, there was a sudden influx of American lawyers and professors in Istanbul, and the strata of Turkish society who could afford to send their children to Robert College nodded knowingly to each other. Now that America was at war, would spies from New York, Chicago, and San Francisco be as obvious as the silent, suspicious, square-featured Slavic neighbors from the north or as mysterious as the Orientals from the Far East?[4]

Celik was introduced to one of the "professors" in a night

club, one of many in Istanbul. The American told the Turkish college student that he was gathering a bibliography.

"What's your subject?" asked Celik innocently, in fluent but lightly accented English. The professor named an obscure Italian poet. Celik said it was a name with which he was unfamiliar. They chatted awhile. Small talk. After an hour they separated. In the Fall of 1942 after classes had resumed, Celik was invited to visit the apartment of another American friend. The visiting bibliographer was present.

"How would you like to help us?" the professor asked as they sipped cocktails. "We're here working for the Allied cause and we know your sympathies. We have checked you out."

Celik wondered how he might assist the Allied cause; he was only a university student and had no access to enemy agents or information that could be used by his hosts. For his first assignment he was asked to become acquainted with a beautiful young lady who claimed to be married to a Canadian.

"One of your friends, who is also working with us, knows her. He will arrange for the introduction. Find out if she plans to leave the country."

Celik chuckled, remarking how it smacked of E. Phillips Oppenheim. "How well should I get to know her?" he asked. He was told that it was up to him.

"By the way," the bibliographer asked, "how's your Italian?" He handed Celik a copy of the *Divine Comedy*. "Read this and translate, please."

The multilingual Turkish student read and translated to the satisfaction of his hosts. Finally, flushed with liquor, Celik found the courage to ask if the Americans were from OSS. The two agents stiffened. "Wha— where . . . where did you hear about OSS?" stuttered the bibliographer. "Who else in Istanbul knows about OSS?" The agents looked at each other, and the American whose apartment they were visiting suddenly turned grim.

"Celik," he snapped, "you're never to mention that name again! Forget about OSS! But first tell us where you heard about OSS?"

The young Turk allowed as to how most of his fellow students at Robert College had been discussing the arrival months earlier of the additional American professors, and in discussions amongst themselves they tried to imagine which of their new teachers were spies. Occasionally, the newspapers reported that a body had been fished out of the Bosporus, and youthful imaginations wondered which one of the OSS agents posing as professors might have done in the floating corpse— which surely must have been an Axis agent.

Some weeks later Celik was introduced to the young lady in question as "Ted Andrews," a member of the American Embassy Staff. In time they had an affair, and during their first night together she wondered aloud as they lay in each other's arms if "Andrews" was really an American (he had explained his slight accent by claiming that he was born in Europe where he had lived most of his life).

"Why do you ask?" he replied, wondering if she had seen through his cover.

"Darling," she whispered, "it's just that you don't make love like an American. They don't know how, and they are not sexually powerful like European men."

Soon after their first assignation, she asked "Andrews" if he could obtain a Canadian passport for her. Her "husband" was back in Canada, and she was all alone in Istanbul with no connections at the Canadian Embassy. "You must know somebody there," she asked her newfound lover.

Celik passed on her request to his OSS contacts, and a visa was obtained for her departure by way of Syria and other Middle East points en route to Canada. After she left Istanbul, Celik asked his contacts who she really was and learned that his mysterious Austrian-Turkish beauty was really an Abwehr agent. She also had been responsible for the execution of several American airmen who had been shot down in Austria. While she was living there, she had been a Nazi counterspy infiltrated into the resistance.

She had been an OSS target for quite some time, but in neutral Turkey her person was inviolate. Once outside Turkey, in Allied territory, she was subject to arrest and trial. She was arrested when her bus stopped in Damascus and was executed as an Axis spy.[5]

8

On them shall come at midnight
A strange and sudden fear;
  When, waking to their tents on fire,
They grasp their arms in vain,
  And they who stand to face us
Are beat to earth again;
  And they who fly in terror deem
A mighty host behind,
  And hear the tramp of thousands
Upon the hollow wind.

—WILLIAM CULLEN BRYANT (1794–1878):
Song of Marion's Men

In Europe, Asia, and North Africa, active resistance to the Axis invaders slowly germinated and, finally with proper cultivation, grew into secret armies. They were called guerrillas, partisans, the underground, the resistance, and a host of other names depending upon the enemy-occupied country.

Although the term "urban guerrilla" was not in use during World War II, there were rural guerrilla movements in the Soviet Union, the Balkans, Central Europe, North Africa, Southeast Asia, and China. And in Western Europe and in the few major cities of North Africa where the resistance was made up of workers and intellectuals, a widespread movement of urban guerrillas flourished—as much as any clandestine organization is capable of doing in nations occupied by a powerful enemy.

By early 1942 it was agreed by the Allies that the resistance movements held great possibilities for aiding the war effort, although their activities would have to be determined by conditions prevailing in any given region. As clandestine saboteurs in densely populated areas or as armed guerrillas in open, forested, or mountain country, they constituted a grave danger to the Axis. The resistance forced the enemy to maintain large numbers of troops as an occupational force, thus preventing their employment on the main battle fronts.

The underground also sabotaged the enemy war effort. The first of these functions was achieved by open warfare and by attacks on enemy lines of communication which required, in turn, the deployment by the enemy of additional troops away from the battlefronts. The second important function of the resistance was discharged by acts of terrorism against the enemy—assassination, demolition, work stoppage, damage to supplies, the spread of resistance sentiment directed against the enemy, and shoring up the morale of subjugated peoples.

Early on, at least a year before Pearl Harbor, Britain's SIS had deployed its first behind-the-lines agents in substantial numbers to Nazi-occupied Europe, enemy-held regions of North Africa, and to India for forays into Southeast Asia. After Pearl Harbor, SOE still bore the brunt of the behind-the-lines operations for more than a year because of the inexperience of the new American intelligence organization. Experience was being gained in North Africa by the OSS operation before and after the invasion, and the arrival of Detachment 101 in India about the same time that Operation TORCH was to be launched was a portent of future activities.

But the major emphasis was directed at German-occupied Europe, including the Balkans. Behind the Allied effort in this historically eruptive corner of Europe were two years of secret negotiations culminating in an agreement at Washington in March 1943 between President Roosevelt and British Foreign Secretary Anthony Eden. The agreement stated that recognition of territorial acquisitions by the respective Allied military forces would have to be accorded. In October 1940 Britain had offered the Soviet Union "leadership" in the Balkans in exchange for a "benevolent" Soviet attitude; this was later reaffirmed on November 28, 1943, at the Teheran Conference. At the British–U.S.–Soviet foreign ministers conference in Moscow the previous month, it was agreed that each of the three Allies would act in territories liberated by their respective forces as they judged best.

The Allied aim was to set a fire beneath the enemy in Europe. France and the Low Countries became targets along with Norway and the Balkans. By the terms of the armistice imposed upon France on June 22, 1940, Alsace-Lorraine was annexed to Germany and two French zones were established. The Northern Zone was directly administered from Paris by German occupation forces, and the Pétain government collaborated at Vichy in the unoccupied Southern Zone until the Allied invasion of North Africa. Just before the armistice was signed, Colonel Charles DeGaulle, one step removed from promotion, had escaped to London and established the Free French movement. In September 1941 the French National Committee was established under DeGaulle, who now held the rank of brigadier general.

By the end of 1940 the first resistance movements began to emerge in different localities of occupied France with little regional coordination or national cooperation, although Britain's SOE immediately dispatched agents to assist the small anti-Nazi underground forces. In the summer of 1942, OSS and SOE began working together in an effort to organize the French resistance, and by late 1943 the intelligence agencies of both Allies had set up in London a single SOE/OSS headquarters which in May 1944 was renamed Special Forces Headquarters (SFHQ).[1]

In Belgium and the Netherlands, agents of the British-American SFHQ assisted the resistance which, in Belgium, was directed by Omar Becu, an official of that country's International Transport Workers Federation, who personally enlisted many of the OSS radio operators.

Meantime, the most fertile—and natural—region for resistance activities was the Balkans, whose potential had been recognized by General Donovan during his journey to Sofia and Belgrade in 1940. Organized resistance began in the spring of 1941 when Colonel Dragoljub "Draza" Mihailovic retreated into the Bosnian Mountains with a staff of Yugoslavian Royal Army officers and some regular army units, which later came to be called "Chetniks." However, it wasn't until after the Nazi invasion of the Soviet Union that the first Yugoslav Communist Party (CPY) guerrillas, or *parti-*

zans as they preferred to be called, launched resistance activities under the leadership of Josip Broz, whose underground name was "Tito." By the end of the war Tito's partisans would number more than 793,000 men and women, while the Chetniks would fail militarily and politically, at times siding with the Wehrmacht or engaging in combat with partisans.[2]

A somewhat similar situation held in Greece, which was also factionalized with Royalist, Republican, and Communist elements. The SOE dispatched a number of agents from Cairo to destroy railroad bridges in the war-torn country. Then, after a brief appraisal and second thoughts, they were directed to remain as liaison officers with the anti-Communist National Republican Greek League (EDES) and the Communist-controlled National Liberation Front (EAM) and its military arm, the Greek Peoples Liberation Army (ELAS). Both sides fought each other sporadically.

About the same time—in late 1942 and early 1943—the first two OSS agents of Detachment 101's "A" Group began parachute training for a secret mission into Kachin country in north Burma. Other OSS units would follow Captain Jack Barnard and Burmese radioman Saw Judson into the jungle early in 1943 in what was, for "A" Group, a typical guerrilla operation: blowing up railroad tracks used by the Japanese Army.[3] In England OSS "Jedburgh" teams of two officers and one enlisted radio operator—usually an American, an Englishman, and a Frenchman in any combination, began their specialized training for forays into France. Other advance teams of OSS agents were in training to prepare the way for the invasions of Sicily and Italy and operations in Yugoslavia, Albania, and Greece. Special teams were also being organized to work Czechoslovakia, Hungary, and Austria. By late 1944, OSS operations would be launched full scale in Japanese-occupied Thailand and Indochina.

But the primary mission in 1942 and 1943 was intensive training to participate in various resistance movements around the world. Some OSS activities with resistance movements would have far-reaching postwar implications for Americans, who would learn by bitter experience that their preconceived notions of the nations and peoples to which they would be deployed needed considerable revision.

Nor was their classwork really informative. The American approach to guerrilla warfare in World War II was based on their own history—of colonial soldiers sniping at British redcoats from the safety of the forest; or the Confederate raiders of Colonel John S. Mosby; or the war parties of the frontier Indians of the West and Southwest and their bitter battle for survival against the inroads of the white settlers. In some cases there was antipathy among some OSS recruits, who recalled their Civil War history where guerrillas were as much disdained by the professional soldiers of the Confederacy as they were hated and feared by the Federal troops: Northern General Thomas L. Rosser declared that guerrillas were "a nuisance and an evil to the service;" and General Robert E. Lee, commander-in-chief of the Confederate Army, summed up his low regard for guerrilla warfare in one sentence: "I regard the whole guerrilla system as an unmixed evil."

The early OSS Special Operations (SO) and Operational Groups (OG) units and individual Secret Intelligence (SI) agents were under pressure to learn quickly what their British mentors had acquired over at least a century, if not longer. Throughout history, underground resistance has played a major role in revolutionary movements by directing political activities, performing many different kinds of organizational and operational functions, and, most of all, supporting overt guerrilla warfare. In Athens and Sparta during the Peloponnesian War in the fifth century B.C., underground agents tried to subvert the governments of each other's city-states. Spartan agents working within democratic institutions of Athens were impressively effective in their propaganda and agitational activities, designed to create internal dissension and develop popular distrust of the government.

In China it had long been common strategy for underground movements to form guerrilla bands and organize support among the peasants to overthrow local warlords or corrupt Mandarins. Later, in Europe during the Middle Ages, there were underground resistance movements such as the *Jacquerie,* a loosely knit organization of beggars and thieves.

Southern Germany had its rebel peasants, Italy had the warring merchant-states which instituted all manner of clandestine warfare—and assassination in particular.

OSS personnel had to learn from scratch how to operate in areas of the world which already had a history of resistance movements and guerrilla warfare.

For example, it wasn't until the end of September, 1942, that three British aircraft took off from Egypt with nine officers and three enlisted men of SOE Force 133 in Cairo. Target: the three railway bridges that carried the only north-south railway in Greece used to supply the German and Italian occupation forces in that country and Axis troops in North Africa. This highly strategic railroad link in mid-1942 was being used to transport supplies from Germany and Italy through the Balkan countries into Greece and its port of Piraeus. These supplies were then barged to Crete and loaded aboard small freighters for the nightlong run to North Africa. British intelligence officers in Cairo estimated that Rommel obtained at least 80 percent of his supplies over this route.

It was a bitter period for the British, who were impatiently awaiting Operation TORCH many hundreds of miles removed from the Afrika Korps bases in Libya. Allied forces in Africa, during the months prior to the invasion, lacked both naval and air forces strong enough to overcome the Luftwaffe air cover. If this daring mission to blow up the Gorgopotamos bridge or other structures that spanned chasms at Papadhia and Asopos could be pulled off, it might mean all the difference in making possible a planned Eighth Army breakout at El Alamein in Egypt. With the bulk of his supplies from Europe cut off, Rommel would suddenly find himself unable to maintain pressure against the British offensive, thus forcing him to pull back deeper into Libya to his main supply areas further to the west.[4]

Lieutenant General Bernard L. Montgomery had assumed command of the Eighth Army in August 1942 after the Afrika Korps and its supporting Italian divisions had smashed through the Allied forces the previous May and June. They had captured Tobruk and an inordinate amount of supplies before rolling the Allies back into Egypt, where they finally dug in at El Alamein. The Allies lost 75,000 men killed, wounded, and captured—33,000 in the Tobruk garrison—and all but 65 tanks; the Axis armies lost about 40,000 men. The summer was used as a breather by both sides. Rommel was confident that his 96,000 men, half of whom were Italians, and his 600 tanks arrayed in eight infantry and four armored divisions, could hold the line. Finally, fighting malaria and other maladies, he turned command over to General Hans Stumme and flew back to Germany for treatment.

Meantime, Montgomery began making plans to counter-attack across the minefields and push the Axis armies out of Egypt and further away from the vital Suez lifeline. Late October was his target date, and it was vital that the railroad bridges in Greece, of such strategic importance to the Axis, be destroyed at least a month before the Allied counter-offensive.

The infiltration plan was simple. Three aircraft would carry the SOE group and their arms, explosives, and radio equipment to a drop zone (DZ) which would be marked at night by bonfires set by agents. In the early morning hours of October 1, 1942, one stick of four men parachuted to "signal" fires that turned out to be a shepherd's camp in the hills. In the second aircraft another group of SOE sappers jumped into a DZ marked by bonfires set by a Greek agent working for SIS who was expecting supplies but not a demolition team. The pilot of the third aircraft found no signal fires and turned back to Egypt. Weather conditions on three occasions prevented the final SOE element from parachuting in to join their comrades. Finally, nearly a month later, the remaining members of the mission parachuted "blind" and floated down near an Italian military garrison. They spotted the chutes in the sky and opened fire, fortunately missing these earth-bound targets. The men scattered and reassembled during the day, avoiding enemy troops out beating the bushes for the airborne infiltrators. It took two weeks to make contact with the original group, and by the time all plans had been made to destroy the more vital of the three bridges, the decisive battle at El Alamein had ended on November 4 with the enemy in disarray—losses totaling 59,000 casualties and prisoners, including 34,000 Germans, 500 tanks, and 400 guns destroyed or captured, compared to 13,000 Allied casualties and 432 tanks knocked out by the enemy. When Montgomery's attack began, Rommel immediately flew back to Africa to resume command; his second in command, General Stumme, died of a heart attack when the Allied offensive began.

Although this particular SOE mission had failed to maintain its original operational schedule, the loss of the strategic bridge slowed down the Axis supply line and, at the same time, set the stage for Operation ANIMALS—the large-scale sabotage plan then under study by SOE/OSS Cairo to precede the Allied invasion of Sicily scheduled for the following summer.[5]

Originally organized as a one-shot mission, the first SOE unit in Greece early discovered that there was a resistance organization with guerrillas willing to battle the enemy. Colonel (and later Brigadier) E. C. W. Myers, the SOE detachment leader, arranged a meeting with two Greek guerrilla leaders, Colonel (later General) Napoleon Zervas of the Greek Army, and Athanasios Klaras, also known as Aris, a communist guerrilla commander. Unaware of the existence of the underground until they were met by friendly Greeks, the SOE unit eagerly accepted the cooperation of the two guerrilla leaders, who provided 150 *andarte* (guerrilla) fighting men. The local guerrillas, poorly armed, ragged, and hungry, and in some instances sickly, were elated that the Allies had finally arrived, although Myers was under instructions to exfiltrate his unit by submarine once the mission had been successfully completed. Three men, who had managed to evade capture and refused to surrender when British forces were defeated in 1941 in Greece and Crete, were produced by the guerrillas and offered to join the operation.[6]

Thanks to the intelligence supplied by guerrillas, Myers learned that the bridge at Gorgopotamos, the responsibility of an Italian military unit, was the least guarded and offered the best opportunity. In addition, it was the most strategic of the three spans. Finally, all was ready on the night of November 25, and the guerrillas moved into position. But plans often collapse for any number of reasons; H-Hour at 2300 hours passed as Myers nervously waited for the assault against the Italian guards to begin. The guerrillas, led by SOE sappers, were to attack from two directions and, while the fighting was taking place, the demolition teams would move in, set their charges and fuses, and quickly pull out.

The moon was full and a slight ground fog hung over the area. Fifteen minutes after H-Hour the attack began. It took an hour to knock out the guard detail. At one point during the operation, Myers had to commit his reserve force of guerrillas because of unexpected resistance from the embattled Italians who, as far as the British and their guerrilla comrades were concerned, were not the greatest fighting men in the Axis armies. The bridge was knocked out; the guerrillas and SOE sappers took to the hills, elated with their successful operation. The Afrika Korps supply line remained severed for six long weeks, adding another knockout punch to the serious defeat that Rommel had suffered at El Alamein during the twelve-day battle in the desert that ended on November 4—four days before the landings in the west in Operation TORCH.

At both SOE and OSS headquarters in Cairo, the success of the Myers mission, thanks to a strong assist by the guerrillas, called for a strategic reevaluation. A small stay-behind team would launch what later would be referred to as NOAH'S ARK, ultimately to become part of the joint SOE/OSS Allied Military Mission (AMM) to occupied Greece.[7]

By early 1942 Greece was ripe for exploitation by Allied intelligence. When Italian occupation forces in Albania invaded Greece in October 1940, the Greek population immediately rallied to the call to arms, hiking across the mountains to the battlefields in the north. By year's end the Italian Eleventh Army had been turned around and driven out of Greece and 30 miles into Albania where, backs against a wall of mountains, Mussolini's troops fought for their lives. However, the Greek counteroffensive bogged down because of an inadequate supply system and a poor military staff that was oriented toward defensive rather than offensive tactics.

Greek victories turned sour rapidly, especially after the death of General Ioannis Metaxas in January 1941, at the height of his fame and popularity (which also rubbed off on King George II, the less popular monarch). And when Hitler, angry over the Italians' defeat by the Greeks, decided to invade Greece on April 6, 1941, the king fled the country not to return until war's end. Another cause of the Greek debacle was the fact that Metaxas, actually a dictator despite his popularity, and pro-Axis until the Italian invasion, had refused to permit several hundred senior army officers who had been purged in the thirties to return and fight for their country. These republican officers, all antimonarchical, later provided a resistance nucleus, and the Greek Army, equipped mainly with weapons purchased in the thirties from Germany, would be familiar with enemy weapons after the guerrilla forces were formed—knowledge which was valuable in fighting the Axis occupation forces.

Hitler's strategy was clear as regards Greece. In order to protect his southern flank after he invaded Russia, the Nazi leader regarded domination of the Balkans, including Greece and its islands, as vital to the security of the southern anchor of the German armies. And, of course, the Balkans represented a vital supply route to his troops in Africa, and strategic air and naval bases for the Mediterranean area.

On April 6, 1941, Hitler attacked through the Balkans with twenty-seven divisions, toppling Yugoslavia and forcing Prince Regent Paul to flee to London. Yugoslavia surrendered on April 17, followed by Greece six days later. On May 20 the Wehrmacht invaded Crete, which had been bolstered by additional British troops, and ten days later the Axis controlled the Balkans and the neighboring Greek islands.

By the end of 1941 Greece had been divided into occupation zones: the hated Bulgarians in the northeast, the equally despised Italian Eleventh Army straddling the greater part of the mainland, various islands, eastern Crete, and the capital city of Athens. A Greek puppet government also was established by the Axis.

Famine and tyranny gripped the country, and the volatile urbanites in the cities, with a long tradition of political awareness—and political divisiveness—were ripe for resistance. Into this maelstrom British SOE and SIS elements stepped gingerly, to be followed by the less politically sophisticated OSS American SO and OG units, many of whose team members were Greek-born or of Greek descent. Events in Greece projected the shape of future political events around the world where, barely recognized, free-wheeling and undirected postwar nationalism would be given birth within the Allied-sponsored resistance movements.

Meanwhile, the men who directed operations behind enemy lines in 1942–43 had become aware of the massive logistics problem. Transporting Allied guerrillas would require more than fast boats and submarines to deliver spies and saboteurs to enemy shores—and arms, ammunition, food, clothing, and other supplies to the resistance. The men who directed SOE and OSS were finally faced with the ultimate reality: They also would require their own specially trained navy and air force. Intelligence and paramilitary operations were truly three-dimensional. In the cities and hinterlands occupied by the enemy tens of thousands of resistance fighters were clamoring for revenge, and by early 1943, were demanding arms, ammunition, and supplies necessary to attack and help defeat the hated common foe.[8]

9

If a man have a tent made of linen of which
the apertures have all been stopped up, and it
be twelve bracchia across and twelve in depth,
he will be able to throw himself down from
any great height without sustaining an injury.
—LEONARDO DAVINCI (1452–1519),
Notebook entry describing the parachute

The Allies, through their ability to grant or withhold supplies, exercised a strong influence upon the success or failure of
resistance movements around the world. Fighting as guerrillas,
the members of the various resistance units in different nations
had to rely on more than captured enemy arms and supplies.
The seeds of rebellion and resistance had grown into a garden
of deadly flora waiting only to be harvested and squeezed of
the poison to be spread among the enemy. A British account
of the situation in occupied Europe in 1943 described it
this way:

> Even after three years of privations and repression
> and the ferocity of Nazi reprisals for any act of dis-
> obedience, the spirit of independence was still alive. In
> the mountains of Yugoslavia the patriots continued their
> struggle against the armed forces of the Axis. Guerrilla
> outbreaks in Greece were on the increase. French
> resistance found expression not only in sabotage and
> in attacks on German officers, but also in rioting and
> resistance to forced labour, and in March the report
> that all youths from 20 to 23 would be drafted for
> labour services resulted in the flight of several thousand
> into the mountains of Savoy where they maintained a
> brief resistance against the authorities. Norwegian anger
> at repression and food seizures forced the Nazis to pro-

115

claim a state of emergency during the second week of October as a precaution against outbreaks. Dutch resistance to compulsory labour and the internment of ex-soldiers brought the proclamation of martial law at the beginning of May. . . .

In Denmark the first attitude of icy aloofness was replaced by an active campaign of sabotage and by August throughout the occupied countries sabotage had become so widespread that the Germans demanded the handing over of the culprits to German military courts. . . . These were forces for the Allies as well as the Germans to take into account. Within the European Fortress lay enslaved populations who passionately awaited an Allied assault as a signal to turn against their oppressors with all their remaining strength. It was one of the tasks of the United Nations to keep that spirit alive and to provide the weapons and the leadership which would enable the forces of liberation within Europe to co-operate with the coming invasion.[1]

In London the Combined Chiefs of Staff (CCS) were of one mind in early 1943—the resistance movements held great possibilities for aiding the war effort. Their activities would be determined by various conditions—military, political, and geographic—in any given region. As clandestine saboteurs in densely populated areas or as armed guerrillas in open country, they constituted a source of grave danger to the enemy, and the commanders of the Axis occupation forces were well aware of this threat. The activities of the resistance, therefore, could be equated with factors such as the enemy's determination to destroy the underground movements which "depends upon the amount of supplies dropped to the patriots, which in turn depends upon the military advantage gained by making the enemy employ his forces against the patriots. . . ."[2]

Originally, in August 1940, the RAF had organized Number 1419 Flight at North Weald in Essex, England, to drop agents in France by parachute or by touching down on isolated meadows with the single-engine Lysander aircraft, called a "Lizzie" by British pilots. A year later the original three Lizzies in 1419 Flight had been merged with 138 Squadron to be followed in March 1942 by the establishment of 161 Special Operations Squadron. Secret operations in France required more than submarines and fast boats which had to penetrate enemy shore defenses and the ever-present mobile and foot patrols that were constantly on guard against the infiltrating Allied agents. Air deliveries of secret agents and supplies for the resistance in short order was refined by the RAF into a special military science.

However, it would be left to the U.S. Army Air Force to provide the push for the establishment of larger air-group-size units specially employed for extremely dangerous flying missions to deliver men and materiel behind enemy lines. Allied agents and supplies for the resistance movements would be delivered in increasing numbers; and OSS OGs would not only fly in conventional aircraft to make equally conventional parachute jumps into isolated DZs; they also would be transported on their missions by glider and even in put-putting 180-horsepower Sikorsky helicopters.

Moreover, just as OSS required a certain type of individual to risk his life behind enemy lines, so would the U.S. Army Air Force require unusual flying skills from the men who would be responsible for supplying the resistance movements. Their log books, if they were pilots or navigators, or personal records if they were gunners and other flight crew members, would show terse flight record entries—date, type of aircraft, length of flight, number of landings, and the designation: Combat Mission—SECRET.[8]

The Britain-based USAAF Eighth Air Force Composite Group of two squadrons in 1942–43 provided CARPET-BAGGER missions to the resistance in occupied France and the Low Countries, as well as a handful of missions to Norway. While the U.S. military build-up continued in England during 1942, the RAF employed multiengine Halifax bombers and aircraft of similar size—Wellingtons, Stirlings, Albemarles, and made-in-America B–24 Liberators, along with lend-lease twin-engine Dakotas, or C–47s as they were listed by USAAF, and, of course, the aforementioned "Lizzies" and Hudsons. However, in mid-1942 only one American bombing squadron was deployed to "bomb" the continent with propaganda leaflets or "nickels," as they were called by the British who were skilled in the coinage of military slang. The Americans called these missions "nickeling the Nazis."

During most of 1942 USAAF was involved in the build-up

for Operation TORCH and the few CARPETBAGGER missions that were flown in support of the resistance consisted of twin-engine C–47s assigned to those special supply drops from the Troop Carrier Command. The C–47 targets were generally within three hundred miles of their base in England, a distance well under their maximum action radius. But this extra time allowance obtained by flying relatively short-range missions was provided in anticipation of changing weather conditions, inability to locate a DZ or landing zone because of enemy activity on the ground nearby, or even navigational errors. Nor were courses flown in a straight line because of the locations of enemy antiaircraft positions throughout occupied territory. And, of course, enemy radar was a major consideration which required frequent changes in course on the way to the target.[4]

In the Mediterranean Theater of Operations (MTO), navigation was even more difficult than over Western Europe. In Southeast Asia it was strictly seat-of-the-pants flying by the ATC squadrons of the First Air Commando Force organized in late 1943. However, the pattern of secret air missions to the resistance movements was developed into an exact and closely articulated operation in MTO where few navigational aids were available. Flights from North Africa required over-water flying for four hundred to five hundred miles, then inland for one hundred to two hundred miles to the pinpoint DZ, and most of these flights were made on instruments. For example, RAF Squadron 624 at Blida, an air base forty miles from Algiers, often flew supply missions to Force 133 in the Balkans and to the French resistance in southern France.

On November 17, 1943, Colonel Monro MacCloskey, an officer with the Joint Planning Staff of Allied Force Headquarters (AFHQ), flew his first secret air mission with 624 Squadron, making two supply drops in southern France. The long, tiring flight took nine hours and fifteen minutes, and McCloskey, a West Point graduate and pilot, later carved his niche in the history of the development of secret air missions for OSS.[5]

On a visit to AFHQ at Caserta a short time later, "Mac," as he was known to his friends, stopped at Bari to visit his

old friend Major General Nathan F. Twining, then commanding the Fifteenth Air Force. General Twining had just returned from AFHQ and, while dressing for dinner, he told
MacCloskey that he had been given a "hot one."

"Mac, you've heard about the French *Maquis,* the Italian
and Yugoslav partisans, and what they're doing to help us
win the war?"

"Yes, sir," replied the colonel, recalling his recent flight
with 624 Squadron.

The general spoke about the early RAF effort, dropping
supplies and agents in occupied Europe from bases in England, and the recent movement of modified Halifax bombers
to Blida to support the resistance in the Balkans, northern
Italy, and southern France. "And today," General Twining
continued, somewhat indignantly, "I was directed to organize a bombardment squadron to perform these same missions!"

"Well, what's so bad about that?" MacCloskey interjected.

"Hell, Mac, we're in the strategic bombing business, not
in supply-dropping operations. Practically all our bombing is
done in the daylight. These cloak-and-dagger missions are
flown almost entirely at night and at a very low altitude. It's
a highly specialized project and we don't have anyone in the
whole Fifteenth Air Force who knows anything about it."

"Chief, it's really not as complicated as it sounds," Mac-
Closkey replied. "Now let me tell you how the RAF carry
out these missions."[6]

One hour and two highballs later, the two left the commanding general's quarters for the staff officers' dining room.
General Twining had remained quiet through most of Colonel
MacCloskey's discourse, asking a few pertinent questions but
in the main listening. What MacCloskey didn't know at the
time was that he had talked himself into a job.[7]

On March 25, 1944, Colonel MacCloskey became commanding officer of the 122nd Liaison Squadron, which was
redesignated a Bombardment Squadron and would the following June become the 885th Bombardment Squadron (Heavy)
(Special). By V-E Day, MacCloskey's squadron would have
gone through growing pains of expanding in size to the
Fifteenth Special Group (Provisional) and then being redesignated as the 2641st Special Group (Prov.), supporting

among the Allied behind-the-lines units the OSS 2677th Regiment (Prov.), whose sub-units had parachuted agents, OGs, and SOs in the Balkans, northern Italy, Austria, Czechoslovakia, and southern France.[8]

The 122nd Liaison Squadron had originally been made up of seven twin-engine B–25 Mitchell medium bombers and three B–17 Flying Fortresses; the squadron's pilots, who couldn't hack it in regular air combat units, were reassigned to carrying passengers and official mail on administrative flights between various military headquarters in the Mediterranean area. Nor had the decision to organize the special air missions units been taken lightly. When Lieutenant General Ira C. Eaker assumed command of the Mediterranean Allied Air Forces in January 1944, an increase in the delivery of supplies to the resistance organizations was among the various matters which had attracted his attention. As commander of the Eighth Air Force in England, he had been instrumental in organizing the two AAF squadrons for special operations in Western Europe, covering France, the Low Countries, and Norway. He was convinced that these particular supply operations were well worth the effort, and he wanted Americans "to get some credit in delivering knives, guns, and explosives to the Balkan patriots with which to kill Germans."[9]

Unfortunately, in the vast Allied military bureaucracy there were times when the right hand was unaware of what the left hand was doing. Also, the beefing up of the OSS/SOE effort in the occupied countries continued quite slowly. British intelligence had fewer human resources on which to draw than the U.S. At one point, Project SKIPPER had been launched in 1942 in Canada in an effort to recruit men and women for secret missions with no questions asked about their politics. The two major requirements: language capability and a strong anti-Nazi attitude. In the U.S., OSS recruiters were canvassing the military training camps, and the files of the Foreign Nationalities Unit were continually being scoured for potential recruits.

Although Italy had been invaded in mid-1943 and Operation ANIMALS had been moderately successful, it appeared that the CCS in London and the Pentagon had overlooked the critical air support that the resistance would require for

Operation OVERLORD—the invasion of France and the continent. General Eaker understood the problem better than his superiors in Washington. So, too, did Air Vice Marshal Sir John C. Slessor, who messaged his personal friend, the commanding general of OSS, that the current allotments in the MTO "of a few B–25s are practically worthless and we really require a squadron of heavy bombers sorely. I am convinced that the way the most can be done to divert forces away from OVERLORD is to raise Hell in the Balkans and that invaluable aid to that end would be accomplished by a squadron of American heavy bombers for the Special Operations Force."[10] On the following day General Donovon wrote to the commanding general of USAAF, General H. H. "Hap" Arnold that, "Only [with] the assignment of sufficient planes to bring the total of four squadrons of heavy bombers in the European Theater and at least one full squadron of B–17s in the Mediterranean Theater will our contribution approach the scale of the British effort." The British effort out of England revolved around 205 Group of the RAF which at times consisted of as many as 134 multiengine Wellington and B–24 heavy bombers.[11]

It had also taken much too long for the Allied CCS to realize that a major airborne supply effort to the resistance would be required if the underground of saboteurs, secret agents, and guerrillas was to support OVERLORD, about which they had no specific details, but were eagerly awaiting them. Unfortunately, for more than six months after the Allied invasion of Italy, support for the resistance in northern Italy and the Balkans continued as a nickel-and-dime operation. There were still those in the Pentagon who looked down their noses at OSS and special operations, and this was officially reflected during the decision-making that led to the creation of Colonel MacCloskey's speedily organized wartime command.

One of the generals on the JCS friendly to Eaker wrote on March 22 that some of his fellow officers were dubious about granting the request to beef up the number of secret air missions to the resistance and the increase of support that OSS could give to the guerrillas. Major General H. A. Craig wrote Eaker that "the War Department has been very reluctant to grant this authority, notwithstanding the urgent need for this unit. As a matter of fact, this action has set a precedent, so unless the directive . . . is followed immediately and implicitly, there may be some repercussions."[12] One might question whether the enemy was entrenched behind the artillery-studded west wall along the French coast and in the towns and villages of the Balkans, or in the Pentagon.

Following the pattern established by the RAF, the CARPETBAGGER operation out of England was far less complex than similar operations in MTO which were responsible for supplying the resistance movements in southern France, northern Italy, and the Balkans. In England requests for missions originated either with field agents or at various Country Sections in the London headquarters of OSS. The chief of OSS SO and his counterpart in SOE determined the priority of missions, and targets were then pinpointed by the OSS Air Operations Section (AOS) and forwarded by scrambler phone to Eighth Air Force, which would determine if the missions were possible. Terrain of the target areas and the strength of enemy air defenses near the DZ were major governing factors in this decision. If the targets were approved by Eighth Air Force, the AOS was notified along with the British Air Ministry, which would cancel any proposed RAF missions that might interfere with an agent or supply drop. Meantime, the OSS Country Section would message its field agents of the code phrase or "crack signal" that would be broadcast by the BBC radio. This signal was the prearranged code phase which told the field agent how many planes to expect and when they would arrive at the DZ.

There's an old military adage made famous by Alfred Tennyson in his poem, "The Charge of the Light Brigade,"

Theirs not to reason why,
Theirs but to do and die.

And Colonel MacCloskey was not aware of the high-level politics focused on his new command or the meaning behind the statement of policy made to him by the Fifteenth Air Force Deputy Chief of Staff for Operations, Brigadier General Charles Born: "Mac, we'll give you anything we have in the Fifteenth Air Force to keep you going. But, if you *don't* cut it, you're in trouble!"[13]

In his memoirs, later published as *Secret Air Missions,* MacCloskey, then a retired brigadier general, recalled:

> We hadn't been designated a "Special" squadron for nothing. Everything about the outfit was special. The aircraft had to be specially modified; the crews had to be specially trained; the loads we were to drop had to be specially assembled; and the targets had to be specially identified. We were unique in that in almost 3,000 sorties we never dropped a bomb; and we became more accustomed to looking up at mountain peaks at night rather than looking down on them in the daytime.[14]

It took some time, but by mid-spring 1944, the MAAF units assigned to special operations had perfected their delivery methods. All the effort put forth to drop supplies and agents to resistance groups would have failed unless nearly perfect cooperation existed between the aircraft and the reception committee at the DZ. It was a procedure that OSS personnel had to learn as part of their training. Oftentimes there were no second chances for a drop, nor could the aircraft spend much time "stooging" (orbiting overhead) in the area of the DZ. The DZ had to be ready and identification signals exchanged. Inside the aircraft the dispatchers or "kickers," the men who kicked out the supply bundles, had to time the drops so that the supply packages would not fall out of the DZ and, as often happened in northern Italy and the Balkans, into the hands of nearby enemy units. Although this danger was at a minimum, a poorly executed drop could destroy supplies or scatter them so widely that recovery was virtually impossible.

> The reception committee played an important and often dangerous role in supply operations. This was the group which prepared the DZ, lighted the signal fires or laid out the identification panels or, if it was an unusual daylight drop, maintained contact with the resistance leaders, and arranged for recovery and removal of the supplies.
>
> In Yugoslavia, each DZ was staffed by an Allied (OSS

or SOE) liaison officer, a small party of troops (OSS or SOE), and numerous partisans. In France, reception committees varied in size according to the quantity of supplies expected and the anticipated enemy opposition. The standard committee usually had 25 men for each 15 containers, which was the normal load of one aircraft. The committee went to great pains to protect the DZ from enemy interference. It could not afford defense against air attack, but every possible measure was taken to keep the dropping ground's location secret and to prevent its capture by enemy troops. The technique used by the *Maquis* was more or less typical of that developed by resistance groups elsewhere.

Maquis guards took up their positions around the DZ, roads leading to the area were blocked off, and a watch was kept for enemy patrols. These patrols generally had four or five Germans or French militiamen, but might be larger. On those rather rare occasions when a strong patrol surprised a committee at work, the two groups would fight it out, or the patrol would call up reinforcements. By the time these could arrive, the underground would have recovered the supplies and disappeared. Detection of a DZ would make it unusable for a time, but the patriots kept a constant watch and reported when enemy vigilance had relaxed. . . .

Many times, however, the DZ was either surrounded by the enemy or was in danger of being detected. On such occasions, the fires were not lighted until identification signals had been exchanged. The aircraft, whether the fires were lighted or not, circled over the pinpoint flashing the letter of the day. Upon receiving the proper response by Aldis lamp or flashlight, the crew prepared for the drop. This identification procedure saved large quantities of supplies from falling into German hands, since enemy troops, especially in the Balkans, often discovered the DZs just before or after fires were lighted. Then, even though the fires were burning, the aircraft would not drop because the ground-to-air signal was not given.

Drop zones were located wherever possible in areas least susceptible to enemy discovery. In heavily populated regions, such as Denmark and the Netherlands, the DZs were very difficult to conceal. In the mountain areas of Norway, Southern France, Northern Italy and the Balkans, detection was much less to be feared. Consequently terrain obstacles or difficulties of approach were minor considerations in laying out a DZ. In the

Balkans, dropping grounds were nearly always in rugged mountain country where danger lurked in dark uncharted valleys. The danger was primarily that of terrain and poor visibility. Pilots had to fly at about 600 feet over the DZ, which often was three to five thousand feet *below* the surrounding peaks and ridges. Accidents were few, but occasionally not even the most skillful pilot could avoid disaster.[15]

If high-ranking officials in OSS headquarters in "Q" Building in the Washington, D.C., complex couldn't quite envision the vast special air-missions effort that had been mounted by USAAF and the RAF in late May 1944 on behalf of OSS/SOE, at one point neither could America's highest ranking airman. The event occurred May 25, 1944, while final preparations were being made in London for OVERLORD. In the mountains of Yugoslavia, OSS and SOE representatives at the Supreme Headquarters of Tito's National Liberation Army at Drvar and at the headquarters of Mihailovic's Chetniks were trying to obtain cooperation from the warring Yugoslav factions. Churchill had offered support to Mihailovic early in the war on the basis of information from the Yugoslav government-in-exile in London that the Royal Army general in the mountains had the majority of the population rallying to his side to fight the Nazi invaders. Later intelligence from British agents dispatched to Yugoslavia disclosed that Tito and his Communist-oriented partisans were better organized and were conducting harder-hitting operations against the enemy. Even more important, Tito had the full political support of Stalin. The Russians were eager to send a combination military-political mission to Yugoslavia to assist the partisans. They were also anxious to take some of the credit for the bulk of American arms, ammunition, and supplies that began to arrive in late 1943. These supplies, first in small amounts, built up in 1944 as the special air-missions squadrons began to arrive on the scene in Italy.

The partisans were elusive, fighting from the shadows at night, and falling back into the mountains after launching a successful ambush. But in mid-May Abwehr intercepted a cable from the Yugoslav military attaché in Washington to his Royal Army counterpart in Cairo giving the location of Tito's headquarters at Drvar.[16] As it turned out, sending the cable in the clear was a deliberate attempt to notify the Germans where they could find Tito. With the headquarters of the Communist-led Yugoslav Army of National Liberation destroyed and Tito killed or captured, Mihailovic would once again become the resistance leader to whom they would rally, and the government-in-exile would remain the controlling postwar political influence, or so the monarchists reasoned.

For several weeks the Wehrmacht had been massing troops at strategic locations and had carried out local attacks in preparation for what was intended to be the final stroke against Tito in western Bosnia, where his headquarters were located in a ravine just north of the mountain village of Drvar. The Soviet mission was located about a mile to the northwest, the British SOE mission in a ravine about two miles to the south, and an American Air Force meteorological unit and an OSS detachment on the western outskirts of the village.

However, on the day before the attack, Luftwaffe reconnaissance aircraft continued to circle overhead. This aroused Tito's suspicions, and he ordered part of his headquarters to pull back deeper into the mountains. Then, just before dawn on May 25 (Tito's birthday), Stuka dive bombers struck, one by one, for more than an hour. At dawn Junker-52 transports passed overhead, towing gliders packed with troops of the SS Seventh Mountain Division. Paratroopers of the SS Airborne Jaeger Battalion jumped from the Ju–52, the gliders were released and silently approached the village, whispering in from the south and west, scraping and crunching to a halt on the hillside near the American detachment. The troops in them, armed with light weapons, spilled forth and deployed for action. About one hundred enemy aircraft and gliders were involved, carrying two enemy battalions. Against them the partisans could marshal less than a thousand men, who set up a blocking force, enabling Tito and his staff and the Allied missions to flee into the mountains. One American officer was reported missing.

Meanwhile, a German armored column moved south from the town of Petrovac. Other than helping him in making his escape, Tito's partisans were unable to come to his aid.

In the confusion of the attack and the escape of the Allied missions, radio communications with OSS/SOE in Bari, Italy, were so garbled that Allied fighter aircraft didn't appear on the scene for two days. However, in response to Tito's plea for help, once he and his staff and the Allied missions had regained their wits, more than one thousand bomber and fighter sorties were mounted by MAAF.[17]

The enemy operation, called *RÖSSELSPRUNG* (the knight's move in chess), planned for the command of the Fifteenth Mountain Army Corps and supporting airborne and motorized units to "advance with a number of task forces concentrically in the region of Petrovac-Drvar . . . overcome the resistance of the Red forces and occupy the center of the Red command. In this operation the airborne Jaeger Battalion will parachute at dawn and overcome the resistance of the enemy command, putting them out of action for a long time."[18]

By June 1 Tito and a handful of members of his staff had made it south through enemy forces which had loosely encircled the Prekaja Mountains. Once they had slipped through the German cordon, the partisan leaders hiked across the hills and through the valleys to an emergency airstrip at Kupresko Polje farther south, arriving at dusk on the third. At the emergency strip, British members of Number Two Party Balkan Air Force Terminal Service were waiting to receive any Allied or partisan escapees from Drvar so they could radio Bari for evacuation aircraft. A Soviet C–47 of the Balkan Air Force (BAF) touched down at 2200 hours. Tito and the most important members of his staff boarded the American lend-lease gift to the Russian Air Force and were flown to Bari. The Soviet transport returned for another load along with three C–47s from the Sixtieth Troop Carrier Group command by Colonel Clarence J. Galligan. The tow-headed twenty-four-year-old colonel, at the controls of one of the three C–47s, supervised the evacuation of seventy-four persons that night and seven more planeloads the following night.[19]

The Balkan Air Force had saved Tito and members of the Allied missions from almost certain capture. But in official Washington, little if anything was known about BAF. In the

Pentagon on the day after Tito's rescue, a smiling colonel—an OSS liaison officer to AAF—was ushered into the massive E-ring office of the Chief of the Army Air Force. General Arnold was a busy man, more interested in what B–17s and B–24s were doing to knock out the Nazi war machine than in the operations of the Troop Carrier Command. General "Hap" Arnold probably knew more about air combat operations and strategic bombing than any one man in the War Department, but he was too involved in daily military strategy to know everything about the total AAF effort.

The OSS colonel smartly saluted the Chief, whose nod signaled the officer standing before him to continue.

"Well, General . . . sir," the man from OSS began nervously.

The AAF chief glared with a get-on-with-it-man-I'm-very-busy expression.

"The Balkan Air Force did it again," the OSS visitor declared.

General Arnold looked up from the sheaf of classified papers that he had been studying. "The what . . . ?" he asked.

"The Balkan Air Force," the OSS colonel repeated.

"What the hell is the Balkan Air Force?" the Chief snapped.

The colonel, undaunted, quickly recounted in detail the rescue of Tito and staff for the AAF's senior general. In brief, he explained that BAF was the air force created for OSS, nor was he too far off. Virtually all secret air missions were flown by it on behalf of OSS and SOE and the resistance armies they were trying to create.

10

Mobility is the true test of a supply system.
— B. H. LIDDELL HART:
Thoughts on War, 1944

"We're going in," the blond young officer at the left seat controls of the C–47 advised his co-pilot on the intercom. The co-pilot gulped, flicked the button on his microphone, and repeated the order to the three battered twin-engine transports following behind in the darkness of the night. Below, a T formation of bonfires flickered, splashing the darkness with light from the line of flames.

Colonel Clarence J. Galligan, a crushed "fifty-mission" hat clamped to his head by the pair of oversized earphones, grimly scanned his airspeed indicator which read 110 m.p.h. His left hand tightly grasped the yoke of the control stick. His right hand gripped the throttle as he carefully jockeyed the "Gooney Bird" toward the landing site below. He couldn't see the steep jagged peaks that reached into the sky. He knew that they were there. He knew that the slightest mistouch of the controls, the tiniest deviation from course, could send him smashing into the rocky mountainside overlooking this tiny valley deep in the middle of Nazi-occupied Yugoslavia.

The T signal of bonfires loomed larger as the C–47 lost altitude. Sweat beaded the forehead of the co-pilot, Captain Homer L. Moore. The "old man," at least two years his senior, had gone "ape" by accepting this mission. Who ever heard of landing a C–47 in a valley buried deep between the rugged Dina Alps of Yugoslavia? Sure, at least there's a chance to make a successful landing during daylight hours. But at night?

"Full flaps!" Galligan ordered. The co-pilot hit the handle, and the twin-engine transport suddenly slowed in flight. Galligan leaned forward on the yoke, and the C–47 began to slip in at a steeper angle, rapidly approaching the signal fires on the ground.

"Tell 'em to hit full flaps at four thousand," he said to his co-pilot, who relayed the message to the other pilots in the transports following in behind at five-minute intervals. The C–47 passed over the T fires, and Galligan goosed the throttle just enough to maintain altitude, banked tightly, at the same time straining his eyes to make out the terrain alongside the line of signal fires. There it was. The ground. Rutted and uneven. Good old *terra firma.* He hauled back on the stick, and the C–47 flared out and set down, rolling roughly while he tapped the toebrakes on the rudder pedal to slow and finally stop. A flashlight in somebody's hand beckoned him to follow, and he turned the C–47 with skill born of long experience and taxied off the makeshift runway to the side of the field.

Behind him the second C–47 followed. Then a third; and the fourth C–47 somewhere in the night made its final approach. By the time he braked to a halt, a mob of ragged guerrillas swarmed out toward his aircraft. The crew chief pushed open the cargo door, and chattering partisans, rifles slung over their shoulders, clambered aboard and began passing out crates of ammunition, weapons, and medical supplies to others who hauled away the cargo. In the cockpit Galligan and his co-pilot just sat there. Suddenly they were exhausted from the strain. Half of the mission had been completed. There was still another vital phase that had to be carried out before the coded success message could be radioed back to headquarters in Brindisi.

Galligan watched one of the C–47s come in, and to no one in particular talked the pilot down. "Easy does it," he breathed softly. "Throttle back . . . back . . . back. That's it. Now the brakes. Ahhhhh. . . ." He nodded as the third C–47 bounced along the airstrip. He sweated down the fourth transport the same way.

Partisans rushed to the newly arrived aircraft. Cargo doors were flung open, and crates were quickly removed. Then the return cargo was loaded. Litters were quickly lifted from the shadows and trotted to the plane. Limping men were assisted toward the C–47s and lifted aboard. By this time Galligan was on the ground supervising the operation. He glanced at his wristwatch. It was 0300 hours. The mission called for no more than thirty minutes on the ground. An American, clad in a paratrooper uniform marked by no insignia of rank other than an American flag on one shoulder and a patch lettered U.S. CONTINGENT on the other, handed a burlap sack to Galligan.[1]

"What is it this time?" Galligan asked the American, an OSS liaison officer attached to the partisan unit.

"The usual," the OSS man replied. Galligan could feel the weight of documents. He also knew that the sack contained vital maps and other paper that had been captured from German units which the partisans had attacked.

"Are the 'Joes' ready?" Galligan asked. The OSS man nodded. He stepped back into the shadows and returned with five men dressed in nondescript clothing similar to what the partisans were wearing. These were OSS SI agents returning to their headquarters, the 2677th Regiment (Prov.) OSS, located in a heavily guarded compound on the outskirts of Bari, Italy. They were the real reason for this dangerous, breathtaking flight into enemy-occupied Yugoslavia. Each man, a spy, carried imbedded in his memory vital data about some of the Wehrmacht divisions that were waiting in Greece for orders to move swiftly north to relieve and bolster the German forces spread across the war-torn Italian peninsula.

This was the real reason for Colonel Galligan's secret flight. These "Joes" had to be airlifted out to AFHQ. One of the partisan regiments had been moved to the heights overlooking the valley just to secure it for the arrival of the spies and the landing of the C–47s. It was that important an operation.[2]

Suddenly from the heights above, a flare sizzled into the sky. Then a second. A third. Ghostly white light blanketed the valley, starkly outlining the C–47s as well as the even blacker shadows cast by rocks and trees and ridgelines. The rattle of gunfire echoed down from the heights above, and Galligan and his fellow pilots saw the sparkle of muzzle blasts.

"Get the hell out of here!" the OSS man shouted to Galligan

as he turned toward some of the partisan officers and roared orders in Serbian to move the guerrillas into blocking position and hold off the enemy. Galligan heard orders shouted in the strange tongue as he hastily clambered aboard his C–47, followed by the OSS agents, and dashed through the cabin into the cockpit and quickly settled into his seat. There wasn't time to buckle the seat belt or shrug into his parachute. In fact, there wasn't even time to run through the checklist with his co-pilot. Both men flicked switches on the instrument panel. The co-pilot jabbed the starter button, and the still warm engine whirred, coughed, and then kicked over.

By this time Galligan had his earphones clamped over his cap. "Tell the others to follow us," he snapped to his co-pilot. "We'll take off with navigation lights on so that there'll be no trouble following."

He shoved the throttles forward, and the C–47 picked up speed, rattling like hollow tin down the rough airstrip between the marking fires. No time to warm up. Ahead he spotted tracer bullets. Somebody was shooting *down* at the transports from the heights. The C–47 picked up speed. The tail lifted off the ground. The tachometer moved to take-off speed, and Galligan inhaled deeply as he hauled back on the yoke and felt the Gooney Bird leap off the ground. Now if only he didn't cream into the steep slopes, he thought to himself, and carefully watched his compass heading. The deep shadows of the mountainsides suddenly gave way to the brighter night sky dotted with stars. He exhaled slowly and turned on a heading that led toward Bari, Italy, on the other side of the Adriatic.

"Are the others okay?" he asked his co-pilot. Captain Moore grinned and nodded. Galligan exhaled and relaxed, his teen-age features belying the fact that he was a full bird colonel in the Army Air Force, and one of the youngest group commanders in the one wartime service that was the butt of jokes about the ages of fighting COs who wore eagles or stars on their collars.

Galligan thumbed the microphone button and voiced the code word that his headquarters had been waiting for. The message would be flashed to OSS in Bari, he knew, and to General Eaker's Mediterranean Allied Air Force headquarters.

Galligan's first mission into the rugged mountain peaks of the Balkans took place on the night of April 2, 1944, when two C–47s—Galligan at the controls of one of the Gooney Birds—came down on a rough dirt strip near Drvar in north-central Yugoslavia. The runway, if it could be called that, was marked by the dull orange glow of two parallel rows of wood fires. Only when the pilots dropped below the level of surrounding peaks did they dare turn on their landing lights. German antiaircraft units guarding a nearby railroad would have been alerted by an unexplained light in the mountains, and Luftwaffe night fighters would have been quickly scrambled to investigate, as had happened on occasion.[3]

Drvar was one of a total of thirty-six airstrips that were carved out of the deep hidden valleys of Yugoslavia, including one that was six hundred feet long and ended with a five-hundred-foot drop to the jagged rocks below. There were no fixed navigation aids, and Galligan and his pilots approached their landing areas by dead reckoning. When the sound of approaching aircraft was heard on the ground, the partisans lighted fires to mark the runway, either two parallel rows or a single line. When only one line of lights appeared, pilots landed on the left where the ground had been rolled into some semblance of smoothness. When the mission was completed, and the C–47 airborne, the guerrillas dragged great logs studded with spikes over the runway. If daylight brought a curious Nazi reconnaissance plane into the area, the observer would see only what appeared to be a plowed field.

Then there were the "Joes," or spies, who had to be parachuted or landed in Nazi-occupied areas. However, every now and again one of the undercover infiltrators would prove to be not a "Joe," but a "Jane," the nature of her mission wrapped in even tighter security. Galligan may have been commanding officer of the Sixtieth Troop Carrier Group, but he knew enough not to speak to the spies who were hustled aboard the C–47s, always at night.

In such cases, the aircrews knew only that the mission orders called for delivery of a passenger to a certain designated airstrip. They saw the passenger for the first time when he or she appeared out of the darkness at the edge of the flight line minutes before take-off. The official record tells very little about the "Janes." Were they young or old? Plain or beautiful? The nature of their work still remains a mystery —perhaps for all time.

Aerial delivery of weapons, supplies, and equipment to the partisans was carried out in a number of ways. Bundles of indestructible items were kicked from the door of the aircraft as the pilot slowed to near-stall speed approaching the fires that marked the drop zone. More delicate gear was parachuted to earth. For bulky pieces of equipment—components of portable mountain field artillery pieces among other things—a special carrying rack was fitted to the underside of the fuselage. The equipment was packed in long cylindrical packages with a parachute folded into one end. At the drop zone, the pilot pressed a switch which released the cylinder from the carrier and—hopefully—it would float easily down to the hands of the receivers.

This exterior gear occasionally caused the pilots some uneasy moments, especially if a parachute tore loose prematurely. Once Galligan reported this interesting experience to squadron intelligence at debriefing:

> I was flying along just above the mountaintops when we had a sudden jolt. The airspeed indicator dropped back toward zero, and the nose of the airplane headed for the mountains. I immediately realized that a container chute had opened prematurely, so I dived the plane at a steeper altitude, hoping to rip the chute off. A loose chute would usually rip off at 140 to 150 m.p.h. and this diving maneuver, therefore, was standard practice for pilots in these circumstances.
>
> But this chute didn't fill and billow open, so I pulled up just above the mountaintop at 110 m.p.h. I couldn't hold altitude with the load and the added drag, so I headed for the coast dodging between the mountains. I was still losing altitude when suddenly the plane leaped forward like a colt at a racetrack. The chute had torn loose at last.

Of the four containers under the plane, two held high explosives and detonators. From inside the ship it was impossible to tell which container had lost its parachute. Over the DZ Galligan released his cargo. Three parachutes blossomed forth. The fourth cylinder plummeted to earth to land with a dull thud.

"Thank God," recalls Galligan, "that one wasn't filled with explosives. It hit the ground about 50 feet below our plane."

On another night in late April, 1944, Galligan had taken off on a mission with Capt. Moore occupying the other seat. The target was a crude strip at the bottom of a narrow valley surrounded by towering peaks. Thick overcast covered the area, and they could catch only an occasional glimpse of the fires kindled by the reception party. However, they let down successfully, only to find serious trouble on the ground.

An afternoon skirmish with a strong German patrol had left twenty-two men wounded, all so seriously that they needed immediate hospitalization. While the partisans unloaded supplies from the aircraft, Galligan and the guerrilla leader walked among the straw mats and goatskins that served as pallets for the wounded. There were four British agents in the group of injured and two Americans. The rest were partisans, some bearded, battle-scarred veterans along with a sprinkling of youths still in their teens. Their wounds were unwashed, and the deep scarlet of fresh blood stained the rags that bound heads and thighs and bellies.

"We can take half of them now," said Galligan, "and come back tomorrow night for the others. Let's load the worst of them."

Even as he spoke, an excited partisan carrying a burp gun appeared out of the darkness surrounding the firelight. Gesticulating violently, he jabbered out a message to the guerrilla leader. When the man paused for breath, the leader translated.

"The Germans are back. They are in the village two miles below with half-tracks and armored scout cars. We will have to make a run for it. You must leave immediately or you will lose the airplane."

"How long can you hold them off?"

The leader shrugged.

"Who knows? We will roll rocks from the mountain down on the road. And we have some dynamite and hand grenades. But such things will only delay them. This camp is lost. They are too strong."

Galligan made a decision.

"Start loading the wounded."

With his eye he measured the length of the short runway and the height of the surrounding peaks. It would be like taking off from the bottom of a soup bowl. There was no room to maneuver for altitude. Once the wheels left the ground there was no place to go but up. He summoned the crew chief as the sound of small arms fire floated up from the village below.

"Get everything off the airplane that isn't nailed down. And tell those partisans to hurry up the loading."

"How many do you think we can take?"

Galligan made a second decision as the sound of gunfire below was punctuated by the dull thump of a distant explosion.

"We will take them all—every man."

They made it, with a load of twenty-two wounded men and a runway under the wheels that was little longer than a football field. As the crew chief told the story later, he said that "Galligan simply prayed that airplane over the mountains."[4]

Colonel Galligan's Sixtieth Troop Carrier Group was as much a part of the Balkan Air Force as Colonel MacCloskey's "Special" 858th Bombardment Squadron (H) which was later enlarged to group size. However, BAF soon became a mixed bag of organizations which included, shortly after its organization on June 4, 1944, SOE Force 399 and attached OSS OG detachments from Company B, 2677th Regiment (which at one point was called the Strategic Balkan Services of OSS), an RAF Wing consisting of two British squadrons, 1586 Polish Flight, Numbers 1 and 88 Squadrons of the Italian Air Force which had been enemy units only twelve months earlier, and the Russian Air Group.

The idea for a supporting AAF organization for OSS originated in the War Department on February 14, 1944— somewhat late despite strong recommendations on the heels of earlier overtures made by OSS men in the field. Ordered to use existing assets, MAAF tabbed the 122nd Liaison Squadron for the mission along with its newly assigned commander, Colonel MacCloskey. In official exchanges,

General Eaker noted that the 122nd had "no authorization and no table of organization suitable for such work." Also, the demands of OSS and SOE for missions to the Balkans reflected the increasing importance of supply work. The MAAF commander's solution to the immediate problem at hand was to reorganize the 122nd Liaison Squadron as a heavy bombardment squadron with fifteen aircraft of longer range and greater load capacity instead of the squadron's original seven B–25s and three B–17s.

Higher up the chain of command within the Mediterranean Theater of Operations, Lieutenant General Jacob L. Devers, the deputy commander of MTO, assured the head of JCS, Gen. George C. Marshall, that there would be no difficulty in organizing the new squadron. He emphasized the importance of letting the French and Balkan resistance know that the British were not the sole source of the aid the underground was receiving.[5] Even then, national rivalries had not quite disappeared.

About the same time that BAF was formed, RAF Air Vice Marshal William Elliott was placed in charge of a Special Operations Committee (SOC) to coordinate BAF, SOE Force 399 in the Balkans, the catchall 2677th OSS Regiment whose various companies deployed detachments to southern France, northern Italy, the Balkans, Austria, Hungary, and Czechoslovakia, and the Allied Missions to Tito which included Brig. Fitzroy H. Maclean's Number 37 Military Mission and the OSS Mission to Tito headed by Colonel Ellery C. Huntington. Later, the BAF would encompass combat squadrons that were on call to give fighter and bomber support to the growing resistance armies then beginning to sally forth in great strength and hammer the enemy directly.

But national rivalries increased beginning with the arrival of a Soviet military mission to Bari, ostensibly to bring aid to the Yugoslav partisans led by Tito, who had undergone special Comintern training in Moscow that prepared him for his prewar role as a political agitator and his wartime role of resistance leader. On February 3, 1944, two lend-lease C–47s bearing the red star of the Soviet Air Force touched down at Bari. Out stepped a military mission headed by Andrei Vishinsky, who was under instructions from Moscow to continue into Yugoslavia at the earliest possible opportunity and join Tito's Supreme Headquarters.

Up until the end of 1943 Churchill had leaned toward Mihailovic as the resistance leader in Yugoslavia with the most military clout and political support. Earlier that year he had sent Maclean into Yugoslavia with an SIS and SOE group—all of whom parachuted into the country to establish contact with Mihailovic and Tito. In short order Maclean began to report back to the Prime Minister that the partisans and not the Chetniks were the resistance group to watch. Official U.S. policy was to follow the British lead in Yugoslavia.

In the interim, Churchill and Stalin earlier had agreed that the Balkans represented spheres of influence for their respective countries, and the Prime Minister bowed to the Soviet leader's insistence that Yugoslavia, with a strong Communist-led partisan force, fall under the aegis of Moscow. Churchill, on the other hand, insisted that in exchange Greece fall under the aegis of the British. Few American policymakers in Washington realized the implications, and even Tito took a while to see the light—a situation which after the war led to his complete break with Stalin.[6]

In an effort to seek greater "comradely" political support for his National Committe of Liberation, Tito had sent Milovan Djilas, one of his most trusted lieutenants, to Moscow to work out arrangements for more Soviet support to the partisans. "One of the things that had to be settled in Moscow," Djilas later recounted, "was the organization of supplies from the Soviet Union. Stalin personally ordered that an air route to Yugoslavia should be set up directly from the Ukraine. When the first crew was called to undertake this dangerous route over the Carpathians, German-occupied Rumania, and Hungary, more than a hundred fliers volunteered. Some of them told our mission: 'We shall not fly by night, but in broad daylight!' Shortly afterward, toward the end of April, several Soviet planes arrived in Yugoslavia, dropped materiel, and returned to their airfields in the Ukraine. The Soviet Government had further decided on our suggestion to send them ten Soviet transport planes to Bari so as to fly assistance to Yugoslavia."[7]

Transporting the Soviet mission to Tito's headquarters was easier said than done. Vishinsky pressed for immediate assistance from AFHQ. The Soviets were aware that there was regular air traffic transporting OSS and SOE to Yugoslavia and elsewhere in the Balkans and northern Italy. Vishinsky, on his way to Italy, demanded no less an effort on behalf of his mission. The Soviets stopped at MTO headquarters in Cairo, and again at MAAF headquarters in Tunis, before continuing on the third leg of the journey that began in Moscow and would end at Tito's Supreme Headquarters.

However, Operation MANHOLE, as the project to infiltrate the Soviets into Yugoslavia was called, was delayed by winter storms. In January CCS had informed General Wilson that he was to facilitate the movement of the Russian mission to Yugoslavia as soon as possible after the two C–47s had arrived in Bari. Meantime, Advance Force 133 at Tito's headquarters messaged AFHQ that, winter flying conditions having curtailed supply drops, it would be appreciated if a landing was made in daylight with as great a cargo of additional supplies as possible to provide for the new Allied mission scheduled to arrive. A landing strip could be prepared by partisans at Medeno Polje, southeast of Tito's headquarters. And the additional aircraft could be used to transport wounded partisans back to Italy for more advanced medical treatment.

Operation MANHOLE originally was scheduled for February 3 with the two Soviet C–47s, a third C–47, and six Italian SM–82 tri-motor transports along with an escort of fighter planes. But there were second thoughts on February 1 by Brigadier General Lauris Norstad, who claimed that the landing ground in Bosnia was beyond reach of heavily loaded C–47s and the smaller-capacity Italian transports. General Eaker then suggested that the Russians parachute from the transports, but none of the men from Moscow had received any jump training.

When the two Soviet C–47s finally arrived at Bari, ostensibly to lay over until February 5 and then continue on to Yugoslavia, bad weather had set in. Colonel Socolov, meantime, had gone over the Operation MANHOLE plan with his Allied staff colleagues and immediately complained that not enough fighter plane protection would be afforded by the eighteen P–40s and twelve additional fighters to be picked up over Cutella, some 130 miles up the coast north of Bari. An additional twelve P–47 Thunderbolts were scheduled into Operation MANHOLE to give cover over the Adriatic.

Then it began to snow, and the landing ground at Medeno Polje became heavily blanketed; and the mission was scrubbed again. By mid-February the Soviet group was becoming increasingly nervous and, in an effort to assuage suspicions, MAAF staff officers decided that only gliders with skids could safely land in the snow. The Russians, apparently under strong pressure from Moscow to get on with it, agreed to the glider airlift.

On February 23 at 0900 hours, twenty-three Soviet officers and six British officers of Force 133 were loaded into three Waco CG–4A gliders strung out behind three AAF C–47s from MAAF Tactical Air Command. The C–47s were loaded with 10,500 pounds of supplies to be dropped over the LZ after the gliders were cut loose. Forty-five minutes later the C–47s revved up and began their take-off runs from the end of the Bari airfield. Inside the gliders the Russian officers and their British comrades in arms smiled wanly at each other as the plywood canvas hulks thumped along the ground echoing a hollow drum sound that reverberated until the stubby wings began to grab lifting capacity. Suddenly, the noise halted. They were airborne. Over the Adriatic, Operation MANHOLE was met by twenty-four P–40s and twelve P–47s which paced the slower-moving transports and gliders. Over the LZ a radio signal from the ground notified the transport pilots that they were on the target. Visibility was near zero. The gliders were cut away and whispered their way to the ground, dropping below the thick ceiling to the welcome sight of smoky bonfires on the spreading plain below. The pilots guided in the gliders to smooth landings in the snow. Overhead, the three C–47s were talked down below the clouds, and each made a single pass and unloaded packages to the waiting partisans below.[8]

The Russians had arrived in Yugoslavia thanks to the U.S. Army Air Force flying just another one of many secret air missions—and in an unconventional way. The gliders themselves bearing American markings would be long remembered by partisans at the scene, in the event that, in the interest of propaganda, the Soviets might try to rewrite the facts. After all, the Vishinsky group had tried its best to arrive in Yugoslavia in aircraft bearing the red star of the Soviet Air Force and flown by Russian air crews.

The first two Soviet C–47s that arrived in Italy were stationed in Brindisi (south of Bari), the airstrip used by the Allied air units that would be incorporated into BAF, and from which the Russian air crews flew to Yugoslavia—on two sorties in March and three in April. Although the partisan officials in Bari made high claims for the Soviet supply role, the five sorties in two months were made expressly for the purpose of supplying the Vishinsky group's advance party to Yugoslavia. The supplies came from British stocks that had been earmarked for the partisans. Later, the British and American members of the CCS agreed that the U.S. had greater supply resources and that the bulk of supplies to Tito should be supervised by OSS supply teams.

Meantime, the early OSS arrivals in Yugoslavia quickly learned the difference between the Royal Army insignia worn by the Chetniks and the red cloth five-pointed star stitched on handmade navy blue forage caps or sewn on collars of the ragtag clothing worn by the partisans. After the Soviet mission to Tito had established itself, photographing members of the OSS teams and the Maclean group, and otherwise playing out the role of political commissars rather than military advisers, the members of Tito's headquarters soon began to replace their cloth red stars with metal insignia of similar size and color. It became a standing joke among the OSS and SOE teams that the Soviet supplies had finally arrived: "Tin stars no less; the Russkis are preparing the partisans for a formal march into Belgrade—behind a band."*

Although the lower ranks among the Soviet mission and air units were friendly if not gregarious, there was a constant political tug of war. It was obvious to General Sir Henry

---

*Author's personal observations while attached to OSS in 1944. Soviet officials in Yugoslavia and representatives in Bari on a number of occasions attempted to take credit for providing the supplies of weapons, ammunition and other military equipment delivered by OSS to the partisans.

Maitland Wilson, the senior Allied commander of MTO, that
the Russians were more interested in ultimate political gain
and were unable to support either the Balkan resistance movements or Communist-led movements elsewhere in Europe west
of the Nazi-Soviet front in Eastern Europe, with anything
more than a fraction of what the Western Allies could provide. In the give-and-take of political maneuver, the Soviets
tried to keep their options open by demanding a blank check
as to what they ultimately would provide in the way of
military support to Tito. At one point they wanted permission
to operate not less than twelve fighters and twelve transports
in Italy, but General Wilson fixed this number as the *most*
Soviet aircraft that could be accommodated in his command.
Later, Vishinsky tried to go over Wilson's head and appeal
to Marshal Pietro Badoglio, who headed up the interim
Italian Government, but the Italian leader was taking his
orders from AFHQ.

Wilson was adamant. He reasoned that the only way to
gain some leverage with the Soviets for the establishment
of AAF or RAF bases in the Soviet Union or in Eastern
European territories they controlled was initially to limit the
Russians in Italy. Thinking long-range about future strategy
in the Pacific and the use of Soviet territory for Allied military and air operations against Japan, he reasoned that these
restrictions would still be helpful. When the Soviets finally
arrived in late July with their additional fighter and transport
squadrons totaling twenty-four aircraft, they also brought four
small liaison planes to present to Tito along with two lend-
lease C–47s.[9]

Although the Soviet air units were to operate under BAF,
Air Vice Marshal Elliott complained that this operational
control was "more nominal than real, the Russians throughout
taking an extremely independent line." And there were those
among the Soviets who were so politically oriented that any
slight incident became a provocation.

At Brindisi an RAF vehicle accidently struck one of the
Soviet C–47s, damaging the aircraft slightly. "Provocation!
Sabotage!" loudly accused Colonel Socolov, the Soviet spokes-
man. Allied airmen noted, however, that the Russian officer
didn't wear aviator's wings on his tunic, as did his comrades.
On another occasion, Colonel Socolov asked the BAF com-

mander for permission to fly a training mission to a point off
the Adriatic island of Corfu, and it was granted on condition
that there be no landing or parachuting into Greece. Even
then the Western Allies had become wary. On the night of
July 25, 1944, the C–47 landed in Greece, and eleven Russians were met by guerrillas of the Greek Communist resistance ELAS.[10]

It was a delicate period for the Western Allies, who at that
time were planning an airborne and amphibious invasion of
Greece to cut off some twenty Wehrmacht divisions. At the
same time the Communist EAM/ELAS had begun to clash
with EDES, another powerful resistance organization in
Greece. The commander of EAM/ELAS, Stephanos Saraphis,
reasoned that Russian supplies could turn the tide in the
coming conflict for control of the Government of National
Unity. But Lieutenant Colonel Popov, who headed up this
surreptitious mission, declared that he had no mandate to
promise supplies but would accept a list. Saraphis later wrote,
"within two days lists were provided. But, to the very end,
we never received any assistance."[11]

Perhaps the postwar political scene for Yugoslavia and
elsewhere in the Balkans had been set as early as October
1941, when Captain Duane Hudson, a British SIS agent,
parachuted into Yugoslavia. The following year Major Atherton of SIS was landed on the Montenegrin coast of Yugoslavia by submarine and was later murdered for the gold he
carried. The blame for his murder was directed against a
General Novakovich, one of Mihailovic's Chetnik commanders, who later disappeared. On April 21, 1943, two
teams of Canadians of Yugoslav origin, recruited in 1942
as part of Project SKIPPER, were parachuted "blind" to
make contact with the resistance. In May additional British
teams were parachuted in.

The first American OSS teams parachuted in August.[12]
Major Louis Huot, without any orders from his superiors,
took it upon himself to contact Tito, although Major Linn
Farish had been tapped for the assignment. Marine Corps
Captain Walter Mansfield, a young member recruited from
General Donovan's law firm, established the first American
contact with the Chetniks, which continued officially until

late 1944. The heavy British political impact occurred in September 1943 when Brigadier Maclean parachuted into Yugoslavia to direct the Allied Military Mission. There was no Allied Special Operations Committee in 1943. The British claim to represent the Allies, based upon Churchill's earlier agreement with Stalin about Balkan spheres of influence, caused no end of consternation at OSS headquarters in Cairo until November, when General Donovan, on one of his frequent overseas inspections, established the right of OSS to pursue operations with the partisans independent of Maclean's mission.

Unaware of the intramural politicking among the Western Allies, Tito's headquarters viewed the American presence in a different light, as reported later by Vladimir Dedijer, former Belgrade journalist and confidant of Tito:

> One day, a rather strange man appeared in Partisan territory. He was an officer of the United States Army, a major, who said his name was Huot. He asked to see Tito, but inquired all the time whether there were any British officers in the vicinity. At that very moment a British officer came along. The American immediately asked the town mayor to hide him in another room so that the Englishman should not see him. The town mayor did as he was asked, but was at a complete loss to understand what the American officer was after.
>
> The facts were simple, however. Major Louis Huot had not obtained permission from the Allied command to come to Yugoslavia. He had come on his own initiative to assist the Partisans, whose representatives he had met in Bari. Huot was received by Tito and had a long talk with him, after which he returned to Italy. He kept his word. He sent us over 400 tons of uniforms, medical supplies, ammunition and other items, which could not be found in Yugoslavia, from certain U.S. quartermaster stores. . . . This assistance amounted to more than the total aid we had hitherto received from the Allies. We were planning on further supplies when one day this energetic American disappeared from Bari. He had been posted elsewhere.[18]

The Allied supply effort to the partisans really didn't get off the ground until mid-1944. In an effort to immediately arm the Yugoslav partisans with additional weapons, the

Allies decided to turn over wooden cases of rifles stored in an Italian Army depot in Sicily. Unfortunately, the boxes of weapons were not opened for inspection, and OSS along with the British accepted the entire lot and arranged to ship them to Yugoslavia. Once the rifles were handed over to the partisans, it was discovered that these weapons were old models of castoff rifles from many nations. These weapons had been captured from the Ethiopians during the Italian foray into that African land in the mid-thirties. Most of the Italian rifles in the shipment were unserviceable for one reason or another. By cannibalizing the 40,000 weapons, the partisans were able to assemble some 2,000 serviceable rifles.[15]

In Italy, meanwhile, the decision to supply the Italian partisans in the far northern regions of the peninsula was held off until the Allies were finally stalled north of Rome in the summer of 1944. The *Maquis* in southern France were provided with an arms build-up in preparation for the Allied invasion in August 1944, which would be spearheaded by a large infiltration of OSS agents and OG and SO teams. In Greece, OSS and SOE prepared that devastated nation for a British invasion scheduled after mid-September.

For OSS, the latter six months of 1944 would be the decisive time for secret missions and special operations on a global scale.

11

> Against an army sailing through the clouds,
> neither walls, nor mountains, nor seas, could
> afford any security. A flight of northern savages
> might hover in the wind and light at once with
> irresistible violence upon the capital of a fruit-
> ful region that was rolling under them.
> —SAMUEL JOHNSON: *Rasselas*, 1759

While the OSS effort in Europe was slow in getting under
way, the operations mounted by Detachment 101 in Burma
put the joint OSS/SOE operation to shame. And the China-
Burma-India (CBI) Theater of Operations was at the end of
the mighty Allied supply line, receiving less of the materiels
of war from the United States than any other region. Paratroop training in Southeast Asia was a luxury that Detachment 101 could ill afford. Indeed, the early jump missions
into the jungles were made by men using the Air Force seat-
type chute normally worn by pilots rather than parachutes developed for airborne infantry to be worn on the back and
chest. This supply line for OSS in Burma, was, indeed, the
end of the line.

But there were vital targets in the remote jungles—Japanese military bases, some airstrips, and the strategic rail
system which sent trains rattling across bridges spanning
deep ravines and rivers that during the monsoons turned to
swift, unnavigable torrents. When "A" Group first parachuted
into the jungles in late 1942, the target was the railroad
running north from Mandalay. At one of the bridges that
were to be destroyed, a Japanese patrol surprised Lieutenants
Patrick Quinn and B. V. Aganoor who immediately retreated
into the jungle with the enemy in pursuit. Aganoor fell be-

hind to provide covering fire and was cut off and killed. Quinn managed to escape and make his way back to "A" Group's base camp after several days in the jungle.[1]

Meantime, the enemy had been alerted to the danger from the OSS teams, and local spies were employed to go into the jungle and find the OGs that had begun to raise so much unexpected havoc. Not only aircraft for supply drops were in short supply in CBI in early 1943; so was other equipment. When Captain Jack Barnard's element of "A" Group faced possible interception and capture by a Japanese patrol, they radioed the main OSS camp for rubber boats. None were available. Instead, eight rubber air mattresses were dropped to the party so the OG could escape down the Irawaddy River. Another problem that faced Detachment 101 was communications. Field radios threw out a good signal, but they were powered by dry-cell batteries which lasted only thirty hours in the extreme humidity and heat. And batteries were burdensome to carry, even for the many bearers who were employed by OSS. Preferable were C–3 explosive blocks, ammunition, and field rations rather than heavy, bulky batteries. Small hand-powered generators were tried, but they produced a whining noise that could be heard far and wide in the jungle.

Although some of the Kachin guerrilla units began to use elephants to transport supplies through the jungle, air transport and supply made all the difference between success and failure for OSS. In late 1943 the newly developed C–46 "Commando" had been pressed into service transporting supplies to China over the "Hump," the towering Himalayas. Unfortunately, all the bugs in this new twin-engine transport had not been discovered; it was virtually flight-tested on the dangerous route across the roof of the world. The Air Force began to lose C–46s one by one, and the OSS teams in the jungle found themselves picking up pilots and air crew members who were forced to bail out of craft that had suddenly become disabled in flight. Detachment 101 rescued between 25 and 35 percent of the airmen who were forced to take to the silk to escape crashing with their planes. The Japanese were known for taking no prisoners. Natural hazards of the jungle environment also took a gruesome toll as related in one OSS rescue report:

One fate that befell some of these crew members was unbelievably gruesome. As they parachuted into the tall trees, often 100 to 150 feet high and with huge trunks, their bodies traveled beyond the upper foliage, but the parachute was stopped in its descent, caught upon the branches. A man caught in this position, and hurt as most were, would stay suspended in jump harness more than one hundred feet off the ground, like a puppet. The man could neither drop down nor climb up. The result was a slow, agonizing death. In several cases, by the time 101 people located the hopelessly hung-up pilot, ants had eaten away so much flesh that all they found was a skeleton hanging in a tree.[2]

At the U.S. Army Experimental Station, the cover name for OSS Detachment 101, the requirements increased a hundredfold during the first year after the original group of twenty had arrived in India and established itself in the Southeast Asia region. The increased requirements were for the Burmese and Kachin tribesmen who had been recruited and trained for intelligence missions and guerrilla operations in the tropical terrain. But the Americans in the Southeast Asia OSS unit had built up to five above the original number of men who had arrived in July 1942. Halfway around the world from OSS headquarters in Washington, requests for supplies took three to six months before the sorely needed equipment arrived. The supply situation improved after General Donovan visited Detachment 101 in late 1943; and that's when this first OSS operational unit lost its original commander.

Captain Carl Eifler's health had deteriorated. He had been involved in an accident during an intelligence mission at sea off the coast of Burma: piloting the unit's two-seater L-5, he had crash-landed. Malaria and other tropical diseases had taken its toll of his huge physique, and the pressures and responsibilities had also caught up. He suffered a breakdown, and General Donovan had to face the issue and make a decision, which he did by relieving Carl "for physical and medical reasons." Eifler's original deputy, Captain Coughlin, a lieutenant colonel at the end of 1943, was assigned to direct all OSS operations in the CBI, and Captain Peers, also a lieutenant colonel at the end of the year, was named to command Detachment 101.[3]

The OSS teams and the agents that were recruited and trained at the U.S. Army Experimental Station were everywhere in Burma, and of increasing problem for Japanese counterintelligence. The first Japanese captured after the early enemy campaign that ran the Allies out of Burma in the spring of 1942 was taken by an OSS Group. He was a pilot who had parachuted into the jungle, and from this prisoner the Allies were able to mark and pinpoint for Allied airstrikes some of the cleverly concealed enemy airstrips.

Finally the tide began to turn, and CCS in London approved a major airborne invasion of Northern Burma. Captain Sherman B. "Pete" Joost, who had spent months in the jungle organizing the Kachin tribesmen into guerrilla units, was temporarily assigned to the First Air Commando Force that was then being organized by two AAF mavericks, Colonel Philip G. Cochran and Lieutenant Colonel John R. Alison. The plan called for an airborne division to land deep inside enemy territory and, fresh and ready for battle, to mount hard-hitting operations against the Japanese. Earlier, the 5307th Composite Group, also known as Merrill's Marauders, had surged into the jungle and despite the physical conditioning and special jungle training of these troops, the environment still took a heavy toll.

An airborne operation, on the other hand, would permit the deployment of fresh troops ready for combat and a continuous aerial resupply, which Merrill's Marauders had lacked. Airborne operations by a small raiding brigade led by Brigadier Orde C. Wingate had made all the difference in one jungle campaign mounted in 1943. The Air Commando force consisted of fighter aircraft for escort and close support missions, C–47 transports, L–1 and L–5 liaison planes, and CG–4 gliders which would transport equipment and men to be landed at three LZs—Broadway, Piccadilly, and Chowringhee. Detachment 101's "A" Group had made the first foray deep into enemy territory in late 1942 where the airborne attack, called Operation THURSDAY, would take place.

Colonel William Peers assigned Burmese agent Saw Judson, who had been one of the original pair of OSS agents to parachute into the area, to jump in again with a larger team of specially trained Kachin tribesmen and a group of

Chindits from the airborne division composed of one South African and four Indian brigades. The intelligence and reconnaissance teams would radio word of enemy movements so that the commander of the ground forces, Brigadier Wingate, would have the latest enemy developments noted on his tactical maps.[4]

The airborne invasion of Burma was unique in that no one commander was given direct charge of the entire undertaking. D-Day was March 4, 1944, and the first C–47 took off at 1800 hours towing two heavily laden gliders in what was to be nighttime infiltration and landing. As the transport gained altitude pulling the two ungainly gliders, seventy-eight other CG–4s awaited their turns as they stood drawn up in a double row. After dispatch of the first twenty-four gliders, it would be necessary to await the return of the tugs for further movements. However, an hour before take-off, late aerial recon photos revealed that Piccadilly had been blocked by logs that had been dragged across the field. The Japanese had discovered what obviously was a secret landing field, but the enemy was still in the dark as to how or when the LZ would be used. Wingate abandoned his plan to land gliders at the unserviceable LZ. Although twenty-eight minutes behind the operation's original schedule, Operation THURSDAY continued into the night.

The first wave of gliders carried the commander of 77 Indian Brigade, a small force of combat troops, and a detachment of U.S. Army engineers who would prepare Broadway for C–47s by the following evening. Despite the plans, the glider operation ran into trouble at once. The nylon tow ropes had deteriorated under exposure to the sun and weather and some of them snapped shortly after take-off, forcing the glider pilots to make emergency landings in the nearby ricefields. Also, the use of one tow plane, or tug, for two gliders—a technique that was necessary because there were too few tugs—strained the aircraft in their rapid climb to avoid the nearby hills. Overheated engines and abnormal consumption of fuel made it necessary for the C–47 pilots to release their gliders far short of their destination.

As a result, of the sixty-seven gliders that were airborne thirty-two reached Broadway, nine landed in hostile territory, another nine landed in friendly territory, two were

lost, and fifteen were forced to turn back to Lalaghat airstrip which was one of the two airfields that were used to
mount the operation. And there were other difficulties
at Broadway, according to the official AAF report which
described a field marred by deep furrows and water buffalo
holes that had not shown up in the original aerial reconnaissance photos.[5]

> First arrivals lost their landing gear and could not be
> moved. Later arrivals crashed into the stalled gliders, and
> the field became a shambles. It is remarkable that this
> misfortune did not turn into a disaster. As it was, only
> 31 men were killed and 30 injured of the 539 who landed.
> To avoid more serious consequences, the brigade com-
> mander radioed: 'No more gliders!' The glider fly-in to
> Broadway ended. Fortunately, enough heavy equipment
> was salvaged to permit the American engineers and
> British troops to bulldoze an airstrip 300 by 5,000 feet.
> By the night of 6 March, Troop Carrier Command was
> able to complete the fly-in of 77 and 111 Indian Brigades
> using 44 British Dakotas and 39 American C–47s. . . .
> That same night, 6 March, 12 single-tow gliders landed
> at Chowringhee with no difficulty, and the contingent
> immediately prepared the field as a landing strip sub-
> sidiary to Broadway. It was not intended to use Chow-
> ringhee for more than a few days, and it was abandoned
> 10 March.[6]

Some weeks before Operation THURSDAY, Captain
Joost participated in one night landing rehearsal when more
than a dozen gliders, filled with troops and equipment, were
towed into the sky and then released in a dry run to see if
the actual airborne operation had a chance to succeed. It
worked far better than the first landings at the Broadway LZ.
On D-Day Joost boarded one of the first gliders with part of
the Chindit *Dah* Force which would spearhead the operation.
Seated with members of the *Dah* (knife) Force in one of the
gliders, Joost recalls how the moon was fairly bright and he
could see two C–47s ahead, each towing two gliders.

> We had arrived at Broadway, and below me I could
> see the paddy. I knew it was a hundred yards wide and
> about six hundred feet long. Small enough, but from the
> air it looked positively tiny. Our C–47 started down

and then zoomed up as the pilot evidently changed his mind. We circled once, and then as we turned back toward the paddy, I watched our glider pilot release the tow rope, and without a sound we headed toward the ground. The landing was fine, and the second we came to a stop I was out of the glider. The field was deathly still and not a sound could be heard anywhere. It was an eerie sensation. Everyone jumped out quickly and pushed out glider over to the side of the field to make way for those to follow. The timing called for a landing every two minutes. We had barely cleared our glider when in came another with a long, loud swish and then another and another. Ours had been the third to land and up to number six everything went like clockwork. Then number seven cracked up after hitting a small hummock in the middle of the field. The impact split the glider and the soldiers were spilled out onto the field. Before we could get enough men together to move the wrecked glider, another six or seven came crashing into the pile-up.

Despite the losses caused by the accident, the enemy had no warning of Brigadier Wingate's plans. Although the operation itself was without a cover plan, the forced landing of nine gliders near enemy positions in itself provided an impromptu deception. Two of the gliders came down in the immediate vicinity of a Japanese divisional headquarters, and the enemy naturally concluded that an assault was underway against some of his installations. The airlift itself afforded the British force time to establish itself in the area almost two years after the Japanese had forced an Allied withdrawal. Unfortunately, Wingate did not live to see Operation THURSDAY succeed. He was killed in a plane crash on March 25, 1944, and his remains were not recovered until April 1947.

Flying in that remote region of Southeast Asia, or operating on the ground deep in enemy-occupied territory, had its attendant risks for OSS. A body could disappear forever.

So, too, could a body disappear forever half a world away from Burma in the Italian Piedmont and the rugged Alps of the north central peninsula—especially in winter. The code name of the DZ was LAGOON GREEN, a deep valley in the Dolomite Mountains of northern Italy and a redoubt for 2,000 partisans and their Allies from OSS and SOE. The deep valley, just south of the Brenner Pass, held the most harried regiment of partisans in all Europe in February 1945. They were on the verge of starvation; they were sick, and they were running low on ammunition. Nor had they received any air-delivered supplies since the fall of 1944. At the same time, they were in an ideal geographic location to harass the enemy supply and withdrawal routes through the various passes leading through Udine and Treviso and Verona and the heavily trafficked Brenner Pass.

Weather conditions in northern Italy had scrubbed many a bombing and air supply sortie, and the partisans and their Allied mentors in the field were on the verge of desperation. One message that arrived at OSS headquarters in Bari pleaded, "IF YOU CAN'T SEND SUPPLIES, THEN SEND FOOD. WE'LL FIND A WAY TO FIGHT BUT WE CANNOT FIGHT WITHOUT FOOD."

The narrative statement of Fifteenth Air Force Special Group, commanded by Colonel MacCloskey, reports how Captain Robert "Tex" Stone, the commanding officer at the 885th Bombardment Squadron, and Captain Alan Partridge, the Group Navigator, pulled together a crew of volunteers for a hazardous flight to LAGOON GREEN on the night of February 14, 1945. Three days later another drop would be made. Moreover, this was Stone's fifty-first mission, one over the required fifty which was a ticket home.

> They decided that an accurate drop at low altitude could be made. They volunteered to fly one plane to the target and Lieutenant John J. Koenig and his crew volunteered to fly the second aircraft. The elevation of the reception ground, as shown on the target chart, is 4,200 feet (above sea level) while the surrounding mountain wall is within a two-mile radius, rises to 11,000 feet, a difference of 7,200 feet, less than a mile on either side of the reception. To get into this "hole" it was necessary for the aircraft to make a circling let-down, peeling off in the last stage to a loss of 4,000 feet a minute, cut the power back for a drop at 135 m.p.h. and then with full boost circle out through a mile wide ravine.

One slip, one fraction of pressure on the controls at the wrong moment, and the aircraft would slam into the steep canyon walls. Enemy troops in the mountains shooting up at the multiengine B–24s used on this mission couldn't help but hit their target if the moon was full or partial. Or the enemy could shoot down at the aircraft in the steep valley from the heights above. The distraction of hostile fire, however momentary, could cause the one fatal slip. Few pilots could be expected to remain that calm and steady at the controls when their aircraft is under fire. But the pilots and aircrews of the Fifteenth Special Group were a breed apart. Some were volunteers, and others were rejects from the heavy bomber squadrons who had been tagged "yellow" or "gutless" by their buddies because they refused to fly dangerous combat missions, or they were unable to accommodate physically to high-altitude flying. But day in and day out they flew their unarmed missions, flying low and slow in an effort to deliver the materiel that the partisans needed to wage war in the enemy's rear.

The airborne support to OSS/SOE and the resistance movements was summed up at the time by one of the units in the Balkan Air Force:

> This Group has been fighting the Axis in a method heretofore unheard of. They didn't go flying in tight formations over the target, dropping blockbusters on German industries, nor did they come buzzing down at treetop level, guns ablaze, shooting up convoys, troop concentrations, trains, and other exciting things a fighter pilot does.
>
> No, the boys of troop carrier had another method of evening their score with the Germans; operating with the Balkan Air Force, they slipped in and out among the ever threatening mountain peaks in the still of the night, dropping supplies and frequently landing right in Jerry's back yard. In their own way they dropped bombs that were more accurate than those placed by the world's best bombsight, machine-gunned troops and enemy supply lines not from the sky, but from behind walls, buildings, mountains and ravines, not in person of course but by making it possible for the partisans to do these things. By the continuous flying on the part of the aircrews, in the face of weather frequently more dangerous than the enemy, the partisan forces were supplied with everything from blood plasma to jeeps, when and where needed, on a scale never before possible.

Though thousands of miles from the invasion of
Normandy . . . the partisans were able to divert several
divisions of German forces and keep them plenty well
occupied. Acting as observers, the crews reported all unusual incidents noted on each flight. . . . As a result,
fighters or bombers were sent out to neutralize the target,
sometimes a motor convoy, and frequently an enemy
fighter base.⁷

But it was left to Detachment 101 to experiment with airborne infiltration of the future. One of the best agents in the
Detachment 101 stable was code-named "Betty," and to him
fell the distinction of being infiltrated by helicopter—the only
time during World War II that the few noisy 180-horsepower
Sikorskys were used in a clandestine intelligence operation.
The helicopter, from an air rescue unit, had limited performance in 1944. It could fly no higher than 7,000 feet and
was unable to carry a passenger or cargo if it operated at an
altitude of 3,000 feet above sea level. Nevertheless, it was
used once by OSS.

General Donovan's attitude was to try anything that had
even the slightest chance to work. "His imagination was unlimited," wrote former OSS officer David Bruce some years
later. "Ideas were his playthings. . . . Woe to the officer
who turned down a project because, on its face, it seemed
ridiculous, or at least unusual." And there was a little-known
branch of OSS that was "unusual," directed by Stanley P.
Lovell, a dour New Englander, whose solemn features belied
a sense of humor and a strong belief that the impossible
only took a bit longer.

Lovell's job was to develop unusual ways to kill, maim,
sabotage, and conduct carefully planned mayhem on a scale
large or small. During one of General Donovan's periodic
briefings in the Pentagon to the JCS in August 1943, Lovell
was introduced as OSS Director of Research and Development and proceeded to demonstrate a few of the simpler
booby traps and incendiary devices that he had concocted. One
was a howling, shrieking mechanism that exploded with a
deafening sound; Lovell was surprised to see distinguished
two- and three-star generals—the nation's senior military

leaders—"clawing and climbing to get out through the room's single door." Lovell was never invited back for a Pentagon demonstration during World War II.

As he and General Donovan left the military headquarters across the Potomac from the nation's capital, the director of OSS laughed as he recalled the scene in the briefing room. "I think we overdid that one," said Donovan.[8]

One of the early weapons in the OSS arsenal was an incendiary bomb in the shape of a small book. The celluloid casing was packed with napalm jelly which was fused to an ignition timer set for periods up to seventy-two hours. Another was a sabotage device called the Casey Jones because it was designed for railroad sabotage. Specifically, it was a steel box that contained an explosive charge with a permanent magnet on top so that the entire device could be fastened to the underside of a locomotive and timed to explode as the saboteur desired. This device was refined still further when an electric-eye mechanism was installed so that the bomb would explode only in a tunnel.

Another weapon was a noiseless, flashless .22-caliber pistol and submachine gun for silent killing. At General Donovan's request, one of the pistols was delivered to his office to be presented to President Roosevelt, but in a most unusual way. Donovan brought the pistol to the White House along with a sandbag and was ushered into FDR's office, normal wartime Presidential security measures having been set aside for the chief of American intelligence. The President was dictating a letter when he looked toward the door, saw Donovan, and motioned him in. While FDR was speaking to his secretary, Donovan set the sandbag on the floor and silently fired an entire clip of bullets into it. The President continued dictating to his secretary. When she left the office, Donovan presented the pistol to FDR with a handkerchief still wrapped around the still-hot barrel, explaining at the same time that he had fired off a clip of ten bullets and the firing hadn't even disturbed the chief executive.

The President was momentarily shocked and then pleasantly surprised that a weapon could be brought into his presence and fired without a sound. Then he laughed, asked Donovan to congratulate the man who made the silent killer weapon, and then, as he gingerly placed the weapon on his desk, allowed as how Donovan was "the only black Republican I'll ever allow in my office with a weapon like this."[9]

The cloak-and-dagger effort required more than placing spies in strategic places and, as time went on, it was discovered that certain types of intelligence acquisition required experts with PhDs who were heavy in science and technology. The OSS expertise was of a social science nature and, occasionally, R&A researchers came across bits of scientific information that made little sense to experts in history, government, geography, and economics. There were always fantastic rumors floating around about terrifying secret weapons and atom bombs which were duly reported by the OSS and British agents, but invariably the technical details were hopelessly nonsensical. The reason was obvious. No ordinary spy could obtain the information required for the simple reason that he lacked the scientific training to know what was essential. Only scientifically qualified personnel could search out this type of intelligence, and a Mata Hari with a PhD in physics is as rare in real life as in fiction.[10]

A select group of scientists—code name ALSOS, the Greek word for grove, for Major General Leslie R. Groves, director of MANHATTAN Project—was organized to work with OSS in the acquisition of information about experiments in nuclear physics by the Germans. OSS cooperated with the ALSOS to some extent, offering various leads, but it was the scientists themselves who tracked down the complex information that ordinary agents were not capable of uncovering, much less understanding.

In early 1945 when Allied armies were hammering the Wehrmacht inside the Fatherland, an ALSOS team learned from a French engineer that the Germans had a similar scientific intelligence group in Paris. "I worked for them," the Frenchman told the American scientific team who interrogated him. "All I had to do was to keep them occasionally informed about new inventions and inventors. They called their organization 'Cellastic' and used some Dutch and Swiss people who feigned an interest in buying patents as a front. But it was really a German technical spy ring."[11]

Where in Paris? The French scientist described the building at 20 rue Quentin Beauchart, just off the Champs Elysees, smack in the middle of the French capital. The address was right next door to the Paris headquarters of OSS.

12

> A great part of the information obtained in war is contradictory, a still greater part is false, and by far the greatest part is of a doubtful character.
> —KARL VON CLAUSEWITZ: *On War*, 1832

Without information, OSS would have been a total failure, and the lives of brave men and women sent into the field as agents in and out of uniform would have been jeopardized far beyond the normal risks of operating in a hostile environment. The wartime intelligence agency's R&A section was responsible for providing the detailed information upon which high-level or low-level decisions would be made. However, not all information was correct, and not all policy decisions were the correct ones.

There were personal prejudices among the men of genius and achievement in the polyglot OSS. Basically, these prejudices were political and ideological in nature. Many wartime decisions based on these prejudices came back a generation later to haunt the leaders of the Western wartime alliance.

But in the early forties there was a war to be won, and much of the sophisticated R&A studies produced by OSS was of pertinent use to the nation's military planners in the Pentagon. Operation TORCH had been successful in North Africa, and at the Casablanca Conference, General Eisenhower was directed to prepare for Operation HUSKY—the invasion of Sicily in July 1943 to be followed by the invasion of Italy. The R&A information machine was supported by an IBM information punch card system which at that time was the only high-speed data system of its kind.

Once the green light was given for Operation HUSKY,

R&A went to work and put together the vital statistics about this ancient island separated from the toe of the Italian peninsula by the strait of Messina. But what of the people? Who lived in the tiny villages that dotted the rocky landscape and in the urban centers of Palermo, Marsala, Licata, Syracuse, Catania, and Messina, the coastal municipalities where invasion troops might land and whose docking facilities would play an important role.

Other islands had also been targeted by the Allies. Pantellaria, on the invasion sea route to Sicily, had to be smashed, because it served the enemy as a forward fighter base and early warning center. Corsica and Sardinia also would have to be invaded, since they provided the enemy with a base from which to flank the Allied operation. In Sicily itself those Axis divisions, or their remnants which had been successfully withdrawn from North Africa during the days of defeat in Tunis in April and May, were now waiting for the Allied attack which the Germans expected in one of two places—Sicily or Greece.

How many enemy troops were in Sicily? What kind of beaches were available for amphibious landings? The number of enemy airfields and aircraft? And then there were questions of a nonmilitary nature concerning the people of Sicily and how they would react to an Allied invasion.

There was an organization on the island called the Mafia, whose members were part of the American underworld. Was the Mafia anti-Fascist? If so, could the Mafia, whose own *banditi* often roamed the hills, be pressed into service on behalf of the Allies? How could this secret organization be contacted? The answer to questions about the Mafia was locked behind bars in a state prison in Dannemora, New York, and more specifically in a cell occupied by Salvatore Lucanio, who was serving a thirty-to-fifty-year sentence on sixty-two counts of transporting women across state lines for the purposes of prostitution.[1]

This particular prisoner of the State of New York, alias Charles "Lucky" Luciano, was the Mafia chief in the United States. He reportedly offered his assistance through his attorney, Moses Polakoff, who had contacted OSS. A number of naval officers from ONI, dressed in civilian clothing, visited Luciano at least fifteen times. Most of the later visits took place at the Great Meadows state prison, where the Mafia leader had been moved to more comfortable quarters that also permitted the required secrecy. The conversations all concerned Sicily and people who could be contacted by Allied intelligence agents.* The OSS had no trouble recruiting Americans of Sicilian extraction from the estimated two million who lived in the U.S. in 1943.

When Operation HUSKY, the invasion of Sicily, was firmed up with some information reportedly provided by the Mafia chief, it was just a matter of executing the intelligence side of the plan.

One of the major intelligence operations was a great burst of guerrilla activity in Greece during the month preceding the invasion of Sicily. As part of a cover plan to keep the Axis guessing, CCS ordered the small British SOE group and the guerrilla forces with which they were fighting to go on the offensive. It was hoped by the Allied command that this outburst of activity would deceive the enemy about Allied intent and either draw enemy troops into Greece or keep those on occupation duty in the country. In some measure, Operation ANIMALS did both.

Although the invasion of Sicily would be an Allied affair with the majority of assault forces representing U.S. army, air, and naval strength, the behind-the-scenes operation in Greece was strictly a British affair, and OSS agents did not appear on the scene until later in the year. On June 21, 1943, six SOE sappers attacked the Asopos viaduct under cover of darkness and damaged it critically. It took the Germans, using Polish and Greek labor, two months to make repairs on the structure which carried the vital rail line. But

---

*There have been many conflicting stories about Luciano's role. However, a number of people, including former military intelligence officers who had been in contact with the Mafia chief when he was in prison, appeared before the parole board or wrote to the board on his behalf when he applied for a parole in late 1945 based on "services rendered to the nation." Whether he was promised parole and residence in the U.S. or deportation has never been disclosed. He was deported, and in early 1946 Italian newspapers reported that Luciano was greeted on arrival in Sicily by Don Carlo Vizzini.

the first engine to go across the repaired viaduct crashed through and fell into the gorge. A pier had collapsed either through sabotage or faulty workmanship, and the rail line was out for another two months.[2]

The SOE commander, Brigadier Myers, originally planned to use EAM/ELAS guerrillas to attack through two tunnels. The third of the three practicable approaches was from below the bridge through a gorge that opened into a wide valley. But the Communist leader of the ELAS guerrillas turned down the SOE request for support because of possible enemy retaliation and partisan losses. The guerrilla commander told Myers that the operation could "have no hope of success unless at least 1,500 men were used with artillery and machine guns." But the six SOE sappers proved the guerrilla chief wrong, and the Asopos operation was, by timing, the opening shot of Operation ANIMALS on behalf of the Allied invasion of Sicily. Throughout Greece telephone communications were cut, and of forty-four major demolitions of transportation routes, sixteen were on railway lines. Prime Minister Churchill later claimed that two German divisions "were moved into Greece that might have been used in Sicily."

Operation HUSKY jumped off on July 10, 1943, preceded by a paratroop and glider airborne strike on the night of July 9 with parachute infantry from the U.S. Seventh Army, commanded by General George S. Patton, and glider troops from the British Eighth Army, commanded by Field Marshal Bernard L. Montgomery. Patton's forces were to strike along the southwest coast of the mountainous island and Montgomery's army on the southeast coast. With naval and air support the island could be secured within sixty days. Under Allied military control Sicily then would become the jumping-off place for Operation AVALANCHE—the invasion of Italy. By July 14 the Allies were moving in additional combat and support troops from the total invasion force of 478,000 men against whom were arrayed Axis forces of German and Italian troops numbering between 300,000 and 365,000.

Meantime, the intelligence role, never denied or confirmed publicly by many participants, began when an American aircraft with a yellow silk flag inscribed with a large black L passed over a small village and dropped a packet in front of the church in the weather-beaten square. The following day, July 15, the same aircraft marked the same way passed low over a villa on the outskirts of the same town, and another packet was dropped. As with the first packet, a yellow silk scarf inscribed with a black L was enclosed with instructions written in the *Sigie* jargon of the Mafia. The villa belonged to Calogero Vizzini, known to Sicilians as Don Carlo, chief of the Sicilian Mafia.

Within hours a messenger was dispatched to the village of Cammarata at the foot of a rocky mountain in west central Sicily where he was under orders to contact a group of armed men who lived in the caves and ravines. The instructions written in the hand of Don Carlo were to be eaten if the messenger was in danger of being stopped by the *Fascisti*—Wehrmacht or Italian soldiers—at road blocks. Don Carlo also dispatched another messenger to the Mafia's second in command, Giuseppe Geno Russo, with instructions to take to the hills and join other armed Mafia bands in occupying strategic towns along the main roads of the western half of the island—the American area of military operation (AO).[8]

On July 20 a patrol of three American tanks, the lead one flying a yellow silk flag, approached Cammarata and halted. A lone figure wearing a silk scarf around his neck walked toward the tanks. The hatch on the lead tank opened, and an American officer, cradling a carbine, ordered the Sicilian to halt. He then clambered out of the tank and walked to the elderly Sicilian who, with great ceremony, removed his own scarf and spread it wide so that the officer and the careful eyes scanning the area from the observation slits in the armor behind the machine guns and cannon could see the sign of the L.

The officer, in fluent Sicilian dialect, greeted Don Carlo. Then the questions. Where was the enemy deployed? How many *Fascisti*? What units? Artillery? Machine guns and their positions? Was the enemy entrenched on the mountain overlooking Cammarata? The replies were quickly forthcoming while additional Americans climbed from tanks. Armed Sicilians began to show themselves, but instead of nervousness on either side, there were only smiles and conversation. Several

of the Americans, called *cugini* (cousins) by the armed
civilians, were also of Sicilian extraction.

The enemy on the mountain? No enemy. Only friends. "It
is our mountain," Don Carlo declared emphatically, adding,
"and this is our land."

Although the fighting was heavy in the British area of
operations, enemy resistance was relatively light in the American AO. The enemy's coastal divisions were composed
principally of Sicilian reservists pressed into service by Italy's
dictator, Il Duce. Mafia agents had approached the men in
these various units, and as many as two-thirds of the reservists
in some units deserted only hours after the men from the
villages and the hills had made their point.[4]

By July 23 western Sicily was cleared by Patton's troops,
and he turned the Seventh Army east to assist the British
who had been stopped at Catania. By early August the Italian
divisions began a mass exodus, and on August 11 the Wehrmacht retreated in ships to Italy in what was a Dunkirk in
reverse. By August 17 the last of 100,000 German troops,
9,800 vehicles and fifty tanks were back in Italy. American
casualties were 7,319 killed and wounded; the British lost
9,333, and the Axis lost 164,000 killed, wounded, and captured, of whom 32,000 were Germans. Allied forces also
captured large amounts of enemy supplies. In the campaign the
Wehrmacht had fought both professionally and tenaciously
while the Italian forces, who had shown little desire to fight,
surrendered or deserted in droves, assisted by the OSS connection—the Mafia.

The next step: Italy.

Salerno was invaded on September 9, 1943, and of the
many different OSS missions that went in, two were 180 degrees apart in scope and target—the "McGregor Project"
and a line-crossing operation. Captain Steven Rossetti followed the first wave of American assault troops ashore at
Salerno on September 9, 1943, as the long-awaited invasion
of the European continent by the Western Allies began. Accompanied by three Italian agents, Rossetti was an OSS line-
crosser responsible for escorting spies through enemy lines
or, if need be, from inside enemy lines back to friendly
forces. The agents were new at the job, and Rossetti also

was on his first secret mission for the OSS Fifth Army Detachment. The target was Naples, and Rossetti's instructions were to deliver the agents and their radio to a point eighteen miles south of the strategic port city. Italian agents, later called "bennies" in OSS jargon (every Italian, when asked about something by Americans at Salerno would answer, *"Va bene, va bene"* "That's good, that's good") were dispatched as close to Naples as possible. Coincidentally, Rossetti passed through the town of Avellino, which was the birthplace of his father.

A party of German soldiers fired upon them on the way back, turning the original forty-eight-hour mission into one that lasted nearly a week because the enemy had tightened his defenses around the beachhead. Still Rossetti returned through Allied lines successfully. He made eighty-four infiltrations of enemy lines during the next eleven months.

Meantime, the "McGregor Project" team also had landed with the invasion forces on its more complex mission. The original plan failed because of the unstable and unpredictable tactical situation at the Salerno beachhead. Italy had been in a state of political chaos since July 25. At the height of the Allied operation in Sicily, Italian dictator Benito Mussolini, Il Duce, was toppled from power. The war in Italy suddenly had become one of political intrigue and espionage along with the heavy fighting. The situation was so fluid that high-ranking Allied officers began meeting with Italian Government representatives in Lisbon and, before the actual armistice was signed, inside Rome itself. It was the perfect opportunity to try to wean the Italian Navy away from the Axis before the Germans moved in and claimed the ships for their own forces.

"McGregor Project" had been the brainstorm of Navy Lieutenant John M. Shaheen. He proposed that a team of agents infiltrate enemy lines and establish secret contact with Rear Admiral Massimo Girosi of the Italian *Commando Supremo,* or Chiefs of Staff. Shaheen also was aware that the admiral's brother, Marcello, was a well-known resident of New York City and available to OSS to assist the mission. The original plan was to have Marcello write to his brother and, once the contact was made, arrange for a secret rendezvous between the Italian admiral and a high-ranking

Allied officer. The letter was dispatched by an OSS team in Sicily who used an Italian prisoner as courier. The prisoner had surrendered to the Allies and was willing to undertake the journey to the Admiral's headquarters, which was also in the POW's hometown.[5]

Upon receipt of the letter, Admiral Girosi discussed its content with members of the *Commando Supremo,* who decided to await the outcome of fast-moving events. Shaheen and the team he had put together were unaware that American generals were at that time arranging to meet an Italian Government representative in Lisbon to discuss surrender terms for Rome. He did not even know that General Donovan himself was involved in Allied negotiations with aging Marshal Pietro Badoglio, who had been asked by King Victor Emmanuel III to form a new government after Mussolini's arrest on July 25, 1943. The Allies, in an effort to push Badoglio's administration into making some hard political decisions (such as capitulating to the Allies and requesting German military forces to leave the country), mounted two heavy bombing missions from North Africa. One airstrike knocked out the two railroad yards serving Rome. The second raid, on August 12, occurred as a series of attacks in northern Italy and included the bombing of Milan.

Meantime, U.S. forces in Sicily had cleared the western half of the island. OSS agents arranged a meeting between General Donovan, who was on hand in Sicily as he was for nearly every major invasion, and Benedetto Croce and Alberto Tarchiani, two longtime political foes of Mussolini. They suggested to Donovan that Italians be given the opportunity to fight under their own flag, saying that they would volunteer if they did not have to take an oath of loyalty to the King, whom most Italians disliked. Anti-Fascist Italians, surmised Donovan, could be useful to OSS.[6]

The general also used his organization to deliver a message to Badoglio in Rome. He reminded the marshal of their earlier meeting when the OSS chief was a globe-trotting civilian visiting Italian forces in Libya and Ethiopia. In the meantime, Sicily had fallen, and the Allies had landed in Italy.

Unaware of all of these sensitive high-level negotiations, Shaheen had organized a team of fellow OSS officers composed of a diverse group of characters—John Ringling North of the circus family, football star Joe "Jumping Joe" Savoldi, Ensign E. M. "Mike" Burke, former foreign correspondent Peter Tompkins, Carlos Conti who had fought for the Loyalists in Spain, and Admiral Girosi's brother, Marcello. By September 9 the "McGregor" Mission was ready to secretly penetrate Italy and contact Admiral Girosi personally. Only then would the Allies be free of the threat of Italian naval vessels falling into German hands.

When the first wave of Americans landed at Salerno, the "McGregor" team was right behind the assault force. But these OSS people had never had to reckon with modern combat, except Conti with his experiences in Spain. Enemy artillery fire was hot and heavy, and the OSS team had to retreat under a frightening barrage of exploding shells. The "McGregor Project" had come a cropper. So, too, had OSS penetration of Italy during the tenuous period between the Allied landings in Sicily and Italy's secret surrender on September 2, effective six days later. During this period a series of political events and maneuvering in Rome and elsewhere in Italy delayed the formal capitulation of the new government of Marshal Badoglio. For forty-five days, until the surrender was announced, a confusing political tug of war for control of the government went on. The dearth of hard intelligence from Italy allowed the Germans time to move in heavy infantry reinforcements and even rescue Mussolini from house arrest.

Those forty-five days were fraught with comic-opera overtones, and an indecisive Allied high command, playing out its own waiting game because of few and conflicting intelligence reports, lost the opportunity to capitalize on the overthrow of Hitler's Axis partner. Marshal Badoglio, officially announcing that Italy would continue to fight on the German side, launched armistice feelers in Istanbul and Tangiers and then opened secret negotiations in Lisbon with Allied military representatives who were hurriedly flown to neutral Portugal from London. The Allies pressed for unconditional surrender while offering Italy lenient terms. But they were caught up in the behind-the-scenes interplay of Italian politics and factionalism without knowing exactly what was going on among those who had wrested control from the Fascists.

In Berlin, a suspicious Hitler was surprised by the *coup* in Rome and moved quickly to place as much of Italy as possible under German military control and disarm the Italian forces—this in an effort to protect his Alpine communications to the Balkans. Meantime, anti-Fascist elements in Rome and Milan began to surface and level demands for an armistice upon Badoglio's government. In an effort to gain time to move additional divisions to Italy, the Germans also proposed a meeting of foreign ministers. The Axis "partners" agreed upon August 6 at the frontier town of Tarvisio. Meanwhile, there was an abysmal mutual ignorance of respective intentions by the Allies and Italy's new government. Italian leaders were hoping that the Allies would forget about "unconditional surrender," and the Allies estimated Italy to be stronger militarily than she really was, although the state of mind of Italian troops who surrendered in North Africa and in Sicily should have been a leading intelligence indicator of Italy's will to fight.

Badoglio's Foreign Minister, Raffaele Guariglia, had been in Istanbul and had left behind with neutral diplomatic sources a draft of possible armistice terms. A copy of this document had been obtained by the OSS group in the Turkish capital. As it was written in formal Italian, Turkish student Turhan Celik was sent for and asked to translate it. But events were moving too swiftly, and OSS had the same information that Allied policymakers also had received simultaneously by way of diplomatic missions in Lisbon and Madrid.

On the other hand, one of the items of intelligence that OSS and SIS should have had was a report of large German troop movements that had been obtained by the clandestine United Freedom Front—the anti-Fascist underground. Some 120,000 enemy troops were reported on the march in northern Italy, and General Giacomo Carboni, commander of the four-division Italian motorized corps stationed near Rome, told civilian friends that there was a "potential fifth column" of at least six thousand German civilians in the Italian capital.[7]

On August 20 Major General Walter Bedell Smith, Eisenhower's chief of staff, and British Brigadier Kenneth W. D. Strong, Allied intelligence chief, met secretly in Lisbon with Italian General Giuseppe Castellano. Travelling incognito on a diplomatic train, he had arrived four days earlier after a stopover in Madrid to meet with the British ambassador. General Castellano had no instructions other than to discuss Allied terms. The two Allied generals also had their instructions to make no advance promises but to insist on an "unconditional surrender." The Italian government would just have to trust the Allies' sense of justice.

The Italian general told the generals from CCS that Italy could not split away from Germany without Allied military help. He then suggested that the Allies make two landings—one to the north of Rome, the second to the north of Rimini on the Adriatic. He told Generals Smith and Strong that two such military operations would force the Germans to withdraw toward the Alps and leave Rome and central Italy safe.

During this period of flux, FDR and Churchill were meeting in Quebec; in the industrial north, Italian labor leaders were threatening a general strike because of stepped-up Allied air raids. They demanded that Badoglio enter into immediate armistice negotiations. But the marshal was trying to negotiate more favorable terms on his own. He had even sent a second general to Lisbon to meet again with Allied representatives while Castellano was on his way back to Rome on the same diplomatic train that had taken him to the Iberian peninsula. Marshal Badoglio also was playing his own political game in attempting to bring about the switch to the Allies without formally capitulating while, at the same time, retaining a government that would maintain the monarchy.

Upon General Castellano's return to Rome a series of meetings was held by cabinet ministers in the Badoglio government. The scene was one of near-hysteria and utter confusion on August 27. Out of the policy conferences came a decision to inform the Allies that the Italian Navy would remain in port instead of sailing to Allied ports as demanded in Lisbon by Generals Smith and Strong. Most important, at least fifteen Allied divisions must land to secure Italy from the Wehrmacht. Moreover, one of these divisions should be parachuted north of Rome near Civitavecchia to protect the capital. The ministers also demanded that they must know in advance the date of the Allied invasion so that the armistice could be announced as soon as the troops began to land. With these new instructions, General Castellano departed for Sicily to meet with Generals Smith and Strong on August 31.[8]

The Italian General's instructions from his government were flatly rejected by the Allied military negotiators, although Castellano was told that amphibious and airborne landings were possible to increase Rome's security *if* the Italians could secure control of the airfields and landing sites against any possible German counterattack. General Castellano and his colleague, General Giacomo Zanussi, who had been sent secretly by Badoglio to Lisbon (without his foreign minister's knowledge or consent) for a second meeting with the Allies and who had returned to Sicily with Generals Smith and Strong, flew back to Rome that evening. The Italian generals were unaware that the Allies had already decided to invade Italy at Salerno with a large-scale amphibious force. Operation AVALANCHE was scheduled for September 9 with a smaller and earlier diversionary landing on September 3 across the Strait of Messina in Calabria province.

On September 1 Marshal Badoglio obtained King Victor Emmanuel's approval of the surrender, and the following day General Castellano flew back to the village of Cassibile, south of Syracuse. There he and General Smith signed a "Short Armistice," consisting of only military terms of capitulation and omitting the phrase "unconditional surrender." The armistice was to take effect six days later, on September 8.

Thirty-nine days had passed since Mussolini had been deposed and arrested. Allied intelligence, including OSS, had drawn a complete blank about the substance and content of fast-breaking political events in Italy. If acted upon with a combination of military options open to the CCS, these events might have changed the course of the war in the Mediterranean Theater of Operations. The opportunity to strike was possible; the military assets were at hand.

These thirty-nine days represented one of the biggest OSS failures of World War II.

The next seven days were equally fraught with missed opportunities. General Castellano remained in Sicily with

the Allied commanders to work out details of the airborne
and amphibious landings near Rome. Two days before the
armistice was to become effective, General Mario Roatta,
Italian Army Chief of Staff, received word to his dismay
that the airborne landing would be made by only one Allied
division, while the main thrust of the invasion would be made
at points near the heel and toe of the Italian boot, more
than two hundred miles to the south. So far as he was
concerned, his forces around Rome were not strong enough
to secure the airbases and parachute drop zones.

Under the assumption that the armistice announcement and
all tactical cooperation with the Italians were set as scheduled,
the Allies secretly dispatched to Rome Brigadier General
Maxwell D. Taylor, assistant commander of the Eighty-second
Airborne Division, and Air Force Colonel William T. Gardiner
to make certain that there would be close tactical coordination
at the airfields and DZs held by the Italian Army. To Taylor's
surprise and dismay, he learned that the Italian troops had
not secured the airstrips and DZs. In a personal confrontation with General Carboni, the motorized corps commander,
and General Francesco Rossi, deputy chief of staff of the
Italian Army, the paratrooper general was told that the
Wehrmacht already had moved into the area and controlled
the airfields. Taylor then demanded to see Marshal Badoglio
and was taken to the old general's home to learn that some
of the *Commando Supremo* were under the impression that
the invasion was scheduled for September 12. At 0200 hours
on September 8, Marshal Badoglio asked Taylor to cancel
the airborne operation and to delay the armistice announcement scheduled for early evening of September 8.

At the surrender signing in Sicily, the Italian representative
had agreed that Marshal Badoglio would have to broadcast
an announcement to the Italian people. Subsequent planning
called for a coordination of the Allied broadcast and the
Italian leader's announcement, which would follow by an
hour or two. However, the Allies had informed the Italians
that all they could do was provide an eighteen-hour notice
to the marshal that the Allied broadcast would be forthcoming at the end of that time period. Arrangements were
made for AFHQ to broadcast from Algiers music by Verdi,
which would be the signal to Badoglio. Although this music

was broadcast on September 7, it was not picked up by
Italian radio monitors, and Badoglio was unaware of the
exact time of the Allied announcement when General Taylor
confronted him. That's when the old marshal advised the
Allies to delay their announcement (and invasion) because
he required more time to make "arrangements."[9]

The Italian government was in a state of shock, especially
the cabinet ministers. General Eisenhower at AFHQ in Algiers
was equally dumfounded when he received Taylor's coded
message to scratch the Eighty-second Airborne Division's
operation and Badoglio's message to AFHQ relayed by the
American general to delay the armistice announcement. The
Allied commander canceled the airborne operation but
flatly refused to delay the armistice announcement. Marshal
Badoglio was forced to follow the Allied radio broadcast
from Algiers that Italy had withdrawn from the war and
"has surrendered its armed forces unconditionally." An hour
and fifteen minutes later, Marshal Badoglio announced over
Rome radio that an armistice had been signed and that "all
hostilities by the Italian armed forces against the British and
American forces must now cease." And to confuse the
announcement and the order still further, the Italian leader
ordered that the Italian armed forces "will, however, repel
attacks from whatever quarter they may come." It was as
ambiguous and confusing as the activities of hysterical
Italian officials who had concocted a thoroughly confused
political situation in the space of forty-five days.

On September 9, as Allied troops were storming ashore
at Salerno, a group of panic-stricken Italian government
leaders led by Marshal Badoglio and their Majesties, the
King and Queen, fled from Rome, abandoning the capital
without leaving any clear orders or authority as to who would
command the armed forces and take charge of the city's government. Moreover, Badoglio had even left behind important
government documents that fell into German hands when
the Wehrmacht marched into the city.

This confusing period established a glaring weakness
of Allied intelligence in Italy at a very critical juncture
in the war. An effective intelligence operation in that country
might have saved the day for the Allies. There were no

Wehrmacht troops in great strength anywhere near Rome when the armistice was to be announced and the airborne invasion launched. A panzer division was at Lake Bolsena, 66 miles northwest of Rome, and a parachute infantry division was well south of the city—not, as General Carboni insisted, immediately surrounding Rome. Moreover, the one thing that Field Marshal Albert Kesselring feared most when he received word of the Salerno landings was an air drop on Rome—against which he felt himself to be defenseless. As he later recorded, he nervously "kept his binoculars trained on the sky all . . . day [September 9] watching for enemy planes that never came. . . ."[10]

The failure of OSS in Italy prior to Operation AVALANCHE was apparent to the intelligence agency's director, and he set about to rectify this serious operational defect. Subsequently, the intelligence gap did cost many American lives on the bloody and muddy battlefields at Monte Cassino, the Rapido River, and Anzio. Tens of thousands of American and Allied combat casualties might have been avoided if intelligence had been forthcoming from Rome and elsewhere in Italy in early 1943.

13

It is essential to know the character of the enemy and of their principal officers—whether they be rash or cautious, enterprising or timid, whether they fight on principle or from chance.

—Vegetius: *De Re Militari*, 378 A.D.

The Italian wartime resistance movement, or *Resistanza Armata,* was born in Italy as soon as General Eisenhower concluded his broadcast from Algiers. The anti-Fascist underground, which had existed since Mussolini and his Blackshirts had taken power in 1925, now had additional support from other elements of society. In Yugoslavia the Italian occupation forces were taken prisoner by Tito's partisans with the exception of two divisions. These Italian soldiers joined the Yugoslavs as the Garibaldi Partisan Division and, commanded by a Communist political commissar, gave a good account fighting in the IX Partisan Corps. When Belgrade was liberated a year later, additional Italian was prisoners joined Tito, who acknowledged 35,000 fighting men from across the Adriatic. In France, Italian military personnel joined the *Maquis;* and in Greece, thousands of Italians deserted, but many were tracked down and killed by the guerrillas. Others were taken prisoner by the Wehrmacht. However, some Italians managed to join local guerrilla units, and later a few were hired by OSS OGs which had arrived in Greece in early 1944.

But many of the *partigiani* who took to the hills after Italy's formal surrender were prompted by the same motives as their fellow Europeans—to free their country from a brutal enemy. In this the Italians were no different from the

French, Belgians, Dutch, Norwegians, and Greeks. Politically fragmented because of the multiple political movements and ideologies, many of the partisan groups were organized along party lines. It was a situation which would cause many a problem for OSS and SOE when they began to make contact with the *Resistanza Armata* and deal with the Central Committee for National Liberation (CCLN), which was organized within weeks after Italy's surrender.

The political backgrounds of the partisans tended to vary from one group to another. In many cases individual soldiers banded together when they found themselves separated from their military units right after the surrender, especially if their units were deployed in the mountains. At the time of the Allied landings in Italy, the anti-Fascist resistance movement was composed of several underground parties operating throughout the peninsula. Of these groups, the Action Party's *Giustizia e Libertà* (GL), and the Socialist, Communist, and Christian Democratic groups had taken the lead. They pulled recruits from:

> all those in the population opposed to Fascism on political and/or economic grounds; individual members seem to have joined for one or more reasons: They were attracted by the political program of the group they entered; they were disgruntled by Nazi neo-Fascist economic regimentation; they hated the German invader; or they had been interrupted by the war. These "political" groups organized and took part in active operations, largely in the nature of sabotage, against the Fascist regime and its German protector.[1]

The ground rules for any organization that OSS supported was to bury all political animosities and concentrate on fighting the common enemy. Official British policy, however, was to side with the monarchy and support those in the Italian resistance movement who were royalists at heart. At the same time, a strong Communist-led movement was beginning to make its mark; professionals from the party would become resistance leaders and demand a greater share of Allied weapons and supplies based upon the performance of their units. The problem of local politics caused no end of confusion for America's wartime intelligence agents.

The "McGregor" Mission team that waited in vain for a signal from Admiral Girosi could thank the flux of Italian politics. The Italian navy had been won over with the armistice, and Lieutenant Shaheen turned his attention elsewhere. Specifically, he decided that the U.S. Navy would benefit from technical information about the deadly Italian SIC naval torpedo, which was far superior to anything in the American arsenal. The SIC, or *Silurifici Italiano Calosi*, named after its inventor, Professor Carlo Calosi of the University of Bologna, was a very accurate magnetic-activated torpedo. Its value had even been recognized by the German Navy, which had ordered 12,000 torpedos. These torpedos were designed to explode simply by passing under a target ship rather than on impact. It was the SIC torpedo used by the Germans against Allied shipping on the Murmansk run that had snapped freighters in two at great loss. Technical intelligence had become Shaheen's mission for OSS, and the "McGregor" team began to scour Allied-occupied Italy for samples of the SIC, which they came across in bits and pieces at different navy yards.[2]

But where was the professor? If the Germans got to him first. . . . Caught in the north when the surrender was announced, he was unable to make his way south and, aware that he was known to the Germans and that they would soon be after him, he went into hiding in a convent in Rome. His whereabouts were not discovered by Shaheen until early December 1943, when word filtered to OSS headquarters in Naples that Captain Calosi of the Italian Navy wanted to get out of Rome.

A message was sent to the inventor to leave the convent secretly and head for a tiny resort village on the coast whence he would be taken out of Italy. Eight nights, at the appointed time, he waited in the damp, cold weather and flashed the prearranged signal out to sea. Finally, on January 3, 1944, his signal was answered, and a fast PT boat slid out of the blackness, its bow grinding into the sandy beach. Black-clad figures jumped to the ground and identified themselves. Then he was quickly lifted and pulled aboard, the crew pushed the boat off the beach, and were in turn pulled out of the water. The powerful engines were started and the torpedo boat used by the OSS Maritime Unit (MU) at Corsica sped west to that mountainous island. By January 24, Dr. Calosi, who had shed his naval uniform and title, had been reunited with several other Italian naval technicians in the United States and was immediately put to work developing countermeasures for his torpedo and an improved similar weapon for the U.S. Navy.[3]

Following the initial failure of the "McGregor Project," Peter Tompkins, one of the members of the team, dropped out and began on his own to recruit and train Italian agents for crossing the lines to collect battlefield tactical intelligence. Meantime, he chafed at the bit while waiting for permission to launch a project that would land agents by parachute, or submarine, or MU boat well behind enemy lines. Compared to the majority of his colleagues, Tompkins was ideally suited for his role either as spymaster or spy. He had grown up in Rome, spoke fluent Italian, and knew the city intimately. A former journalist, he had joined OWI, and from his vantage point as a civilian at AFHQ in Algiers, he had closely watched the Allies mishandle, out of ignorance and stupidity, their political policy toward the French military leaders who surfaced to power in North Africa. Many of them had been associated closely with the discredited Vichy government.[4]

It was at this point that he switched from OWI to OSS and found himself with the "McGregor" Mission whose highly motivated but amateur intelligence operatives had crapped out in their plan to establish contact with Admiral Girosi. Shaheen and his group went one way, and Tompkins established his own operation within OSS. Left to his own devices, he managed to elude some of the incompetents who were then being assigned to OSS by the military because the War Department would not assign them anywhere else. Tompkins had just been offered the job of organizing and directing all SI operations in Italy when General Donovan arrived on the scene because of the impending Operation SHINGLE—the invasion of the Anzio beaches some thirty miles from Rome.

From the September 9 invasion at Salerno, it had taken the Allies four months to inch up the Italian peninsula and cross the Volturno River, stumbling against the formidable Wehrmacht Winter Line anchored in the rugged, snow-capped Apennine Mountain range. The German forces were entrenched within the shattered remains of the monastery atop Monte Cassino and elsewhere on the towering peaks. North of the Winter Line were additional German troops, and Nazi-occupied Italy was firmly within the grasp of the Axis, which had been reborn on September 12 when, in a daring airborne assault with Stork gliders, Captain Otto Skorzeny had landed with ninety Nazi paratroopers and rescued Mussolini. Il Duce was flown back to Germany, met with Hitler, and was ordered to reestablish his Fascist regime and once again assume the post of head of state under German supervision. The Allies expected that an amphibious landing at Anzio would flank the Germans and force them to pull back from the Winter Line, while the U.S. Fifth and British Eighth Armies would move forward and take Rome—an operation that would have succeeded the previous September, as originally planned, but failed because of the lack of hard intelligence at the time.

That failure still disturbed General Donovan when he met with Tompkins several days before Operation SHINGLE and declared that an OSS agent should be in Rome *before* the invasion to coordinate intelligence and partisan operations. In October a radio had been smuggled into Rome by an Italian agent, but an experienced man from OSS was necessary to direct the operation. Tompkins was that man. He was flown to the OSS base in Corsica and transported by an MU torpedo boat to the Italian mainland. Two days later he was in Rome. It was January 24, 1944, and the Anzio invasion had begun.[5]

In the mountains of northern Italy partisans awaited assistance from the Allies which was slow in forthcoming. The OSS detachment attached to the Fifth Army and commanded by Colonel Ellery C. Huntington, Jr., was concerned more with collecting tactical intelligence from line-crossers. British "A" Force teams and a handful of SOE groups had penetrated north, but most of the contacts were with thousands of escaped Allied POWs who had regained their freedom when Italy had surrendered; by winter they were moving from one hideout to another to escape the Germans and the

Fascist mobile police. It was the mission of "A" Force to collect these POWs, and with the assistance of guerrillas and the underground, exfiltrate them out of Italy and into Switzerland where they would be interned in greater comfort.

In the fall of 1943 OSS was reorganized along the British pattern with great emphasis on SOE-type operations. Combat intelligence was desperately needed by the Allied forces, and Italian agents were recruited with the assistance of the *Organizzazione della Resistanza Italiana* (ORI) which helped send the first Allied mission to the north. In the south, where the Allied-controlled Italian Government was located at Brindisi, a group of disbanded regular army officers had set up an intelligence organization called the Military Information Service (SIM), which was to provide some agents for later OSS missions. If the Allied behind-the-lines operation was slow in getting started during the winter of 1943–44, there were many reasons other than heel-dragging by OSS. The air-supply system had yet to be organized, and the autumn and winter months in northern Italy provided formidable flying weather which curtailed a large number of sorties.

The Italian CCLN, which Tompkins finally managed to contact shortly after he had settled down inside the Eternal City, presented plans for "large secret armies in the field." The Allies were in no position to accommodate a partisan army in the field for many reasons, chief of which was the need to play a waiting game while the huge supply effort was directed to England in preparation for Operation OVERLORD—the invasion of France and the establishment of the long-awaited Western Front. By the time the Allies had broken out of Anzio, where Captain Rossetti had spent 129 days working with line-crossers, Rome was about to become a prize on June 4, 1944, to be followed by the Allied landings at Normandy two days later.

Much of the intelligence about enemy troop movements to Anzio had been collected by Tompkins. On several occasions he was able to radio information to AFHQ for relay to the Allied forces on the beachhead, which checkmated several enemy counterattacks, especially the first attempt by the Germans to push the Allies back into the sea in early February 1944.

Although Tompkins had set up a near-perfect OSS operation in Rome, other problems faced OSS in the various listening posts at which agents were stationed. Specifically, the single major problem was the amateurish errors in action and judgment made by OSS people themselves. Perhaps successes outweighed failures, but of failures there were many. After the invasion of Italy, General Donovan issued an assignment to a recent recruit to OSS as if it were a trip to the supermarket.

"Wild Bill called me in," recounted a retired military officer, "put his arm around me and said: 'Do you know anything about Spain? We don't know what's going on over there. Why don't you go and see what you can find out?' That's how I wound up in Lisbon on my way to Spain. I hadn't gone to any espionage school. I went in cold. My orders were to follow the streetcar tracks on Santa Anna Street to a fork in the road and continue until I was in front of a new building.

"I went to the end of the line . . . and saw the new building in front of me. I walked in and as I stepped inside, two krauts in uniform blocked the door and a third asked me what I was doing there. 'You're in the Germany Embassy,' he told me. I knew I wasn't because I had passed the German Embassy on the way. I apologized and calmly walked out the door, which opened before I touched it. I went back to the fork, took the other road, and wound up in front of another modern building. This was the American headquarters, and I recounted my adventure to the man in charge, who said: 'Do you know you're the first person to go into Gestapo headquarters and come out on his own?' "[6]

In another *faux pas* also in Lisbon in 1943, OSS reportedly penetrated the Japanese Embassy and left evidence of the entry. The Japanese, discovering that somebody had entered their diplomatic offices, decided that a low-level military attaché code might have been compromised and changed it. The upshot of switch in ciphers was that the U.S., which had been read major Japanese diplomatic codes prior to Pearl Harbor, did not break the new code until the fall of 1944—a year after OSS agents had tried their hand at second-story work. This was the result of a typical case of bureaucratic jealousy. Prior to Pearl Harbor, General

Donovan had not been privy to the secret of the penetrated
Japanese diplomatic codes. Nor had the Army ever advised
OSS that the Japanese military attaché code out of Lisbon
had been cracked and was read regularly and, therefore,
it wouldn't be wise for OSS to try to penetrate this particular
embassy.[7]

As for political involvement in the affairs of other nations,
the OSS record left much to be desired in 1944–45. Allied
intelligence had discovered in early 1944 that pro-Axis Hungary might be willing to surrender to the United States before the Wehrmacht would invade and assume administrative
control over the country. The mighty Red Army was slowly
pushing west, and the Germans wanted a secure area in their
rear. Hungary, on the Axis side, had wanted to get out of the
war after the Allied landings in North Africa, and soundings
were privately made to OSS in Switzerland. It was decided
to parachute an OSS team, code-named "Sparrow" Mission,
into Hungary to meet with that country's leaders to discuss
terms. Colonel Florimond Duke, a forty-nine-year-old World
War I pilot and in early 1944 head of the OSS Balkan Desk
in Washington, volunteered to head up the risky mission to
a hostile country. He selected as his companions from the
OSS Labor Desk Major Alfred M. Suarez and Captain Guy
T. Nunn, who had been given permission to undertake this
mission by their section chief, Major Arthur Goldberg.
Suarez, a radio technician and veteran of the Spanish Civil
War, and Nunn, a magazine writer who spoke excellent German and workable French, had both passed their parachute
training course and proudly wore the parachutists' badge
on their uniforms. Colonel Duke, on the other hand, was
to make his first jump. And they would jump "blind." There
would be no reception committee below, unless it was unwanted; and in that case they would be in serious trouble.[8]

They parachuted into Hungary in March, met with a ranking general too late even to discuss terms, because the Germans had made their move, and on March 19 the trio gave
themselves up as POWs. Their cover story: They had been
parachuted to the wrong place. They were supposed to have
been dropped into northern Yugoslavia. Advised by Hungarian officers, who had known the reason for their visit, that
they might as well forget their mission, they were able to

divest themselves of $6,000 worth of gold louis d'or coins and rid themselves of their radio. Then they were turned over to the Germans who, suspicious, first moved them to a political prison in Vienna and threatened to execute them as spies. However, they stuck to their cover story and insisted that they were bonafide POWs, as they were in uniform when captured, and claimed protection under the Geneva Convention. After four months of intensive grilling and threats, they were transferred to *Oflag IV C* in Colditz Castle. This famous prison, situated on the Mulde River between Leipzig and Dresden, housed 350 Allied POWs.[9]

There, the "Sparrow" Mission sat out the war, while in nearby Rumania OSS set up a headquarters in Bucharest under Lieutenant Commander Frank G. Wisner. His local problems included having a bullet fired by a Russian soldier smash through a window. Wisner, pistol in hand, dashed out and waylaid a Red Army man in his cups trying to steal one of the OSS vehicles. When prevented, the culprit fired another shot.[10]

The adventures of OSS people were as varied as their assignments, but some assignments ended tragically. There were those in the organization who craved adventure and this is what they got. And, of course, there were a number who got more than they bargained for. Such was the experience of the men who had volunteered for the "Dawes" Mission—the revolt that failed.

14

I have eaten your bread and salt
I have drunk your water and wine,
The deaths ye died I have watched beside,
And the lives that ye led were mine.
—RUDYARD KIPLING:
Departmental Ditties, 1886

By August 1944, OSS planners began to take a long hard look at Central and Eastern Europe. With the second front open in France and Operation ANVIL about to invade Southern France, the attention of SFHQ in London was focused upon Poland, where an uprising in Warsaw had begun on August 2, and Czechoslovakia, where British SIS and SOE "A" Force 399 reported increasing partisan activity in the mountains of Slovakia. In Hungary, "Sparrow" Mission had disappeared, and Colonel Duke, Major Suarez, and Captain Nunn were in enemy hands. Another mission to Hungary and a mission to Czechoslovakia were authorized by SFHQ, and the requirements and carrying out of the operations were handed down the chain of command to the headquarters of OSS 2677 Regiment in Bari. What followed represented the needless loss of lives, because these men were ill prepared to take on an operation of the magnitude of the "Dawes" Mission, with the ancillary "Day" and "Houseboat" Missions thrown in for good measure.

After the American and British invasion forces had broken out of the Normandy beachhead, Allied intelligence strategists reasoned that it was time to disrupt the enemy behind the lines whenever and wherever possible, not only where Allied armies were fighting in the west. Although British agents had been working the Central and Eastern European area since 1941, the Polish Section of SOE early on had recruited a number of Poles as Allied agents in 1940. Three were prepared to parachute into Poland in December 1940, when the mission was scratched at the last minute, just as they were standing beside the twin-engine Whiteley strapping on their chutes. Cooler heads had prevailed at the Air Ministry; it was believed that the range of the slow-flying aircraft was barely sufficient to make it to Poland and back in the event evasive flying was required over occupied Europe and Germany.

On the night of February 15, 1941, a longer-range RAF Wellington bomber took off carrying Polish Army Lieutenants Stanislaw Krzymowski (code name Kostka), Jozef Zabielski (code name Zbik), and a political courier, Czeslaw Raczkowski (code name Wlodek). Six hours later, early on the 16th, they parachuted close to the town of Bielsko in Western Poland near the prewar border with Germany. Representing SOE and the Polish government-in-exile's Sixth Bureau (Intelligence), they became the first Allied agents to penetrate Eastern Europe. During the ensuing twelve-month period forty-five additional agents were parachuted with two tons of arms, explosives, and communications equipment, and $1,660,-850 in bills, 1,775 louis d'or gold coins, and 885,000 German marks, the money earmarked for intelligence operations by the rapidly growing underground.[1]

Elsewhere in occupied Europe, British agents were following a similar pattern with much of their information forwarded to the new American intelligence organization. If OSS had anything to learn from the British, it was "Do it!" Whatever the consequences within the diplomatic area, reasoned Britain's intelligence officials, the Foreign Office was there to make whatever representations were required. The United States, on the other hand, was concerned with following formal procedures in its dealings with the Allies, especially with the Soviet Union. Nor was the State Department unaware that the Soviet Union had staked out Eastern Europe and the Balkans (with the exception of Albania and Greece) as areas of wartime and postwar Russian political influence. In 1944, therefore, the United States formally asked the Soviets for permission to deploy American "military missions" to Czechoslovakia, Hungary, and Rumania under the pretext of searching for and repatriating downed airmen. By the end of July 1944, the Soviets reluctantly agreed to permit a U.S. "military mission" to fly into German-occupied Czechoslovakia to evacuate a number of downed fliers who had been collected by the partisans. The "military mission" became the official cover story for the ill-fated "Dawes," "Houseboat," and "Day" Missions.

At OSS headquarters two teams were organized and prepared and briefed for a flight to Czechoslovakia in mid-September. The "Dawes" Mission was headed by U.S. Navy Lieutenant Holt Green with Sgt. Joseph Horvath, Slovak interpreter, and Pfc. Robert Brown, radio operator. Mission: Aid the resistance in Slovakia—the eastern region of the country—and collect intelligence information. "Houseboat" Mission was commanded by SI Lieutenant John Krizan, *nom de guerre* for Czech-born U.S. Army Private John Schwartz, Lieutenant Jerry Mican as a second SI agent, and Navy radioman Sp(X)2/c Charles Heller. Mission: To penetrate as far as possible into Bohemia—the western half of Czechoslovakia—and conduct secret intelligence gathering operations.[2]*

In Czechoslovakia during the summer of 1944, British "A" Force teams had collected a number of American airmen who had bailed out of their crippled aircraft and Allied military personnel of other nationalities. They had put them up in a hotel in Banska Bystrica, a small city of some 17,000 population nestled in the Low Tatra Mountains of Slovakia. It was the perfect cover for the OSS missions, for nearby was a former Luftwaffe airfield at Tri Duby, six miles away. On September 17, 1944, the six OSS agents, all dressed in U.S. military uniforms, boarded three B–17s of the Fifteenth Air Force Special Group at Brindisi. The three Flying Fortresses had been loaded the day before with medical supplies, arms, ammunition, and other materiel for the partisans. At 0600 hours the aircraft took off one by one, and over the Allied air base complex at Foggia on the Adriatic coast north of

---

*All after-action reports of this nature were classified SECRET and other than those personal copies which many participants managed to retain, these reports are now in the archives of CIA and unavailable to researchers.

Bari, the special mission slipped into a formation of four-engine B–17s and B–24s heading for bombing targets elsewhere in Central Europe. Six hours later, as the formation flew over western Slovakia, the three special mission B–17s peeled away from the formation, let down over the mountains, and one by one touched down on the abandoned airfield. It was 1000 hours, notes the official after-action report and "Operational History of the American Military Mission to the Czechoslovakian Forces of the Interior (CFI.)" "Upon arrival at Tri Duby the mission was given a very cordial welcome and congratulations on a flight made into an area completely surrounded by the enemy."[3]

Lieutenant Green lowered himself through the forward crew hatch of one of the bombers and dropped lightly to the ground. The local people and partisans applauded but were shoved aside by an elated group of ragged American airmen, all of whom stopped short when they identified the OSS leader's uniform.

"What the hell's the Navy doing here?" one of the airmen asked. They watched curiously as another pair of legs wriggled from the hatch and a figure dropped beside the naval officer. It was radio operator Charles Heller clad in Army clothing, a green Navy jacket with the letters U.S.N. stenciled on the back, and a white sailor's cap on his head. While the partisans began to assist in unloading the aircraft, the "Houseboat" Mission slipped away to set up shop in the city. Lieutenant Krizan had returned to his native land for the first time in five years.

After the aircraft were unloaded, the operational history continues, "The planes then returned to their base, taking all evacuees present." The authors later estimated that sixty men were evacuated.

For the rest of the month Lieutenant Green organized his operation and met with partisan leaders who were using the Slovakian city as a brigade headquarters.* But the sound

---

*Unknown to the OSS people who arrived in Czechoslovakia, the Russians had been very active in the area and had helped the partisans to organize. Also, two brigades of Slovak troops, trained and equipped in the Soviet Union, were flown in to support the resistance.

of enemy artillery fire in the distance worried Green, and it appeared to Horvath and Brown that as the days passed the distant thunder grew louder—and closer. Meantime, guided by an "A" Force team scouring the countryside, a number of additional Allied military personnel had been delivered to the town by Lieutenant Davies of "A" Force. The majority were Americans, but the group included four POWs who had escaped from enemy prison camps—two New Zealanders, and two Frenchmen who were both wounded. The "Dawes" team radioed OSS headquarters in Bari requesting an evacuation flight for the twenty-six men, more supplies for the intelligence unit, and another delivery of war materiel for the partisans. Green also asked for a second radio operator, explaining that since his arrival he had made many contacts with the resistance and had learned locations of a number of POW camps. Moreover, Green pointed out, in order to gather this information, he would have to move about the countryside. If he had another radio operator, he could leave the other radioman at his base to relay his intelligence and receive instructions from headquarters in Bari during his forays in the field.

The OSS radio station in Bari acknowledged receiving Green's reports, including his message about the Allied repatriates. Several days later he radioed another urgent message for an evacuation aircraft, this time adding that the enemy was beginning to close in on Banska Bystrica from three directions. Fair weather conditions in the area eliminated any flying hazards, and with the enemy coming closer, messaged Green, "This request should be complied with immediately." The OSS mission commander also pointed out that while he could still use a second radio operator, it was not advisable to send in additional people because of the rapidly changing tactical situation.

An evacuation mission had been laid on following Green's original request on October 1, but weather conditions at Brindisi had grounded all aircraft. Meanwhile, as the days passed, OSS headquarters in Bari for some unaccountable reason decided to put together a heavy mission to Czechoslovakia despite the warnings of the deteriorating tactical situation in the vicinity of the LZ. The airlift would consist of six B–17s filled with more supplies, fourteen additional OSS personnel representing three new penetration missions, a civilian war correspondent and his Navy photographer, a British "A" Force officer, and two officers from the OSS operations center in Bari who would return the same day after they had a chance to confer with Green and assess the situation on the ground. The aircraft, escorted by thirty-two P–51 Mustang fighters with a long-range mission capability, followed the same pattern of joining a scheduled bombing mission before leaving the formation to land in Slovakia.[4]

Major Walter Ross and Lieut. B. W. Duranian from OSS headquarters in Bari conducted their business with Green while the six aircraft were unloaded. They boarded with the twenty-six repatriates, and the six B–17s took off under cover of darkness, their crews relieved once they were airborne. They, too, had listened nervously ¡to the rumble of artillery echoing off the distant slopes. It was the sound of enemy guns, and these crew members of the special mission aircraft preferred to take their chances in the sky.

When the B–17s left, there was on the ground in Czechoslovakia a total of twenty OSS people, the war correspondent and his photographer, and one "A" Force officer from SOE. Thirteen of these OSS intelligence operatives would die, some tortured horribly and executed in a Nazi concentration camp by the Gestapo; three others would be captured and survive; two would barely escape with their lives through the enemy's intensive antiguerrilla hunt, and the war correspondent and his photographer also would forfeit their lives.

Joining the "Dawes" Mission was Navy Lieutenant James Gaul, an SO officer assigned to assist Lieut. Green; Second Lieutenant Frank Perry of SI with instructions to penetrate into Austria; Captain Ed Baranski, commanding the SI "Day" Mission, which also had been laid on to operate in Slovakia, and his three SI team members: radio operator Pavletich, interpreter Thoms, and Thomas Novak, a native of Slovakia attached to the "Day" group.

Another group of SI agents with the mission of penetrating into Hungary was commanded by Second Lieutenant Tibor Keszthelyi, assisted by Sergeant Steve J. Catlos and two Hungarian agents recruited in Rome—Monsignor Moly, a

priest, and Paul Cora, a radio technician—and Private First
Class Kenneth V. Dunlevy, an SI radio operator and cryptog-
rapher. Two SO officers, Captain W. A. McGregor and
Lieutenant Kenneth Lain, had been included in the "Dawes"
Mission personnel package as instructors to the CFI partisans
in the use of American weapons and equipment. Lieutenant
Lane Miller was attached to OSS from the Fifteenth Air
Force Air Crew Rescue Section. Joseph Morton, an Associated Press war correspondent, and PhoM 1/c Nelson Paris,*
a Navy photographer assigned to cover the "military" mission's activities in Slovakia, rounded out the complement
behind enemy lines, along with British Army Lieutenant
Robert Willis with orders to join SOE "A" Force 399.[5]

What happened to Missions "Dawes," "Houseboat," and
"Day," and the Austrian and Hungarian penetration operations, and to these OSS agents and their British and partisan
colleagues, was committed to an official record in May 1945
by two of the survivors, Sergeant Steve J. Catlos and Private
First Class Kenneth V. Dunlevy, while memories were still
fresh. Their exciting and tragic narrative continues:

თთ თთ თთ

6–7 October 1944
We were selected to be on the second flight into Slovakia
about ten days before take-off. We had practically *no briefing*
on the Army of Liberation, their operations, or about the
topography, weather, political or economic conditions in that
area. During those ten days we were standing by with very little
idea of the purpose of the mission, the personnel or any pertinent details. This was understandable from a security point of
view, but from a personal point of view, it made it difficult
to get ourselves set for such an important assignment. On

---

*The report submitted by Catlos and Dunlevy listed the rank
or grade, name, and military serial numbers of all U.S. personnel
on the second flight of October 7. Pavletich, Thoms and
Thomas Novak were probably not the true names of these SI
agents, nor were those of Monsignor Moly and Paul Cora, who
were to penetrate into Hungary. This was not the first time
that OSS had used Catholic priests for sensitive missions. The
report is included here with very little editorial change.

6 October, the 15th Air Force said they were ready for a flight of six B–17s, with an escort of thirty-two P–51s. The afternoon of the 6th we loaded our equipment into the planes. Besides our personal gear, our load consisted of Marlins, bazookas, ammunition, medical supplies, and gasoline for the Slovaks. We also loaded clothing to be given to the ACRU [Air Crew Rescue Unit] which picked up stranded flyers.

On 7 October at 1000 we took off. . . .

It was good flying weather and we had no difficulty until we approached the area of the airfield. For some minutes we could not locate it. Finally, by following the Hron Valley and by seeing smoke from signal fires, we spotted the field. It seemed that, although no one was visible a few moments before, thousands of people sprang out of nowhere to greet us. Among this group there were at least 200 people with cameras who took pictures of us. Tri Duby was a training field built by the Germans to train Czech flyers. It was suited to fighter aircraft, but scarcely for B–17s. The runways were makeshift—built of earth. The twenty-six people to be evacuated were loaded. . . . This took about 30 minutes, and during this time, the escort fighters circled above us. One B–17 was stuck in the mud for about an hour and took off alone later, but returned safely to base.

Lt. Green assigned some of us to live in the villa requisitioned by the CFI for the American Mission in Banska Bystrica. The rest were assigned to a hotel near Army Headquarters. From the moment we landed, we noticed that artillery and machine gun fire was clearly audible in the distance, about 10 kilometers away. On the way to Banska Bystrica (hereafter called BB), we noticed many tank traps and other concrete military installations for defense that had been built by the Slovak Army. The villa and the Noroday Dom Hotel in BB were completely modern and the villa, which had been Gestapo Headquarters when the Germans were there, was extremely modern and well-kept in every respect.

It was apparent to us in these first few days of organizing ourselves, that Lt. Green had not desired or expected so many men . . . we felt that this large mission had been sent out without the full consent or advice of the men who were already in Slovakia. There was no ill feeling about this, but it caused a complete reorganization of plans because of the danger of our position.

8 October 1944

Because of enemy pressure, Lt. Green was advised by CFI to move all equipment not immediately necessary to Brezno, 42 kilometers up the Hron River. Gaul, Mican, Catlos and Dunlevy left with these supplies for Brezno in a truck. Davies and Willis, two British Army leftenants from "A" Force in Italy (British equivalent of OSS), who were bringing their equipment to Brezno, were also on this truck. The following day, Mican was recalled to BB for analysis and intelligence work. We set up an emergency radio station in Brezno immediately, as did Willis, who made contact with Force 399 (similar to "A" Force) in Bari. Dunlevy did not try to make contact, since it was considered only an emergency set-up.

9–14 October 1944

We stood by in Brezno. Our stay during this time was uneventful, but we did notice much activity on the part of the inhabitants against the pro-Nazi elements in the city. We also noticed that in BB, which took the form of forcing these pro-Nazi elements to build tank obstacles, clear roads and, near Brezno, build an airport. We had the distinct impression that we were extremely welcome as Americans, and we were treated well in every respect. On 10 October, Lain and McGregor stopped at Brezno where they were busy instructing the Slovaks in the use of care of weapons. . . . Those men returned to BB on the 13th with us. Joe Morton came with these men on the 10th to get his typewriter, which we had brought on the truck, and returned the same day to BB. Paris also came with Lain and McGregor and made a complete photographic record of the weapons and training.* On 13 October, a few hours before we left Brezno, Lt. Green and Maj. Schmer of the British Army Force 399 visited Brezno on their way to the front. Schmer was the leader of the British "Windproof" Team assigned to penetrate Hungary. After visiting the front near Telgart, Green and Schmer returned to BB at the same time we did. They reported that there was no fighting in the Telgart Sector, but that the town had been three-fourths destroyed by fire, set by the retreating enemy. We returned to BB because the pressure seemed to

---

*Because of the variety of weapons, explosives, and equipment, OSS utilized the training experience of SO officers McGregor and Lain. Both men had joined OSS from the infantry.

be relieved in that area, and to help Horvath and Brown who had been overworked at ciphering and transmitting cables to Bari.

While we were in Brezno, Moly and Cora, the agents, had left for Hungary after being briefed by Tibor. Pavletich, Thoms, Novak and Baranski ("Day" Mission) had left for Evelen to procure intelligence in that sector. Morton had been writing articles on the people and their anti-Nazi effort. The military and political situation seemed to be the same in BB. The Slovakian people still had infinite faith in the Russians, and believed that they would keep their promise of sending two parachute divisions, should the enemy at any time threaten to overcome them. While we were gone, two Czech Parachute Brigades (about 2500 men), trained in Russia, and fully equipped with Russian-made sub-machine-guns and 37 mm anti-tank and anti-aircraft guns, had been flown in at Tri Duby and Brezno airfield in C–47s. The two promised Russian divisions never appeared at any time that we were there.

14–20 October
We stayed in BB during this time performing routine duties. Some military personnel drifted in—airmen, prisoners, and internees of the Slovaks in Bratislava. Many of these airmen were released from camps . . . by the Slovak Army of Liberation which had begun to form in September 1944. Other airmen were able to contact Partisans after bailing out while on a mission. Lt. Shafer, 15th Air Force, was hit on his 13th bombing mission on Friday, 13 October, and abandoned ship at 1300 hours. Two British agents, Jack Wilson and Keith Hensen, came to BB on the 20th with some airmen. They were very surprised to see us, apparently having no information that Americans were in BB. Some of the airmen who came to BB objected to the fact that during their briefing before taking off, no mention was made of our American mission being in BB to help them. They were briefed on escape routes to Hungary, but not on the area they were in. An Australian who was working with the Partisans identified Wilson as a bonafide English citizen. Wilson was supposed to have been dropped into Austria in civilian clothes, but by mistake, was dropped into Slovakia, 120 miles from his pinpoint. Hensen had escaped from a German prison in Slovakia after having been captured and sentenced to death. A few days before the 20th, Green

requested by radio to Bari, the evacuation of these men, 19 American airmen and 2 British agents, and added an urgent appeal for supplies. Green sent several messages at this time, requesting an immediate operation into Slovakia before the airstrip at Tri Duby was lost. It is worth while to mention that we were well aware that the Germans had excellent Direction Finders, and informers in BB who knew of our operations. They undoubtedly had a complete record of our dispatches, etc. Our receiver was consistently jammed by the Germans. It was apparent to all of us that this airfield would soon be lost after we were bombed by Stukas. During these six days we transmitted to Bari over a thousand cipher groups a day on battle order and intelligence.

20–26 October 1944

On 22 October, the 21 evacuees were taken to the Tri Duby airport, as it was expected that the 15th Air Force would try to make a landing. On this day there was intermittent bombing. These men were brought back to BB after a fruitless wait, when it appeared to be a greater risk to stay at Tri Duby than to stay in the town. The Slovakian workers managed to keep the field in usable condition by filling in bomb craters. All men of our second group from Bari, and the 21 evacuees were to be returned to the base in Italy, leaving only Green, Horvath, Brown, Krizan, Mican and Heller at BB. There was also a great deal of pouch material, maps, reports, etc., to be brought back. At Tri Duby we waited on the operation until mid-afternoon on both the 24th and 25th—then the operation was given up. Permission was requested of the Russians to evacuate these men through their territory, but this was never granted. There were many C–47s coming and going for the evacuation of Russian personnel and certain CFI officials. We learned later that the 15th Air Force had bombed Bratislava, about 200 air miles from BB, on the 24th, which made us feel that they could have laid out an operation for BB as far as weather was concerned, or that after their bombing mission, they could have picked us up at Tri Duby. As all organized resistance collapsed, CFI officials told Green that government and army personnel were moving to Donovaly, a resort about 25 kilometers north of BB. It was here that they hoped to reorganize and regroup their army, but the Partisan leadership seemed inadequate and consequently Donovaly became merely a temporary refuge.

Pro-Allied people throughout Slovakia began an underground movement to hinder the enemy's operations, and in each village there were agents of this movement, but these agents were often ignorant of their comrades' identity, even in a nearby village. When the Americans and British were racing across France late in the summer of 1944, plans were made for an uprising to occur at the most favorable time seen by the leaders in Bratislava. A few days before the first of September 1944, resistance on a large scale began and the enemy was driven back from a large area in central Slovakia. All garrisons were cleared and many pro-Axis people interned, as well as many Germans taken prisoner. This was successful for about 5 weeks, until the enemy started counter-offensives from three directions. The two Czech brigades brought in from Russia were first-class soldiers, but the enemy strength was more than they could withstand. The other Slovak elements of resistance proved unequal in courage and equipment to the opposing forces. We felt that the impression of the Slovaks, which was that the Allies were going to send a quick victory, was rapidly lost under enemy pressure, and as the army retreated through their own villages, many men went back into civilian life and tried to disguise their military position. It seemed that these people never had any real ardent desire to keep on fighting, but only to retrieve prestige as not having given in to the enemy before. The Germans took advantage of this demoralization by trying to establish order and letting men resume their normal civilian ways of living. Many times not a single shot was fired at the Germans during these disorganized fights. In many places in the Hron Valley where defenses and installations had been built, no use was made of them.

26 October 1944

The government and army officials of the CFI evacuated BB and moved to Donovaly. Green was advised of this and desired to stay with them as long as possible. Heller, Krizan, Gaul and Mican had gone to Donovaly on the 25th and made billeting arrangements for our party. Up until the last minute, Gaul was trying to get the Russians to evacuate us as soon as possible. CFI officials asked that personnel be limited as the food situation was critical. When nothing else seemed possible, all mission and Air Corps members moved to Donovaly by bus. It seemed only a matter of hours until BB and Tri Duby would be occupied by the enemy. The OSS personnel stayed in a resort hotel on the third floor at Donovaly. The airmen and British lived in civilian houses in the town. We set up immediate contact with Bari, stated our predicament and the loss of Tri Duby airfield.

27 October 1944

Enemy reconnaissance planes spotted the CFI concentration of approximately 3000 men, and strafed and bombed on the road between BB and Donovaly. There was an attempt to bomb an emplacement of four A/A guns in Donovaly, but the FW–189 which did so released its bombs short of the target because of intense flak. During the entire day, Stukas, FW's and ME–109's were busy from BB to Donovaly, strafing and bombing.

28 October 1944

We made contact with Bari, at 0300, and this proved later to be the last contact we were to make with our own equipment. We explained the seriousness of the situation, and that we were leaving this area in hopes of finding a more stable resistance group with whom we might work. Green briefed all of us on CFI information, and the party of 37 was split up into four groups for ease of movement. These groups were designed to have their own radio communications, but actually only two sets were in order when we departed. These groups were to be headed by Green, Ken Lain, McGregor, and Perry. At 0600, we left Donovaly with hundreds of other people. We walked into the mountains, the lower Tatra Range. After 10 miles, the order was given to lighten packs at Norynica, as the enemy was reported to be in a valley that was necessary for us to cross. This was done to hasten our movement. We were following a large group of people on the assumption that they were making for the Russian lines. Much food was given away, mostly by airmen who were too lazy to carry it, and we all regretted this later on. There was slight confusion here as to what was worth carrying and what was not. We had been told by the Brigade officers that we would reach the Russian lines in five days, so we felt that we had enough food. During that time, Lt. Perry ordered Catlos to destroy and dispose of the radio he was carrying. This proved to be an unwise move, as the radio might have been of invaluable help later on. All motion picture film that was not developed was destroyed

here. Paris left his motion picture and still cameras hidden
with a Slovak civilian at Donovaly. He retained the lenses
(which he later lost) and a small Contax camera.

We started down the mountain side into the valley where
we encountered Slovak troops who were fleeing from the
Germans and were trying to reach home. We met a civilian
whom we took on as a guide, because he said he knew
the mountain terrain in this area. We lunched on K rations
and proceeded up another mountain, guided by this civilian.
We proceeded up another mountain at the end of this valley
and about half-way to the top decided to camp for the night.
The weather on this day had been favorable to keep us hidden
from the enemy, but the low rising clouds and drizzle soaked
us all to the skin. We had no tents or shelter.

29 October 1944

We started to the top of the mountain about 6,000 feet
high. On top of the mountain we met many people coming
from different directions, also fleeing the enemy. In this
area we saw great quantities of guns, ammunition, grenades
and enemy gear strewn on the sides of the trails. It seemed
to us that if the enemy had so desired, he could have an-
nihilated all of us very easily. The weather was very bad—
rain and sleet, visibility zero—which was in our favor, hiding
us from possible strafing. These large groups of people, made
up of Partisans, Jewish refugees from Hungary, women and
children, greatly handicapped us in our movement to a place
of safety. We were trying to make a Partisan camp, said by
our civilian guide to be near Brasiva. By mid-afternoon we
reached the first outpost of the camp and were refused admission until Green established our identity as Americans. At
this time our civilian guide left us, as this was as far as he
intended to go anyway. At this point the Partisans, who were
made up mostly of Frenchmen and Russians, were disarming
any soldiers from other areas who still had guns, ammunition,
or other equipment.*

---

*After the Allies landed in Normandy, many POWs escaped
from their prisons and slave laborers from their factories. Unable to make their way back to their countries of origin, they
banded together and either fought as guerrillas or foraged as
freebooters and bandits. This would explain the presence of
Frenchmen and Russians, although the latter were in Czechoslovakia for the purpose of assisting the resistance.

The camp was made up of bunkers, which were huts excavated from the sides of the mountains. Some of our boys were ill from exposure, and the commissar of the camp allowed us to use bunker facilities, but most of us preferred to stay in the open even though we were soaking wet. This was also true of the boys who were ill. The smell and the dirt inside the bunkers was unbearable. Also, we preferred to stay by ourselves to protect our equipment from being stolen. It rained and sleeted incessantly during the night and we spent long hours trying to dry our clothes piece by piece. It was almost impossible to make a fire in the rain, so we used some of Paris' film which we thought was in excess of what he needed. At this camp was the Russian mission to CFI at BB, and remnants of the Czech Brigade were regrouping and reorganizing there.

30 October 1944

We were informed by the Brigade that they were planning to make a march for the Russian lines, thought to be about a week's march away. Again we met with Maria Gulevics, a Czechoslovakian girl of about 23, whom we had known slightly in BB as a member of the CFI Headquarters. She had worked as liaison between the Russians and CFI because of her linguistic abilities, and spoke fluent Czech, Russian, German and Hungarian. She had been of some help to us before in Donovaly as an interpreter, and had become very friendly with Lieut. Keszthelyi. She was at this camp, and through her help, we managed to get a bunker cleaned out and spent the night there.*

---

*Maria Gulevics, an attractive blond Carput Rus, was a schoolteacher before the war. Prior to the uprising in Slovakia, she was closely associated with the underground and became very familiar with the behind-the-scenes political situation in Slovakia before the arrival of the OSS missions. Added Catlos and Dunlevy in their report: "Maria was assigned to us as an interpreter by the CFI general staff when the revolt collapsed. We are certainly grateful to her, because it was through her linguistic abilities and resourcefulness that we managed to obtain the minor cooperation we did from the Slovaks and Partisans, especially after their military operations collapsed in disarray. Her daring adventures into and through German infested areas in our behalf was something that would have been impossible for us. She is undoubtedly most responsible for our being alive today."

31 October 1944

In the morning we drew some provisions from the Brigade. For these provisions a small amount of gold was paid. Each man in our party had been issued five 20 franc (gold) Napoleon pieces, plus 1000 koruns of Slovak paper currency. Also the airmen were given 100 koruns a day for spending money by Lt. Green. The people were extremely anxious to get the gold pieces and the exchange worked out very favorably for us. At noon we left with approximately 600 Brigade members and Partisans. The Brigade marched slowly—halting for long intervals while the patrols went out ahead to scout—and we waited behind in the cold and wet. Our physical resistance was beginning to weaken from lack of sleep and food, and from the dampness of the weather, but our spirits were still high. After 15 hours of marching and wet weather, we reached a point on the crest of a mountain, about 15 kilometers west of Dumbier Mountain. There was nothing but sheer drops on each side, except the way which we had just come up. We needed rest and decided to descend one of those sides.

1 November 1944

It was 0300 hours, and we were so cold in the wind and snow that we wanted to get back down below the timberline for shelter and to build a fire. Many of our boys had badly frozen feet and hands by this time and we were afraid of pneumonia developing. We managed to get down the steep slide by walking, sliding, rolling and tumbling. Here Morton and Gaul narrowly escaped serious injury as boulders were dislodged above by horses and men. A horse that had lost footing came tumbling down from above—missing Gaul by inches. The rest of the group followed when they saw us descend. We finally came to the timberline where we spent the night in the woods. The food shortage was acute, principally because all of the food that had been issued to the Brigade had been lost during the night. This food had been packed on a horse led by a deserter from the SS troops. He was assigned by the Brigade to lead the horse and stay with our group. We ate what we could find, including many pack horses that had been converted into steaks. We moved a few kilometers down towards the valley and spent the night—again a rainy one.

2–5 November 1944

Our people moved further down the valley into a hut which was a shelter from the sleet and rain, but not a very safe position from enemy patrols. Two of the flyers, Lt. John Drezner and S/Sgt. Jurgen, were very ill—being delirious and showing symptoms of influenza. We stayed at this hut for several days, awaiting the Brigade's next move. We needed this rest badly. Green, Catlos, Horvath, Tibor and Maria, and some of the airmen took daring chances raiding farms and going into the village for food. We found a calf which we purchased. Besides the two sick flyers, many of us had diarrhea, sore feet, and muscle pains from over-strain.

5 November 1944

The Brigade moved to another point about an hour's march up the mountain from the hut, to an abandoned lumber camp. Gaul sent Mican to live with the Brigade and serve as liaison. We remained at the hut and while some of our men were on food patrols an abandoned German radio truck was found. It had been wrecked either by the retreating enemy or by looters, but we did manage to salvage some batteries, gasoline, a charger, and souvenirs. The batteries proved too strong to operate our set and were given to the Brigade. We also found two German MG–34s (machine guns) which Catlos set up ready to fire near the cabin. The Slovaks took these to what they said was a more advantageous point. This did not please us, because we would rather have protected ourselves than rely on them.

ᆼᄵ ᆼᄵ ᆼᄵ

15

In a retreat, besides the honor of the army,
the loss of life is often greater than in any two
battles.

—NAPOLEON: *Maxims of War*

Slovakia was hostile territory even for Lieutenant John
Krizan, although this was the land of his birth, and he spoke
the language and understood the mores of his forefathers.
Although he commanded the services of partisans, he trusted
no one—only his own instincts. He had wanted to remain
behind and continue his SI mission as an American spy.
But Lieutenant Green, as senior officer, believed that every
OSS agent who spoke the language would be an asset to the
group, and he ordered Krizan to don his uniform. It was
the consensus among the OSS people that if they were caught
in uniform, the Germans would imprison them as POWs rather
than execute them as spies. However, many SI agents carried
L-pills, lethal rubber-coated tablets filled with a fast-acting
poison that one might take at his own discretion in the event
of capture and subsequent torture. Swallowed whole, they
were not dangerous, and would pass through the system.
But one bite . . . Several British SOE agents had taken their
own lives when they were about to be captured. Some OG
and SO personnel also carried the L-pills.

The last message to Bari transmitted by OSS equipment
advised: "MOVING INTO MOUNTAINS. ENEMY PUR-
SUING. THIRTY-SEVEN AMERICANS, INCLUDING
AIR FORCE PERSONNEL, SPLITTING INTO FOUR
GROUPS." Then the names of the officers who would com-
mand each group.

Weather had turned to rain and sleet on November 1, whittling away at the health of many of the airmen who were not up to the rugged life for which the OSS people had been trained. On November 7, Krizan, Lt. Shafer of the Air Force, and four other airmen, guided by two partisans, went on patrol. The partisans, moving about 500 feet ahead of the Americans, passed into the woods unaware that Germans were hiding in the timber. When the Americans came abreast of the enemy patrol, the Germans ordered them to halt, drop their weapons, and raise their hands above their heads.

Krizan thought fast. His wallet held $500 in U.S. currency, and a tiny slip of paper with a number of vital, coded radio recognition signals. Unobtrusively, he pulled his wallet from his pocket and tossed it into the underbrush. But an alert German soldier spotted the wallet and just as unobtrusively picked it up, glanced at the currency contained within, and shoved it into his own pocket. Krizan exhaled with relief. The enemy soldier, he reasoned, would keep the money and toss the wallet away. He was never more wrong.

After the capture of Krizan's patrol, the Catlos-Dunlevy narrative continues, the commander of the Russian-trained Czech Brigade requested that the Americans move from their hut to the camp they had set up.[1]

ᎧᏉ   ᎧᏉ   ᎧᏉ

6–9 November 1944

While moving two heavy batteries on horseback, Catlos fell through a rotten bridge into a stream with his horse and injured his back severely. Our quarters in the camp were very cold and wet, but the boys' morale was high at most times. The Brigade furnished us with rations. We paid well for them, but it was worth it. Morton had a dispatch case full of his writings stolen during the night and no trace of it except a small brown notebook which was picked up beside a trail several days later. He later rewrote this material at various places along the way.

11 November 1944

The time set for drawing rations was 0900, and we were going to break camp with the Brigade and move toward the

Russian lines at noon. Recon showed the Germans were planning an attack on us at any time. When we were getting
our gear together, ready to move on, Green was told . . . that
departure was advanced to 1000 instead of 1200. Shortly
before 0900 we saw some of the Brigade moving toward the
top of the mountain. We had just been issued our rations
and had not had time to distribute them among our men.
Being told to move immediately, we did so, leaving much of
the food behind. It was just as well, because about 500
yards from the camp slugs started whistling past our ears.
The Germans were right behind us. The Brigade scattered in
all directions. We had never seen such panic and disorganization—there was no leadership whatsoever. We reached the
summit of the mountain without any casualties at 1200 and
were greeted by a raging blizzard which seemed to be getting
worse by the minute. We had great difficulty in keeping ice
from forming on our eyebrows and beards, since we had
not shaved for some three weeks. We tried to cook a leg
of venison given to us by the Partisans, which we had cut up
and put into hot water for a stew. The water had just begun
to warm up when firing broke out close to us, and we divided
up the raw hunks of meat, put them into our pockets and
started along the top of the mountain. It was difficult to see
the men ahead of you on the trail. About 1400 the same
flyers who were ill before, again became delirious and said
that they could go no further. At this point it is well
to mention that the flyers as a group had, for some time,
felt that it was to our disadvantage to stay with the Brigade,
because it was much easier to spot a large group than a small
one, and they did not think that the many stops and their
disorganization afforded much for the future. But Green felt
that these disadvantages were outweighed by the advantages
of getting food, having some protection, and being with men
with some knowledge of the country. Also, the fact that there
were many Russians with the Brigade meant that it would be
easier and safer to cross the Russian lines with them.

Believing that death would result from freezing and starvation, the flyers requested Green's permission to go back into
a village where they had heard that some men had been
successful in hiding some time before. . . . All of the airmen
at this time decided to go back to this village and asked for
Green's consent to leave our party. After a brief conference
with the airmen, Green consented, but only reluctantly, as

he felt that the Brigade knew where they were going. Ken
Lain and McGregor asked Green's permission to accompany
the airmen and this was granted on the grounds, we think,
that they would be guides and would assist those that were
ill. Both of these men, Lain and McGregor, were in good
physical condition. Then all of this party left us, including
Hensen, the British agent. They went back the same way
we had come. Wilson stayed with us. At this time, some
of the airmen said that they would rather be German prisoners and have a warm meal and a place to sleep, than face
such hazards as we were now going through. It must be
remembered that some of these men had been in German
camps before, where they had been treated rather decently.
The morale of our OSS group was still high, and we don't
remember of ever hearing such statements from any of our
people. We were determined never to give ourselves up as
prisoners. The weather was extremely bad, the blizzard raging, and darkness overtook us. We all grew anxious about
the men who had left us because the way back was completely
obliterated by the high wind, driving snow and sleet. We were
afraid that they might freeze after losing their way. Our
OSS group now consisted of 13, and Maria and Wilson. We
proceeded with the Brigade until 1800, when it became
dark. Advance scouts said they had lost their way and we
should retrace our steps. Our morale and spirit was at a very
low ebb now, it was so cold and our hunger was so great
that most of us wanted to sit this one out. After rechecking
with the scouts, it was decided that we would descend from
the mountain and seek a place to camp for the night in the
timberline. We did this and reached a thickly wooded area
at midnight. To reach this point, we were forced to cross
a mountain stream many times and, as a result, our feet
were swimming in our shoes and many got bad frostbite
from which they never completely recovered. This injury
to the feet was a contributing factor to their inability to march
and played a great part in their ultimate capture. During this
march, 83 in the Brigade had done what we wanted to do—
sit it out—and we later learned that they all froze to death.
Many of the pack horses were abandoned and also left to
freeze.

This night we discovered that some of our limited food
supply had been stolen by Partisans and the Brigade personnel.
Green told us that we could do likewise and not be outdone

by this bunch of bandits with whom we were forced to travel. But he gave this order only after trying to buy some food through the Brigade commander for gold, dollars or koruns. The Brigade Colonel and his staff merely laughed at Green, stating that his men did not have food for themselves. We knew this to be untrue.

Because of the critical food situation and lack of equipment and sickness, many members of the Brigade were permitted to return to their homes on their own.

12 November 1944

The next day the Brigade commander appointed a Czech lieutenant and two soldiers to join our party to guide and assist us. The Brigade left the following day, as did the Colonel and his staff.

13 November 1944

After consulting with the new members of our party, it was decided to go to a point where we might survey enemy positions and concentrations, and to find the best possible route of evasion for an escape through the lines.

We did not make this trip, since we thought it best to keep the party together and regroup and wait until the rest of the stragglers had cleared out of the area.

14 November 1944

We started to march on empty stomachs, frozen feet, and in general poor physical condition. After moving a few kilometers down the valley we met some French Partisans and they gave us a meal of horsemeat and bean soup. We met the Colonel here once more and found most of the Brigade intact. They were all planning to move on to Dolnia Lehota where there was reported to be no enemy. Shortly after 1200 we started for this village. Due to bad feet, some of us had difficulty in keeping up with the pace of the Brigade. At 1900, after a long march over mountains and through sleet and snow, we came to a wooded place about 7 kilometers from Dolnia Lehota. Here we were informed that the enemy was occupying the village.

15 November 1944

Again disillusionment and disgust with the Brigade. After a lengthy debate with the Colonel, Green decided to remain here for the night. The Czech lieutenant, Vladimir, and his two boys, Pavlo and Tibor, together with OSS Lieut. Keszthelyi and Maria, went to the village to scout for food and information. All we had to eat that night was a couple of spoonsful of half-cooked beans. Life seemed useless, morale was very low, and yet we had faith that these people would return with food the next morning. Vlad and his two boys returned laden with food. Also they had some good news. Lieutenant Keszthelyi and Maria had stayed at a farm house just on the edge of the village to try for more food and look for a possible hideout. We were going to be allowed to stay in this house for the time being. That night we started for the farmhouse where we joined Maria and Tibor. Here, for the first time since leaving Donovaly, we had all the warm food we wanted and slept in a warm shelter. We will never forget the kindness of the Slovak farmer who took us in. Tibor and Maria had made a trip to a mining camp the day before to inquire about a hideout. They had again met the Brigade, but by now there was only a remnant of the former number. They told Tibor that we could have some space in the house.

16–17 November 1944

At 0600, we moved to the mining camp which was 7 kilometers from Dolnia Lehota. There were about 800 people, half Partisans and half Brigade, at this unworked antimony mine. There were two nurses in the Partisan group who dressed our feet, for which our men were most grateful, and we shall never forget their kindness. The nurses said that they had never seen such bad feet.* Vlad heard of another hut about 45 minutes' walk up the mountain from the camp.

18–30 November 1944

After securing permission from the Partisan commandant, we moved to this hut. The hut was very crude, but comfortable, with stove, water, and all we needed. At this time we picked up some body lice which stayed with us until we got behind the Russian lines. Through the Partisan radio, we learned the state of the war in Western Europe and also on the Russian front, via BBC. We attempted through a

---

*Dunlevy had been hit hard by frostbite and subsequently lost a toe. As for the nurses, reported the authors, "We later learned from some Partisans that both of them were captured by the Germans and killed."

TR-1 radio to contact Bari, but our power-pack had burned out because of exposure to constant dampness. There was commercial power here which we could have used had our own sets not been destroyed. We sent out food patrols to the village of Dolnia Lehota. Some of the boys' feet healed almost completely here, yet there were many men who were in no condition to move. During the following two weeks the Brigade remnants remained at the headquarters in the mine, except for a few who were reported to have arrived at Myto about 20 kilometers from Dolnia Lehota. Time passed with only sorties into the village for food, and convalescence for our party. On 28 November, the mining engineer's son brought a note to Green stating that Major Schmer was at Headquarters. Schmer managed to penetrate Hungary for a very short distance when they were ordered to return to BB via a pre-arranged code signal from BBC. The CFI collapsed before he could return to BB and he and his men joined some Partisans near Polomka. Schmer learned of our location from one of the Czech Brigade near Polomka. After speaking with Schmer, Green decided to accompany him to Polomka where, with a British radio, there was a possibility of getting a signal to base. The Czech who told Schmer of our position said he had identified us as Americans because one man was wearing a jacket with U.S. Navy on the back of it. This type of jacket was the one that Gaul and Heller always wore, as Schmer himself had remembered back in BB. On 29 November, Schmer, Green, Horvath, and Brown went with a guide to Polomka. On the morning of 30 November, at 0830, the Germans made a surprise attack against the mine headquarters and routed all men there, killing approximately 40 and wounding many more. About 0700, Lieutenants Mican, Keszthelyi and Gaul had gone to Headquarters to try to find an escape route, and were caught in this attack. They jumped out of the windows in the Headquarters building. Tibor had two bullet holes in his trousers, one slug had been deflected by a pocket knife. They circled through the woods to try to get back to our hut where we were. Without knowing what had happened to Tibor, Gaul and Mican, we left the hut at 0930 and started up the Dumbier Mountain, on whose slopes we had been living. The snow was deep and no trail visible. It was very difficult travelling because some of the men still had infected feet. Maria had an especially bad infection, but never complained. Throughout the whole time she was with us, this remarkable girl was courageous, uncomplaining, and a great morale booster for our party. We met several people who had been at the mining headquarters during that time and we asked for information about Gaul, Tibor, Mican and Perry. Perry had gone to Dolnia Lehota the night before with a Slovak soldier for food. No one knew of his whereabouts, but reported Gaul and Tibor okay. They did not know where Mican was. After an hour, Gaul and Tibor caught up with us. When we reached the timberline we were forced to turn back to the hut because the snow was impossible. On the way back to the hut we found Mican wandering along our path. Mican was dazed from overdoses of sulfa drugs which he had taken for a bad bronchial congestion. We would like to say here that Mican showed fine courage and willpower against the greatest odds of ill health throughout these hardships. We hoped to go to Polomka and join Green and the British. We spent the night at the hut and the next morning we started for Polomka via Bystra and Myto. We had no guide, but Gaul was very skillful at using maps and compass and led us through some very dangerous areas. Gaul drove us and kept us moving, and in many ways, seemed a first-class officer for such a trip. We saw no German patrols, and shortly after noon we met a guide in the woods who claimed he knew the way to Myto. We also met another civilian on the road who was standing near a single telephone line running back into the woods. We didn't know the purpose of this, but believed that he telephoned our location to the Germans.* The guide was not certain of the route to Myto, but with Gaul's help we finally reached there. Gaul and the guide went into the village and the rest of us stayed in a sheepherder's hut half a kilometer away. We finally came to Myto about 2100. Gaul was gone three hours, in which time he secured some food and found some refuge for the three sickest people in our party—Maria, Paris, and Miller. When they went to the village they were refused shelter because the people had changed their minds, saying they were afraid of

---

*Gestapo and other German security agents roamed the hills, and this particular "civilian" probably reported the presence of the Americans by telephone which enabled the German patrols to reach them so quickly.

retaliation if the Germans learned about their harboring Americans. Maria, Paris and Miller returned about 0700 the next morning, after a very difficult walk to our hut.

1–3 December 1944

We learned of a hunting shack in the mountains near Myto where three Jewish Partisan boys were hiding. Gaul went with the guide, and his Slovak soldier who had been with us, to inquire about the possibility of our living there until we were better able to go on to Polomka. Myto was half-way between Dolnia Lehota and Polomka, and we thought we could successfully march there after a few days of re-cuperating here. We were granted permission to stay at this shack.

4–12 December 1944

We moved from the sheepherder's hut to the shack, where we lived until the 12th. On 5 December, Gaul and Catlos went to Polomka to try to contact Green. On the way they had several interesting experiences while evading enemy patrols and outposts. At Bacuk, machinegun fire came very close to hitting them, and once while following a railroad line (which we were assured by the Partisans had been blown up by demolitions) they narrowly missed meeting up with a German armored train. In Polomka they were treated hospitably by the natives until the arrival of some 500 German troops on a train interrupted their mission. . . . On 10 December, Green, Gaul, and Willis ("A" Force) went back to Myto and Catlos remained at Volky Bok. On the night of 7 December, Green had made contacts through the British radio in Willis' custody. This proved to be the last contact between Bari and our party. In this message Green gave our position and re-quested medical aid if possible. On 12 December, Tibor and Mican were surprised by an enemy patrol and captured while leaving Myto to return to our shack. Gaul had brought a letter from a Slovak girl named Margaret, assigned to the British by the CFI, which was a letter of introduction to a Protestant minister in Myto . . . to enlist his aid in the purchase of some horses to help bring out our ailing party to Polomka. Gaul then assigned Tibor and Mican to make this contact, instructing them to return the same evening, al-though the two men had asked if they could remain over until the following morning. About 1900 on the evening of 11

December, Mican and Tibor entered Myto under cover of darkness. The next morning as they were leaving, just before dawn, a patrol surprised and captured them. It was likely that Mican, in a weakened condition, had needed to rest during the night. It is possible that these men may have been betrayed by the minister with whom they talked. We had heard that there were many pro-German people in Myto.

When Tibor and Mican did not return, Gaul, Willis and Dunlevy went as close to the village as possible, but found no trace. Meanwhile, Catlos in Rejdova learned from a Slovak that Tibor had been seen in BB in a Gestapo prison on 23 December; Mican nor any other American was with him. This is the last trace we had of either of these men. Gaul and Maria went to the village early in the evening of 12 December, and learned from the people in a house in which they stopped that Tibor and Mican had been captured. The patrol and the captives had started up the trail toward the place where we were hiding, but turned back because of the snow storm, which was probably very lucky for us. Gaul and Maria returned to our shack and Gaul ordered us to move immediately. This was about 2200 and by midnight we were well on our way.

13–14 December 1944

On the way to Polomka we had several close calls with enemy patrols. For two days we struggled along toward Polomka, spending the night near Bacuk in the forest. We had a civilian guide on this mission and a small boy. The guide proceeded into Polomka and arranged for our accommodations there. He notified the mayor of the town of our arrival. The mayor sent out another civilian to guide us to a hunter's shack near Volky Bok, approximately 6 hours' march up the mountain from Polomka.

15–26 December 1944

About 2 hours hiking above our shack was a winter resort hotel at Volky Bok. This hotel was two stories high and had about 50 rooms. Schmer, Leftenants Zenopian ("A" Force), Willis, Davies and Margaret were living there. Brown, Green, Horvath and Catlos were sent to live with them. This was an advantageous spot for signal fires; the British had pinpointed the top of Volky Bok for an expected drop. Fires were burning in this area every night from the 18th through the 25th. The drop was actually made on the night of 26 December, after our men were captured. We never received anything from this drop because it was made in the Hron Valley where it fell into German hands. During this time between the 15th and 25th, we ran many food patrols, but we could not move because of illness in our party.

While on food patrol in the vicinity of Polomka on 17 December, Lt. Gaul, Joe Morton, and Ken Dunlevy with some Slovak natives, whose help had been solicited in carrying food from our rendezvous to the shack, were surprised by an enemy patrol. On our way down the mountain to the rendezvous we met and were informed by a Partisan patrol that an enemy patrol had been sighted in a valley adjacent to the one we were in, but was thought to have left the area. This patrol had gone up the adjacent valley, circled across the lower foothills approaching the mountains surrounding the shack where we lived, and was returning to Polomka by way of the valley we were in. The Partisan patrol was not spotted by the enemy.

We were in a clearing just 40 yards from a wooded mountain slope to our right and the Germans were 125 yards above us, heading down towards the valley. When we first observed the enemy, the Slovaks immediately exclaimed "*Nemci!*" (Slovak for Germans), threw off their packs laden with food, and fled into the woods. We were so completely surprised, freezing in our tracks for a few seconds. Then we also dashed for cover in the woods, our group and the patrol observing each other simultaneously. When the natives threw down their packs and began their mad dash, the enemy shouted "*Alt*" and immediately began firing at us with sub-machine guns and automatic rifles. We were under accurate enemy fire for almost 30 seconds. Dunlevy was the last man to reach cover. He was still suffering from a shoulder injury that he had received early in November and his backsack was so laden with food, as were those of the other men, that it was necessary to abandon it to enable him to move faster. He had difficulty in doing this because the snow was so deep and they also had to cross a creek in order to reach cover. Dunlevy rolled over and over in the snow, making himself a difficult target and, at the same time, freeing himself of the pack and scrambling to the safety of the forest. The slugs fired by the enemy were kicking up a spray of snow all around him—some no more than a yard away. We were unarmed except for a small Italian Beretta carried by Morton who pulled it free and emptied the clip in the enemy's direction. We were unarmed at this time because we had received information from the Partisans that the probability of contact with the enemy here was very remote, and guns were excess weight when carrying food.

We went on deeper into the woods and mountains. Morton's inadequate shoes easily tired him and he had to rest often. Gaul remained at his side and ordered Dunlevy to continue on. At one point during this trek up the mountain Morton and Gaul were feared to have been captured. They were met later by Dunlevy while attempting to find their way back to the shack without a guide. This was our first trek into this area and, of course, it was unfamiliar territory. We met some Partisans two hours later and they led us along a path which they said would take us to our shack. We walked up this path for 30 minutes and discovered that it was the same trail we had taken on our way down from the shack that morning. Dunlevy had been chewing tobacco and left a trail of tobacco juice in the snow—a welcome sign. Upon returning to the shack at dusk, we were told that the Partisans had reported our firefight and that *they* had dispersed the enemy. We later learned that the Partisans had hidden in the woods and observed the shoot-out. We decided to remain in the shack until something better turned up, and the surrounding villages near by seemed free of the enemy.

On 24 December all men were invited to the shack by Gaul for a Christmas Eve Party except Willis, Brown and Dunlevy, who remained at the hotel to build signal fires. Among the following people who attended the Christmas Party were: Lt. Green, Lt. Gaul, Joe Morton, Heller, Horvath, Steve Catlos, Miller, Wilson, Paris, Major Schmer, "A" Force Leftenants Zenopian and Davies, Margaret, Maria, and Partisans Stonek, Rudy, and Pavlo.

This party lasted until shortly after midnight. Christmas Day we were all together in the shack for holiday dinner. Gaul conducted a very nice religious service before dinner and we sang Christmas Carols in Hungarian, Slovakian, English and German. After dinner Dunlevy and Catlos returned to the hotel with Zenopian, Davies and Maria to help them get the signal fires started. There was some feeling of

jealousy; Maria had been with our group for a long time
and resented Margaret's intrusion into her domain. Maria
preferred to go up in the mountains away from Margaret.

On 26 December, at 0830, all those in the shack, except
the Slovak soldier, Pavlo, were captured. The following story
was told to us by Pavlo:

> Joe Horvath and I were standing by the stove cook-
> ing breakfast in one room of the shack while the others
> were rising from bed and preparing for breakfast. It was
> about 0800 when we heard a terrific burst of machine
> gun fire and slugs came through the roof. All of the
> people huddled in the corners of the hut, but Major
> Stonek (Partisan officer) and I were wounded. Whether
> any of the others were, I do not know. The Major and I
> showed each other where we were wounded and then I
> ran and picked up my automatic machine pistol. Dash-
> ing through the door on the opposite side of the cabin
> from which the firing came, I was forced to abandon
> my gun because I could not get through the camouflage
> of pine trees placed around the shack. Fleeing to the
> woods some hundred meters from the shack, I hid where
> I still had a good view of the hut. In about five minutes,
> the enemy, some dressed in peasant clothing, descended
> to the shack and entered with sub-machine guns ready
> for action. There was no firing from inside the shack.
> Lane Miller was washing in the stream beside the hut
> and when the firing began, he raised his hands in sur-
> render and was forced into the shack at gunpoint. After
> twenty minutes passed, 14 people were marched out of
> the hut which was set afire and taken in the direction of
> the hotel. I started making my way to the same place,
> keeping under the protection of the woods at all times.
> The snow was as deep as 8 feet in many places, so I
> nearly froze to death, since I had only a woolen under-
> shirt besides breeches and boots. Knowing the other
> Americans and British were at the hotel, I hoped to con-
> tact them somewhere near there. At 1530 or 1600, the
> enemy passed me on their return trip from the hotel to
> Polomka. Finally I arrived at the hotel, only to find
> that it, too, was burning. I met some of the Partisans
> who had returned to find out what had happened and
> was told that the Americans and British were at a
> forester's house about an hour's hike from the hotel. I
> started for this place, meeting Zenopian and Davies on
> the trail about half-way from the hotel to the house.

27–31 December 1944

Maria, Catlos, Dunlevy, Davies and Zenopian attached themselves to a Partisan group whose leader Zenopian knew. At 0800, two more Slovaks from the patrol arrived at the hotel, warning of danger from a concentration of Germans in the neighborhood. We made preparations to leave. From our position on Volky Bok we could see on another mountain top where there was a concentration of some 300 Germans in uniform. Mortar and light artillery fire was being aimed at the hotel. At 1000 hours we left the smoking, charred shell of the hotel and took to the woods where we watched through binoculars a skirmish between Germans and Partisan forces commanded by Demko, a Russian Partisan captain. At 1230 smoke still hung over the hotel fired by the Germans. At 1830, Partisans informed us that a major and soldier were badly wounded and were coming down the trail. We went out to meet them, but found only Pavlo. We could not find out what they meant by "the Major."*

Catlos, Dunlevy, Zenopian, Davies, Rudy, and Maria attached themselves to another Partisan group, whose leader also was known to Zenopian. It was the leader's request and we deemed it wise ourselves, and remained with the group a few days, living at the forester's house and in bunkers we had built, until we decided to march to the Russian lines. On 31 December, the alternative we faced was to stay with the Partisans and face slow starvation and an enemy attack at any time. They had orders to remain in this sector. Or we could start for the front lines. We wasted little time in deciding in favor of moving to the front. Our area was surrounded by the enemy and we understood they had orders to completely annihilate the Partisans. Catlos forced the

---

*In the shack when the enemy came upon it and the shooting began, were Lieutenants Green and Gaul, Major Schmer of the British "Windproof" Mission, SIS agent Wilson, Horvath, Heller, Paris and AP correspondent Morton, and Margaret, along with Partisan Major Stonek and Partisan Rudy. Miller had been caught outside and escorted into the shack at gunpoint after he surrendered. The other two men who made up the 14 people taken prisoner observed by Pavlo, who had escaped, were probably two Partisans who regularly visited the shack during their patrol between Volky Bok and Polomka. After they completed their patrol they would receive breakfast at the shack.

issue with the British; Leftenant Zenopian was unwilling to leave this area . . . Davies opted to leave with us. Either from fear of being left alone with the Partisans, or by a wise change of mind, Zenopian decided to come along. His unwillingness to undertake the hazardous trip to and across the lines was based on fear of cold and hunger and the hardships which we would undoubtedly have to endure. But thanks to his and Maria's assistance, a so-called Russian Intelligence Officer attached to the Partisan group was persuaded to guide and assist us to the front and through the Soviet lines. The Partisan leader also assigned a member of his group to go with us and act as a guide, or in any other capacity we thought necessary. Meantime, Pavlo, the wounded soldier from the Brigade, had been placed in the home of another forester who promised to care for and hide him. Maria also had arranged this, and gold to pay for food and medical care was presented to the forester.

1–5 January 1945

We left this area and started for the Russian lines at 0700 on 1 January 1945. Our group was made up of the following people: Catlos and Dunlevy of the American Mission; Davies and Zenopian of the British Mission; Maria; Sasha, Russian Intelligence Officer; Yanno, Slovak Partisan assigned to guide us; Rudy, member of the Czech Brigade and one of Stonek's men, Gregor, Josef, and Fritz, Partisans who later deserted our group; and a wounded 19-year-old Partisan. All were in uniform except Maria.

The weather was poor and visibility limited, ideal for travelling through many clearings which were in clear view of enemy observation posts. By early evening we had passed through the ring drawn about the Partisans by the enemy, and that evening we arrived at a farmhouse between Pehorela and Sumiac and passed the night here. We were guided at this time by Sasha, who was familiar with this area. He planned to take us across the main valley and across the Hron River before dawn on the morning of 3 January. After a comfortable rest in the farm house—we needed it, too, as we had walked 25 miles up, over and down mountains that first day—we started the next morning for a hut where we intended to remain until just before dawn of 3 January, when we then would cross this valley.

At 0400, with Sasha guiding, we started on what we

knew might easily end in death, capture, or serious wounds. At first light we succeeded in reaching the opposite side of the valley, having successfully crossed the main road, railroad, and Hron River. The former two obstacles were very well patrolled, and we were most fortunate in slipping across. After crossing the valley, we hiked on, bearing southeast. Shortly after noon we stumbled on to a forester's cottage. We were quickly waved away and told to return later. After fifteen minutes he came into the woods, explaining that a German patrol of 25 men had just left his house not more than five minutes before we arrived. The patrol was combing the woods and might pass through this area again at any time. We bought some food from the forester who gave us directions to Rejdova. We knew there was an underground leader there, with information about the location of the Russian front in his sector. As darkness was going to overtake us before we could possibly reach his village, we sought out shelter and found a hunting shack in the mountains. The next morning we heard machine-gun fire in the valley below us and moved on although our Partisan guide did not know this area as he claimed. We stumbled on Rejdova by late afternoon.

Enemy troops had been quartered in the town but they had been moved out because of a supposed typhus epidemic. Villagers were most cordial, giving us food and lodging. The people here refused money for anything; it was the first time anywhere that the people had not tried to get all the money or anything else we had to offer. Also it was here that Catlos was offered a hiding place and refuge until the Russians arrived. The front was only 35 kilometers away. Catlos and Dunlevy decided that one of them should remain behind while the other would attempt to return to OSS Headquarters in Italy and report on the Mission's activities and to report the capture of the men. Catlos remained behind. Informed that this was a very dangerous region in which to attempt crossing the front, we found a man to guide us to the next village where he would secure another guide who would take us to yet another village closer to the front. There, he in turn would secure another man for the same purpose. At this point Sasha, Josef, Yanno, and the wounded boy decided to change into civilian clothing and walk home or through the front lines on the main roads.

6–18 January 1945

After the group left Rejdova, Catlos went into hiding there, during which time he came down with dysentery which lasted about two weeks.*

19–25 January 1945

On 23 January, about 5,000 Germans were bottled up in Rejdova by the advancing Rumanian troops. Catlos' host became nervous about hiding him and he was told that he would have to leave. Catlos said that he could not go into the village in an American uniform and his host presented him with a fur hat and a topcoat. Picking up a bale of straw from the barn for camouflage, he walked through the village and to the edge of the town. Then he realized that it would look suspicious for him to try and walk away from the village carrying a bale of straw. He entered the last house on the edge of the village and asked the woman who lived there if he could borrow the axe that was stuck in a block of wood in front of the house. This way he could continue up towards the woods, posing as a woodchopper. From 23 to 26 January he remained in the woods with very little to eat, almost freezing to death. He was liberated by the Rumanian troops on the afternoon of 26 January.†

After Catlos volunteered to remain behind on 5 January, Zenopian, Davies, Dunlevy, Gregor, Fritz, Rudy and Maria left Rejdova bearing southeast. Our way to the lines was now an extremely hazardous one. The enemy was building bunkers in the lower mountains and the wooded areas were becoming very sparse. We were fortunate in finding a guide at the next village who took us to Petermanovce, 20 kilometers from the front. We stayed in this village the night of 5 January and the next day, when our contact in this village travelled to the front to learn firsthand the possibilities

---

*While Catlos was in hiding in Rejdova he was without medical attention. However, posing as a Hungarian (a language he spoke fluently as a second-generation American of Hungarian descent), he received sympathy from a German soldier, who gave him two opium pills to ease the pain and discomfort.

†Rumania and Hungary had become Axis satellites in 1941 and provided divisions which fought with the Wehrmacht in Russia. However, when the Soviets in their march westward invaded Rumania and the Bucharest government capitulated on August 23, 1944, Rumanian military commanders immediately allied their divisions with the Russians.

of crossing. After returning from Bystre, a village 6 kilometers from the front, he advised us that it would be very hazardous to cross at this time. The mountains levelled into plains and were only sparsely wooded, providing very little cover. Enemy troops were retreating rapidly and sometimes fled through the woods. The front was expected to reach our position in a day or two. Consequently, he advised us to hide in an iron mine near the village which had been abandoned for almost 100 years. He promised to supply us with food, and on the night of 6 January, he guided us to the mine. Westward movement of the front came to a standstill the next day. It was most discouraging, as we were anxious to contact the Russians as quickly as possible. We had all been infested with lice for nearly two months, and were suffering from exposure and malnutrition. On 10 January, Maria decided to visit the village, don peasant clothing, and walk to Bystre the following day on the main road, hoping to make contact there and secure information about military operations on the front and the possibility of our moving closer to the action. She returned 2 days later; and she told us that she had found a hiding place 6 kilometers from the front.

On 13 January we went to Bystre where we were met by Yanno, who was armed but clad in civilian clothing. He had arranged for us to live in another iron mine near the village of Bystre. Here we remained until the front passed us by 10 days later. On 23 January we walked into Bystre, only to be greeted by Rumanian troops who had been fighting on this sector of the eastern front. We were disappointed at first in not having contacted the Russians, who we thought would effect our immediate evacuation to Italy. Later, much to our disgust, we learned what it is to cross the front into Russian-occupied or controlled territory.

We requested the Rumanians to take us to Divisional Headquarters as soon as possible. Maria then walked 7 kilometers to Stitnik where a Russian Headquarters was located and made arrangements for us to go there for identification and to receive orders for moving well behind these Allied lines on the Eastern Front. The next day the Rumanians sent us to Reszyno where we crossed the Hungarian border for the first time. Rumanian Divisional Headquarters had been set up only a few hours before, and high ranking staff officers were just arriving. We stayed with the Rumanians until 25 January, and were then taken to Rimavska Sobota where we were released to the Russians.

26 January–10 March 1945

We were questioned many times by Russian intelligence officers. We also saw, for the first time, quantities of American lend-lease equipment being used by the Russians. Dunlevy was even issued a pair of patent leather U.S. Navy officer's dress shoes. On the evening of 29 January we were pleasantly surprised when Catlos arrived, announcing that the Rumanians had pushed through Rejdova three days earlier. On 30 January, the Russian Headquarters was moved nearer the front, locating at Lucenec on the border of Hungary and Slovakia. Here Zenopian complained of several physical ailments and asked to be hospitalized. We were not in favor of this and wanted to continue on to a place from which he might be evacuated as soon as possible. Reluctantly, we entered the hospital after we had been told that the care was good, and the living accommodations would be the best the Russians could provide. After entering the hospital, Zenopian was taken elsewhere—supposedly to a higher command. . . . But before leaving, he did ask and received assurance that he would be given hospital treatment upon arriving at this supposed higher command.

From 1 February to 10 February we remained in the hospital, hearing nothing until we finally demanded that we be taken somewhere to contact our people. As time passed, it seemed apparent that they had not sent any message to our liaison officers requesting verification of our identities or our evacuation. On 10 February we were taken to Janskiser, Hungary, which was a Russian [NKVD—Secret Police] counter-espionage headquarters. Maria was the only one of us questioned, as she spoke Russian and the NKVD spoke no English. We had briefed her many times about what she might or might not tell them about our operations. By this time she knew our story better than we did; she had told it so many times. She knew exactly how much might be disclosed to them, or anyone who inquired about our presence in this part of Europe. If any further information was requested, she knew that she could refer the questions back to us to reply directly. The Russians were very rude and inconsiderate of Maria at times; we were restricted in many ways while in this village and very poorly fed.

After 10 days in this hell-hole we were taken to Tura near Hatvan, Hungary, to a commission set up by the Russians for the sole purpose of handling escaped Allied POWs, or people liberated by the advancing Soviet armies throughout this part of Europe. Many French, some Dutch and English were here when we arrived, but we were the first Americans. Although this commission was supposed to arrange and effect evacuation and repatriation of Allied peoples it was just like all the other things the Russians tried to organize. As one former POW, a British sergeant so aptly put it: "The Russians couldn't even organize a Christmas Club." Finally, on 6 March we received our travel orders, together with seven other British military types, for transportation to Odessa. While stopping over at Bucharest on 10 March, enroute to Odessa, Catlos contacted the Allied Control Commission which obtained our release from the Russians.

ໜ   ໜ   ໜ

The OSS foray into Czechoslovakia turned out to be a mission ill conceived and poorly planned. Those who returned were lucky; they survived the revolt that failed.

16

"... all enemies on commando missions, even
if they are in uniform, armed or unarmed, in
battle or in flight, are to be slaughtered to the
last man."

—ADOLF HITLER to his
generals, October 18, 1942

Prior to his capture, "Houseboat" Mission's Lieutenant
Krizan, moving freely about dressed as a local in his role
as an American spy, couldn't help noticing how the Communists had tightened their control of the resistance movement, promising supplies and Red Army divisions that never
materialized other than the two brigades which finally fell
apart beneath the massive effort by the Germans to crush the
partisans. Earlier, Captain McGregor and Lieutenant Lain
had expressed their dismay when they tried to instruct the
partisans how to handle the bazooka.

"They're afraid of these weapons!" the SO captain reported to Lieutenant Green. "We handed 'em out one day,
showed them how to use these tank and bunker busters and
then the next day we found them strewn about the area."

Added Lain angrily: "Thrown away, godammit!"

During his forays around the countryside seeking information, Krizan had discovered that the Soviet agents and their
fellow Communists who controlled the partisan movement had
ordered the guerrillas *not* to accept or use their American
weapons. The ugly spectre of politics and policies beyond the
comprehension or competence of the OSS missions had
surfaced in Central Europe as it had other regions of the
continent. But because of the press of fast-moving events in

Slovakia and the retreat of the partisans and the OSS missions into the mountains, the two SO officers never did learn at that time why their guerrilla allies had discarded American arms.

McGregor and Lain later were captured along with the sick airmen they had escorted down the mountain to surrender to the Germans. These airmen were in uniform and therefore were POWs in the full sense of the term. The intent of the SO officers was to assist the airmen as far as one of the villages in the Hron Valley and leave them there.

"Then we'll catch up with you," McGregor told the "Dawes" Mission commander. Green agreed. It was the last time the fleeing OSS teams saw the two infantry officers. Escorting the airmen down the steep trails, they ran into a large enemy patrol and were ordered by a Wehrmacht officer to surrender along with their fellow Americans. It was the end of the line; they dropped their weapons and raised their arms above their heads as ordered. In uniform, they were considered by the German troops as just another one of the thousands of escaped POWs or downed airmen roaming Europe during that period of the war.

The airmen and the OSS officers were returned to a POW camp until they were liberated by advancing Soviet forces in mid-April 1945. Taken for just another pair of Americans, Lain and McGregor maintained their "cover" as unlucky observers on bombing missions whose ill-fated aircraft were shot down by Luftwaffe fighters.

After Krizan was captured and tossed away his wallet with the incriminating code list, he and the airmen were marched to the nearest German headquarters. As they were escorted into the valley, Krizan whispered to the airmen in front of him that he couldn't explain his reasons but would his fellow captive claim him as a member of his crew. "Okay," came the whispered reply from the airman, a B–24 bomber pilot. Krizan and the pilot traded whispered conversation before they were interrupted.

"I don't know anything about airplanes," Krizan muttered softly. "Just make sure that you give me a job on the plane to fit my rank."

"You're the bombardier," the pilot replied to the Army enlisted man impersonating an officer in more than name, rank and serial number. Schwartz, alias Krizan, didn't know the difference between a tricycle landing gear B–24 Liberator bomber and a conventional two-wheel tail-wheel B–17 Flying Fortress. After giving this idea some thought, Krizan decided that if he was questioned about bombing targets and bomb-sights his interrogator would quickly see through his ignorance.

"Do I have to know anything?" Krizan asked moments later. Reluctantly, the pilot nodded.

"Stille!" one of the German soldiers shouted, prodding Krizan with his rifle.

A few minutes later Krizan stumbled deliberately against the pilot and they both fell to the ground.

"Just give me a job on your crew where I don't have to know too much," Krizan said as they untangled on the ground.

"Co-pilot," came the terse reply as they slowly got to their feet surrounded by hollering and menacing Wehrmacht soldiers. The file of American captives moved on and Krizan, turning over the pilot's reply to his question, accepted the idea, stifling a chuckle at the same time.[1]

Three days later the American POWs were taken to Bratislava, a Czech city on the Austrian border less than 100 miles from Vienna. The airmen and Krizan were put through interrogation before they were individually questioned at length. Standing before a Wehrmacht intelligence officer, a colonel, Krizan again repeated his cover story.

"I am Lieutenant John Krizan, U.S. Army Air Force," he announced adding his serial number.

"That's a Slovak name, isn't it?" the colonel asked. Krizan nodded. The questions followed one after the other. Do you speak Czech? Krizan nodded. Where are your parents from? He explained that they had been born in the States, and that he was third-generation Slovak. His replies were short and concise, consisting of "yes" or "no" or of one, two, or three word sentences. He'd fall back every few minutes on the prerogatives of a POW—name, rank, and serial number. He had to keep from answering their queries as long as possible, otherwise his strong accent might give him away. The enemy wasn't stupid. An American, or one who claimed to be a Yank, with a strong accent might raise additional questions, questions that easily could give birth to suspicions. They could take him for a spy, especially if the word had filtered to Bratislava that OSS teams were operating in Czechoslovakia. Whatever he did, Krizan knew that he had to maintain his cover story—a co-pilot whose B–17 had been shot down while on a bombing mission. During the time they had been on the move, he had absorbed details from his fellow captives. Now if only the "crew" didn't blow his cover. He exhaled a sigh of relief when he thought about the wallet. It was gone, and the code with it. He had his dogtags. They would suffice. After all, who could prove that he wasn't Lieutenant John Krizan? His dogtags had his cover name, his address in the Bronx, his serial number, blood type, and religion. He was pleased with himself; everything appeared to be going his way.

Krizan's carefully established cover and his OSS training as an SI agent meant that he had to forget who he really was. The Germans somewhere had a record of John Schwartz, a husky 24-year-old Slovak who had served in the anti-Nazi underground in his native country in 1939 until the Gestapo had picked up his trail. He escaped to France and decided that the only way he could remain out of the Gestapo's reach was to join the Foreign Legion. The Legion accepted aliases from recruits who, in turn, received anonymity and a safe haven against unwanted intrusions from a checkered or questionable past. After the fall of France in 1940, he found himself in a POW camp for French troops and again wondered how long it would take before the Gestapo finally caught up with him. His only alternative: Escape. He made his way to the United States and joined the U.S. Army to continue his personal war against Fascism.[2]

A natural recruit for OSS, he soon found himself in Washington, D.C., at secret training centers in the area and, by virtue of his enlistment in the U.S. Army for the "duration and six months," he had received coveted citizenship. Parachute training followed, and then the plan for "Houseboat" Mission. After his capture he wondered whether or not he would ever enjoy the citizenship bestowed on him by his adopted country. The interrogation finally ended; and Krizan alias Schwartz (or was it the other way around, he thought to himself) awaited an uncertain future. A week later he and his "crew" were transferred to the infamous Rosaulerlandau Prison in Vienna rather than to a POW camp. Obviously, the enemy intelligence officers had their suspicions raised and if one member of the crew was suspect, so was the group. They remained at the prison, constantly interrogated, until one day in February 1945, he was confronted with the pilot of his "crew" who appeared somewhat unsteady on his feet and badly bruised. His cover was blown! Or was it?

"I had to tell them, John," was all the pilot said, his downcast eyes and bowed head explained that he had broken under enemy interrogation.

"Tell them what?" Krizan asked, his impassive features hiding his fear that he had been discovered.

"That you're not one of us," the downcast pilot abjectly replied before he was led back to his cell. Krizan then became the object of intensive interrogation. His questioners were good, damned good. They led him on, building up the suspense. February ran into April and he still stuck to his cover story. He was questioned for weeks. They suspected that he could speak Slovak. They even addressed him in this language he also understood. But he stuck to his name, rank, and serial number. They learned he spoke French, and when an interrogator-interpreter tested Krizan's knowledge of the language, he reported back that the prisoner "speaks with a strong *American* accent."

Krizan was held prisoner through the cold winter months with men imprisoned for political and other reasons. Some remained in the same cell with him for months; others were taken out for "interrogation" and never returned. In one sense, Krizan was at least "safe" for a time in enemy hands. As long as they didn't know who he really was. . . .

Interrogation increased toward the end of February 1945. Prisoners were cruelly beaten up before his eyes with the warning that he could expect a similar fate if he didn't own up to who he was. The Gestapo still hadn't been able to break his cover.

On March 20 a pair of Gestapo inquisitioners finally confronted him with the evidence of his guilt—the slip of paper with the code that was in the wallet he had tried to throw away. The evidence was damning.

"You're OSS!" one shouted. "We know your organization!

"Your headquarters is in Bari. Your unit is the 2677th Regiment. Your intelligence chief has an office on the fifth floor. His name is Colonel Howard Chapin; Major Otto Jake is his deputy.

"You might as well talk. We know everything!"

Krizan was stunned. "Will they shoot me in uniform?" he asked himself. "Shall I play along, give them a story?" It was a time for a quick decision, and Krizan opened up with what he thought was plausible and what the Gestapo wanted to hear.

"OSS?" he replied, shrugging his shoulders. "What's that? I don't know any Colonel Chapin." Then he finally owned up to the code.

He told his inquisitors that had had been given the slip of paper the previous October by a British officer in the Czech mountains to pass on to a major he was supposed to meet on another mountain. "I never met the major," Krizan admitted. "I just didn't want to get caught with this piece of paper. It looked like a code to me." He hoped they would buy his story—or he was as good as dead.

"Ah, so it's a British code!" exclaimed one of the Gestapo agents, flushed with satisfaction.

"I guess so," a dejected Krizan admitted. "All I know is that I was supposed to pass this on to a British major. I never did meet him."

The two Gestapo agents, smiling because they had finally "broken" the case, ordered Krizan returned to his cell. They had a complete file—they thought. They knew all about OSS in Bari either through intelligence or from the OSS people captured earlier in Czechoslovakia—vital information probably obtained through torture. A British major with "A" Force had indeed been killed. Unknown to Krizan, his fellow agents, including "Windproof" Mission chief Major Schmer, had been executed in Mauthausen concentration camp, and with everybody involved dead, the Gestapo had no way of tracing back to doublecheck the OSS agent's story.[3]

Krizan was saved. His underground contact in prison, an Austrian medical doctor, was released before Vienna fell to the advancing Russians. The prison guard detachment tried to buy its own safety by releasing all political prisoners. In Budapest, the prison guards and the Gestapo had murdered their political prisoners before retreating, but they were caught by the Red Army and summarily hanged without any trial.

It was now April 5. The commander of Rosaulerlandau Prison didn't want to meet the same fate. Krizan's contact told him prior to his own release that if the American ever got out, he would have a place to hide until Vienna was liberated. A package of cigarettes delivered to Krizan would be the signal that the underground contact had himself reached safety. That pack of cigarettes was personally delivered by the prison commander himself.

At this point Krizan made his pitch for freedom. He warned the prison commander of certain death unless he freed the OSS agent, and any other Americans in the prison.

"Release us all as political prisoners," Krizan suggested, "and I'll give you a letter signed by me, an American officer, that you were kind to us in prison."

Soviet artillery rumbled in the distance. The prison commander needed no further urging. Krizan and two American airmen were given release papers describing them as political prisoners, and on April 15 in the dead of the night they were set free. Krizan led the POWs to his underground contact and then holed up with other Americans until Vienna was captured by the Russians. He, too, was interrogated at length by the NKVD before being returned to Bari by way of the USSR.*

---

*On August 30, 1964, Schwartz, Catlos, Lain, and McGregor returned to Donovaly, Czechoslovakia, the scene of their OSS adventure in World War II, for their first meeting in 20 years. Their reunion came about as a result of the celebration of the 20th anniversary of what Czechoslovakian historians call the Slovak National Uprising. Despite the very critical report of the role of the partisan forces submitted by Catlos and Dunlevy, a classified document unavailable to the official sponsors of the anniversary, the Czech government officially considers

Another "dead" agent had come back to life!

Although there were other OSS agents and teams less fortunate than Krizan, a few close calls were experienced by a number of men who were captured and tortured—and didn't break. Hitler's 1942 message was interpreted either liberally or strictly. One OSS OG team in Italy was captured by the Germans while on a mission to blow up a railroad tunnel on the line running south from Genoa. A year after the war, the remains of the fifteen-man OG team, all American GIs of Italian descent, were discovered at the spot where they had been executed and dumped into an open slit trench. Each man, his hands bound behind, had been shot through the back of the head.

Another OSS officer, Captain Roderick G. Hall, had been betrayed by his Italian agent. After twenty-one days of torture, he died; and Gestapo forced an Italian doctor to sign a death certificate which listed the SO officer's death as "heart failure."

As for the members of the "Dawes," "Houseboat," and "Day" Missions who were captured in Czechoslovakia, they were all tortured and finally executed by the Gestapo in the notorious Mauthausen concentration camp near Linz, Austria.

During this period one of the strangest stories of torture and guts was experienced by T/5 Salvadore Fabrega, who had been captured along with his radio operator, Sgt. Oliver Silsby. As part of a three-man OSS team led by Captain Howard Chappell, "Tacoma" Mission was parachuted into the lower Italian Alps in late December 1944, to take over the region that had been worked by Captain Hall until his sudden and mysterious disappearance. This was not a "blind" jump. On the ground was a reception committee from "Aztec" Mission headed by Captain Joseph I. Benucci. After a briefing on the local situation, the "Tacoma" team moved on to its AO and immediately began organizing partisan

---

the revolt against the German occupation a heroic and successful event. The Czech government presented each of the four American visitors with a medal commemorating the 20th anniversary of the uprising and a mountaineer's axe, the symbol of the Slovak Partisan Commander's authority.

forces which were supplied with air drops arranged by
Chappell.

During the first two months of 1945, the partisans led by
the "Tacoma" team raised hell in the area. Additional German troops were brought in to track down the guerrillas and
on March 6, after a heavy gunfight, Chappell's team was
captured along with some of the partisans. Chappell later
escaped but was recaptured after he had been wounded
while trying to evade enemy patrols. Despite a bullet in one
leg, Chappell, a former college football player, tackled his
captor and killed him with his bare hands by breaking the
German soldier's neck. Chappell escaped again and joined
up with the "Aztec" Mission.

Meantime, Fabrega and Silsby were brought to Gestapo
headquarters in the area. Fabrega was tortured severely
by the Nazis who not only wired him to a small hand-
cranked generator, but brutally beat him with fists and
clubs. Throughout, he maintained that he was an American
airman who had been shot down and was trying to escape
capture when he just happened to be caught along with
the other Americans and partisans. Several days earlier,
"Tacoma" Team had managed to evacuate a number of
Allied airmen through the underground railroad established
by the resistance. The experiences of the airmen he had
assisted was the cover story he assumed.

But when the Nazis couldn't make Fabrega admit that he
was not what he claimed to be, he was forced to witness
the torture and beatings of partisans and a horrible "meathook" execution along with the hangings of two Italian
guerrillas who had slept beside him only 48 hours earlier.
During the brutal meathook execution, he was made to
watch four Nazis lift a partisan to the back of a small
truck while a fifth member of the Gestapo torture team
rammed the point of a meathook under the jaw of their
victim. The meathook was fastened to a rope strung from
a tree limb. The truck was driven out from under the
victim leaving the partisan wriggling his life away at the
end of the rope, his toes barely touching the ground. In
an effort to crack Fabrega, the Gestapo indicated that he
soon would be next if he didn't talk. He remained silent,
expecting to meet his Maker at any time. For ten days he

was alternately tortured and threatened, and at one point a traitor among the partisans was placed in his cell in an effort to break through Fabrega's cover. The Gestapo knew that OSS teams were working that area of northern Italy and causing heavy damage to Wehrmacht supply and communications lines. Still he didn't break.

He was then moved on March 16 from Belluno to a prison camp in Bolsano, where he was told he'd be interrogated and tortured further, and executed if he didn't talk. Then, in what is one of the strangest OSS adventures and examples of personal heroism, Fabrega was offered an opportunity to escape and refused, and related in the citation for his Distinguished Service Cross:

> . . . Near Brunico the driver, who besides being the chauffeur for the SS commander in Belluno, also acted as a spy for the American mission and on numerous occasions had furnished valuable intelligence items and forewarning of impending raids, tried to persuade Technician Fifth Grade Fabrega to escape with him to the Partisans, but this he refused because he realized the importance for the American mission to retain the services of a spy in the SS command in Belluno. . . . His . . . unselfish action in refusing to escape when facing further torture and possible death, in order to further the aims of the mission to which he belonged, is in keeping with the highest traditions of the Armed Forces of the United States.

At Bolsano Fabrega met Silsby and a British SOE officer. He thought Silsby had been killed along with Captain Chappell. While in the concentration camp he also discovered the name of the local agent who had betrayed Captain Hall and other partisans and OSS units. During the final weeks of the war, when the enemy knew this was the end of the line, various Italian Fascists, Gestapo officials and agents, and SS troops desperately seeking safety attempted to turn themselves in to American POWs. Others attempted to escape only to become victims of a blood bath at the hands of partisans who had thousands of personal scores to settle. The betrayer of Captain Hall was confronted by Fabrega and confessed before he was led away by the partisans.[4]

When S/Sgt. Frederick A. Mayer, his faced scarred, swollen, and blue from a severe beating and his back scarred by whiplashes, reported to his superiors on May 3, 1945, "Greenup" Mission had nearly cost him his life. It all began in late 1944 when Sgt. Mayer and four buddies, Sergeants Hans Wynberg, George Gerbner, Alfred Rosenthal, and Bernard Steinitz, had become disenchanted with inactivity in OSS. They were shipped to Italy and assigned to the OSS Special Reconnaissance Battalion which at that time had few behind-the-lines missions laid on. Intelligence operations and management at the time left much to be desired. Intelligence professionals in OSS field units were few and far between, and this factor, along with a paucity of intelligence information from which mission operations could be planned, immediately curtailed whatever grandiose ideas the "big picture" planners in Washington or London had envisioned.

Like the typical GIs they were, the five OSS paratroopers and intelligence specialists griped about their lack of assignments—especially as each of them spoke at least two European languages, and they all had foreign residence in their backgrounds. Their loud protests, which they also presented in writing, was brought to the attention of Lieut. Colonel Howard M. Chapin, an operations officer who was busy setting up a German-Austrian Section at 2677 Regiment's Bari Headquarters. The five men were individually interviewed by Chapin and his staff and then sent to a training base near Brindisi for special SI agent training. Mayer teamed up with Wynberg as his radio operator, and a third agent was attached to the team, an Austrian who used the name Frank Martin.

During their training the five men split into three groups, with Gerbner and Rosenthal in the second group, and Steinitz who would train with a third unit.* As their missions were Top Secret, the teams were separated several weeks after their joint specialized agent training had gotten under way. Mayer

---

*During the special SI training of the five agents earmarked for missions to Austria and Germany, they were told in late January 1945 of the execution of the members of the "Dawes," "Day" and "Houseboat" Missions, indicating that OSS had received this news either through its own or British sources.

and Wynberg were scheduled for a mission to Innsbruck, Austria. This was an important communications center for the near-by strategically located Brenner Pass through which the Wehrmacht in Italy and the Balkans received supplies. Moreover, it was virtually impossible for the Allies to close the Brenner Pass, no matter how many bombing missions were mounted. It was a heavily defended area.

By the fall of 1944 intelligence had been obtained about Nazi plans to build a *reduit*, or last-stand fortress, of underground bunkers and other secret areas that could hold thousands of men. The members of the "Greenup" Mission had been well briefed about their target, and they knew exactly what was most important. Compared to some OSS operational errors of the past, the "Greenup" team was well prepared and equipped—that is, if the mission went as smoothly as planned by the operations desk. They had their radios and extra batteries, winter clothing, skis (as they would be dropped in the Alps some thirty-odd miles south of Innsbruck), and other·necessary equipment. Over their U.S. Army uniforms they wore white ski parkas for camouflage. At the end of February 1945, "Greenup" Mission was parachuted into Austria.

But the penetration did not come off as smoothly as planned. The three agents were dropped in a valley along the Ferner glacier just south of the target, but one package of skis was lost. With only two pair of skis available, they lashed some of their light equipment and the radio transmitter to one pair of skis. Martin pulled the load while Mayer and Wynberg followed, struggling for hours through the extremely deep snow, before they arrived at a small village about thirty miles from Innsbruck. After a day-long rest the agents moved out again until they reached a village closer to Innsbruck which also was Martin's hometown. There Martin located Wynberg and the radio transmitter with trusted friends before he and Mayer left for Innsbruck.

Inside the city they set up an organization of agents, couriers, cutouts and sources of information. Mayer and Martin worked fast and on March 7, ten days after they had parachuted into Austria, the "Greenup" radio relayed the first of a regular series of reports. A factory assembling Me–109 fighter planes had halted production because parts were not forthcoming. Wynberg broadcast the location of the assembly plant, and it was bombed. Information about troop trains moving into Italy to reinforce the Wehrmacht, as well as the identification of the military units aboard the trains, permitted Allied generals to revise their order-of-battle information and plan their strategy accordingly. Other trains were "marked" by Mayer's agents, and Fifteenth Air Force bombers had a field day.

On April 5 the "Greenup" Mission radioed: "ALL MOVING TARGETS DISPERSED DAILY BETWEEN NINE AND THIRTEEN HUNDRED GMT. SUGGEST CHANGE BOMBING SCHEDULE." Later they learned that Gestapo Chief Heinrich Himmler and Italy's Fascist leader, Mussolini, had arrived in Innsbruck, which started the intelligence analysts in Western capitals and Allied military headquarters wondering what was up among the Axis leaders.[5]

Finally, on April 20 the Gestapo caught up with Mayer, who had discarded his role of a Wehrmacht officer on leave to recover from wounds. Fluent in French, he had assumed the role of a French foreign worker—accent, identity papers, and all. A courier observed Mayer's arrest and managed to get a warning through to Wynberg, who packed up the radio and escaped minutes before the Gestapo arrived. The German security organization had picked up a number of anti-Nazi suspects, and while torturing one of the prisoners they had learned about Mayer's spy ring without linking "Greenup" Mission to OSS. Martin also managed to elude the Nazi security police, and having found the man they believed to be the major Allied agent in the area, the Gestapo leaned on Mayer with a vengeance. For four days he was beaten, lashed with a whip, water-tortured, and painfully strung out on a torture rack. Still he refused to break.

On April 24, south Austria's highest ranking Nazi official, Kurt Primbs, invited the battered American spy to lunch with him and Franz Hofer, the *Gauleiter* or political chief of the Tyrol. Even the Nazis were aware of the handwriting on the wall during the final weeks of the war in Europe, and it was every man for himself in the contest for survival. Hofer told Mayer that he might be interested in entering negotiations with the Americans for the surrender of the Tyrol and, of course, a guarantee of his own safety. Mayer said he could assist in arranging such a surrender, but as an act of faith he wanted a message delivered by one of the agents among the many who had been organized by the "Greenup" Mission. The message, which was delivered to Wynberg at his new hideout, was transmitted to OSS Bari and read: "PRESENTLY IN GESTAPO HANDS BUT WILL GET OUT ONE WAY OR ANOTHER. DON'T WORRY. . . ."

Three days later, the beatings and torture having been halted, Mayer was transferred to the Reichenau concentration camp outside Innsbruck. On April 29, he learned that *Gauleiter* Hofer was about to address the people of the Tyrol and exhort them to make a last ditch stand against the approaching American forces. His Gestapo guards, anti-Nazis who had been working with the resistance organization with which "Greenup" had been cooperating, escorted Mayer to the *Gauleiter*'s residence minutes before he was to go on the air. The chief of the "Greenup" Mission didn't waste words: The public would never follow the *Gauleiter*'s exhortation to continue fighting for the Nazis; Hitler had committed suicide, and Admiral Karl Doenitz had succeeded him as Führer. The war was all but over. There was nothing left but unconditional surrender, the OSS agent told Hofer. The *Gauleiter* said he would tell his people to surrender to the American advancing troops if Mayer would place him under house arrest and guarantee his safety while in the custody of the "Greenup" Mission. Mayer agreed, and World War II in the Tyrol was all but over—almost.

The U.S. Army's 103rd Infantry Division was fast bearing down on Innsbruck on May 3, 1945, and there was a danger that the Austrian city might be shelled if the division's advance column did not know of the *Gauleiter*'s unconditional surrender to the Allies. Having changed back to their U.S. Army uniforms, Sergeants Mayer and Wynberg, with Mayer wearing his officer's rank for effect, organized the surrender of Wehrmacht units dug in on the approaches to Innsbruck. Unaware that the OSS mission commander was only a sergeant, the G–2 of the 103rd Infantry Division three days later wrote a letter to Colonel Chapin describing how "Lt. Fred Mayer performed a very valuable service for the Army . . . holding *Gauleiter* Franz Hofer and his staff in custody awaiting the arrival of American troops . . . and through this contact it was possible (1) to order the German troops on the western edge of the city to cease all resistance and admit the American troops . . . without opposition and (2) to obtain a statement from the *Gauleiter* Hofer for a radio broadcast [to the German forces] . . . to lay down their arms."[6]

Thanks to Frederick Mayer, the only blood that was shed at Innsbruck was his own. When asked by one of the 103rd Division's staff officers what had happened to him, Mayer's terse reply with an appropriate pause between words: "hit by Gestapo . . . truck, I think." For a few days this rejoinder always brought a chuckle from those who asked how Mayer came by the ugly cuts and bruises that had unbalanced his features. The questions suddenly came to an end when the word was passed along at division headquarters that it really was the Gestapo that had tried to break Fred Mayer.* But his torturers broke first.

---

*Hitler's full message to his generals about executing commandos or SOE and OSS agents was a Top Secret order. The two additional items in this order are as follows:

"If it should be necessary initially to spare one man or two, for interrogation, then they are to be shot immediately after this is completed.

"In case of non-compliance with this order, I shall bring to trial before a court-martial any commander or other officer who has failed to carry out his duty in instructing his troops about this order, or who has acted contrary to it."

General Alfred Jodl, Hitler's Chief of Staff appended: "This order is intended for commanders only and is not to fall into enemy hands."

General Wilhelm Keitel's endorsement: "Commando raiders captured by the Wehrmacht troops are to be handed over to the Security Forces."

As a prosecutor at the Nuremberg war crimes trials, General Donovan had the satisfaction of participating in the trial of Dr. Ernst Kaltenbrunner, a high-ranking SS official and deputy to Gestapo chief Heinrich Himmler. Kaltenbrunner was charged with responsibility in the deaths of the OSS agents captured in Czechoslovakia and executed at Mauthausen concentration camp. He was hanged October 16, 1946.

17

The bridge could have been anywhere in Nazi-occupied
Europe. However, this bridge spanned the Albert Canal on
the rail line southeast of Antwerp, an important port and
communications center in Belgium. In the distance a whistle
howled the signal of an approaching train. At each end of
the bridge stood a Wehrmacht guard. The whistle howled
again, its loud *woo-woo* carried by the night air. The guards
caught the sound of the approaching train still some miles
distant. But they never caught the sound of running feet, nor
did they catch sight of the shadowy figures that erupted
from the darkness.

One moment the guards were standing at their posts. The
next moment they were expertly slammed with knives, silently
pushed into the lower rib cages of their bodies—on the
left side below the heart—and it was all over. They slumped
dead to the ground. The killers joined other figures moving in
the night.

The train whistled again, nearer now. The dark moving
figures disappeared into the night. The train rumbled on to
the steel trestle. It was jammed with troops from the Low
Countries on their way to new duty in Italy. It was the
summer of 1943 and the Wehrmacht was bolstering its
divisions in Italy. The Allies were hammering away at Sicily

before jumping off against what Winston Churchill had described as "the soft underbelly of Europe."

Inside the train the Wehrmacht soldiers were silent, brooding men. They had nothing to be happy about. They didn't know exactly where they were going, but as long as they were heading south they didn't care. Any place was better than Russia.

When the train reached the half-way point across the trestle, a splash of flame erupted. It was the last thing the two German soldiers operating the locomotive were to see in this life. The explosion tore apart the steel trestle; the engine left the tracks and toppled into the water, pulling a string of cars packed with screaming humanity. The cries of horror were obliterated by the rending of steel.

Hours after word had reached Wehrmacht headquarters in Berlin that the troop train had been sabotaged, a report of the incident was handed to a tall, thin officer whose gold oak leaf insignia and service branch pin denoted a major in the U.S. Army, Judge Advocate Corps. Major Arthur J. Goldberg studied the message from behind thick-lensed glasses and nodded his crew-cut head. He opened a folder stamped TOP SECRET and wrote the date of the sabotage incident.

In the Labor Section of OSS in Washington Major Goldberg leaned back in his chair, his hands clasped behind his neck, and contemplated the next in a series of sabotage operations. He also recalled a few years back to the early thirties, when he had been graduated from Northwestern University law school. Instead of going into private practice, Goldberg had joined the labor movement as a lawyer and carved out a niche for himself during the depression era when the American labor movement was beginning to flex its muscles and organize membership in the old CIO.

In the course of his service as a union lawyer, Goldberg had carried on lengthy correspondence with labor leaders in Europe. When they visited the United States he was called upon to meet with them, escort them to various cities, and then set up formal arrangements whereby the labor unions of Europe would maintain contact with their brother unions in the United States.

The European labor movement was old, at least half a century older than the relatively new unions in the United

States. Unlike union leaders in the U.S. who came up through the ranks of the workers, Europe's labor leaders were in the main cultured, well-educated Socialists who idealistically looked toward the day when governments would control all means of production, and well-meaning intellectuals would govern their respective nations—in peace.

These men were *not* Communists. They intensely disliked what the Reds stood for, and they, in turn, were hated by Communist leaders in their respective countries. European labor organizations were also feared by the Fascists. The reason: Labor represented a threat to totalitarian rule of the right or the left.

After the war began the labor movements of Europe fought the German invaders, although in most European countries before the war, entrenched conservative parties representing big business and inherited wealth had tried to smear the Socialist labor movements with a Communist tag.

During the thirties, when both the United States and Europe were slowly pulling out of a devastating depression, Arthur Goldberg had built up a solid friendship with many important labor leaders and organizations in Europe. He didn't know it at the time, but he was also building up what would become part of a secret Allied army behind Nazi lines.

A few months before Pearl Harbor, Goldberg had been contacted by George K. Bowden, a well-known Chicago attorney, who wanted the labor lawyer to meet a close friend who was visiting Chicago. The meeting was held in Bowden's office. The visitor was the Director of COI. Donovan didn't mince any words.

"I understand you have a lot of contacts in Europe," he said.

Goldberg nodded.

"Will they fight Hitler?" Donovan asked.

"They're fighting him now," Goldberg replied.

"I haven't heard about this," the White House emissary noted.

"But Hitler has," declared Goldberg. "They fight in their own way."

Through his contacts abroad he had begun receiving letters posted from neutral countries like Portugal and Switzerland and Sweden, outlining Hitler's mad plans.

After Pearl Harbor Goldberg entered the Army. He wanted a combat assignment. In fact, his transfer had already been arranged to one of the new combat divisions being formed when Bowden again contacted him. He insisted that the young captain wangle a leave and visit him in Washington. It was that important.

Goldberg met with Bowden. The older man came right to the point. He told the young labor lawyer that he could be of greater use to the United States if he would join the supersecret OSS. He said that Goldberg's contacts in Europe were now needed in the worst way. He didn't have to spell it out. Goldberg knew that he could organize his contacts as no other person could. In fact, he realized that he could personally damage the enemy even more than as an infantry company commander. He accepted and within days found himself in Washington at the OSS headquarters complex at 25th and E Street, N.W.

And it was a confusing organization that Goldberg joined. The Wall Street types whom he met looked upon Goldberg with suspicion. They just didn't trust anybody with a labor background. However, they soon learned to respect the Army captain who began to get things rolling. The first thing he did was to submit a lengthy memorandum to Donovan outlining the reasons why the European labor movement could be organized to work for the Allied cause.

"We can take advantage of the hatred of Hitler by members of the European labor movement," he wrote. "The strength of this resistance comes from the working people. They fought the rise of Fascism from its inception. They are its implacable enemy. . . . In fact, the working people of Europe have unparalleled access to strategic information. We must remember that they man the ships and the trains which transport the men and materiels of war. They pour the steel, dig the coal, process the food and make the munitions which are the sinews of war."

He proposed that an OSS Labor Desk be established to contact the labor forces of resistance; collect strategic information; foment sabotage, spoilage, noncooperation, slowdowns, and guerrilla warfare; and, finally, prepare for the Allied invasion of Europe.

It was a great plan. The only thing that was wrong with

it was that some of the bankers and Wall Street brokers in OSS brought heated opposition to any contact with organized labor which they believed might become left-wing oriented. Goldberg defended his plan.

"Who else have we got behind enemy lines?" he asked. Then he pointed out that it was now late 1942, and it would take at least two years before special sabotage teams could be created with enough men to do the job that anti-Nazis were fully capable of carrying out the day after tomorrow.

Goldberg had moved his files from his Chicago office to OSS in Washington. In the metal cabinets were letters from men whose names the Gestapo would have paid a fortune to know. Some of these formed the nucleus of the secret agent corps that OSS would come to rely upon.

Soon the coded orders from Goldberg were radioed to London and Geneva. Agents were to contact certain men throughout Nazi-occupied Europe. So that there would be no mistake, Goldberg sent a lengthy physical and very personal description of each man to be contacted in the event that the Nazis might have arrested a particular labor leader and replaced him with a plant.

It suddenly occurred to Goldberg that the remote possibility might come up when the outcome of a truly important mission could depend upon a personal meeting between himself and an important labor leader who would trust nobody but the head of the Labor Division. In one meeting with Donovan, Goldberg outlined this possibility. Donovan didn't waste any time replying. It was possible and anything that was within the realm of possibility called for preparedness.

"Start training and keep yourself in shape," the general ordered.

Goldberg knew what this meant. He had to be physically in shape to leave Washington at a moment's notice for Europe on a secret mission behind enemy lines. There was no time to take any parachute training. He was too busy for that. However, he found time to study the manual for secret agents. He became a crack shot with pistol and rifle and learned the rudiments of demolition work and the operation of radio equipment. He began a daily program of physical exercise. If and when the time came, he'd be ready.

Meanwhile, he continued to work at his desk as spymaster for the anti-Nazi labor movement. The daily operations, all listed TOP SECRET, blended one into the other. The rail operation was most important. Twice a month on schedule as regular as the mails, an obscure Austrian track-walker checked into a little inn on a Swiss mountainside near the Austrian border. The inn was not far from the end of a rail spur which extended into neutral Switzerland from occupied Austria. In a back room of the inn, the Austrian rail worker talked for hours at a time with an OSS agent who worked directly for Goldberg's labor division.

He was the last link in a spy chain that covered the whole transport field in Austria and included former rail union officials, locomotive engineers, and section hands. The Austrian, a former union official who a decade earlier had become a friend of Goldberg's, poured out vast amounts of information about Nazi troop movements, location of the always mobile sections of the German General Staff, damage assessments from bomber raids, the location of ammunition dumps, and other highly strategic information.

This information was radioed back to Washington to Goldberg's division. Assessing it was some other department's job. What Goldberg did was keep a copy of the information in a folder marked with the alien agent's name; it was part of the record of his underground labor army.

As part of the vast R&A collection center, the OSS Labor Desk provided an accurate picture of various European resistance movements as seen through the eyes of the labor officials who had gone underground. The men who worked the Labor Desk had arranged for Belgian labor leader, Omar Becu, to direct the resistance movement in that country some months before the Allied invasion of Normandy. In one R&A report prepared with the assistance of the OSS Labor Desk, the Belgian underground was called "one of the best organized in Europe." The report continued:

> Sabotage of the country's communication system and of its industry . . . and the organization of strikes are the principal operations of the active resistance movements. Certain resistance groups, however, while partici-

pating in these activities, have specialized in the planning of military operations to be launched at some opportune moment in the future. The sabotage groups as a result of the nature of their operations are made up primarily of industrial workers, who form separate clandestine groups according to their trades and their geographical location. A trade union underground is known to exist, and it may have connections with the workers' sabotage groups. . . .

Although no accurate estimate of the strength of the active resistance formations is possible, it appears that their total effective membership does not exceed 10,000. . ; . One of the principal reasons for this growth can be found in the fact that many young men have preferred to join the clandestine groups and live as outlaws rather than be sent to the Reich as deported workers. . . .[1]

Early on, the Germans had scoured the occupied nations of Western Europe for workers to man the Nazi war production machine. Somebody had to replace Germans of military age who were fighting for their Führer, and Western Europe represented an endless pool of trained workers. Before the Allies invaded France, 600,000 Belgian workers had been deported to Germany and, noted the R&A report, "As a result of the German labor deportation decrees ranks of the Belgium resistance movements have greatly increased since 1942. Men who would not have joined the underground under normal conditions have preferred to live as outlaws in the mountains rather than be shipped as laborers to the Reich. The Ardennes are the main hiding place of these resistance groups who are known under the French name of *Maquis*. The various resistance movements have helped to organize the *Maquis* into operational units and supplied them with food, clothing and arms."

This R&A analysis of the Belgian resistance also noted that the Communist underground appeared to be the most powerful and "the only political party containing separate resistance groups . . . according to reliable reports the Communists' supply of arms and ammunition is larger than that of any other clandestine organization."

Two months after the Allied landings in France, the R&A

report carried a lengthy section provided by the OSS Labor Desk:

> The sabotaging of communication systems stands out as the most important activity of the various active resistance movements in Belgium. Railroad sabotage has disrupted transportation in Belgium to such a degree, that the German authorities have resorted to almost daily appeals to the railway personnel for cooperation. . . . Besides the sabotage of the country's communication system, Belgian patriots have been particularly successful in the organization of strikes. These accomplishments have been primarily due to the fact that the Belgian patriots do not incite workers to indiscriminate strikes, but attempt to organize them for the attainment of specific demands. Requests for higher wages, better working conditions, more food, and other similar demands, have served the patriots as motives for calling strikes, most of which have ended by German compliance with 'the workers' requests.[2]

Noted the Nazi occupation officials in Belgium: ". . . acts of resistance, far from being spontaneous, are committed by the vanguard of a well-organized army of criminals."

> The most continuous and probably most effective sabotage was that directed against the French railroads. Attacks were made to derail German troop and supply trains, to cut tracks, blow bridges, and damage locomotives . . . railway sabotage was greatly accelerated in 1944 and tied to a certain extent with the Allied air offensive against enemy transportation. Damage done by saboteurs compared favorably with that inflicted from the air. In the first three months of 1944 the underground sabotaged 808 locomotives as compared to 387 damaged by air attack. However, in April and May, air attack was stepped up and accounted for the damaging of 1,437 locomotives compared to only 292 put out of action by saboteurs. Between June 1943 and May 1944 a total of 1,822 locomotives was damaged, 200 passenger cars destroyed, 1,500 cars damaged, 2,500 freight cars destroyed and 8,000 damaged. . . . A report by the Vichy police records that during October and November 1943 more than 3,000 attempts were made by patriots to wreck some portion of the railway system.[3]

The German commander in the west, Marshal Gerd von Rundstedt, made it clear that rail sabotage was cause for concern and would become more serious at the time of the Allied assault. A measure of its seriousness was the partial substitution of German uniformed railway workers for employés of the *Société Nationale des Chemins de Fer*, the French national railway system. Between February and June, twenty thousand German workers were brought in, chiefly to check locomotive sabotage. As D-Day approached, OSS headquarters became more concerned with coordinating rail sabotage to relate directly to military operations. In May, OSS headquarters reported that 571 rail targets were ready for demolition, and thirty road cuts were prepared.

> In addition to accomplishing the specific acts of active sabotage, Resistance leaders hoped to complete the disorganization of the French railroads by planned non-cooperation of the railroad trade union and management. It was estimated that in those ways serious dislocation of rail traffic in France might be maintained for eight to ten days after the Allied landings.[4]

In France, during the two weeks before D-Day, Allied bombers struck at the rail net. The attacks stretched to Belgium, but Allied intelligence analysts estimated that the Wehrmacht still had "three times the rail capacity needed for military traffic, four times the required number of cars, eight times the required locomotives, and ten times the required servicing facilities" to move reinforcements toward the Normandy beachhead. French rail workers who were secret members of the resistance began removing cotter pins from railroad equipment of all types so that by D-Day the enemy's rail transportation system was on the point of total collapse.[5]

Despite the ample evidence of active resistance forces in enemy-occupied countries, given a push by OSS and SOE, there were still those in the Allied high command—British and American—who had their doubts as to how effective the resistance forces would be on D-Day or thereafter. A steady flow of information about events in France, for instance, was regularly transmitted to OSS in mid-1942, at least five months before the invasion of North Africa. Lieutenant Commander Tom Cassady, in his role of U.S. naval attaché in Vichy, France, made four secret trips into occupied France to the north. Other agents were working the same beat, and it was a period when OSS had decided to go it alone without any assist from SOE—when official State Department policy favored General Henri Giraud over General Charles DeGaulle as leader of the French government-in-exile. At the same time, Virginia Hall, a correspondent in Vichy for the *New York Post* and an American citizen, had been working for SOE since early 1941 as a contact for British intelligence agents. When the Germans launched their Operation ATTILA in occupied Vichy, France, as an answer to the Allied Operation TORCH, Miss Hall escaped across the Pyrenees to Spain with "Cuthbert." She had lost a leg in an automobile accident some years earlier and moved about wearing an artificial limb which SOE agents had nicknamed "Cuthbert."[6] Tipped off by her "friends" in the Vichy police, she was able to warn British agents that certain roads were patrolled or certain meeting places suspect. When the Wehrmacht marched into Southern France in Operation ATTILA, the incoming head of the Lyons Gestapo, Klaus Barbie, declared that he "would give anything to put his hands on that Canadian bitch."[7]

In time, despite a serious setback in the summer of 1943 when the Gestapo arrested leaders of the factionalized French underground, the resistance grew into a powerful *armée secrète* that after D-Day was able to put 200,000 fighting men into the field. In fact, there was more emphasis before June 6, 1944, on supplying the partisans in the Balkans than on resistance in Western Europe.

Planners on the CCS tended to be cautious in drawing up the strategy for Operation OVERLORD; they decided to regard the resistance as a bonus and to place no reliance on the underground in France to accomplish strategic objectives. One CCS committee thought in terms of a national uprising—that sabotage by the resistance could not be regarded as a strategic weapon unless "backed by a general strike or by a rising on a national scale." Again, the political spectre as the joint British-U.S. committee declared that such an uprising would be desirable from a military standpoint but also might be politically objectionable. Added a French military officer assigned to OSS: "The favorite notion of mass uprisings posited the existence of universal courage, whereas courage only inspired a few men —as it has always inspired the few rather than the many."8*

Four months before D-Day, CCS still considered that resistance activities must be regarded as a bonus although thousands of young Frenchmen had taken to the hills and forests in 1943 to escape a German labor draft. These were some of the backbone of the *Maquis* or *Maquisards,* named after the thorny Corsican bush of the same name. Also, in February 1944, Colonel Joseph P. Haskell, chief of Special Operations for OSS was still concerned about the relatively small scale of the American contribution to behind-the-lines operations in France.

He feared especially the political repercussions on American-French relations of allowing the British to continue supporting the Resistance. The State Department two months later warned the Joint Chiefs of Staff that the impression was gaining ground among the French that, whereas the British were doing everything possible to arm the French patriots, the United States was holding back for political reasons. Thus in May, 25 more U.S. aircraft were assigned to Special Operations over the protests of Air Marshal Sir Arthur W. Tedder who, doubting the value of the Resistance movement, considered the increase unjustified.

Air Marshal Tedder's doubts were unquestionably shared by many in the Allied command, and the effective-

---

*The French officer's comments surfaced with something of a shock 27 years later when, in 1971, a lengthy four-hour film opened to capacity audiences in Paris. Entitled *The Sorrow and the Pity,* this critical film depicts the do-nothing and collaborationist attitudes of a large segment of the French population during World War II. The French Government, short of censoring the volatile documentary, limited its exposure to a single movie house which played to packed audiences. According to long-time Paris resident, Colonel Dan. C. Biondi, U.S. Army (Ret.), many Frenchmen are claiming that they served in the resistance, and a steady "trade" in certification and authentication continues today.

ness of the Resistance as revealed after D-Day was very generally regarded with surprise.[9]

With a direct link to European labor groups prior to D-Day in France, another facet of OSS operations was launched in late 1943 and reached a crescendo of training in early 1944. In London, SFHQ organized Operation JEDBURGH—three-man Allied teams, international in the full sense of the word, which would be parachuted into France immediately before and after D-Day to organize the resistance and supervise the delivery of arms to the guerrilla forces. The JEDBURGH teams, or "Jeds" as they were called by the Americans in OSS, consisted of an Englishman, a Frenchman, and an American, of whom two were officers and one an enlisted man radio operator. Trained in guerrilla tactics, leadership, and demolitions, the Allied teams were organized to coordinate their operations behind German lines with the invasion forces in their advance across France. "Thirteen teams were dropped into France in June 1944, and eighty more followed," one British historian notes. "Total casualties were only 21 dead. . . ."

Among the "Jeds" were Frenchmen who had labor connections in their own country—especially when the OSS Labor Desk, which had moved part of its operation to SFHQ in London, learned that near Lille, France, nearly three thousand miners were available for work with the resistance once the moment was ripe for action.[10] Before Operation JEDBURGH had become a reality and not a just a few active agents in France, one of whom was Major Peter J. Ortiz, one of the handful of recruits with colorful backgrounds similar to that of soldier of fortune Charles Sweeny. A former officer in the French Foreign Legion, he was wounded in action fighting *les Boches* and then was taken prisoner when France fell in 1940. He escaped from POW camp in Austria, made his way out of France to the United States by way of Lisbon, joined the Marine Corps, and obtained an Officer Candidate School commission.

When he returned to France as an OSS SI agent, parachuting into his native land, he carried with him a carefully prepared wardrobe in order to appear an ordinary Frenchman. Thanks to the experiences of the British who passed on some of their expertise to the fledgling American intelligence organization, OSS had developed a number of techniques to assist agents who had to operate in a hostile environment.

The "Moles" at OSS headquarters in London were responsible for preparing the physical accouterments that were part of the cover identities of agents. They turned out clothing that made OSS agents into Danish fisherman, French miners, Austrian peasants, or Wehrmacht officers or soldiers. Their Nazi uniforms were so perfect that they were indistinguishable from the real thing. The "Moles" collected their huge wardrobe from people who had escaped from occupied Europe; and in New York City other OSS agents scoured secondhand clothing shops, buying European clothing, suitcases, fountain pens, shoes, and anything else that a spy might need to maintain his cover behind enemy lines. In their fourth-story garret near OSS headquarters on London's Grosvenor Street—a few doors from General Eisenhower's Supreme Headquarters Allied Expeditionary Forces (SHAEF)—the "Moles" sat hunched over clothing and expertly sewed false pockets and cut down oversized clothing to a better fit for the agent being prepared for a penetration.

They also ran a printing press in their garret with an expert counterfeiter—said to be on "leave" from a prison cell—who put together false identity cards and documents that were able to pass close scrutiny by enemy security police. Among these documents were working papers for agents who would pose as laborers in German factories, and ration books. To add realism, the "Moles" themselves carried these documents to be used later on Top Secret missions in their own pockets to give them a worn appearance. On many occasions they even wore clothing prepared for agents to give it that "used" look.

Ortiz's first operation in France as the radio operator for a three-man team called "Union" Mission, helped set the stage for the follow-on Operation JEDBURGH. The "Union" team, composed of Ortiz, and British Colonel H.H.A. Thackthwaite, a former schoolmaster, were parachuted on the night of January 6, 1944; the French member of the group, Pierre Fourcaud, followed by sea. Their mission in the Haute Savoie region of France was to impress on the *Maquis* that organizing for guerrilla activity, especially on or after D-Day, was their most important duty. The "Union" Mission found one *Maquis* group of three thousand men anxiously awaiting the invasion and the supply of arms that the Allied intelligence group promised would soon be forthcoming. Of the three thousand, about five hundred were lightly armed, Ortiz noted. By D-Day the entire group was heavily armed, and their weapons included mortars.[11]

Although Ortiz and Thackthwaite had parachuted into France clad in civilian clothing, they had taken their uniforms with them, and the British officer later claimed that he and his American colleague were "the first Allied liaison officers to appear in uniform in France since 1940." On one occasion Ortiz was stopped by a German patrol and despite his perfect identity papers which the enemy soldiers didn't even question, they insisted that he open his suitcase. In it was his Marine Corps uniform! Ortiz opened the suitcase and stepped back and, unnoticed, slipped his L capsule out of his pocket and into his mouth. It was only a matter of moments and then. . . .

The officer leading the patrol lifted out Ortiz's uniform coat which had been folded inside out, the inner lining of the coat showing, rather than the Marine globe and anchor insignia, campaign ribbons, or his officer's insignia of rank pinned to the shoulders. The German draped the coat over his arm without unfolding it, intent on looking for weapons or a radio. Nor did he take any note of the forest-green trousers, also part of the Marine uniform which had been seen but rarely in France even before World War II. After the German officer had gone through everything, he dropped the still folded coat back into the suitcase and nodded to Ortiz that he could leave.

His British colleague later reported that Ortiz was proud of his uniform and occasionally wore it into some of the towns visited by "Union" Mission. One evening, he met some Germans in a bar, and playing out his role of a collaborationist, he pumped the enemy officers for information. During the heavy drinking bout the Germans insulted everything that the U.S. represented; finally, never having met one, a German officer actually insulted the U.S. Marines. That was too much for Ortiz. He abruptly excused himself, returned to his hideout and put on his Marine Corps uniform, which he hid under a raincoat. Then he jammed a pistol into his pocket and returned to the bar where he had met his German drinking partners. They were still there when he walked in and moved to the bar where he ordered a drink. Turning slowly, he shrugged out of his raincoat and, at the same time, pulled out his pistol. Alone, he faced the startled enemy officers resplendent in his Marine Corps uniform. Slowly, the Wehrmacht officers began to comprehend that standing in front of them was an American officer—wearing an American uniform. A United States marine.

"We've been drinking toasts to Hitler all night," Ortiz declared. "Now I want to offer a different toast. To the President of the United States!" He raised his glass, and gesturing with his pistol he carefully watched the Germans slowly raise theirs and, at his insistence, offer a second toast to the United States Marines. Then Ortiz slowly backed out of the bar, his pistol warning the enemy officers that any false move and somebody could get hurt, or even killed. He departed from a side exit and escaped into the night with the satisfaction that it would be a long time before this group of enemy officers would again insult the United States —or the U.S. Marine Corps.[12]

Before too long Ortiz was in the thick of it. The German security services had discovered that "Jean Pierre" and the American Marine officer were one and the same. After the OSS agent led a *Maquis* raid in which a troop train was destroyed, and transportation along a two-mile section of track was halted for three days, a price of 150,000 francs was placed on his head, and within weeks it had been raised to half a million.

The Allied "Union" Mission predated Operation JEDBURGH by half a year, but the British SOE which had been recruiting agents in Europe since the fall of France had discovered early on that British intelligence people and other nationalities easily worked together on secret missions in enemy-occupied territory. As it turned out, the three-man JEDBURGH teams, which numbered eighty-two Americans from OSS, turned out to be one of the most successful operations of its type during the war—and one of the better organized OSS operations.

By early February 1944, the first "Jeds" began to arrive at Milton Hall, an old English manor house about 100 miles from London. Within ten days the full complement of British and French military personnel, and some French, Belgian, and Dutch "civilians" with a military cast to their shoulders had arrived, and training began in earnest. Operation OVERLORD—the invasion of France—was in the planning and preparation stages, and the "Jeds" had less than ninety days to shape up. Some of the men had to drop out for a week of intensive jump training at an RAF school near Manchester. Graduation was a series of jumps from an aircraft.[13]

But on arrival at Milton Hall, the "Jeds" first had to mate up with compatible colleagues, and some of the teams ended up with two Americans of the trio, or two British. Among the "Jeds" who trained at Milton Hall and later parachuted to France were Captain Paul Cyr, the first American "Jed" to jump into France. He obtained a photostat of the Wehrmacht fortress defenses at St. Nazaire which he immediately channeled back to Allied commanders by crossing through enemy lines and personally delivering the plans. Navy Lieutenant Mike Burke had volunteered for the "Jeds" after serving with OSS in Italy. Captain William E. Colby and two French partners were parachuted by error into an enemy-held city and lost their supplies, which landed on roofs of houses in which Wehrmacht troops were billeted.[14]

And Lieutenant Roger Hall parachuted into France to join a "Jed" team whose leader had been wounded, only to discover that instead of landing well behind enemy lines, he had landed behind his own lines. The U.S. Army's Second Armored Division had broken through and overrun the sector. Although the "Jed" team had radioed SFHQ in London that they had been overrun by friendly forces and a replacement for the wounded officer wasn't needed, the message had been slow in reaching the operations officer responsible for the SO teams. The official excuse: It took time for messages to pass through "channels."[15]

Other frustrations plagued the OSS agents and teams

in the field, and high-level policy decisions also took time to pass down the chain of command and frustrated men who were giving their all. Although carefully selected starting in late 1943, OSS field personnel—SI agents and members of SO and OG units—could not help but become personally involved with the causes of the resistance groups they were assigned to support, often at great risk. Even the more urbane and experienced men of Britain's SOE succumbed to this human frailty, often placing them at odds with official government policy toward the resistance. The "political" side of the war would have its repercussions as the global conflict reached its benchmark in mid-1944 with the opening of the Western Front.

The political design is the object, while war
is the means.
> —KARL VON CLAUSEWITZ:
> *On War*, 1832.

On May 6, 1943, a Luftwaffe Ju–52 transport loaded
with armed guards, four Allied officers, and a handful of
British Army enlisted men—all prisoners of the Germans—
flew eastward from Germany. Three landings later, the
twin-engine aircraft rolled to a military airfield on the outskirts of Smolensk in German-occupied Russia. On the following morning, the Allied POWs were escorted to near by
Katyn Forest to view a scene of war at its most horrible—
the aftermath of the Soviet invasion of Poland nearly four
years earlier.

When the Red Army, in concert with Nazi Germany, invaded Poland in September 1939, the Soviets crushed resistance in the area of operations which was theirs by
agreement with the Germans. During the campaign the
Russians captured 200,000 Poles who were shipped to a
hundred-odd POW camps in eastern Poland and in the Soviet
Union. However, Stalin ordered three POW camps set up
expressly for the confinement of Poland's officer corps,
composed of the defeated country's educated middle and
upper classes. Approximately 15,400 Polish officers were
rounded up by the NKVD secret police troops. At a POW
camp in Kozielsk, 5,000 officers were interned, 4,000 at
Starobielsk, and 6,400 at Kalinin. Through the winter of
1939–40, the NKVD carefully screened the POWs. Six joined

the Communists and some four hundred indicated that they would side with the Russians.

That left 15,000 anti-Communist officers, the potential postwar leadership of Poland. They all disappeared during March, April, and May of 1940. By the summer of 1941 the Soviet Union was desperately battling her former ally in a war of survival that carried the Wehrmacht through Smolensk and deep into Russia, to the very gates of Moscow.

In 1943 the Germans found the bodies of 4,143 Polish officers buried in mass graves in Katyn forest. Seeking to turn their grisly discovery into propaganda, they ordered this small delegation of Allied POWs to be taken to Smolensk. Two were West Point graduates and Regular Army—Lieut. Colonel John H. Van Vliet, Jr., and Captain Donald B. Stewart, both captured several months earlier in Tunisia. The other two were Lieut. Colonel Harvey Stevenson, of the British Commonwealth South African Forces, and Captain Stanley S. B. Guilder, a Russian- and German-speaking Scottish doctor in the Royal Army Medical Corps, both captured at Tobruk, in North Africa, in 1941.[1]

Although suspicious of their German captors and aware that their trip was intended for propaganda purposes, the Allied officers reluctantly had to conclude that the Germans had not committed this atrocity. Independent postwar investigations supported their wartime observations. The evidence indicated that the NKVD, using German ammunition and Red Army three-bladed bayonets, had brutally executed nearly five thousand Polish officers POWs from the Kozielsk prison camp.

"I hated the Germans," recalled Colonel Van Vliet. "I didn't want to believe them. At that time, like many other Americans, I more or less believed that we could get along with Russia. When the Katyn story broke while we were still in prison camp, we believed the whole thing to be one huge, well-managed desperate lie formulated by the Nazis in an effort to split the Western Allies from the Soviet Union. We knew that the Germans would do their best to convince us that Russia was guilty. The way it turned out, it was the Nazi pot calling the Russian kettle black."[2]

Fourteen months after the Allied POWs had visited

Katyn Forest, the Wehrmacht was being rolled back across Eastern Poland by the Russian forces of Marshal Konstantin K. Rokossovski's First White Russian Front just east of Warsaw and Marshal Ivan S. Konev's First Ukranian Front further to the south. This 450-mile advance, however, had overstrained Russian supply capabilities and the offensive came to a temporary halt.* The leaders of the Polish government-in-exile in London had authorized the Polish resistance to decide when to launch a general uprising; the time had arrived, resistance leaders decided, in late July 1944. It was also time for the resistance throughout Europe to rise up against the German invaders and occupation forces in their respective countries, especially as the Western Front had opened the previous month with the Normandy invasion. On July 22 the Polish resistance had intercepted German radio messages ordering a general withdrawal to positions west of the Vistula River, the site of the Polish capital of Warsaw.[3] In Warsaw, some forty thousand resistance fighters in the Polish underground, with stocks of food and ammunition, awaited a signal from their commander, General Tadeusz Bor-Komorowski who appeared to be waiting for the sound of Russian artillery in the east. Russian warplanes began bombing German positions during the final days in July. On July 27 the Soviet Union signed an agreement in the Kremlin with representatives of the Polish Committee of National Liberation, which had been established several days earlier by the Russians to usurp control from the exiled government in London.[4]

The resistance forces of General Bor-Komorowski owed their allegiance to their London-based government. Organized Free Polish forces flying combat missions against the Luftwaffe out of bases in Britain, and supply missions to the Polish underground and other Allied resistance forces from bases in England and Italy, and Polish infantry divisions had

---

*As it turned out, the death of the Polish officer corps—for political reasons, to erase future opposition—curtailed the fighting capabilities of the resistance army. The Soviet armies which pushed the Germans westward across Poland might have saved many Russian lives if the resistance forces of the Polish Home Army had been used to fight the Germans on a large scale.

seen combat in North Africa and were fighting in Italy and France. As a counter to the exiled Polish government, in what was the first in a pattern for the conquest of other East European nations, the Kremlin had established a number of governments of national liberation. Except in Yugoslavia, these new leaders of Communist governments would return to their homelands on the shoulders of the Red Army.

Meantime, as the Russians moved west they met up with elements of the Polish Home Army fighting as guerrilla resistance forces. In mid-July the Soviets agreed to furnish new arms and equipment for nearly two divisions of the Home Army which had linked up with the Soviet commander of the Third White-Ruthenian Front in the Wilno area of eastern Poland. In an *aide memoire* submitted to the British Government on July 25, the Polish government in London noted that "According to mutual agreement these units . . . were shortly afterwards to return to the front as units of the Polish Army under orders of the Polish Government in London and the Polish Commander-in-Chief, and under operational orders of the Soviet Supreme Command. Meanwhile, on the 17th the Soviet authorities arrested the Staff of the Home Army from the Areas of Wilno and Nowogrodek."5

Soviet broadcasting stations also had been urging the Polish people to drop all caution and launch their general uprising against the common enemy. On July 29 Radio Moscow broadcast an appeal from Polish Communists to the people of Warsaw, declaring that the guns of liberation were within hearing and that "all is lost that is not saved by active effort. . . . By direct active struggle in the streets and houses . . . of Warsaw the moment of final liberation will be hastened and the lives of our brethren saved."6

Unfortunately, the Polish exile government was neither a smooth-functioning nor viable administration and had been at odds with its British host on a number of issues. Among them was a plan developed by the Home Army commander in Poland in September 1943 proposing an uprising assisted by the air force. "Our entire military effort outside Poland," he wrote, "should be subordinated to providing air assistance

in the event of a rising." The distance between Allied bases
in England and Italy was not taken into account, nor such
considerations as the availability of aircraft. A reply was
sent back to the Home Army commander six weeks later
which noted that if all went well "the Polish Air Force may
be in a position to support a rising by the beginning of
1945; such support will only be feasible if the relevant plans
and timing are fully accepted by our allies. . . . At present,
on political grounds, the British do not want to commit themselves."[7]

When the resistance organization inside Warsaw finally
was goaded into launching the uprising, it was done without
any thought of the consequences. What if by some chance
the Soviets, who were about ten miles away at the end of
July, could not (or would not) aid the uprising? What if the
Allies in the West could not provide supplies by air? But
despite these questions, the uprising was launched by General
Bor-Komorowski on the afternoon of August 1, 1944.

> At exactly five o'clock thousands of windows flashed
> as they were flung open. From all sides, a hail of bullets
> struck passing Germans, riddling their buildings and
> their marching formations. In the twinkling of an eye
> the remaining civilians disappeared from the streets.
> From the entrances of houses our men streamed out and
> rushed to the attack. In fifteen minutes an entire city of a
> million inhabitants was engulfed in the fight. Every kind
> of traffic ceased. As a big communications centre where
> roads from north, south, east and west converged, in the
> immediate rear of the German front, Warsaw ceased to
> exist. The battle for the city was on.[8]

From that point on Warsaw became a political pawn, as
five hastily concentrated German divisions were moved into
and around the city to crush the revolt. The situation soon
became grim for the Poles in Warsaw—and London—who
had not considered the realities of the tactical situation in
the West. "Many conferences had been held on this subject,
hundreds of telegrams exchanged, urgent couriers sent back
and forth," wrote one historian,

> yet when at last the moment for the rising arrived, it
> turned out that the plans were irrelevant and the real

situation very different from what had been foreseen.

All the Polish military plans had been based on the assumption that help by air from the Polish and Allied squadrons would only be possible if the Western Front was to the east of the Rhine, which would reduce the flying distance considerably. This condition had not been fulfilled and the Allied air bases were still in Britain. The transfer of the dropping operations to Italy had afforded access to southern Poland but did not alter the position of Warsaw. The shortest distance to the Polish capital from London is 950 miles, from Brindisi 880 miles. Even the heaviest bombers, used for night flights, could not fly this distance both ways unless they were specially adapted. However, the Polish representations took no account of this factor. Some even asked once again for the Parachute Brigade to be dropped and for the Polish Air Force to be sent to Poland, although they must have known that it was quite impossible.[9]

General Kazimierz Sosnkowski discussed the problem with the British and then messaged Warsaw that he was "demanding drops, combatant status, parachute help, our air force. . . ." Churchill proposed an emergency air-supply drop but he cabled Stalin that since Russian troops were right outside the city, where they remained as soon as the uprising was launched, a Soviet supporting attack "may be of help to your operation."[10]

Stalin turned a deaf ear to Churchill's message just as he did to Polish Prime Minister Stanislaw Mikolajczyk, who was in Moscow at that time trying to reach terms with the Kremlin, which had recognized the new Communist government in Poland. When Britain and the U.S. proposed a massive supply effort and asked for permission to have aircraft land at Soviet airstrips on a shuttle from England and Italy, Stalin at first refused. The Western Allies now began to see the writing on the wall.

The Poles were desperate. A hundred Poles had been trained along with the JEDBURGH teams. They were to be parachuted to France under the auspices of SOE and OSS to join up with many of their expatriate fellow countrymen who were also fighting with the *Maquis*.

These teams, code-named BARDSEA, were highly skilled and competent underground fighters, all tough, all good shots, all trained in demolition and parachuting. General Stanislaw Kopanski tried to obtain the services of the BARDSEA group through a formal request made to Colonel Theodore Palmer of OSS London, who was urged to intervene with his superiors so that the Americans could provide SO and OG teams to embattled Warsaw.

The BARDSEA Poles had been overtaken by events beyond their control, as much as they would have preferred assignments to Warsaw rather than to France. Unfortunately, this sort of waste of well-intentioned effort is inevitable in war, and both the logistics of the problem and the politics made their deployment an impossibility.[11] Events in Poland were beyond the scope of OSS and, as it turned out, beyond its competence; SOE had assumed responsibility for intelligence out of Poland in 1940.

At OSS operations centers in London and in Bari, officers and men worked around the clock preparing SO and OG teams and supply packages, in the event there might be a change of heart somewhere topside—at CCS, at Whitehall, or even in Washington. In the Brindisi operations center of the Fifteenth Special Group, a state of readiness prevailed, in the event a mission to Warsaw was commanded—or, in AAF parlance, "fragged." Supplies to the Italian resistance were curtailed as a result of the Polish crisis at a time when the Allies were moving ahead north of Rome.

Even a Soviet liaison officer in Warsaw pleaded with Stalin for Russian aid. "After acquainting myself with the general military situation," declared Captain Konstanty Kalugin of Czarny Group 66804 on August 5,

> I come to a conclusion—that in spite of the heroism of the Army and the entire Warsaw population—there are still needs which if made good would permit a speedier victory over our common foe. These needs are automatic arms, ammunition, grenades, anti-tank weapons. Drop arms on: Wilson Square, Invalids Square, Ghetto, Krasinski Square, Zelazna Brama Square, Napoleon Square, Mokotowski Field and Cavalry Barracks in Powisle and Bielany. Recognitions signals: white and red sheets. German air force destroys the City and kills civilian population. Direct artillery fire on Vistula bridges, in the Warsaw area, on Saski Garden, Aleje Jerozolimskie, as these are the main channels of movement for

the German Army. The enemy is bombing from Okecie
and Bielany airfields. The heroic population of Warsaw
trusts that in a few hours time you will give them armed
support.[12]

Stalin remained intransigent about the use of airfields
behind Russian lines by Eighth Air Force bombers making
a supply run to Warsaw. It was obvious that once the
uprising was crushed, so, too, would be the resistance; and
the new Polish Committee of National Liberation and its
Lublin Government automatically would assume full political
control without any opposition.

Biding his time despite world opinion against his waiting
game in Poland, Stalin finally authorized a shuttle flight.
However, there also had been opposition to an air drop from
senior Allied commanders.

General Eaker, after studying the possibility of daylight drops by the Fifteenth Air Force, concluded that
the danger was too great. No fighter cover could be
provided for the target areas, which were 770 miles from
Fifteenth Air Force bases and beyond the range of
heavy bombers unless equipped with bomb-bay tanks. All
he could promise was to use the night efforts of special
operations to the maximum. General Spaatz suggested
that a supply drop might be combined with the next
shuttle mission from the United Kingdom to Russia, but
the principal effort in August seems to have come from
MAAF. All available aircraft were assigned to the
work. Two squadrons of the 205 Bomb Group (RAF)
and 148 Squadron (RAF) supplemented the activity of
1586 Polish Flight. These units succeeded in completing
84 of 170 attempted sorties; but delivery of 100 net
British tons [2,200 pounds] resulted in the loss of 30
aircraft. In September the entire 205 Group participated
in supplying Warsaw, but the effort was small. Less than
23 tons were delivered by 19 successful sorties in 47
attempts. Of the 10 aircraft lost, eight were by 1586
Polish Flight.

The Eighth Air Force made one mass drop to Warsaw.
On 18 September three groups of 110 B–17s were dispatched, of which 107 dropped 1,284 containers, with
the loss of two planes. The B–17s, protected by one of
the three groups of escorting P–51s, continued on to
Russian bases and then returned to the United Kingdom

via Italy. This drop was reported as having achieved a high degree of success, but the Russians claimed that at least 50 per cent of all supplies dropped by the RAF and AAF fell into German hands. The mission of 18 September had afforded some relief . . . but General Spaatz reported that further drops were urgently needed. General Arnold did not favor a continuation of the Polish missions because they detracted from our offensive effort and subjected the AAF to possible heavy losses. Any further assistance, he believed, should be dependent upon the date of relief of Warsaw. At the end of September General Marshall believed that at least one more mission should be made to relieve the desperate situation in Warsaw. But it was too late for a trickle of supplies to be of such assistance to the city.[13]

On September 30, 1944, all resistance ended. Of the 40,000 men and women of the resistance forces in the city, about 15,000 were killed and 200,000 of the one million population were killed and wounded in the heavy fighting. The Germans lost 10,000 killed and 9,000 wounded, and reported 7,000 missing.[14]

After the Warsaw uprising was crushed while the Soviets deliberately did nothing, Allied leaders in London and Washington, their suspicions about future Soviet policies confirmed, found themselves faced with another serious problem. Both SOE and OSS had built up the resistance forces in occupied Europe—and inadvertently had aided the Communist underground. At SFHQ, many operations officers had come to the conclusion that they had contributed to Communist strength in northern Italy, France, the Low Countries, and in the Balkans. Specifically, the OSS operations officers had responded well to the glowing reports of their agents in the field, and had provided the wherewithal required by the SO and OG units to arm partisan allies. In Italy, for example, there was fear at 2677 OSS Regimental headquarters in Bari that at war's end the political power in the north would probably fall into the hands of those who had at their disposal the greater amount of weapons and ammunition, rather than to those leaders supported by the majority of the people.

In Greece in 1944 the Communists or *Kommunistikon*

Komma Ellados (KKE) hid behind the National Liberation Front called *Ethnikon Apeleftherotikon Metopon* (EAM), a label deliberately designed to give the movement a national and nonpolitical appearance. Military support for this non-political movement was given by the partisan arm or *Ethnikos Laikos Apeleftherotikon Stratos* (ELAS). ELAS, the military arm of the front organization, recruited former Greek officers, and the guerrillas, according to one historian, spent more time hiding in the mountains and remote valleys than in fighting the enemy.[15] In the fall of 1943 the first American liaison officers returned with members of the British mission who had left Greece to attend a strategy conference in Cairo. Until that time Greece was strictly a British show. However, with the two American OSS officers on the scene, the British Military Mission became the Allied Military Mission. In December 1943 Major Gerald K. "Jerry" Wines parachuted into Greece to become the deputy to the British colonel commanding AMM. The OSS Operational Groups began to arrive in Greece in strength in the spring and summer of 1944—seven OGs of twenty to thirty men each and, after Major Wines was injured in a fall from a horse, the OGs came under the command of Colonel Paul West from OSS in Cairo.[16]

One of the first OGs to arrive was "Chicago" Mission, led by Major James G. L. Kellis. In early 1944 the OSS team infiltrated into Greece behind Kellis, who crossed the Greek-Turkish frontier at the end of December 1943. After contacting the guerrilla forces, mostly ELAS units, they set up a vital railway bridge for demolition, destroyed the structure, and halted the movement of chrome mined in northern Greece and destined for factories in Germany.

Another operation, "Stygia" Mission, was infiltrated at a period when ELAS and opposition EDES political movements and their respective partisan forces were battling each other for control of the countryside. It was a time when the British presence was quite tenuous because of London's support of the monarchy and the Greek government-in-exile.

And a typical OG team, codenamed "Staircase" Mission and led by Captain Andy Rogers, fitted into the special operations pattern by demolishing its bridge targets before exfiltrating back to 2677 Regiment headquarters in Bari in a

Greek *caïque*—a small motor-sailer used for fishing and hauling along the coast. Among the sailors who captained the *caïques* crewed by Greeks who worked for OSS was movie actor Sterling Hayden, whose *nom de guerre* was Captain John Hamilton, U.S. Marine Corps.

During this period the American OGs arrived with many second-generation Greeks among them. And not too soon. Some of the guerrilla units had been decimated in a three-way war between ELAS, EDES, and the Germans, and just before Major Kellis had arrived on the scene the National Republican League's EDES *Andarte* had withdrawn to a small area in Epirus. It was the mission of the Greek-Americans to support the guerrillas and get them to fight the enemy instead of each other and, if possible, to keep EAM/ELAS from becoming strong enough to seize political control in Greece after the German defeat or withdrawal.[17] The OSS Americans had their work cut out for them, especially in their dealings with ELAS *Andarte* guerrillas.

> Throughout the war years EAM and ELAS resorted to typically Communist methods by which to increase and maintain their numbers. The occupying armies provided them with the first essential, a suitable psychological undercurrent. The very presence of the invaders created resentment in the Greek people; their barbarous behavior turned resentment to hatred. EAM, raising the banner of resistance, persuaded the citizens to flock to the colours; those who refused were either dubbed traitors and collaborators, their houses burned and their families slaughtered, or were compulsorily enlisted. . . .
> For leaders also ELAS looked to the disbanded Greek regular Army, drawing into their ranks experienced officers and NCOs whose political views were watched and influenced by commissars. Once the citizens had been recruited they were subjected to intense propaganda and political instruction so that many were converted who started the war with no allegiance to Communism. Propaganda was also directed at the world at large and succeeded in giving the impression abroad that the movement was solely devoted to resistance.[18]

Major Wines discovered that the fighting ability of ELAS fell far short of claims, and much of its field operations were directed toward absorbing existing guerrilla groups of other political affiliation, and battling them if they didn't join the front organization.

Originally, twelve Greek-Americans had parachuted into the devastated country, and within a matter of months— by late April 1944—about 250 were roaming the country looking for trouble from the enemy. They grew beards like their Greek kinsmen's. At night they sabotaged the railway lines, blowing up the trains that the Germans were using to evacuate troops and supplies. Off nights were spent raiding Wehrmacht warehouses and ammunition dumps. They had names like George Portolos, Spyros Drakos, Theodore Pippinas, George Pappitsas, and Sam Vakakas— and they were at home in Greece. Some had left the country as children; a few bore typical American names such as Jim Drake and Bill Johnson.

Before they had parachuted into Greece, OSS had detached these men to the Second British Commando group; they received jump training at the Parachute and Intelligence Schools the Allies maintained in Palestine and at Oujda, the Algerian town near Oran. Experienced in the use of heavy infantry weapons, they regularly knocked out German trains by firing bazooka shells into locomotives with unerring accuracy and spraying the rest of the armored trains with equally murderous machine-gun fire. They were so successful that the German locomotive engineers never went more than ten or twelve miles an hour through the passes and over the bridges that spanned deep gorges—guarded all the way by pill boxes every three kilometers and strands of barbed wire along the tracks protected by anti-personnel mines.[19]

In early October 1944 an OG team led by Lieutenant Jack Ganaris infiltrated the railway line out of Salonika which was guarded every fifty yards by machine-gun posts and reinforced every kilometer by concrete flak towers, some on hillsides commanding a wide field of fire. The OG team had quietly moved into the area and spent several nights hiding in caves as they inched ever closer to the guarded railroad line. On the night they were scheduled to make a final foray and blow the rails, and any train that happened to come along, an alert German sentry in a flak tower spotted the OSS paratroopers. He opened fire, wounding Corporal Louis Lenares, who was gripped more by anger at having been observed than pain and hurt from his bullet wounds. Rising to his feet and gripping his Marlin submachine gun, Lenares triggered off short bursts and knocked out the enemy machine-gun team, killing three men in the flak tower. But other enemy positions along the route picked up the sound of the firefight, and flares were fired into the sky overhead; other German sentry posts on the surrounding slopes began shooting.

"Pull back!" shouted Lieutenant Ganaris. "Rendezvous! Rendezvous!" The OSS team had selected a cave as a rendezvous point in the event that they had to scatter if discovered or if they had to take to the hills after the rail line was blown up. In a spate of broken-field running, Lieutenant Ganaris dashed toward Corporal Lenares, but stepped on a mine which exploded beneath his feet, hurling him another twenty feet where he fell to the ground unconscious, bleeding from more than a score of wounds. It was shortly before dawn when he came to, awakened by the throbbing pain of his wounds and the early-morning cold and chilling dew that had settled on his bloody features. The Wehrmacht patrols that had raced to the scene had missed finding him and Lenares in the darkness. Unable to stand, he dragged himself in the direction of Lenares, stumbling across the corporal's body. He was dead. The OSS officer reasoned that it was unwise to remain with daylight soon to break. He crawled into a small shed used by track-repair crews. The day passed. That night members of the OSS team, which had been observing the area from the slopes during the day without spotting the lieutenant's body, decided to make one final sweep of the area. The patrol came across the shed and found the OSS officer waiting, a .45-caliber automatic cocked and aimed at the entrance. Ganaris wasn't about to give up without a fight to the death. The patrol carried him away, across the mountains to an airstrip and he was evacuated to Bari.[20]

Among the Greek-Americans there were also a few experiences that touched even the gruffest of exteriors. Several of the OG team members came across relatives whom they had neither seen nor heard from in years. One of them working with an *Andarte* group chanced upon his brother whom he hadn't seen in years and they exchanged information about the welfare of the Greek and American branches of the family. Sergeant George Karakitos, who had left Greece as a boy, found himself near his home village and stopped in to visit his mother despite the enemy patrols in the area. Corporal Steve Martaishis, left behind in a cottage when he took sick, was dozing when his father walked in. And one of the most unusual meetings occurred when Corporal C. Antinopoulos, a member of the first OG to parachute into Greece, landed a short distance from his grandmother's village, which he had not visited since he was a child. Not knowing whether she was still living, he decided to visit the village and her cottage. He discovered that she was still alive, but blind.

"I am Charles," he announced himself to the old woman. "I've dropped in to see you."

"Charles Antinopoulos?" she asked, disbelieving what she heard. "You are joking and playing tricks on an old lady. He is in America."

"But it's really me, grandmother," he explained, as she ran her gnarled fingers over his face in an attempt to see what her ears had told her.

"How came you here?" she asked, still not believing. "The Germans are everywhere."

"I came from the sky," he said, "by parachute from an airplane."

The old woman had never heard of a parachute, and when other relatives soon arrived after hearing that an American soldier was in the cottage, he left it to his kinfolk to explain to the old woman that it was possible to jump from an airplane and with a parachute land anywhere in the world.

Finally she was convinced. "Such crazy notions these days," she sighed. "But I wish I could see you, my boy."[21]

Family reunions were secondary to the mission at hand. In the field, Lieutenant Tom Stix of the "Stygia" Mission early discovered that as brutal as were the Germans and the Bulgarian troops they used for police details, the guerrillas were equally cruel. The majority of the guerrillas were simple mountain people and lowland peasants, and for the mountain men, torture of the enemy was viewed as a "sport." There were a number of incidents of OSS liaison officers having dispatched a prisoner who was being tortured; many of the other Allied liaison officers later reported that they too, had deliberately shot enemy prisoners rather than leave them to the Greeks.[22]

In July 1944, one of the OG units came across a village where the parents of a member of the team had lived before emigrating to the United States. He finally met what was left of his parents' families. Two weeks earlier, the Germans had made a sweep through the area and indiscriminately shot up the village, killing men, women and children. Several villagers were left hanging as a warning not to harbor guerrillas in the future. Later, out on patrol, the OGs surprised a fifteen-man enemy patrol, and after the shooting stopped the OSS had nine prisoners whom they marched back to their headquarters in the village. As the Germans approached the village, they began to hold back out of fear. But the OSS men prodded them to move on and marched them down the dusty, sunwashed street. People suddenly appeared, hurling rocks and spitting at the prisoners and identifying them as part of the German unit that had shot up the village.

One of the Greek-Americans on the team spoke to the villagers in their own dialect, trying to calm them down. "They are war prisoners," he explained. Then a fifteen-year-old girl came running up and shouting, struck one of the Germans. She pointed out two more. They had raped her and her mother, the cousin and aunt of the OSS team member whose parents had come from this village.

"Move 'em out," he said to his buddies as he pushed the three German soldiers away from their fellow captives. Then he marched them to the small square, followed by most of the villagers, who had blood in their eyes and demanded of their neighbor-one-generation-removed that he turn the prisoners over to them. He refused. They moved in closer, menacing. He raised the muzzle of his sub-machine gun upward and fired off a short burst which brought the angry and growling crowd to heel.

"Over to the wall," he told the German soldiers, gesturing with his airborne trooper's "greasegun." The three enemy soldiers silently shuffled up against a wall, their features pallid as if they knew their time had come. The OSS trooper called to his cousin and asked her if she was sure that these were the men who had raped her. His aunt broke through the crowd and confirmed her identification.

"Move back," the OSS paratrooper shouted, motioning with one hand for the villagers to get behind him. Then, he pulled the half-empty clip from his weapon and inserted a fresh one with twenty rounds, striking it with the palm of his hand to make certain it was attached correctly. He pulled the bolt and slid a round into the chamber and then, muttering over and over again "You goddamned Nazi bastards," he executed his captives with three short bursts. Then, pulling his pistol from his holster, he stepped over to each body and fired a single shot into the faces of the presumably dead men, the .45 slug splattering blood and violently messing up the features of the executed victims.

Without a word, the lone OSS Greek-American turned and followed the direction taken by his buddies. The crowd of villagers, the women clad in black, parted as he passed through them, his eyes focused straight ahead. Behind him the villagers were silent, and somewhat shocked at the abrupt justice they had seen meted out. It was not their brand of justice; they would have tortured their captives first and, as it was done in the mountains, beheaded their victims. They were puzzled by this version of "American" justice.

As most of the team were also Greek-Americans, nothing more was said about the incident, nor was it ever included in an OSS operational report, although a number of similar incidents did occur in Greece.[23]

Living among the partisans in enemy-occupied territory encompassed more than the normal hazards posed by the enemy.

19

Now it is not good for the Christian's health
to hustle the Aryan brown,
For the Christian riles, and the Aryan smiles,
and it weareth the Christian down;
And the end of the fight is a tombstone white
with the name of the late deceased,
And the epitaph drear: "A Fool lies here
who tried to hustle the East."
—RUDYARD KIPLING: *Naulahka*, 1891

In Burma, the operations of Detachment 101 in the
tropic environment continued apace with Allied military
operations in that part of the world. The Japanese were
still in Burma in force in 1943 and Wingate's airborne
Chindit expedition in the spring of 1944 with OSS participation was considered a gallant but largely wasted effort.
Critics complained that the same results could have been
obtained by smaller commando or guerrilla forces without
having committed five British Commonwealth brigades
which had been ground up in the process.

But the critics were unaware of the serious recruiting
problems that OSS faced in 1943. The big recruiting push
was required for Operation OVERLORD and the continuation of pressure behind enemy lines in the Balkans and
Italy. Even the OSS build-up in China continued slowly
and it was not until late 1944 that many of the American
"Jeds" were reassigned to China to participate in operations
similar to those in France with the *Maquis*. However, in
Asia OSS was faced with a paucity of information about the
area and its peoples other than what could be gleaned from

268

the handful of anthropologists and a somewhat larger corps of missionaries who had lived and traveled in the Orient.

Dealing with Asians was a new experience for OSS whether they were the simple Kachin or Naga tribesmen or the more sophisticated and, by western standards, corrupt leadership of the Kuomintang of China or their Communist enemies also fighting the Japanese. And OSS people also discovered in Asia, as it did elsewhere around the world, that some of the people and tactics to be used did not fit with the American ethic—they had to work with the Mafia in planning and carrying out the invasion of Sicily; in 1944 they hired Corsican criminals and smugglers as agents in southern France.[1]

The men who worked closely with agents in Detachment 101 soon discovered that, especially in Asia, there was more than they anticipated to buying and bargaining for assistance and intelligence information. They learned that all services had a price tag attached—called by many names, including *kumshaw* or "tea money"—which was nothing more than a piece of the action for everybody connected with a particular project. Many of the men assigned to Detachment 101 in 1944 were horrified to learn that OSS was in the business of trading in opium. In fact, many of the X-2 staff of the intelligence agency, if they had known, would have deplored such a questionable practice—many had worked in the United States and overseas for the Federal Bureau of Narcotics, which was responsible for stamping out drug trafficking. The Japanese in Burma had issued paper currency which was of little value to the tribesmen up-country, who always traded in opium or other items of value, traditionally using silver coins or ingots as money. The men in the original Detachment 101 group had learned from the British that they would do well to go into the hill country armed with silver coins and opium; the narcotic was prized as a palliative by the tribesmen, who suffered from a complex of maladies.

Simply stated, paper currency and even silver were often useless, as there was nothing to buy with money; opium, however, was the form of payment which everybody used. Not to use it as a means of barter would spell an end to our operations. Opium was available to agents who used it for any number of reasons, ranging from obtaining information to buying their own escape. Any indignation felt was removed by the difficulty of the effort ahead. If opium could be useful in achieving victory, the pattern was clear. We would use opium.[2]

Without the free-wheeling operations of OSS Detachment 101, it is doubtful whether the Allies could have cleared northern Burma of the Japanese and curtailed enemy operations in this strategic area. A Presidential Distinguished Unit Citation covering the period May–June 1945 related that "Under the most hazardous jungle conditions, Americans of Detachment 101, Office of Strategic Services, displayed extraordinary heroism in leading their coordinated battalions of natives to complete victory against an overwhelming superior force; . . . they met and routed 10,000 Japanese throughout an area of 10,000 square miles, killed 1,247 while sustaining losses of 37, demolished or captured 4 large dumps, destroyed enemy motor transport, and inflicted extensive damage to communications and facilities." All told, the 566 Americans and their nearly 10,000 Kachin guerrillas and agents had accounted for 5,447 enemy confirmed killed and an estimated 10,000 killed and wounded. Losses were 18 Americans and 184 Kachins and Burmese killed.

While the operations of Detachment 101 were well under way in mid-1943, OSS emphasis was directed against a new target in Southeast Asia—Siam. The Japanese had entered Siam without trouble. The Siamese leaders, who had taken control of the country in a coup in 1932, believed that they could accommodate to the Japanese presence and political demands. Tokyo proposed an Asian "co-prosperity sphere" to the western colonial areas of the Far East, substituting Nippon's hegemony for that of Britain, France, and the Netherlands. The establishment of a constitutional monarchy headed by former army major Luang Pibul Songgram, who became the pro-Axis Prime Minister and virtual dictator of the country, led to treaties of friendship and nonaggression with the United Kingdom in 1940 and Japan the following year. Siam's weakness prevented any independent policy and forced the country to cultivate the goodwill of both Britain and Japan, although in London the Foreign Office looked upon Siam as falling within the British sphere of influence. While Japan geared for war, in 1941 Siam's policy was neutrality and independence, though its businessmen—in league with the regime—were glad to conduct extensive business with the Japanese.[3]

Japanese military leaders, in planning the conquest of Southeast Asia, considered Siam a bonus; few occupation troops would be required to maintain order in a "friendly" country. However, there was opposition to the Japanese in Siam, and it surfaced in Washington two days after the attack against Pearl Harbor. The Siamese minister, instructed by his government, delivered a declaration of war to the State Department which was deliberately ignored. There were global political problems more important than the one posed by this backwater Asian nation whose diplomatic representative in Washington, it soon was learned, was pro-American. Siamese students in the U.S. formed a Free Thai Army, and COI, without any plan for incorporating these students, enlisted their services and began training them as agents. Meantime, SI and R&A had picked up a number of academics and missionaries with experience in Siam, including Major Nicol Smith and Lucy Starling in 1942. Smith, a lieutenant when he joined COI, had traveled extensively in the area and had written a book, *Burma Road,* while Miss Starling had served as a missionary. Smith had spent some time in Vichy France before the Allied invasion of North Africa, during which time he had surveyed southern France as a future intelligence target. In early 1943 two Thai businessmen arrived in Kunming, China, where they contacted U.S. Government officials who, in turn, introduced them to the OSS mission.[4]

Within days the coded cables began to fly thick and fast between Washington and Kunming. Siam was a big blank in the intelligence picture, and this was the first hard information about the situation in that country. Moreover, OSS learned that Siam was ripe for a secret mission by SI, whose agents would receive support and protection of high-ranking Thais in the Siamese government. Even Lieutenant Smith was surprised when he was offered an opportunity to return to Asia—and possibly to Siam—which had been designated an OSS target.

The entire thrust of the mission to Siam was transferred to Detachment 404. It had been set up in Kandy, Ceylon, by Colonel Coughlin in 1944 to direct all OSS operations in Southeast Asia. A secret training camp for Thai agents had also been set up in the remote hill country fifteen miles away from the OSS headquarters in Ceylon. It took nearly six months for the original group of OSS agents, recruited from among Thai students in the U.S., finally to return to their own country. Three of the five agents made it; two were killed on the long trek out of China.

An anti-Japanese underground, whose only weapon was passive resistance, had sprung up in Siam and numbered among its members senior police, army, navy, and government officials. One of the Thai agents enlisted the Regent, Luang Pradit, in the OSS venture, and he was given the code name "Ruth." The Thai agents, two of whom reported personally to General Donovan in Washington some weeks later, were supported with a major SI operation programmed around the Siam government's own intelligence organization, the military services, and even the police. Major Richard S. Greenlee, recruited from Donovan's law firm, and Major John Wester, a long-time Asian hand, were selected in Washington for the Bangkok Project. In December 1944 they were flown to the Gulf of Siam in a Catalina flying boat, from which they transferred to a Thai Coast Guard launch for the rest of the journey.[5]

Once in Bangkok, Greenlee and Wester met with Siamese officials, including agent "Ruth," the Regent, and were handed a package of intelligence documents that pinpointed the location of all Japanese forces inside the country. The information was so important that Greenlee radioed OSS headquarters in Kandy for permission to return with the package of priority intelligence; Wester would stay in Bangkok and man the radio. A Catalina flying boat pick-up in the Gulf was made five days after his arrival, and Greenlee immediately flew on to Washington, where he personally reported to his former civilian boss in Q Building at the 25th and E Streets complex. Greenlee returned to Bangkok

in April 1945, bringing with him another agent, Captain
Howard Smith, born in the village of Nan in northeast Siam
of missionary parents.

Major Wester's months of nearly solitary confinement
in Bangkok—even the most fleeting public appearance of a
white man would have been noticed by the Japanese—
caused a physical and mental breakdown. Siamese officials
working with OSS blamed themselves for his isolation. With
exquisite logic they decided the problem was Wester's lack
of female companionship—secret agents do not live by intelligence work alone—and in an effort to make amends and
prevent a similar problem in the future, the Thai officials
set up a new headquarters for the OSS mission: a well-
guarded house, somewhat luxuriously appointed, staffed with
eight young ladies who were to be more than mere secretaries
to the Americans.[6]

The extremely high level of intelligence data that came
out of Siam enabled OSS R&A to develop perhaps the most
accurate and complete profile of any target nation in which
operations would be launched. By early 1945 the intelligence
files on Siam covered all aspects of political, military, economic, and social affairs. In an estimate of the success of
Japanese aims in Siam, an OSS R&A analysis reported:

> The Japanese have succeeded in making Thailand a
> base for military operations in Burma and for carry-
> ing supplies to Malaya. As her shipping is driven from
> the seas Japan is more and more dependent upon Thai
> railroads to carry materiel and troops from Indochina to
> ports along the Indian Ocean. So dependent is Japan upon
> this overland route that she built two additional lines, one
> across the Kra Isthmus and one across the mountains to
> Burma, connecting Bangkok with Moulmein. Thai ports,
> rivers, and highways are likewise used by the Japanese
> military. They find Thai airfields especially valuable as
> bases for servicing and regrouping aircraft used in
> Burma. In addition the Japanese have drawn large
> supplies of food and some materiel from Thailand for
> their garrisons and their troops in the field.
> On the other hand, the Japanese have received
> practically no support from the Thai navy and air force
> and very little from the army. Thai troops have under-

taken to defend the Kengtung border against the Chinese, but they have not done so in the spirit or with the intention of fighting Japan's war.

In fact the Thai army has reacted so coolly to Japanese overtures and aims, and has shown such indifference to sabotage directed toward Japanese communications and installations that the Japanese had to take over control of Thai railways, and request the right to increase their garrison troops from ten thousand to fifty thousand. Of late Japan has decreased the equipment furnished the Thai army and has increased her suggestions that Thailand prosecute the GEA war more vigorously. The Japanese evidently fear that the unresponsiveness of the Thai military will in time develop into open hostility directed against them. If that time comes Japan will be faced with the alternative of relinquishing Thailand without a struggle, thus giving up a base of great strategic importance, or of fighting the Thai and by so doing lose yet more goodwill on the continent of Asia.

In spite of the protests and even the resignations of a few cabinet members, the Pibul Songgram government acquiesced in Japan's demands for entry into Thailand and signed the Offensive-Defensive Alliance Japan presented. Thereafter it adopted a pro-Axis policy in the belief that Japan's power in Asia was supreme and would be likely to continue so, and that it was to Thailand's best interests to collaborate. But the Thai government never gave Japan the full cooperation she desired; although it yielded to Japan on foreign affairs it contrived to retain control of Thailand's internal administration. The high point of Thai collaboration was probably reached in November 1943 after the transfer of Shan and Malay (Burmese) territory to Thailand, and after the impressive Greater East Asian (GEA) Conference in Tokyo which secured the adoption of the Joint Resolution signed by the puppet governments of Asia.

But privately the majority of the Thai people, including the officials, remained anti-Japanese and totally unreconciled to the invasion of their land. Japan's successive naval defeats and the fall of Mussolini shook the confidence of the Thai government as well as of the people in the wisdom of a pro-Japan policy. Pibul Songgram became increasingly unpopular because of his appeals for closer collaboration with Japan and because of his totalitarian rule. On 22 July 1944, following the fall of the Tojo cabinet in Japan, the Thai National Assembly overthrew the Pibul government by an adverse vote on a domestic issue. On 29 July the Assembly replaced Premier Pibul with strongly anti-Japanese Kuang Aphaiwong, who thereupon formed a cabinet of officials who shared his political views. At the same time vacillating Prince Adityn resigned from the Council of Regency of which he was head. This left able Pridi Phanomyong (Luang Pradit Manudharm) the sole regent and power behind the cabinet. He had resigned from the Pibul cabinet in December 1941 rather than approve the alliance with Japan, and he had steadfastly refused to collaborate with the Japanese by accepting a political post thereafter. The Assembly representatives effected this change in government by constitutional means and they acted within their treaty rights; nevertheless they exhibited unexpected boldness in overthrowing the militaristic, Japanese-sponsored Pibul regime and setting up in its stead a civilian, democratic, liberal government made up of officials of known anti-Japanese sympathies.

Because the Japanese dominate Thailand militarily the new Thai government must observe existing treaties and meet most of Japan's demands, lest the Japanese take over the administration of Thai civil affairs. The Japanese wish to avoid this contingency, not only because they are hard-pressed elsewhere and short of administrators, but also because they do not want a break with the only non-puppet government in Eastern Asia. So they tolerate the change of government although it constitutes a political defeat for Japan; they know that the Thai people through their representatives replaced officials who collaborated with Japan from policy with those who collaborate from necessity. Japan has attained her political goals in Thailand, but her political controls will last only so long as her imperial troops can dominate the Thai army.[7]

Additional Americans were brought into Siam to organize resistance operations in the northern part of the country along with a British SOE unit deployed as a gesture by the Foreign Office more to show the Union Jack than anything else. The OSS, which had learned well from SOE and SIS, was in full command of the situation in Siam right up to V-J Day on August 15, 1945.

This wartime collaboration between senior officials of the Siamese Government and the United States contributed to the increased postwar role of the United States in Southeast Asia. Nor did the American role in that part of the world stop in Siam and Burma. Toward war's end in 1945, OSS teams were fighting in China with guerrillas and in Indochina assisting a wispy figure of a man known as Ho Chi Minh. Indochina, a French colony first staked out in the middle of the last century, had come under Japanese rule on July 2, 1941, at a high-level conference in Tokyo. France had fallen the previous year and the Vichy regime was at the mercy of the Axis powers and soon-to-join member of the club, Imperial Japan, which had its own imperial designs for all Asia. Demands were made by Japan for military control of all of Indochina: Laos; Cambodia; and along the western reaches of the South China Sea, the Vietnamese areas of Hanoi and Tonkin China in the north; Annam and the ancient Vietnamese royal capital of Hue in the center; and Cochin China in the south, encompassing the area around Saigon and the Mekong Delta. Later in July Japanese warships and transports landed first-line troops, who were garrisoned in the central and southern provinces, with a huge troop and naval build-up at the French naval base at Cam Ranh Bay some eight hundred miles equidistant from Manila, Hong Kong, and Singapore. A total of 125,000 Japanese military personnel were landed, contrary to the July 2 agreement with Vichy that only 40,000 troops would be stationed in Indochina. The Indochinese colonial administration suddenly found itself bereft of all authority by the Japanese, and all French military forces were disbanded with the exception of a few units to be used as colonial police. The costs of occupation were paid from the Bank of Indochina which, under French control, had virtually owned the entire colony. As a crowning blow, the Japanese declared that all export trade henceforth would be conducted exclusively with Japan, and larger tracts of cotton and rubber-producing lands were requisitioned. Except in name, Indochina had become Japanese territory.[8]

Indochina in 1942 was an enigma to American planners. Few Americans could even locate the colony on the map, and it was left to R&A to produce a profile of the area and an estimate of its future importance to U.S. military operations. In Chungking, China, in late 1943 Nicol Smith, now a major, met a Vietnamese woman he later described as a beautiful Annamese. The occasion was a dinner party for visiting OSS Commander Halliwell (actually Colonel Paul Helliwell who later was OSS chief of intelligence in China) and China's intelligence chief, General Tai Li. She was introduced as Madame Robert Meynier, the wife of a French intelligence officer, and the daughter of a "priestess princess," whose uncles were reputedly both wealthy and politically powerful in Indochina. She reportedly had been rescued from an internment camp in France by commandos who lost three English and seven Frenchmen in the raid. As it turned out, however, the OSS teams sent to Indochina during the final months of the war preferred to support the guerrillas commanded by Ho Chi Minh rather than the pro-French political factions represented by Madame Meynier and her family.

On March 9, 1945 the Japanese, impelled by mounting distrust of the French administration and by rapid Allied advances in Burma and the Philippines, seized full control in Indochina. Anxious to prevent a complete administrative breakdown in the colony, the Japanese military headquarters began to encourage all French officials and technical workers in the government and in private companies to remain at their posts "to work under the same conditions as before." And to strengthen their position, the Japanese launched an intensive effort to promote a rift between French and native resistance elements, and to enlist the support of the Indochinese peoples with promises of "independence" as soon as conditions permit.

During the final year of the war Japan discovered that Indochina had become of vital strategic importance in the defense of her conquests on the Asian mainland. Japanese military control in Indochina, besides facilitating military operations in China, protected important escape routes for more than 600,000 Japanese troops stationed in the Netherlands East Indies and continental Southeast Asia. Japanese intelligence also had learned that the French Governor General, Admiral Jean Decoux, had been in contact with General DeGaulle's government, now back in Paris, and with the Allies. Moreover, the Japanese went so far as to accuse the French forces in Indochina of failing to fire on American military aircraft, harboring American airmen shot down over Indochina, and assisting Allied submarines in their raids on Japanese shipping along the coast of Indochina.[9]

By the end of March the situation had come to a head, and the French armed forces of forty to fifty thousand troops —two-thirds of them native—concentrated in the northern provinces of Tonkin, tangled with the Japanese. The native troops, who had been used for police duties, remained loyal to the French during this critical period rather than side with the Japanese who had promised eventual independence to the occupied western colonies. As elsewhere, when Japan first occupied Indochina the natives were told that their new masters were "now able to extend wholehearted cooperation to the people . . . who have been groaning . . . under foreign oppression." At first, the majority of Indochinese responded to Japan's Greater East Asia slogans and promises of cheap goods and considerate treatment. They quickly became alienated by the brutal treatment they received and the deterioration of their economy under Japanese exploitation.

When Japan finally moved on March 9 to crush any resistance in Indochina, it was the signal for OSS to make its move. Indochina came under the control of OSS China, headed up at the time by Colonel Richard Heppner. In 1945 a large number of former "Jeds" had been assigned to China, and the operation in North Asia was, according to those who had been associated with it, "a free-wheeling organization, especially in such out-of-the-way places as Southwestern China."[10]

The official OSS record of operations in Indochina during the closing months of World War II, if it presently exists, is in the hands of the successor Central Intelligence Agency. Because of the lengthy and controversial American involvement in postwar Indochina, these files have been sealed from all but those men closest to the White House. However, rumor abounds and what is fact and what is fiction about the OSS role in Indochina for years has been difficult to ascertain.

One question that goes back to World War II and the administration of President Franklin D. Roosevelt is the official American policy toward European colonies in Asia during this period. Secretary of State Cordell Hull wrote in his memoirs that on October 13, 1944, OSS proposed to FDR that resistance groups in Indochina be given every assistance. The President told Hull that "we should do nothing in regard to resistance groups . . . in relation to Indochina. You might bring it up to me a little later when things are a little clearer."[11] Six months later Roosevelt was dead, and many people who were familiar with the situation in China and Southeast Asia know that during those six months OSS personnel had been in steady contact with Ho Chi Minh. Reportedly Ho made four secret visits to OSS headquarters in Kunming in late 1944 and early 1945. Colonel Paul Helliwell, chief of OSS SI operations in China, later confirmed "several contacts" his section had made with Ho during the winter of 1944–45.

Among the Vietnamese agents trained by OSS was American-educated Dr. Phan Quang Dan; even Ho's best guerrilla leader, Vo Nguyen Giap, was in regular contact with OSS people attached to the underground leader's headquarters.[12] In exchange for "services rendered"—intelligence information and the cooperation of Ho's small guerrilla forces—the underground leader welcomed several OSS teams who parachuted into his camps to work with the guerrillas and rescue downed American airmen. Several months before the Japanese surrender there were five OSS teams operating north of the Sixteenth Parallel and in close cooperation with Ho and Giap, including Captain Lucien Conein, who led a daring raid against a Japanese divisional headquarters at Lang Son on the China border.[13] With a strong assist from OSS, the small guerrilla bases around the Tonkin villages of Cao Bang, Bac Kan, and Lang Son in early 1945 became bases for hit-and-run guerrilla operations against the Japanese. Heretofore, they had been bases from which agents went into the field to collect intelligence about Japanese movements and intentions. But on December 22, 1944, Giap formerly created the first platoon of guerrilla fighters of what later would become the nationalist Viet Minh army. This initial guerrilla unit of thirty-four men was called the Vietnam Propaganda and Liberation Unit, and for the first time the term "liberation" had come into play in colonial Southeast Asia.[14] Actually, the aim was "liberation" from France as well as from Japan.

Meantime, the British also had been active, and SOE Force 136 was parachuted into Indochina along with a number of Frenchmen to assist the men on His Majesty's service behind enemy lines. By the time the war ended, the majority of American OSS people in Indochina were on the side of the underdog—Ho Chi Minh and his Viet Minh nationalists. For one thing, the Americans had been working closely with Ho's people and there was a mutual admiration. Also, one young lieutenant, a radio operator, had spent quite a bit of time with Ho and recalled some time later how he replied to the Vietnamese nationalist's questions about the Declaration of Independence and the Constitution. Ho was in the process of composing for his area of about-to-be-liberated Indochina a Declaration of Independence from France which, when completed, resembled in terminology the one preserved in Washington, D.C.

Immediately after the Japanese surrender, Ho requested that OSS transmit a message for him to the United Nations then meeting in San Francisco:

> National Liberation Committee of VML (Vietnam League) begs U.S. authorities to inform United Nations the following. We were fighting Japs on the side of the United Nations. Now Japs surrendered. We beg United Nations to realize their solemn promise that all nationalities will be given democracy and independence. If United Nations forget their solemn promise & don't grant Indochina full independence, we will keep fighting until we get it.

Ho's message radioed by OSS was signed "Liberation Committee of VML."[15]

However, shortly before the Japanese surrender, Pierre Messmer, General DeGaulle's personal representative, parachuted into the Tonkin region of Indochina and was arrested and imprisoned by Ho's guerrillas. One of the OSS detachments operating with the guerrillas refused to intervene despite Messmer's pleas, and the incident did not go far toward smoothing Franco-American relations.[16]

A week after the Japanese surrender, Major Archimedes L. Patti and a small OSS team were parachuted into the Tonkin area to supervise the evacuation of a number of downed American airmen. With Patti was another representative of the French government, who had a frustrating experience just trying to obtain air transportation out of China. American military officials had deliberately held up Major Jean Sainteny from his official visit to Hanoi. After several days he had a Free French bomber placed at his disposal, and took Major Patti's OSS team with him, expecting that his American friends might be of some assistance because of the close association France's strongest ally had with the Indochinese guerrillas. Sainteny, two years earlier, had established contact with Ho, and they had exchanged letters about the postwar relationship of the Indochinese peoples with Paris. But Sainteny also found himself engulfed in problems with the Indochinese, and the difficulties that he encountered were not made easier by Major Patti's outright refusal to use his good offices to assist the French officer.* In fact, the American OSS teams made no secret of where their sympathies were directed in any showdown between the Indochinese and the French.[17]

The stand taken by OSS in Indochina was further exacerbated by Colonel Helliwell, who later declared that the French were more concerned with "keeping the United States out of Indochina than they were about defeating Japan."[18] A few weeks after V-J Day, Major General Phillip E. Gallagher visited Hanoi from China and politically and publicly insinuated himself on the side of the Indochinese. Gallagher, according to the French version of events during that bitter period, went so far as to propose to Ho Chi Minh that General Donovan's very powerful economic interests would help reconstruct Indochinese railroads, roads, and airfields in exchange for economic privileges. Ho is said to have rejected this offer.[19] The American correspondents who began to arrive in Indochina after V-J Day also took the side of the Indochinese.

But in Paris there were powerful forces girding to resume control over the colony. Indochina and all of its wealth tapped and untapped was owned by the major French banks,

---

*Major Sainteny had worked closely with OSS in France and was at a loss to understand the attitude of the men he met in Indochina and in China toward him personally.

and these powerful institutions were not about to permit the loss of this valuable colony; there were troops in France awaiting transportation and sailing orders. Nor did France recognize the winds of nationalism that were blowing like a typhoon through the undeveloped areas of the world. These two opposing ideologies were bound to clash, and they did. The United States was as naively drawn into the controversy between the French and Indochinese as America later would be drawn into the Vietnam conflict of the sixties and early seventies. Sainteny described the attitude of the OSS Americans in Indochina in 1945 as "infantile anticolonialism which blinded almost all of them."[20]

There also was anti-French sentiment in sleepy, mountainous, and sparsely populated Laos. In March 1945 Oun Sananikone, elder son of the wealthy and politically powerful Sananikone family, had secretly made contact in Bangkok with OSS agents. He asked for OSS agents and arms to be parachuted into Laos. However, nothing came of this request.[21] It wasn't until a month after the Japanese surrender that a ten-man OSS mission arrived in the Laotian capital of Vientiane and curtly ordered the handful of French colonial administrators to get out of the city and halt their interference with the nationalist Lao Issara political party. The OSS team obviously came from the same anti-French pro–Ho Chi Minh group that had raised the hackles of French representatives Messmer and Sainteny only a matter of weeks earlier.

Another indication of the touchy nationalism in Laos occurred when OSS Bangkok dispatched Major Jim Thompson to Vientiane, where he originally was to parachute if the war had not ended when it did; there he was introduced to other Lao Issara nationalists. The nationalists were raiding the French from Siamese territory across the Mekong River from Vientiane; in order to complete his field inspection of the political situation, Thompson crossed back into Siam where he met anti-French Prince Souphanouvong of Laos. The Prince asked for official United States intervention and support for the removal of the French from Laos. This meeting in the home of the Thai governor of Nong Khai, across the river from the capital of Laos, became the first in a long series of conferences with OSS and with American diplomatic representatives after the intelligence organization left the area. It also was cause for strained relations between Paris and Washington, with the French Government expressing strong suspicion of United States political aims in Indochina.[22]

By the end of 1945 all of the OSS teams and other American military personnel had been withdrawn from Indochina, but, according to one report, not without incident.

Colonel A. Peter Dewey, the ranking OSS officer in Indochina, was killed in September 1945—ambushed by Indochinese under questionable circumstances. This turned out to be one of the first incidents of nationalist rebellion by the anti-French elements, who may have mistaken the OSS commander for a French officer. He became the highest-ranking OSS officer to die violently and the first American postwar casualty in what later became South Vietnam.[23] It appeared that few if any Americans really understood Asia or orientals, and despite the tremendous R&A back-up in Washington, the OSS people in the field were unable to grasp the winds of change and the political situation in their respective AOs.

An earlier tragic incident occurred on August 25, 1945— ten days after the Japanese had officially surrendered— when a four-man OSS team in Central China commanded by Captain John Birch tangled with a Communist patrol. Birch, son of missionaries who had worked in China, spoke the language fluently; as an Air Force intelligence officer, he had served on a number of sensitive assignments until he was transferred to OSS in early 1945. According to Amos Melton, who worked with Birch as an Army Air Force counterintelligence officer, the OSS captain led a small team of three men to enter a Japanese headquarters and seize maps of an airfield and other installations. As they approached the headquarters they were ordered to halt by a patrol of Chinese Communist troops which outnumbered the OSS team. What happened is described best by two of the Americans who accompanied Birch on his final mission for OSS.

Joseph Sample related how the Chinese were "understandably disturbed by what seemed to them to be an unwarranted intrusion of their area and demanded an explanation." Birch's ability to speak Chinese fluently resulted in harsh words after the OSS officer tried to bluff his way out of what Sample called a "difficult situation."

Unfortunately for Birch, and later U.S. foreign policy, a full-scale civil war was brewing in China, awaiting only the defeat of the Japanese before the Nationalist armies of Chiang Kai-shek and the Communist route armies of Mao Tse-tung squared off for an all-out war for survival and political control of all China. "The mission should have been routine," added Sample in April 1961, when the true story of the death of John Birch finally surfaced. "Some of these Chinese Communists probably had never seen an American before and Captain Birch's bluff ended in harsh words, which led to insults, and insults to arrogance until finally, in a fit of rage, the Chinese Communist leader shot Birch."[24]

Perhaps Captain Birch, despite his long years of residence in China and ability with a difficult language, never really understood the people among whom he had grown up when his parents were missionaries in that far-off land. Added Sample: "Birch was a man with no particularly distinguishing characteristics—a little stiff perhaps, with not a very high regard for the Chinese, and somewhat self-important, but nothing unusual. If he had strong political convictions, they were not in evidence."[25]

The winds of revolution and nationalism and a deep hatred of occidentals no matter what their nationality was all-pervasive throughout Asia at the end of World War II, and especially among deeply indoctrinated Communist revolutionary forces. Birch was nothing more than an object of this hatred and, if he had not been fluent in the language, the intrusion of the OSS patrol might have passed with no more than a warning and forceful request that the three Americans and their Chinese guide and interpreter turn around and return whence they came.

Instead, he was killed, and right-wing elements in the United States turned his death into martyrdom. An anti-Communist ideology based upon a series of myths sprang up about the heroic American soldier, whom the founder of the John Birch Society called "the first casualty in the Third World War between Communists and the ever-shrinking

Free World." William P. Weiss, Jr., the OSS officer who had assigned the mission to the Birch team, declared that Birch was "just as much a hero as any other American soldier who died for his country." But Sample emphasized that there was "no real object lesson in Birch's death and certainly no glory." The other American on the team, Gustav J. Krause, allowed as how Birch brought about his own death "and he didn't die the hero he was supposed to have died."[26]

The irony of the story of the death of this home-grown American "martyr" is that he died ten days after World War II ended. Perhaps this twentieth century irony was best expressed fifty-four years earlier by Rudyard Kipling; that it definitely was not good for Birch's health to tangle verbally with the larger Chinese patrol:

> And the end of the fight is a tombstone
> white with the name of the late deceased,
> And the epitaph drear: "A Fool lies here who
> tried to hustle the East."

20

War, war is still the cry,
War even to the knife!
—LORD BYRON: *Childe Harold,* 1812.

If the Orient was an enigma to OSS personnel assigned
to North or South Asia, there also were gaps in the intelligence picture in Europe, despite the deep penetrations of
American and British spies and those agents hired by the
secret services of each nation. SOE had parachuted into
France 366 French, English, and Canadian agents; 80 died
in landing and 15 were killed in battle. These agents were
supported by an estimated 100,000 French underground
workers, of whom 35,000 were women. The significance
of the underground was not lost on those who were responsible for developing intelligence information for the decision-
makers at CCS.[1]

Not that the underground could produce intelligence
information on demand. In many cases it was difficult for
the underground to provide certain pieces of intelligence,
because, rarely informed of overall Allied strategic plans,
their objectives were narrow. Agents had to be parachuted
into enemy-occupied territory with certain intelligence requirements. Once on the ground, they would contact the
underground which, in turn, would provide the agent with
food and shelter, and assist him in obtaining the information required by CCS. Once the information was obtained,
the agent would be smuggled out of the country with whatever maps or other documents he and the underground
had been able to obtain. An effective escape-and-evasion net
would provide this service.

Americans in the employ of OSS learned more about intelligence operations than the imagination could conceive. Sabotage operations were of great importance, and the most difficult selective targets were taken out as easily as destroying a bridge or warehouse during a nighttime raid. After D-Day in Normandy, the French resistance was assigned two major tasks—to sabotage the German war effort on the one hand, and protect from German destruction such objects and installations which, on the other hand, would be of value to the Allies at a later date. Wherever it could be avoided, facilities that could contribute to French postwar recovery were not to be destroyed, and unnecessary losses of the population had to be kept to a minimum in order to maintain the morale of the resistance.[2]

Blackmail and bribery were used by OSS agents; intelligence operations at times was a dirty business. Finances also played a very important part in resistance and intelligence-gathering operations. Hard currency, such as American dollars or British pounds—and gold in the form of louis d'or or sovereigns—was a regular part of the supply packages delivered to the resistance. Even German occupation marks were delievered to the resistance for use in operations behind enemy lines. Hard currency in World War II was exchanged on the black market for local money or, when necessary, the imported dollars, pounds, Swiss francs, or gold was paid directly for services rendered. One agent in Yugoslavia reported that it was no trouble to use dollars or gold pieces "since there was invariably a market for 'good money' in the towns." In France, the underground was able to exchange dollars for francs by using diplomatic channels. In one case, in April 1943, the underground received $45,000 in U.S. currency. It was turned over to a friendly attaché in the Hungarian legation in Vichy who, in turn, carried the dollars in a diplomatic pouch to Switzerland, exchanged the money into francs at the black-market rate, and brought the money back to France.[3] In fact, the amount of money dispensed by OSS is mind-boggling.

The underground in Poland received, mostly by airdrops, $34,823,163 in American money and gold, 1,775 gold sovereigns, 19,089,500 German marks, 40,569,800 Polish occupation zlotys and 10,000 Spanish pesetas. Of this huge amount of money for intelligence and other resistance operations, $1,763,200 in American money and gold was lost when the aerial resupply aircraft were shot down during a secret mission or the package of money parachuted to the ground did not fall into friendly hands.[4] Of course, some of the "friendly" hands reportedly had sticky fingers—and the money stuck to them, since the money came from unvouchered funds, of which OSS had a virtually unlimited source for the asking.*

In March 1945 a mission to northern Italy by a heavy bomber, from the 2641st Special Group, commanded by Colonel MacCloskey, resulted in the loss of a quarter of a million dollars in gold. It was inadvertently dropped to the wrong partisan group and never recovered.[5] And in one of the most celebrated scandals to come out of OSS operations in World War II, two Americans were charged with killing their team leader for the $16,000 in gold that he allegedly had on his person, and which rumor had raised to as high as $150,000. The ill-fated "Sparrow" Mission's three agents each carried $2,000 in gold coins in their money belts and turned it over to a Hungarian contact in Budapest rather than have the Germans take it from them. After the war the money was returned to an American officer in Hungary.[6]

Political intelligence-gathering was, for many OSS R&A people in the field, a risky business. Not only personal risk, although this was part of any possible "dangerous and haz-

---

*Although unvouchered funds were tightly controlled at the source by those of Donovan's banker friends who managed OSS finances, monies that reached the field had a way of disappearing —some of it reported "lost" during delivery or in an operation. A number of scandals investigated were hushed up, but a good number of foreign agents employed by OSS obtained a solid postwar financial start that catapulted them into successful business careers. Of course, many of these men had signed contracts with OSS, and this information has been used to pressure them into providing the CIA with needed information from time to time. It goes without saying that a few OSS personnel also benefited financially, and some parlayed their nest eggs into successful domestic and international business enterprises, often with some of the underground and resistance people with whom they had worked.

ardous duty" overseas for which they had volunteered, but a risk for those back in Washington who would receive the information from which important strategic decisions would be made. If the information was wrong because of many factors bearing upon the secret agent's likes and dislikes, political and family background, and other factors that would make for unobjective reporting, massive failures could result. And OSS agents had time and again proved themselves wrong in the field or were, because of naiveté, unaware of the real meaning of the events that were occurring constantly all about them. Political reporting in Asia was extremely difficult, less so in North Africa, Europe, and the Balkans. Once agents in the field fell into the trap—as many of them did—of siding with the political hopes and aspirations of the resistance organizations to which they were assigned, in time they lost their own sense of judgment, proportion, and credibility. Political partisanship by many Americans in OSS ultimately took its toll.

Events in Yugoslavia, for example, angered Lieutenant George S. Musulin, who in October 1943 was the third OSS agent to parachute in to Chetnik territory and join General Mihailovic's guerrilla army. He had been preceded by Captain Walter R. Mansfield two months earlier and then by Colonel Albert B. Seitz who parachuted to the Chetniks in September 1943. Musulin vented his anger at what he considered a doublecross of Mihailovic by the United States government and Britain. Actually, the three Americans had become caught up in big-power politics, more as pawns than shakers and movers of events. However, most field agents in OSS would have preferred the latter role; some did attempt to insinuate themselves and their beliefs into local political affairs.

Keeping order in Yugoslavia—a strategic country through which passed the main rail line to Greece and the Mediterranean—was an important goal for the Germans. In addition to the regular German occupation forces and, before Italy's surrender in September 1943, the Italian Army's divisions, there were elite SS troops, Bulgarian and Hungarian military divisions, and the Croat fascist police, the *Ustashi* supported by the Gestapo. The presence of the Chetniks in Croatia forced the enemy to maintain about 200,000 German and satellite troops in the region, and not until the Italian collapse did the Germans consider partisan leader Tito to be a more formidable foe than Mihailovic.

In dealing with these resistance forces, the Germans also tried to exploit the national rivalry between Serbs and Croats. The Croat *Ustashi*, which was violently anti-Serb in sentiment, was given a free hand in raiding Serbian villages. Tito, a Croat, and Mihailovic, a Serb, also were caught up by traditional national rivalries. The Germans offered rewards for the capture of top resistance leaders and placed a price of $50,000 on the heads of the Chetnik and partisan leaders. The Germans also imposed a harsh reprisal program on the population for all subversive activities. A military order declared that for each German soldier killed by the resistance, fifty to two hundred Yugoslavs would die. Terror ran rampant throughout Yugoslavia, and the Wehrmacht supported by the SS, Gestapo, Bulgars, and *Ustashi*, regularly conducted mass arrests and executions. The wartime population in Yugoslavia declined by 10 percent.[7]

As in any clandestine operation, OSS agents learned early on that the enemy's own security police were constantly on the lookout for Allied agents, and on many an occasion German spies had penetrated the resistance. For example, the German *Sicherheitdienst* or SD security police successfully deciphered the code used by Tito's partisan headquarters for internal communications and, therefore, they often were aware of a partisan attack before it took place. The Germans almost captured Tito at Dvar, Bosnia, in June 1944 after one of their spies infiltrated Tito's headquarters in the role of a partisan.

Prime Minister Churchill was originally a strong supporter of Chetnik General Mihailovic, and until the first three Americans joined the royalist unit in 1943, the British liaison officers on the scene carried the day. The change in Britain's attitude toward the Chetniks was due to a field assessment by the SOE group in Yugoslavia. They reported back to Churchill that the growing partisan force, although Communist-oriented, was beginning to move into full gear and had demonstrated its capabilities rather successfully. In short, the partisans were aggressive fighters and the Chetniks were not. Mihailovic's tactics were aimed to keep reprisals at a minimum and the Chetniks carried out most sabotage and hit-and-run attacks in such a way that the local inhabitants would not be blamed. Sabotage of trains was carried out in isolated areas, far from the nearest villages and towns, and explosions on barges on the Danube River always occurred many miles from the craft's home port. Mihailovic also wanted to hold off any general uprising until the Allies invaded the Balkans, a favorite plan of Churchill's; but the only invasion occurred in Greece in late 1944, when British troops were landed to bring about a ceasefire in a civil war between the Communist-led EAM/ELAS and the non-Communist guerrilla organizations.[8]

Yugoslavia's future course was launched in November 1942 when Tito announced the creation of a Council of National Liberation which he said would be a "provisional government," a ploy deliberately taken before the Teheran Conference, where he hoped to present the Allies with a *fait accompli*. At this conference the Allies once and for all discarded any plans to invade the Balkans, but to increase support to the resistance. Churchill's own SOE agents delivered their assessment of the resistance in Yugoslavia with a candid evaluation that the Communist-led partisans were in all paramilitary way far superior to the Chetniks. At that point, the predominant Allied support swung to the partisans, and enabled Tito by late 1944 to field eleven Lenin Brigades which grew into corps and armies by war's end.[9] A part of Captain Mansfield's accurate assessment of the political problem underscored the local situation:

> The difference was not merely ideological. Serb officers charged that Tito had welcomed into his ranks former Croat traitors and *Ustachi* who, the Chetniks charged, were responsible for Yugoslavia's downfall in 1941. Tito, on the other hand, justified his attack on the Chetniks by claiming that they were collaborating with the German occupateurs. (Tito also charged that Mikhailovich cooperated with the Nazis and Fascists.)
>
> Both Tito and Mihailovic were jockeying for Allied support. Allied missions and supplies were parachuted to both guerrilla groups. Now that Britain as well as Russia appeared to be siding with Tito, we Allied representatives with Mikhailovich stood in the middle of a chaotic situation. Mikhailovich, ignoring the British, turned to me in his anger and pleaded for more

American teams to come in and see for themselves what his guerrillas were doing.

I radioed his requests to Cairo but privately felt that the issue must be settled on a much higher plane. I felt it would be a sorry situation if Allied missions on both sides found themselves using Allied equipment to deśtroy each other rather than the Germans. Could there not be some meeting ground, some point of settlement? Our only lever with guerrillas in the field was supplies. I hoped for some geographical settlement under which Tito would stay in Bosnia and to the north, and Mikhailovich in Serbia, his stronghold. Submission of such a plan to Mikhailovich would be a ticklish proposition, however, for the reason that he claimed to be the legal commander of all Yugoslavia, not just Serbia. Furthermore, Tito's forces were now threatening to push into Serbia.[10]

From the time he had parachuted into Yugoslavia to join the Chetniks, Mansfield participated in bridge demolitions and ambushes with Mihailovic's guerrillas as the only means of assessing their fighting capabilities. The following month, upon arrival of Colonel Seitz, they both observed close up the Chetniks' prowess as fighting men. As many of Mihailovic's forces were members of the Yugoslav Royal Army when the Germans invaded in the spring of 1941, they had the professional expertise with weapons—but they possessed few machine guns, mortars or good rifles. Moreover, the Teheran Conference was coming up and with Britain suddenly swinging full support to Tito, and with the aerial resupply to the Chetniks suddenly coming to an end in mid-September, the two Americans decided that they had better split up and head for the coast where they could meet a boat that would take them back to Italy. The U.S. Government would require their report in order to make the proper decisions at the forthcoming November conference between FDR, Churchill, and Stalin. American policy was to support both factions as long as they were fighting the enemy and not each other; but it turned out, two meetings between Tito and Mihailovic failed to solve differences, and the two groups continued fighting each other when they were not battling German forces. Mansfield didn't make it back to home base until February 12, 1944, nearly two and a half months after the conference ended.[11] Colonel Seitz finally reached a partisan headquarters and was flown out the following month.

In a different OSS role, Captain John Blatnik trudged the mountains and valleys of northern Yugoslavia in 1944–45 in a series of adventures, one of which recalled an earlier visit to the land where his parents were born and the village of his ancestry.

In mid-1944 Blatnik arrived in Bari, Italy, and was immediately assigned to an operational group so that the men could get to know each other and begin their training together. The assignment was a tough one and required a team of men who could function smoothly. Their target was the Trieste and Slovenia area along the northern Adriatic coast. The Nazis were up to something and the Allies had to know exactly what was going on. An OSS team was to be parachuted into the area by the dark of the moon. The group would stick close to the large enemy headquarters and report what was going on at all times. It was a ticklish surveillance job. The coded information would have to be radioed back to Bari; but the enemy would be monitoring the airwaves and once mobile Wehrmacht Direction Finding (DF) trucks began picking up a fix and cross-triangulating, there was a good chance that the Allied radio operators and their equipment could be discovered. Capture was an unpleasant thought.

It was shortly thereafter that Blatnik made his first combat jump into enemy-occupied territory. He watched his teammates pile out of the side door of the black-painted C–47 and disappear into the night. Then it was his turn. He stepped toward the cabin door, one hand sliding along his static line (ripcord) attached to the cable running the length of the cabin. Then he was at the doorway. The slipstream coming through the door whipped against his pale features. He patted his breast pocket somewhat unconsciously, and his imagination reassured him that his L-pill was where it belonged in the event he was captured—the small capsule of deadly, swift-acting, but painless poison he could take in the event he faced capture and questioning at the hands of the Gestapo. Blatnik stepped out into the night. He felt the blast of cold air and then the welcome jerk of his opening chute took his mind off other things. Below him he noted that five fires outlining a *T*-signal flickered on the ground. This was his drop zone, and by the time he landed the other nineteen men on this OG combat team were on the ground with their weapons gathered up. The German commander in the area also knew that something was up. Gestapo informers had been busy. While Tito's partisans kicked out the marking fires, Blatnik assembled his men to give them their instructions.

Blatnik had been selected for this particular operation for one reason. He had been through the area as a youngster when his mother had brought him back to Yugoslavia. Working with Tito's partisans, Russian officers, and Winston Churchill's son, Randolph, a British liaison officer, Blatnik was to relay vital information back to OSS headquarters in Bari. His orders were to obtain intelligence. How he got it was of no concern to OSS in Bari. All that operations wanted was enough valid information on which to make cold, hard evaluations to pass on to the Allied Forces Headquarters in Naples so that the Air Force and Army commanders could make decisions accordingly.

The Italian Theater of Operations consisted of the U.S. Fifth Army commanded by General Mark Clark. Also under his command was the British Eighth Army, the famed "Desert Rats" who won a decisive victory over Marshal Rommel at El Alamein. The scales in Italy were precariously balanced— there were just enough Allied troops to keep the Wehrmacht pinned down in the bitter and rugged mountain fighting north of Rome, but any sudden influx of enemy troops could tip the scales in favor of the Nazis. Nor did the Allies have any troops to spare from the western front in France. Therefore, whatever Blatnik's team did in that small sector of northern Yugoslavia was vital and important to the entire Allied war effort. However, these are big-picture details that a lowly behind-the-lines intelligence officer is never told, nor can he even guess. He's just another guy doing his job as best he can.

It was October 1944 when John Blatnik and the team, whose members called themselves "Blatnik's Chetniks," piled out of a C–47 one chilly night. On the ground the first touch of icy winds blowing out of the mountains greeted the Americans. They were in for a rough time ahead. With a huge force of Tito's partisans to do the actual fighting, Blatnik's team went to work. Four-man American demolition teams, escorted by partisans, began blowing up bridges and rail communications in the event that the Wehrmacht might try to reinforce in Italy with troops from the Balkans. Each night partisan headquarters moved to a different location, and Blatnik accompanied the Allied team of Soviet and British officers. The Russians, he couldn't help but note, had provided the partisans with a little something from the USSR. Every one of Tito's troops wore a small red-painted metal star on his cap. They fought with captured weapons as well as British and American weapons and ammunition. Rations were parachuted by American aircraft. So, too, was ammunition. But, Blatnik wryly noted, the Soviets began taking credit for what the Americans and British were providing in the way of fighting equipment.

On one occasion a German division was sent into the area to clean out the partisan force. It was obvious that the enemy had been tipped off about the guerrilla army headquarters, for the Nazi troops battered their way through stiff partisan resistance and headed directly for the secret command post. Artillery fire slammed into the area. Machine guns chattered, and from the craggy razorback ridges the sound of riflefire drew near as the enemy troops tightened the noose and closed in. Enemy aircraft flew overhead, dumping bombs that rocked the hideaway. It was only a matter of time before the headquarters would be overrun. Blatnik nervously cradled his submachine gun in one arm while he thumbed the pages of a code book with another. His radio operator also fidgeted as he continued sending Blatnik's message advising OSS headquarters in Bari of impending trouble.

The fact that one division was in action in the Trieste area was important in itself. The Germans had not previously had any divisions deployed in that sector. Moreover, one division in action meant that another was in the area—in reserve. This was what AFHQ wanted to know. It was obvious that these divisions were from other areas in the Balkans and on their way to Italy—possibly to tip the scales. OSS OG teams in northern Italy also had been committed to action to bottle up the enemy in Yugoslavia.

Finally, it was time to stop sending radio messages and fight. He carefully placed the code book on the radio set, and his operator pulled the pin on a thermite grenade and gently set it on the well-used Top Secret cryptobook. They dashed away, feeling relief when the fire grenade softly exploded and began consuming the code book and eating into the guts of the radio transmitter.

Enemy shells began dropping into the immediate area, and Blatnik and his radio operator hurled themselves flat on the ground. Dirt and rocks dropped on their bodies and hot shrapnel sizzled past and slammed into the rock outcroppings. They finally made their way to a small detachment of partisans and Russian and British officers. This was the headquarters guard, and the partisan officer in charge said there was a small chance of getting out through the mountains if the Allied officers and enlisted men were willing to shoot their way out and then begin a rugged climb up above the timberline and down the other side.

"What about the rest of our men?" Captain Randolph Churchill asked the partisan officer.

The Yugoslav shrugged his shoulders. "They have either been killed or captured or infiltrated their way through enemy lines to safety," he replied. "They will expect us to try the same thing by attacking from the heights in a downhill rush. We will do the opposite and retreat over the mountain."

It was getting dark. The enemy now had outflanked the area, and small outposts were dug in on the heights above. The motley Allied force would have to climb upward and shoot its way through, and then be long gone before daylight. They began moving out shortly after dark. It was miserably cold. The men hadn't eaten all day. Yet, the will to survive kept them going.

By dawn the following day they had passed through enemy outposts and had reached the other side of the mountain. It was a familiar village that Blatnik and the partisans furtively entered, and the officer from Minnesota went directly to a house he had visited twenty-three years earlier. While the partisans set up a guard around the village in the event Germans were nearby, Blatnik knocked on the door of the cottage. An elderly woman, fright etched on her face, cautiously peeked from a small window and recoiled at the sight of a tall, dirty, and bearded man wearing some sort of uniform with a small U.S. flag sewed on one shoulder and a strip of lettering on the other.

"I'm an American," the voice came through the door. "Open up, I am hungry." The voice carried the local dialect. The woman opened the door and the tall man had to stoop a bit to avoid hitting the low lintel. Another elderly woman appeared; John Blatnik was in the home of his two aunts, in the village where his father was born. But he couldn't identify himself to his own kin. There was always the possibility that the Gestapo might find out and take reprisals against his family. It was one of the roughest moments of his OSS service and tore at him inside. However, he was entirely correct in not revealing his identity to his aunts. A Nazi garrison was located six miles away. Moreover, the enemy regularly sent troops into the village.

Later, Blatnik ran across a downed American airman. He spotted a furtive figure pawing bits of food from a farmer's pigsty. The man's bearded features were drawn, but his mud-caked leather jacket and the battered hat shoved back on his head could belong only to an American airman.

Blatnik slowly drew near the airman. "Need any help, buddy?" he softly called out. The American froze and then turned. His jaw dropped, dumbfounded. Blatnik motioned with his shoulder and turned so that the airman could see the American flag. Surprise turned to relief and tears clouded the airman's eyes. He told Blatnik that he was a tailgunner on a B–24 Liberator. His plane had been shot down two months earlier. He and two of his crewmates were hiding in a culvert outside of the village. One of the men, the navigator, had injured his back in the parachute jump to safety. Afraid to make a fire, the two airmen had bundled the injured officer in burlap sacks to keep him warm. The only food they had eaten was what the two ablebodied Americans could scrounge from pigsties or dig up in the fields. They had been about ready to give themselves up to the enemy. At least a Stalag POW camp was better than starving to death.

"We'll get you out," Blatnik told him. He didn't know how. First he had to communicate with Bari. That meant that he would have to get a message through either the partisan courier system or find another OSS team with a working radio. Meanwhile, heavy fighting had broken out in the Trieste sector as the partisan army battled the Germans to a standstill. In one respect it was a one-sided battle: the Nazis outgunned the guerrillas. On the other hand, the partisans had been able to destroy bridges and railroad track and keep roads closed so consistently that the Wehrmacht Balkan command couldn't reinforce troops in Italy for a major offensive that Hitler's generals had planned.

A few days later the rest of Blatnik's team began assembling. None of the Americans had been killed or wounded, but all of these OSS paratroopers had had close calls. Eight of them had shot their way through the tightening enemy noose. Blatnik decided to keep his group on the go; it would be more difficult for the Germans to spot them. As they moved from village to village they began collecting a motley group of American airmen. Wounded men were dumped somewhat unceremoniously into oxcarts, but it couldn't be helped. The OSS team couldn't tarry too long; the Gestapo and *Ustashi* secret police were everywhere.

The mountain trails began to get rougher. Men lifted the oxcarts over rocks to keep from jolting the wounded men. Native drivers refused to travel more than two villages away from home for fear of being stopped by *Ustashi* on the return trip without proper travel papers. Every few miles Blatnik dickered with local villagers for oxcarts and drivers. Slowly, they continued on their journey as other Americans came out of hiding and joined the group. When the trail grew too steep for carts, stretchers were made and the ablebodied carried the wounded. It was a stumbling wagontrain saga of determined men crossing through hostile land, as winter began to move in.

Blatnik kept his eyes open for possible landing fields where planes could come in and haul them out. At one point, he succeeded in getting a message out by courier. It was relayed to OSS headquarters in Bari, where operations officers were following his OG team's progress on a map. When the message finally came in to evacuate the downed airmen and Blatnik's team, the plane was virtually ready and waiting for take-off.

The tall Minnesotan had ordered holes filled in and the

field leveled enough for even a bumpy landing. The aircraft was in sight and waiting for a recognition signal from the ground when one of the men on Blatnik's team came running up. "Captain," he huffed breathlessly, "there's an enemy column heading this way."

There was only one thing to do—move out. The wounded were hurriedly gathered up and once again the weary caravan hit the road. Finally, they reached a safe airstrip. When the OSS team and the airmen were finally flown out, Blatnik had spent three months running from the enemy, occasionally fighting—but successfully accomplishing the basic intelligence mission for which he had been originally sent into enemy-occupied territory.[12]

Whenever SO or OG detachments saw action, they were—by the nature of their brand of warfare—usually on the run, with the enemy a short distance behind. After Major William E. Colby completed a difficult period in France as a "Jed," he was assigned another difficult misson with the Norso group—a special-operations mission to Norway. The Scandinavian country was occupied by several divisions of German troops, and a 1944 intelligence study reported:

> Evacuations of the children and the aged from coastal towns for reasons of military safety have been reported. More significant have been the executions and the taking of hostages. The best-known of these measures was the arrest and deportation to Germany of 1200 Norwegian Army officers by order of the Commander in Chief of German troops in Norway, and the deportation of the Oslo students to Germany. In spite of the fact that the Oslo University controversy had been the concern of the Norwegian Government, the arrest was carried out by the German military and police, with Norwegian units playing a subordinate role. While this action has now been suspended, a recent report states that the Germans have begun to take "free hostages" among the students and teachers at Trondheim College. The German authorities have been enabled to make a verbal defense of their old political line of racial collaboration in Norway, despite these measures, by pointing to the Quisling government as the representative of Norway. Hence in his reply to the Swedish note of protest on the Oslo students, Ribbentrop in-

sisted not only that Germany was acting for her own
military interests as occupant, but also that she was
defending Norway's interests against disloyal subjects,
and that therefore the Swedish government had no right
to speak for Norway. By representing herself as both
military occupant and ally of Norway, Germany has
been enabled to prepare the territory for the stage of
military administration while maintaining her attempts
at collaboration. Hence it has been recently reported that
even the German military authorities in Norway, including the Commander in Chief of the German troops,
Fälkenhorst, has decided to support the Quisling regime
unequivocally as the only possible government for the
crisis; the government, in return, is cooperating with the
Wehrmacht in decentralizing the Norwegian administration in preparation for its use by the local German military commander.[13]

Although the Norso Group, the majority of whom were
either Norwegians or Norwegian-Americans, were aware
of the difficulties faced by citizens living in a country under
military occupation, they were advised that they would see
little city or town life. Their mission was strictly hit-and-run
—to blow up a vital rail line that could be used to carry
German reinforcements to southern Norway, from whence
they could be shipped to Europe to bolster the nearly defeated
German armies on the Continent.

The Norso group, referred to in official reports as the
"Rype" Mission, trained in Scotland on snow-covered slopes
in the foothills of the Grampian Mountains, so that those
who had not been assigned from the Ninety-ninth Mountain
Battalion at Fort Hale, Colorado, could perfect their skiing
techniques. Based at OSS Area P, the name for Dalnaglar
Castle near the town of Blairgowrie, the Norso group was set
up with two British liaison officers, with Major Colby in command, Lieut. Tom Sather as his executive officer, and
Lieutenants Blain Jones and Glenn Farnsworth as section
leaders. They were joined shortly afterwards by Lieutenant
Roger Hall and Colonel Hans Skybo, a Regular Army officer
of Norwegian descent, and Colonel Bolland, a stiff-backed
West Pointer, both of whom would lend the necessary authori-
tative military clout that would be helpful in carrying out the
mission.[14]

And there were the usual political problems that OSS, working through SFHQ, had to iron out as the Norsos began training for "Rype." The British Foreign Office viewed Scandinavia, and especially Norway, as a nation that fell within England's sphere of influence. The Norwegian Army High Command, which had been working hand-in-glove with England's military services ever since the landing of the British expeditionary force in Norway in April 1940, and the subsequent Allied withdrawal from Narvik on June 8–9, was very much opposed to the OSS mission. More so because the Norwegian government-in-exile feared that any appearance of Allied soldiers might touch off an uprising which, as the tragic Warsaw experience the previous August and September had shown, could not be adequately supported.

After a period of training that began in late 1944, the Norso group was ready by mid-March, as World War II in Europe moved into its final weeks. The specifics of the "Rype" Mission had been laid on—a parachute drop on Lake Jaevsø in northernmost Nord-Trøndelag, with a reception party by the resistance instead of a "blind" drop. The British had turned down a request to transport "Rype," and this refusal was to cost the lives of ten Norsos and fifteen AAF airmen in a series of disasters that put only twenty men in the field. The original plan was to fly thirty-three Norsos to Norway in eight B–24 Liberators, each carrying a "package" of men and supplies. Colby briefed his officers, "all capable of independent operation in the field, on skis, for forty days without help, completely self-sufficient." He assigned Hall to command the remaining twenty men, designated Norso II, to await orders to join Norso I.

On March 25, 1945, the Norsos took off from England. Four of the Liberators dropped on target, one flew off course and dropped its "package" into Sweden, and three returned to base at Harrington after navigators were unable to find the DZ. A second try was made seven days later, and all aircraft returned without finding the DZ, except one which crashed in the Orkney Islands when two engines failed, killing six Norsos and seven members of the eight-man aircrew. A week later four Norsos, including Lieutenant Jones, and the eight-man crew of the B–24 were killed when the aircraft slammed into a mountain eight kilometers from the DZ.

Colonel Skybo was furious, commenting to Hall that he had insisted on sending the Norsos in two months earlier. He bitterly disclosed how SFHQ "gave me the runaround about 'political considerations.' I begged them for Norwegian pilots and British planes to fly the sorties, they turned me down cold."[15]

Meantime, Colby and the nineteen men with him, including Lieutenants Farnsworth and Strather, had established contact with London, reporting that their drops also were bad, men and equipment scattered, and much of the supplies lost because the container chutes had not been hooked up by the aircrews. Colonel Skybo told Hall that the fault lay with inexperienced personnel, replacements, and that an investigation was underway. The cause of the tragic flights was due to an oversight by SFHQ Air Operations. Many of the earlier special air-missions crews in England had completed their fifty missions and had returned to the United States for training on the new B–29s, or transfer to bomber squadrons about to be deployed to the Pacific and China for the final push against Japan after Germany surrendered. The replacements were completely inexperienced, and SFHQ had not insisted on a special training program. These green air crews were asked to fly missions during that one time of the year when weather conditions close to the Arctic Circle were at their worst. Also, SFHQ AOs might have insisted, but did not, on having the "Rype" Mission transported by the experienced crews of an AAF Air Transport Group of twin-engine C–47s commanded by a veteran Arctic pilot who supervised a large airlift called the "Norwegian Project" in 1944. That airlift had been launched at the request of the Norwegian government-in-exile to transport police troops, supplies, and a field hospital to Kirkenes from northern Sweden. After the Normandy invasion, Sweden had quietly granted aircraft landing privileges to the Allies.

The project was organized by the U.S. Military attaché to Sweden, Brig. General Alfred A. Kessler, Jr., and was commanded by Colonel Bernt Balchen. Ten C–47s and crews were based at Kallax airfield near Luleå, Sweden and began operations on 12 January 1945. Most of the police and the field hospital were transferred to Kirkenes by 18 January, but the C–47s

remained in operation until 31 July. By that time they
had flown 572 sorties and landed 1,418 men and more
than 1,181 tons of supplies at Bodo, Kautokeino, Kirkenes and Banak. In addition, the C–47s dropped 41.3
tons of supplies to patriot groups.[16]

It appears that SFHQ, OSS, and the Norsos were unaware
of the "Norwegian Project," which also supported some of the
45,000 members of *Milorg,* the Norwegian resistance organization. Since 1940 *Milorg* had been heavily supported by SOE,
which sent in more than four hundred agents by parachute
and boat or secretly overland from Sweden.[17]

Colby's Norsos, assisted by a small *Milorg* group, managed
to destroy the Tangen bridge on the Nordland Railway—
which Colby later described as "the world's smallest bridge"
—in a single raid, and three kilometers of track on another
go-round; the Germans, alerted, sent a number of patrols
into the field to find the elusive OSS operational group.
Traversing extremely rugged terrain heavy with snow, the
Norso I team engaged the enemy in a running gun battle.
In late April Colby decided that he would hole up in a small
village and hold it as a fort from which to waylay the
enemy, who was then in the process of organizing a withdrawal from Norway. There were upwards of 400,000 Germans in Norway toward war's end. These troops might have
prolonged the war a few weeks if they had been able to reinforce the Wehrmacht divisions that were falling apart before
the Allied battering rams on the Eastern and Western fronts.

Colby's advisory about digging in at the village brought
a quick reply from SFHQ: No! Colby was adamant. *He*
was on the ground and *not* the men at SFHQ operations.
"I am here," he radioed back to London. "I know what I
am doing. I know I can do it; the resistance wants me to
do it, and I intend to do it!"

The reply from London: Colby had his orders, and if he
disobeyed he would be subject to strong "disciplinary action
upon your return."* Days later the Wehrmacht decided to
surrender *en masse,* and Hall and the Norso II group finally

---

*Major Colby later received the Silver Star, America's third
highest combat decoration, for "gallantry in action"—despite
his altercation with OSS headquarters in London.

made it to Norway after the Germans had given up. At the end of April 1945 the "Rype" Mission and the Norsos had the "honor" of accepting the surrender of tens of thousands of enemy troops.[18]

21

One can never foresee the consequences of
political negotiations undertaken under the
influence of military eventualities.
—NAPOLEON: *Political Aphorisms*

Until early 1944 SOE, by virtue of its long experience in
clandestine huggermugger, provided much of the behind-the-
lines intelligence to OSS. The British had recruited American
foreign correspondent Virginia Hall in 1940 and, using the
code name "Diane," she operated successfully in the Vichy
area until the invasion of North Africa. She was well known
to OSS agents working the same area as a journalist rather
than as a British agent. Whether or not the OSS attempted
to recruit her during that period is lost to history, but she did
continue her activities on behalf of SOE—and later jointly
with OSS, when in March 1944 she led two American officers
back to France where they made a boat landing on the coast
of Brittany and linked up with the *Maquis*.

Although a marked woman, her physical disability no
problem other than one of identification not in her favor, she
originally had volunteered to parachute back to France for
OSS with "Cuthbert" tucked under an arm. She had been
identified as a spy by the Gestapo during her previous assignment for SOE. However, on this second mission she assisted
in the supply and training of three resistance battalions, and
on occasion accompanied the *Maquis* on hit-and-run raids
against the enemy.*

---

*Virginia Hall is the only woman ever to have been awarded
the Distinguished Service Cross, the nation's second highest
combat decoration. After an active period in France, she was

The British were ever alert to signing up Americans for SOE and SIS, often to the later embarrassment of OSS. One longtime American resident of France was Ernest Floege, born in Chicago in 1898 and a member of the AEF in 1918 who remained in France after World War I. He settled down, married, raised a family, and operated a successful trucking and bus business until the fall of France in 1940. He escaped to England and was immediately snapped up by SOE as a perfect profile for an agent. His fluent English was marred by a typically French accent and, it goes without saying, his French was equally fluent. Trained by SOE, he was parachuted back to his home region on June 13, 1943, as chief of the SACRISTAN "circuit," as the British called their secret missions. Using the code name "Alfred," Floege was soon joined by a radio operator, a young French civil servant whose code-name "Narcisse" was the cover for André Bouchardon.[1]

Although Angers was home for both Floege and Bouchardon, they made their secret headquarters in the village of Mee, about twenty miles away. For six months their intelligence net, or *reseau,* in the jargon of the resistance, functioned admirably, with Bouchardon as radio operator. However, in late December 1943 during a routine police roundup of people in Angers to check identity documents, Floege's son was among those who were detained. He was a member of the *reseau* and a courier for SACRISTAN and on his person were incriminating documents. Under torture he broke down and incriminated the entire net, and confessed that the circuit had received seven arms drops during the past months. Most of the men that young Floege knew were rounded up while an all-points bulletin was issued by the *Sicherheitdienst* to pick up Floege senior and Bouchardon. Forewarned, Floege managed to escape the SD roundup of Allied agents, but Bouchardon, dining in a restaurant and unaware of young Floege's arrest and confession, abruptly had his meal interrupted by the covey of Germans who descended on the restaurant.

As far as he was concerned, the game was up. Bouchardon

---

finally captured by the enemy when Wehrmacht patrols converged and overran the area where she was hiding. She survived prison camp after torture by the Gestapo.

pushed away the tiny table, splattering his dinner and wine across the small dining room, and rushed the SD group. Taken by surprise, they were bowled apart like tenpins as he charged like a fullback through the Germans and made it to the door, when another group of SD police surged into the restaurant. He grappled with two of the SD police, while others drew guns and fired at the struggling SOE radio operator. One bullet lodged in his thorax and two others slammed into his thighs—more flesh wounds than disabling, but enough to bring him down. Blood bubbled from his lips; he coughed more blood, and the SD security police pulled him off the floor and rushed him to a waiting automobile. A dying man, so they reasoned, and if they could get him to Gestapo headquarters before he expired, they might be able to wrangle additional information from him. Perhaps it would be worth the effort.

But the security police had failed to reckon with Bouchardon. Dumped into the back seat with one SD guard, he sat slumped in a corner while blood drooled from his mouth. Occasionally he coughed and moaned; what appeared to be the sound of a dying man lessened the alertness of the enemy security police. They didn't see Bouchardon slowly pull his revolver from beneath his jacket. He didn't stand on ceremony and order them to raise their hands and all that. Bouchardon actually thought he was dying and saw this as his opportunity to take three hated members of the Gestapo with him. He shot the man beside him on the back seat, turned his revolver on the second man beside the driver, and finally shot the driver in the head, all in a matter of moments, as fast as he could pull the trigger. The automobile careened out of control and then came to a crashing stop. For minutes Bouchardon lay there in the wreckage surrounded by three dead men. He tried to move his limbs. Nothing happened. When his strength unexpectedly returned, he crawled from the wreckage, managed to gain his feet, and then slowly limped away from the vehicle. He made his way to a safe house, and within days was contacted by Floege, who had given his radio operator up for lost.

Medical assistance was unavailable. They escaped the SD net and the underground railroad used to exfiltrate downed Allied airmen passed the two key members of the SACRIS-

TAN circuit to Paris where they were able to lose themselves among the occupied city's several million residents. From there, they went on to southern France through the VIC line, an escape route for agents that had been operating for two years. In late February 1944 Bouchardon made it across the Pyrenees, much of the trip by foot, with the bullet still lodged in his chest. Floege was by his side all the way.[2]

Once evacuated, Bouchardon was operated on in England and quickly recovered. He and Floege joined Operation JEDBURGH and returned to France, heading up a new SACRISTAN circuit. They parachuted into Doubs on May 6, one month before D-Day. While in training for the "Jed" operation, Bouchardon was not only recruited into OSS along with his American-born partner, but he also was enlisted into the U.S. Army.*

There were other colorful OSS agents in France before and after D-Day. Women found dark-eyed E. W. Poitras, code-named "Paul," most "irresistible."[3] With SOE agent Emile Minerault, called "Raymond," he turned one of the poorest-managed underground railroads for moving agents through France into one of the most efficient.[4] And there was action aplenty for the fifteen-man OG units, including one that was parachuted onto the forested plateau of Vercors, southwest of the city of Grenoble. This OSS unit jumped on the night of June 28, 1944, along with "Jed" team "Eucalyptus," commanded by British Major Desmond Longe, assisted by his fellow Englishman Captain A. E. Houseman, a bilingual French-American radio operator named A. E. Pecquet, and a Frenchman.[5] It was as ill-fated a mission as the one that followed two and a half months later to Czechoslovakia with a heavy loss of OSS agents.

The operational plan set up by the new joint OSS/SOE

---

*Without the usual red tape of an induction center in the U.S. and the long training that followed, André Bouchardon immediately became a sergeant in the U.S. Army, and shortly thereafter was promoted to staff sergeant. The unusual administrative program that made this possible, sparked by the OSS and very quietly established, had as its ultimate reward a coveted prize—American citizenship. Citizenship was granted automatically during the war to all those foreign nationals who served in the U.S. armed forces.

headquarters (SFHQ), organized two months earlier on May 1, deployed these two non-French-speaking British officers with long SOE experience to work with a very large group of resistance fighters. Heretofore, Long and Houseman had worked behind enemy lines with small resistance forces, and with the assistance of English-speaking members of the underground they had been able to perform admirably. Now, they were presented with a problem—3,200 *Maquis* on the forested plateau towering above Grenoble in the distance. The newly established SFHQ joint-operations center, suffering from the usual management problems associated with any military bureaucracy, had not taken into consideration that French-speaking officers should head up any secret military mission to so large a resistance force. The SFHQ plan for the four weeks following D-Day was to drop as many as possible of the OG, SO, "Jeds," and British Special Air Service (SAS) detachments, similar to the OSS OGs, into France. The operations people at SFHQ were following the military battlefield axiom of shoving into the line as many fighting bodies as possible. But SFHQ neglected to advise its own people on the ground that "Eucalyptus" was on the way. The Allied unit arrived at night unannounced and unexpected, parachuting blind without any reception on the ground.

Once on the ground they couldn't help but stumble into the *Maquis,* now calling themselves FFI under command of EMFFI or *État-major des Forces Francaises de l'Interieur.* The Vercors FFI, commanded by French Army Colonel Huet, had been attacking enemy movement in the area and then falling back to the safety of their *reduit* on the plateau. But a cardinal rule of guerrilla warfare is *not* to hold ground, not even the high ground, but to ambush and run and then harass and run again, slowing the enemy's movements so that he can be fixed on the tactical maps. Once fixed, other more conventional tactics and weaponry by regular military formations can be brought to bear. Colonel Huet was a traditionalist, and holding ground, the high ground of Vercors, was all that was within his military competence and understanding. But the enemy commander had decided that if he could eliminate the resistance forces he had pinpointed on the plateau, he could maintain his lines of communication south to the Mediterranean coast. He had three divisions in the area and an airfield at Valence from which aerial surveillance of the plateau disclosed the *Maquis* encampments scattered under the trees.

At the Vassieux DZ in the sector, the *Maquis* began converting it into an airstrip for C–47 landings of supplies. Instead, on July 14 an airdrop at the Vassieux DZ deposited a thousand containers of guns and ammunition and clothing but none of the heavy weapons that the *Maquis* had asked for: 60mm and 81mm mortars, bazookas and longer-range 50 caliber machine guns. Nor had the air drop gone unnoticed by the enemy. Within minutes after the last parachutes had collapsed over the containers they had set on the ground, Luftwaffe Me–109 fighters roared out of the sky and began low-level strafing passes of the DZ, killing and wounding many of the *Maquis* who had dashed into the clearing to collect the containers. Enemy artillery also zeroed in on the DZ, and then the elements of three Wehrmacht divisions which had been moved up slowly began to close in on the Vercors *reduit*. By July 18 the noose was tight; the *Maquis* had lost many killed and wounded, although they fought well and determinedly from the jagged rocks along the cliff tops of the plateau.[6]

In one ambush, the OSS OG in ten minutes had killed more than a hundred of the enemy. Three days later the enemy surprised the *Maquis* by landing a score of Stork gliders filled with a total of two hundred SS troops smack on the plateau in the middle of a heavy rain that continued without let-up for two days. The heavily armed SS troops opened up a pocket that forced Colonel Huet to shift his forces to meet the new threat, thus weakening his own positions in his effort to hold the high ground. In a final assault on July 23, the enemy troops overran the plateau, taking no prisoners, and burning and torturing. One of "Jed" radio operator Pecquet's female assistants was caught by the enemy and her belly sliced open; she was left to die, as he would later describe it in a still-classified report, with her guts round her neck. How many casualties were suffered by this particular OSS OG detachment is locked up in CIA files, but Pecquet's report that the OG "had a terrible time whilst in the woods, but . . . to leave the Vercors can be considered a more dangerous feat," spells out the end of this mission.[7]

The battlefield for OSS OGs and SO teams in a sense could not compare with the lonely life of the SI agent who penetrated into Germany and, in the guise of a German civilian or a Wehrmacht or Luftwaffe officer, collected vital strategic information or, if he had crossed through the front-lines on a lower-level tactical intelligence operation, constantly faced death from the air attacks and artillery shellings of his own side. There were too few of these operatives working in the "black." Actually, the problem was one of supply. If a hundred secret agents were needed for "black" operations inside the heart of the Third Reich, OSS Personnel Section would be fortunate if it could come up with even twenty-five possibilities. Where does one find a man who is strong enough mentally and physically, and having that special ability and intelligence needed to handle himself in a hostile environment? Who speaks German like a native and even knows Germany—Berlin for example—like the lifelines etched in his features or the scars of the Gestapo carved into his flesh? He would have had to be a German or, as it subsequently turned out in late 1944—he *is* a German.

Both the British and American intelligence officers scoured the POW camps for recruits among the anti-Nazi prisoners. What it meant for OSS was organizing a special section within SI which would have to carefully screen the candidates and then investigate their backgrounds by whatever limited means was available. A procedure was set up in England; later in an isolated area in France on the German border, facilities were built to prepare those anti-Nazi soldiers and civilians to return to their homeland as spies. However in the eyes of the suspicious OSS spymasters, their new German agents were defectors, turncoats and, using the most denigrating of terms, traitors. They could be trusted only up to a point.

During the Battle of the Bulge in December 1944, specially trained German troops, all English-speaking, were parachuted behind American lines, and in a few instances created havoc during attacks on unsuspecting GIs. Wehrmacht intelligence, using the Lehr-Regiment Brandenburg clad in Red Army uniforms, operated tactical and even strategic reconnaissance and fighting patrols behind Russian lines. However, for the Western Allies to deploy numbers of spies in Germany or behind Wehrmacht lines required the skill and preparation of which neither SOE or OSS SI was capable.[8] The concentration, therefore, was on finding individual anti-Nazi POWs, German refugees, or even Americans of German extraction. And with that special instinct with which spies are endowed, they were to be capable of surviving within the hostile enemy environment. Lieutenant Roger Hall related in his memoirs an assignment he was given by Mr. Terry, OSS operations chief in London for the "Jeds."

"Just between you and me, I don't happen to approve of the plan, but it's not for me to decide," Terry explained to Hall. "This is it briefly. Our boys have gotten their hands on seven captured German officers, three lieutenants, three captains, and one major, to be exact. After extensive screening and intensive questioning, it has been ascertained that they are now anti-Nazi, anti-Hitler and pro-us. They will receive special training, then be dropped in ahead of our forces. Their mission will be to infiltrate German units and send back whatever intelligence they can gather."[9]

One such mission to Germany on March 19, 1945, cost the life of OSS agent Platoon Sergeant Frederick J. Brunner. He was scheduled to parachute at 2317 hours from an A–26 medium bomber, which was shot down over Germany. He was carried on the record as "missing in action" until his grave was found in 1946 in Germany. The formerly SECRET and now declassified history of Army Air Force aid to European resistance movements also covers a number of agent drops starting on March 19 by two squadrons flying out of Dijon, France, which "dropped 82 agents, equipped with radios, at key locations in Germany."[10] Brunner, a German-speaking Marine, was one of these agents, but other than this brief tidbit of information about American spy Frederick J. Brunner in Marine Corps casualty records, no record exists other than those OSS SI files in the custody of CIA.

And another Marine, Corporal James S. Sweeney, was killed in action "during the period 29–30 March, 1945, between 2008 hours and 0745 hours at Mannheim, Germany, while attached to the 7th U.S. Army." Corporal Sweeney was participating in a line-crossing operation, escorting agents for penetration through the lines into Germany.[11]

Some OSS agents were more fortunate. They were captured by the Germans—and, for unknown reasons, were *not* executed. Major Ortiz returned to the Haute Savoie region on August 1, 1944, as second in command of "Union II" Mission headed by an Army major but including four fellow Marines, all sergeants: John P. Bodnar, Frederick J. Brunner, Robert E. LaSalle, Jack Risler, and Charles R. Perry. Perry was killed a few days later during operations in the area of Col-des-Saises in the French Alps.

Sixteen days later "Union II" Mission was surrounded by the Gestapo in the tiny village of Centron, south of Lake Geneva, where the OSS team had made its headquarters. The Germans called upon the Americans to surrender or be killed. Ortiz, in command at the time, had to make a decision which went against his grain. If he didn't surrender, he feared for the lives of the villagers—he recalled the destruction of Lidice in Czechoslovakia in 1942 after the assassination of *Gauleiter* Reinhard Heydrich, the Gestapo overlord of the country. Also, there was the more recent mass execution of seven hundred inhabitants of the French village of Oradour-sur-Vayres in retaliation for the killing of a German officer which was all too well known to Ortiz.[12]

> Ortiz surrendered because he believed that if he and his men shot their way out of the entrapment, local villagers would undoubtedly suffer reprisals for German deaths which a fire fight surely would have produced. Brunner, however, managed to escape the trap, swam a swiftly flowing river to the other side of the village, and travelled across 15 miles of enemy-held territory to reach the relative safety of another resistance group.
>
> Upon their capture, Ortiz and the others passed through a series of German POW camps before they finally arrived at Marlag-Milag Nord. This was a group of POW camps for Allied naval and merchant marine personnel in Westertimke (Tarmstadt Oest), which was located in a flat, sandy plain between the Weser and Elbe Rivers, 16 miles northeast of Bremen.[13]*

---

*Ibid., p. 747. Ortiz received the Navy Cross for the original "Union" Mission in early 1944 and in lieu of a second Navy

Brunner's successful escape was followed by active participation with the French *Maquis* in the liberation of Albertville for which he was later posthumously awarded the *Croix de Guerre* with Silver Star by the French Government.[14]

On August 21, five days after Ortiz and most of "Union II" Mission were captured, Second Lieutenant Walter W. Taylor was taken captive in a shoot-out. He was the last of four Marines captured in Europe, all of whom would survive the war upon liberation in April 1945. Taylor had been assigned to the OSS intelligence team attached to the 36th Infantry Division which landed with the U.S. Seventh Army in the invasion of Southern France at Cannes-Nice on August 15. As a line-crosser, Taylor and his section chief and a Marine sergeant attached to the team, sneaked behind enemy lines in an effort to learn whether the Wehrmacht would stand and fight or retreat. Along with an agent recruited from the local *Maquis*, Taylor headed for his target—the town of Grasse, fifteen miles inland and west of Nice.

> I was to stay behind with the agent and the Citroen (a car the two had "liberated"), accomplish the mission of taking him in and waiting and then taking him out; and then we were to get to the 36th as fast as we could. The agent had been leading the Resistance fight against the Germans ever since the landing and was absolutely exhausted, falling asleep time and time again while we were briefing him . . . At dawn the next morning, the agent and I headed for the town of St. Cezaire, which was declared to be in the hands of the Resistance and where I was to let the agent down and wait for his return from Grasse. However, during the night, due to Allied pressure on Draguignan and Fayence, what evidently was a

---

Cross for "Union II" he was awarded a Gold Star, for which the citation reads in part: "When he and his team were attacked and surrounded during a special mission designed to immobilize enemy reinforcements stationed in that area, he disregarded the possibility of escape and, in an effort to spare villagers severe reprisals by the Gestapo, surrendered to this sadistic *Geheime Staats Polizei*." The French Government also made Ortiz a Chevalier of the Legion d'Honneur and awarded him the *croix de guerre* with palm. He was honored by Great Britain, which conferred on him Officer of the Most Excellent Order of the British Empire.

company of Germans had taken up positions in St. Cezaire. On approaching the dead-still town by the steep and winding road, we ran into a roadblock of land mines; we both thought it was Resistance, and the agent took my carbine and jumped out of the car to walk toward the line of mines. He lasted just about 10 feet beyond the car and died with a bullet through his head. I still thought it was the trigger-happy Resistance but started to get out of there . . . even faster when I finally saw a German forage cap behind some bushes above the road. But the car jammed against the outer coping, and a German jumped down on the road in front of me and threw a grenade under the car. I tried to get out of the right door and luckily did not, because I would have been completely exposed to the rifle fire from the high cliff on that side above the car. The grenade exploded and I was splashed unconscious on the road.* When I came to, I was surrounded.[15]

During the ride to Grasse for interrogation, Allied aircraft continuously strafed the vehicle in which Taylor was traveling as a POW. During the excitement of the attacks by friendly aircraft, the OSS Marine managed to stuff an incriminating document behind the seat cushion of the vehicle. Although

---

*In a letter written to the Historical Branch at Marine Corps Headquarters on May 31, 1966, Taylor related how the hand grenade had shredded his left thumb and that some twelve fragments had struck his left leg "6 of which at last count remain." He also wrote that for some years he felt guilt for the death of the French agent who was killed, adding:

"It might be interesting to note that when I have thought about the incident of my capture I have always pictured us as coming down a long hill and seeing, across a wooded stream valley, the site of the road-block with men in uniform scurrying about and climbing the cliff-embankment. I have always blamed myself for thinking them to be Resistance and not recognizing them as Germans . . . and thus causing our trouble and the death of the agent. However, after years of trying, in 1963 I returned to the scene and found that the reality was quite different from my image, that the road did not go down the opposite side of the valley, that there were no trees, that the actual site of the road-block is completely invisible from any part of the road until one is within about 20 yards, in other words that I could not possibly have seen men . . . scurrying or been aware of the block."

suffering from painful grenade wounds, he was subjected to intensive interrogation which ended when he vomited on the uniform of his inquisitor. The next 20 days were spent traveling to Italy, and stopping at six different German and Italian hospitals for treatment of his wounds. At the end of November he was sent to the same POW camp where Ortiz was confined.

On 9 April 1945, the prisoners at the Westertimke camp were given three hours to move out of camp because of the imminent approach of British forces. The suddenness of this move disrupted the escape plans of Taylor, who had prepared and laid aside false identity cards, maps, compass, civilian clothes, food, and other items necessary for an escape between 15 and 20 April. By the 10th, the Germans had moved the prisoners out and onto the road toward Luebeck, northeast of Hamburg. Taylor, Ortiz and another man planned to leave that night. During the afternoon, however, continuous Allied strafing of the area created such confusion that the three Americans were able to break from the column in which they were marching and make for the nearby woods. . . .

For eight days, the men hid in the woods and moved at night, intent on evading German troops and civilians. The escapees waited to be overrun by British forces and made some attempt to find Allied front lines, whose positions were uncertain and, from the sound of the gunfire they heard, were constantly changing. When they could not make contact with the British, the escaped POWs returned to the vicinity of the camp from which they had been moved. Their food soon gave out and two of the party became sick from drinking swamp water, whereupon they returned to the camp to find it, to all intents and purposes, in the hands of the Allied prisoners. Merchant seamen and ailing military personnel had replaced the nominal guard left behind by the Germans. In fact, on the night that the runaways returned, the British prisoners took over the actual guarding and administration of the camp. On 29 April, British forces liberated the prisoners. . . .[16]

Although there were many Americans in uniform who served with OSS behind enemy lines, the best secret agents were those anti-Nazis who worked for the Third Reich in positions of responsibility or who were privy to information of great value to the Allies. To find such a person was a coup and good fortune befell one OSS station chief.

But one of the best spies that OSS had inside Germany and highly placed in the Foreign Ministry was described by OSS intelligence chief in Switzerland, Allen W. Dulles, as a diplomat "who had the kind of access which is the intelligence officer's dream. . . ."

> He was an official in the German Foreign Office in Berlin and his job there was to screen and distribute for action the cable traffic between the Foreign Office and German diplomatic posts all over the world. Since the messages to and from German military and air attachés in Tokyo were also generally sent through Foreign Office channels, he saw these, too, and they became of great value as the war in the Far East was still to be fought out. He was frequently sent by the Foreign Office as a courier to Switzerland as well as to other posts, and it was on one of his courier trips to Switzerland that he succeeded in making contact with us, having convinced himself that in his way he could contribute to the fall of the Nazis, whom he hated.[17]

"George Wood," the code-name for Dulles' VIP spy, was a short, balding, and nervous individual who at his first meeting with Dulles at OSS headquarters in Bern turned over to the American intelligence official 186 separate items of information. "You gentlemen will ask whether these dispatches are authentic and if so how I was able to get them," the German Foreign Office official told Dulles and his assistant, Gerald Mayer, as they slowly sipped wine in the OSS chief's study. "They came from material which crossed my own desk in the Foreign Office." He also described how, as an assistant to the *Auswaertige Amt* liaison officer for all the German military services in Berlin, he saw an unending stream of documents and cables across his desk, the yield of German missions abroad, war plans, submarine routings, Luftwaffe strength and flight movements, progress reports from military government in all occupied countries, and in short, the completed secret cabled inventory of a warring nation.[18]

If OSS agent "George Wood" provided the background of data about Nazi Germany's decline, then the final scene of the OSS drama in Switzerland began on February 25, 1945, when Dulles and a close associate, Gero von Schulze Gaevernitz, a naturalized American of German birth who remained in Switzerland throughout the war to supervise family business interests and to volunteer his "special services" at the appropriate time, met with Major Max Waibel, an important member of Swiss Military Intelligence. The meeting was held at Waibel's request. Inasmuch as Dulles and Waibel had become close friends, the trio dined in a quiet restaurant near Lake Lucerne. Waibel informed Dulles that he had received very reliable information that certain high-ranking German generals in Italy had put out peace feelers through an Italian businessman, Baron Luigi Parilli. During the ensuing weeks Dulles was informed that the prime mover in the peace feelers was SS General Karl Wolff. As a test of Wolff's sincerity, and of the clout he carried in the German Army in Italy, Dulles sent a message back to Wolff via Baron Parelli that the most important Italian resistance leader captured by the SD, Ferruccio Parri, and OSS Major Antonio Usmiani, be released and brought to Switzerland. The captives were located in different parts of northern Italy and their release would indicate to Dulles exactly how much command Wolff exercised in German military councils.[19]

On March 8 the two men were taken from their cells, each expecting to be led to a firing squad or the gallows, and were bundled into a German staff car with SS officers as escorts and driven to a point along the Swiss frontier, where they were met by a member of Dulles' staff. The negotiations continued and Wolff conferred in Zurich with Dulles personally. In an effort to keep direct communications open, Dulles suggested that an OSS agent with a radio be permitted to set up shop in Milan and a German-speaking Czech, Vaclav Hradecky, code-named "Wally," was smuggled into Italy's largest industrial center. But instead of setting up shop in a safe house, out of sight of the enemy, Wally was put up in the quarters of General Wolff's *aide de camp*, Captain Guido Zimmer.[20]

Nor did everything go according to plan. Gestapo chief Heinrich Himmler had been tipped off that Wolff was in

contact with the Allies, and the SS general was summoned
to Hitler's headquarters in Berlin on April 17 after missing
a meeting originally scheduled for April 2 because of the
Gestapo's suspicions. The delicate negotiations, called Operation SUNRISE, almost came a cropper as Washington ordered
all contacts with the Germans broken off, and SUNRISE
began to set. Two days later Wolff returned from Berlin, having talked himself out of trouble and execution as a traitor
to the Third Reich. The same day, April 23, he entered
Switzerland incognito to meet Dulles again and sign the
surrender terms; but Dulles, handcuffed by instructions from
Washington, was unable to negotiate officially with the SS
commander. Wolff remained in Switzerland until April 27,
and then returned to Italy. Stopping at Cernobbia for the
night, Wolff was bedded down in a villa when partisans interrupted the delicately balanced OSS end-the-war scenario.
Wolff's villa was surrounded, the partisans opened fire on
the villa, the key man in the plan, and his staff who had
the authority to authorize the early surrender of all German
military forces in Italy. Wolff was able to telephone Dulles
in Switzerland of the attack; Dulles radioed Donald Jones at
OSS headquarters in Milan, and Jones raced to the rescue
like the U.S. cavalry. The tragi-comedy of errors in the
making was finally halted by OSS SI agent Jones, code-named
"Scotti," who stepped in and stopped the shooting once the
partisans recognized him.[21]

The partisans were not aware that the men in mufti in the
villa were General Wolff and members of his staff. That he
was an important German official was apparent from the size
and style of the staff cars transporting the party. Jones managed to obtain the release of the Germans without disclosing
to the partisans that they had within their grasp one of the
two senior German generals in Northern Italy. It was apparent to the OSS agent that the partisans, angry after years
of battling the Germans in the hills, would take their revenge
on Wolff despite the high stakes involved. Meantime, Washington had switched signals, and the flat-out unconditional
surrender demand which had curtailed the SUNRISE negotiations was amended, and Dulles was authorized to reopen
negotiations with the Germans. But Wolff had left for Italy.
Thanks to the OSS radio net, SI agent Donald Jones had

received word that Wolff and his party should be put aboard
a plane, to be dispatched from AFHQ in Caserta; there they
would sign the surrender documents. But Wolff was worried
about the situation at Bolzano and the tenuous balance with
the partisans, who might attack his own troops and his headquarters. Instead of accepting the Allied offer to fly south, he
empowered his adjutant, Major Wenner, and Lieutenant Colonel Viktor von Schweinitz, another Wehrmacht staff officer, to
fly to Caserta and sign the surrender documents. On April
29 the two German staff officers put their signatures on the
documents, the surrender to take place on May 2.

During this hectic period, OSS radio operator "Wally" had
been moved from Captain Zimmer's quarters to SS headquarters in Bolzano and, hidden with his radio transmitter in
a third-floor closet, he watched history unfold through the
broken windows smashed by the concussion of falling bombs
dropped by Allied aircraft. The bombs had fallen so close on
April 29 that several German staff officers had been killed, and
in one desperate radio message to OSS the next morning
"Wally" reported that explosions had occurred only fifty
meters from his hiding place, and if the Fifteenth Air Force
didn't halt its raids against the enemy headquarters then
"Wally ist kaput!"—"Wally is finished!" If the bombs didn't
get him, a German firing squad would.[22]

Elsewhere in the Greater Milan area, Captain Emilio Q.
Daddario, an OSS SI agent code-named "Mim," had taken
custody of Italian Fascist Marshal Rudolfo Graziani, who
had slipped away from a party of German troops escorting
out of Italy the physical wreckage of Il Duce and his mistress,
Claretta Petacci, and other high-ranking Italian Fascists.
Mussolini, dressed in a German soldier's greatcoat and wearing a Wehrmacht helmet, sat in the rear of a truck along
with other *Tedeschi*. The German troops ignored their once-
famous ally. The truck was stopped at the town of Dongo
and searched. The Italian dictator was recognized by sharp-
eyed partisans who inspected the men in the truck in their
search for fleeing Fascists.[23] Justice was being meted out
during those final days, and Mussolini and his paramour were
executed by a partisan leader on April 28. Later the same day,
mass executions by firing squad of the Fascist leaders who had

been in Il Duce's entourage were held in the same square where SS troops had executed fifteen Italian hostages two years earlier.

Also disappearing during this turbulent two weeks just before and after the armistice was the so-called "treasure of Dongo" which Mussolini's convoy was transporting—reported to be an estimated $90 million in gold bullion and foreign currency. Word had spread at the time that the "treasure" captured along with Il Duce and his Fascist cohorts was turned over to Dante Gorreri, a Communist underground leader in Como, by Pietro Terzi, a leader of the Fifty-second Garibaldi Brigade, which was Communist-supported. (Also alleged in later years were the "mysterious" murders of several partisans connected with the movement of the treasure. During a sensational trial in Padua, Italy, Terzi testified that his brigade "decided to hand the treasure to the Communist Party because the Communists had fought harder than anyone else.") [24]

What the Communist Party had received from the treasure was a postwar bankroll that included $1,600,000 in Italian lire, $4,059,234 in French francs, $184,897 in Swiss francs, $149,345 in American currency, $396 in Portuguese escudos, $140 in Spanish pesetas and $13,075 in British pounds—a total of $6 million in currency, plus the gold bullion.

Along with the vanished $90 million treasure was the disappearance of *Fascisti* who were summarily executed privately—and publicly—between April 25 and May 6, 1945. Some 2,000 were reported to have been killed in Turin and 500 in Milan; in all of German-occupied Italy the anti-Fascist bloodbath reportedly totaled 40,000, although the true figure is probably lower. [25]

As the walls of the Third Reich crumbled and Allied troops began liberating the living dead in the Nazi concentration and extermination camps, few of the American GIs were prepared for the visual horror, the animal sounds of the prisoners, and the stink of death they came upon at hellholes like Buchenwald, Dachau, Hof, and Bremen, to name a few. Not even OSS appeared to have been aware of the prevailing conditions within the camps or of the extermination centers and their gas chambers and crematoria. An October 1944 OSS R&A

report about concentration camps in Germany noted generalities, including outdated data as much as five years old. This report called concentration camps one of the "fundamental institutions of the Nazi regime."

... They serve to detain or eliminate, without indictment or trial, and without possibility of appeal, any person within the reach of the Nazi machinery inside or outside Germany. By virtue of this constant threat to the life of every citizen, regardless of his real guilt or responsibility, the concentration camps exercise terroristic influence far beyond their physical boundaries.

The actual number of interned persons provides no clue to the numerical strength of the anti-Nazi opposition in Germany. . . . Chief among the inmates were always great numbers of Jews, for it was against this group of citizens that the Nazis first directed their terror; recent reports, however, indicate that few Jews remain in the German concentration camps, having for the most part been either executed or sent to Polish camps. . . .

Life within the camps . . . is thoroughly regimented. A 13-hour work day is devoted to heavy labor including considerable war work. The food and medical care are sub-standard.

In addition to the primary function of imprisoning enemies of the state and certain others, concentration camps also serve to train SS men in brutality, in methods of breaking civilian resistance, and in experiments for rendering opposition elements harmless. Until 1940 every member of SS Deathhead Units (*SS Totenkopf Standarten*) spent at least three months of his training as a guard or officer in a concentration camp. . . . An order prescribing discipline and punishment for use in concentration camps . . . *Disziplinar und Strafvollsug für das Gefangenenlager* . . . is important in revealing the official attitude of camp authorities toward prisoners, but its application is limited by the fact that every SS-man is at once judge and executioner who can punish the prisoners at any time. SS men have given prisoners impossible orders and then have slain the prisoners when the orders were not carried out. SS men have shot prisoners on the spot without previous warning or questioning. In short, the official camp orders or penal regulations have no binding effect upon the guards and officials. The prisoners have no rights, no protection,

and are subject to the arbitrary power of the SS administration. . . .

The death penalty is meted out for sabotage, attacks
upon SS personnel, disobedience to orders, refusal to
work, etc. . . . Suicides occur frequently, because the
SS administration encourages the practice. Prisoners
placed in solitary cells are often given a length of rope.
Prisoners who are disliked by their *Blockführer* (cell
block leader) may be given a rope and ordered to kill
themselves. If they are still alive on the next day, they
are beaten up by the *Blockführer* and the order is repeated. This sometimes goes on for weeks, until the
prisoner commits suicide, or the *Blockführer* tires. . . .²⁶

Finally, the R&A paper, which cited many foreign sources
for its information, reported that "a reasonable estimate of
the present number of prisoners in the German concentration
camps within the 1937 boundaries of the Reich (before
Austria and Czechoslovak Sudetenland were annexed) ranges
from a low of 170,000 to a high of 370,000. . . . Since there
are large numbers of prisoners of non-German nationality
known to be in German concentration camps, it is impossible
to give a nationality breakdown of the prisoners in the concentration camps."²⁷

At the time this report was written, the death camps in
Germany, Austria, Czechoslovakia, and Poland were murder-
ing tens of thousands of inmates each week as fast as they
arrived. If the scope of the death camps was a well-kept Nazi
secret, it appears that much of the high-level intelligence
collected by OSS failed to include information about the
concentration camps and their death factories. It was a failure
in intelligence-gathering that was to shock the world when
American GIs and British and French troops liberated the
pitiful survivors of the death camps. The authors of OSS
R&A Report No. 1844 had been failed by SI, the one section
whose spies, even if in limited numbers, had penetrated the
Third Reich. Nor, it appears, had specific intelligence about
details in the death camps been unearthed by British SIS.
That there were death camps was nothing more than "rumor,"
although various Jewish organizations had evidence both hard
and soft about the deliberate exterminations in the concentration camps. And not even the Allies' Supreme Commander

had been presented with a report containing hard intelligence about Nazi concentration camps. On April 10, 1945, General Dwight D. Eisenhower, General Omar Bradley, and General George S. Patton flew to XX Corps headquarters at Gotha, Germany. It was just another stop on a front-line tour of units and various division and corps headquarters. At the XX Corps headquarters, they were briefed by Major General Walton Walker, corps commander, who then suggested that they all visit the concentration camps at nearby Ohrdruf Nord, just liberated. Patton agreed, commenting to his colleagues on "how bastardly these Krauts can be" and emphasizing that the stories couldn't be believed "until you've seen this pesthole yourself."

> The stink of death was overwhelming even before the Americans passed into the stockade, where some 3,200 naked, bony corpses lay in shallow graves. Others, covered with lice, were sprawled in the streets. Eisenhower paled at the sight. Until then he had only heard of such horrors. Aghast he said, "This is beyond the American mind to comprehend."
>
> Bradley was too revolted to speak, and Patton walked off and vomited. Eisenhower, however, felt that it was his duty to visit every section of the camp. . . . The general turned to his companions. "I want every American unit not actually in the front lines to see this place. We are told that the American soldier does not know what he is fighting for. Now, at least, he will know what he is fighting *against!*"[28]

Clearly, the passing off of the Nazi concentration camps in a bland report was not up to the standards of R&A. The United States and the free world were taken unawares when Allied troops came across the first concentration camps in Germany.

22

Fortresses are the tombs of armies.
—*Anonymous military maxim*

With the war's end in Europe only a matter of time, OSS managed for a brief time to become caught up in a figment of its own and the enemy's imagination. From OSS headquarters in Switzerland, in one of his many reports based on information by his chief spy, "George Wood," Dulles described the problems that the Germans were having just administering the affairs of state. Many Nazi bureaucrats had set up new offices in southern Germany, and the problem was liaison between the newly established bureaucratic centers and Berlin.[1] Heavy Allied air raids also added to the communications problem.

Meantime, in September 1944 OSS R&A delivered a report to the front office in Q Building announcing the possibility that the Germans might fortify their alpine areas and make a last-ditch stand from the safety of the mountains. Added to the R&A report were several additions which were nothing more than intelligence indicators and estimates of what might happen given certain conditions within the realm of possibility.[2] First of all, some military activity was underway in the remote mountain areas. Tunnels were being blasted and roads were being dynamited into the side of the steep mountain slopes; and the sound of all of this labor and heavy construction work was heard almost all the way to Switzerland.

The OSS officers attached to Dulles's Swiss headquarters (they were officially serving as "military attachés," or in some such other innocuous capacity) had spotted the mountain areas that had been fortified by the Swiss—and they were not even

325

at war. The Swiss had carved out a fortress system in the Alps that was most impressive. "And if the Swiss can do it," reasoned the OSS types in Bern, Geneva, and Zurich, "so can the Germans." Even more important, this R&A report, although predicting an end to hostilities in Europe by mid-1945, warned that if the enemy managed to become entrenched in his mountain redoubt, it could cost more Allied casualties than all of the ground fighting in Western Europe up to that time. And the war could stretch on for an additional six months or more.[8]

The enemy *had* made plans to use the mountains as a last-stand redoubt, but only with small forces and on a small scale. Meantime, Nazi leaders proposed to Hitler that they center their military forces and government in the alpine area where they could hold out for years, and in time obtain better armistice terms from the Allies. Western newspapers began publishing reports about Hitler's "hideaway" in the mountains, and in due time Nazi officials, receiving feedback about the Western press from their diplomatic missions in neutral countries, decided that digging a huge fortress area in the mountains made good sense. Goebbels's propaganda ministry moved into action and additional stories came out of Germany about the alpine fortress under construction. High-ranking Nazi generals who should have known better began to believe their own propaganda. As for Allied intelligence, once the stories began to spread within the Third Reich a concerted effort was made to pin down the source and come up with facts, facts, and more facts. Amidst all the propaganda, the Abwehr "leaked phony blueprints and bogus intelligence data to American agents who seemed most ready to accept the stories about the Redoubt."[4]

One American magazine, *Collier's,* in late January 1945 reported an elaborate fortress system of huge caverns, tunnels, and an outside road system. Moreover, the cream of Hitler youth was undergoing special training as guerrillas. These Nazi guerrilla forces were to be called "Werewolves." Even the august *New York Times,* which does not consider an event as news unless it had been first published in that paper, reported via military correspondent Hanson Baldwin that after the fall of Berlin, the Wehrmacht would shift its combat operations south to the *Alpenfestung* or mountain fortress.

In official military circles, press reports like that in the *Times* underscored a lengthy intelligence report whipped together by the Seventh Army G–2. In what was an obvious misreading of enemy capabilities, the G–2 reported:

> . . . Himmler had ordered provisions for 100,000 men and the area was to be defended by "eighty crack units of from 1,000 to 4,000 men each." Himmler was seeing to it that the best arms Germany could produce were earmarked for the Redoubt and sealed trains bearing armaments were arriving from the Skoda works. "Many of those trains" were seen to be carrying a new type of gun. Elaborate underground ordnance shops run by hydroelectric power were being built and a report alleged that an aircraft factory capable of producing a "complete Messerschmitt" was in operation. The terrain would aid the defense and the Nazis could draw upon the Po and Danube valleys, Western Czechoslovakia, and the upper Balkans. The Redoubt Center's combat personnel would number between 200,000 and 300,000 veterans of the SS and special mountain troops "thoroughly imbued with the Nazi spirit," who could expect to fight fanatically to the last man.[5]

In April 1945 the *Times* again reported on the *Alpenfestung,* and correspondent Drew Middleton wrote that stories going about Allied headquarters in Paris told of a National Redoubt that was more strongly fortified than Monte Cassino, one of the toughest battles fought in Italy during World War II for the remains of a bomb-shattered monastery on the high ground. In Allied headquarters the debate continued on and on about the enemy's last-ditch stand, and too many people believed it, although OSS in Europe finally tended to downgrade the mountain fortress theory. Not so other military and civilian agencies, including OSS in Washington. Nor is there any documentation that OSS thinking early on ran counter to what many high-ranking military people believed about the existence of the *Alpenfestung.*[6] By mid-April as the surrender talks with General Wolff progressed in fits and starts, the U.S. military tended to side with OSS that there was *no* redoubt—and this one possible stumbling block on the road to surrender was finally hammered out.

World War II came to an end in Europe on the evening

of May 8, 1944, with the signing of the surrender documents by monocled *Generalfeldmarschall* Wilhelm Keitel who was accompanied by *Generaladmiral* Hans-Georg von Friedenburg of the Germany Navy, and *Generaloberst* Hans Jurgen Stumpff of the Luftwaffe.

But OSS operations in Europe did not end with the German surrender. A number of OSS detachments were deployed throughout the three Western occupation zones of Germany. Former SI agents and OG and SO paratroopers searched for paintings and other valuables and national treasures which the Nazis had stolen. Baron Rudolf von Ripper of SI, who had first seen action as an aerial gunner flying against Franco during the Spanish Civil War, was given the assignment of tracking down escaped Nazi war criminals. It was an assignment the OSS captain relished.

Other OSS people had been deployed to Asia beginning in late 1944 and early 1945. Captain Walter R Mansfield, after his tour of duty with the Chetniks, was shipped off to China in December 1944 and assigned to a Chinese guerrilla force with Corporals Cedric Poland and John Owens and two local interpreters to assist the Americans in communicating with these strange people. Although most of the Chinese guerrillas were willing to fight, many others were not—unlike the fervent anti-Nazi attitudes of the Chetniks and partisans whose paths Mansfield had crossed in Yugoslavia. Nor was his introduction to "the pocket" where his group would operate as simple as infiltration into Yugoslavia by parachute. Mansfield's OSS detachment was driven 750 miles toward its destination, and then it was another 200-mile hike across rough terrain with coolies packing additional supplies.

The Japanese stuck to the main roads, and at one point on their march into the interior toward "the pocket," the OSS team and its guerrilla force passed a roadside bivouac area where five hundred enemy troops were bedded down for the night. Unfortunately, there were not enough guerrillas to attempt an attack. As Mansfield soon learned, the majority of Chinese had bad eyesight and therefore were quite inaccurate with their weapons. And when they moved out on their first patrol, most of the coolie bearers deserted the first night. The Chinese guerrilla chief had not bothered to pay the bearers, something which Mansfield took care of personally thereafter, without any further loss of coolies. He also had his regular altercations with Chao Szu Ling, the guerrilla chief in the area who, once *his* "army" had been armed with weapons dropped to Mansfield and bolstered by new recruits which the Marine captain trained, absconded one night while Mansfield was on a patrol. He took every last weapon and, as Mansfield couldn't help but notice, as Chao's forces grew stronger thanks to American training and equipment, the tempo of his operations against the enemy softened. It was obvious that Chao was building up his own private army and becoming a local warlord.[7]

Mansfield and a patrol tracked Chao some miles, and in a personal confrontation the angry Marine captain forced the return of much of his materiel. He and Chao then agreed to split "the pocket," each taking half of the area as his own AO. In one major ambush in March 1945, Mansfield and his three hundred-man guerrilla force waited in hiding alongside a stretch of road which the enemy used regularly. They selected a spot which the OSS team's senior Chinese guerrilla officer said was too close to a Japanese garrison two miles beyond. Also, Mansfield had set up a daytime ambush—something the Chinese had never tried before and which they questioned. After waiting nearly two hours in the cold of North China, Mansfield decided to give it another fifteen minutes before he ordered his men to withdraw.

"I decided to take one more look down the road through my binoculars," wrote Mansfield. "About a mile or so away, a small stretch of the road was visible before it disappeared again into the hills. My glasses passed over it and just as I was moving on I thought I saw something moving in the road. Quickly I swung the glasses back and could hardly believe my eyes. There, moving down the road toward us, was a group of men—marching! They were still too far away in the distance for me to distinguish how many."[8]

Instead of a convoy ambush, the guerrillas were told that they had fifteen minutes to reposition themselves for a personnel or troop ambush, and move in closer, especially before the enemy troops rounded a bend and came into view. But Mansfield's senior Chinese guerrilla officer, who was against the plan from the very start, refused to cooperate. While Mansfield and his two fellow American OSS corporals moved the machine guns into position and deployed a handful of men to a little finger overlooking the road about two hundred feet from their original position, his guerrilla officer stood pat. He refused again to deploy fifty men closer to the road. It was only after the three Americans personally moved in closer to the road that the Chinese officer released fifty men to join the OSS team.

"Now the Japs had rounded the bend and were coming down the straight stretch about 600 yards away," Mansfield continued. "For the first time I got a good look at them and was amazed. It was an almost unbelievable sight! About 100 Japs were marching four abreast in perfect formation, with no point guard or flank—just as if they were putting on a show for Emperor Hirohito himself! Spaced behind them at 20-yard intervals were three 75mm, horsedrawn guns, and three caissons. All the men were equipped, however, with rifles or light machine guns." Through his binoculars Mansfield observed an officer striding at the head of the marching men, a Samurai sword swinging by his side. About 150 yards away they crossed a bridge and kept coming.[9]

"Chenzai, Chenzai!" whispered the guerrilla officer tugging at Mansfield's shoulder. "Now, Now!" the guerrilla demanded but Mansfield brushed his arm away and declared emphatically in a low voice, *"Meyo! Meyo!"* "No! No!" In order to save face, the guerrilla officer had finally joined forces with Mansfield. Mansfield wanted the enemy column closer because the Chinese were such poor shots. The Japanese continued marching forward—singing. They approached the hundred-yard mark. Then ninety . . . eighty, and Mansfield's upraised arm dropped, signaling the guerrillas to commence firing. He leveled his submachine gun at the middle of the enemy column and squeezed off one short burst after another. The heavier machine guns also opened up from the finger and raked the Japanese column. Enemy soldiers dropped to the ground, dead or wounded. About ten of the enemy were dropped on the first burst and Mansfield couldn't help thinking how a small group of well-trained Marines could have knocked off at least twenty-five or thirty at the first go-round.

The enemy soldiers were well-trained; the survivors of that

first fusillade hurled themselves off the road into a ditch. Mansfield ordered two of the light machine guns repositioned so that the enemy hiding in the ditch could be flanked and placed under more accurate fire. Three Chinese guerrillas were lost as they tried to run the machine guns across an open stretch of road to outflank the enemy in the ditch. Within minutes both machine guns were set up, but the guerrillas continued with their rifle fire even though there was nothing to fire at. The enemy soldiers were too well hidden under cover of the ditch.

"I will never be able to understand what happens to a Chinese soldier once firing has started," Mansfield commented on this experience. "No matter how many engagements he has been in, or how much experience he has, he seems to go hog-wild on automatic fire and acts like a rookie all over again. No amount of training seems capable of changing that. Once again, I became furious as I watched them wasting precious lead, hitting nothing, and disregarding our signal to cease fire."[10]

Meantime, the guerrillas had gotten out of hand. Armed with bazookas for what originally was a truck-busting ambush, they began firing rockets and one "whoompf" after another, followed by loud explosions echoed off the rice paddies. One of the men in a two-man bazooka crew in typical Chinese style became excited and had to get in his innings. No sooner had he fired than the next bazooka-man took this as a signal and triggered off his own rocket. Mansfield ran along the ambush line waving his arms for the bazookas to cease firing. Then he waved on another element of guerrillas to move forward after the machine guns had raked the ditch, killing more of the enemy. The guerrillas ran to the ditch, hurling grenades. Moments later there were about seventy or eighty bodies in the area, while the survivors had crawled off. Instead of immediately gathering up the enemy rifles, the guerrillas began to strip the dead Japanese and loot their bodies despite the possibility that the enemy had heard the firefight and dispatched reinforcements. As Mansfield shouted for the guerrillas to withdraw, the first incoming whoosh of shells from small knee mortars and the explosions that followed fell among the Chinese. They quickly fled into the hills and then regrouped around Mansfield who ordered the light machine guns set up to cover their withdrawal. He remained with one pair of guerrilla machine-gunners while his two corporals stood by the other pair of gunners.

Damage to the enemy: About eighty Japanese killed, more than fifty rifles captured, and several machine guns and other equipment—and the Samurai sword which Mansfield made it a point to snatch as he ran past the body of the dead enemy officer.[11]

But expanding guerrilla warfare activities in China was a lost cause in 1945. There was a three-cornered war going on as the Communist route armies and the Nationalist armies battled both each other and the Japanese. Few Americans could foresee the coming struggle for control of the huge Asian country and population. As far as OSS was concerned, the enemy was Japan, and that's where attention was directed. A handful of *Nisei*, American-born Japanese, were sent to the Far East by OSS to participate in "black propaganda" operations. They manned radio stations set up in the Pacific area to broadcast information to the home islands—and to Japanese troops in China and Korea and Southeast Asia—that was designed to tear down the morale of the people with deliberately concocted lies. Whether "black propaganda" via radio or leaflet drops was as effective as in Europe is questionable. If OSS had plans to infiltrate *Nisei* into Japan by parachute, Maritime Unit PT boats, or submarine, discussion about such operations never surfaced after the war. Taking into consideration the tight control of all intelligence collection by General MacArthur's headquarters, and his low opinion of OSS operations, it is doubtful if any intelligence agency other than Major General Charles A. Willoughby's own GHQ G–2 would have been utilized by the strong-willed general who demanded and was given virtual carte blanche to conduct the operations in the Pacific as he saw fit.[12]

Nonetheless, OSS R&A did address the wartime situation in Japan with a report covering the winter of 1944–45 in the home islands.

For the average Japanese the winter just past was one of constant strain. The weather was said to be the coldest in 25 years; severe earthquakes occurred in Hokkaido and in central Japan; and Allied air raids steadily mounted in scale. War plant dispersal, evacuation, and the destruction of housing facilities in air raids has caused severe dislocation not only in the cities but also in the rural areas receiving the flow of refugees.

Every phase of Japanese life has been constricted by the war. The Government has demanded increased sacrifices of all kinds from the citizenry including a 7-day work week. The first tendency toward dangerous currency inflation since the start of the war followed a recent steep rise in war expenditure. The people, caught between inflated costs, high taxes, and compulsory savings, are finding it hard to make ends meet in spite of increased salaries.

Despite claims that Japan's existing labor supply is sufficient, the Government has continued to take measures to enlarge it. On 10 March 1945 males between 12 and 60 and single females between 12 and 40 were made subject to call for home defense as well as for war production. Previously these groups could only be called up for work in certain essential industries. Much emphasis has been placed on monthly production quotas in war plants, and in November Tokyo promoted the "special-attack spirit" as a propaganda device designed to inspire civilians as well as the military to make greater sacrifices for the war. . . .

Evacuation has reduced Tokyo City's 1944 population of over 7 million to less than 4 million. Compulsory mass evacuation measures, with special emphasis on children and nonessential adults, were intensified after the heavy March air raids demonstrated the inadequacy of shelters and defense precautions. Measures taken to restrain essential workers from fleeing the city indicate a high degree of confusion and terror. Many people have been forced to live in cellars or shacks constructed from debris. Family life has been severely disrupted. . . .

With a reduced number of movies and nightclubs as a result of air raids and Government edicts, the Japanese are turning more and more to the radio for entertainment, but even here they complain about the excessive "sermons and preaching." The populace is constantly told that the war may last ten or twenty years and that "100,000,000 Japanese must be killed before Japan can be defeated."[13]

By June 1945 the Allies had turned their attention to Japan. Negotiations with the Soviet Union toward a declaration of war by Stalin against Japan, a declaration that had been avoided by mutual consent, as it were, so that the warring powers, each fighting the respective allies of the other nation, avoided a dangerous situation. If they had gone to war earlier, an additional front would have opened against the Japanese and a second front for the Red Army would have dissipated the Soviet armed forces which had hurled all military resources against Nazi Germany. The leaders of each nation knew that it was only a matter of time before they declared war on each other, or launched war with a large frontal attack.

However, the OSS was concerned basically with the threat to American military forces in the Pacific. One threat, according to an R&A report issued during the third week in July, was "Japan's 'Secret' Weapon: Suicide." Specifically, the Japanese High Command began to stress in 1944 that the death of an individual in combat should serve a military purpose. That is, any suicide attack should inflict damage on the enemy. If a Japanese soldier is to die in combat, especially in a suicide effort, the least he must do is kill an Allied soldier at the time he gives up his own life. Too often, the Japanese soldier, rather than surrender, committed suicide to no end—without killing his mortal enemy. Soldier's diaries and letters repeatedly referred to the necessity and desirability of death in a hopeless battle situation. On Saipan, a division commander ordered his remaining troops to follow him into the hills where all physically capable officers and enlisted men committed suicide in the ancient tradition of *bushido,* in which *hara-kiri* was the only honorable course in peace or war for the responsible warrior or samurai who has met with failure, whether or not as a result of his own personal actions. *Banzai* suicide charges, another manifestation of the suicide indoctrination, had become commonplace in battle in the Pacific. Officers, and the soldiers whom they commanded, were inculcated with the spirit of accepting suffering and pain in pursuit of their military careers, and to bear physical hardship and torture without flinching. Soldiers were taught from youth that "the way of the warrior is to die," and to "die in battle with a fortress for a pillow."[14]

Expanding on the *banzai* tradition in the Japanese Imperial Army, Navy, and Air Force, OSS R&A issued a SECRET report warning that the High Command had consciously expanded this traditional concept to encompass the employment of suicide tactics as a standard military device, developing "this theme one step further by insisting that a suicidal defense to the last man would meet Allied forces daring to invade the home islands." The OSS report warning the Joint Chiefs of Staff what this one problem might mean for the planned invasion of Japan—Operation OLYMPIC scheduled for November 1945, a landing on southern Kyushu Island to be followed in March 1946 by Operation CORONET, the mightiest amphibious force ever assembled to strike the Tokyo plain of Honshu Island.

The report advised the JCS that the Japanese High Command had gone on record that all air and naval activity would be based mainly on suicide tactics that the nation already had "accepted as a legitimate basic part of ground defense. Already such 'secret weapons' as suicide assault and antitank units, 'human mine' suicide swimmers, suicide boats, suicide planes, suicide flying bombs, and human-bomb gliders have emerged. . . . They are planned to exact the maximum toll of Allied Forces at the most advantageous times."[15]

"Human-mine" suicide swimmers have been used in recent campaigns to destroy landing craft, transports, and cargo ships. These men, generally organized in platoon strength, swim under water in the direction of an approaching landing craft and then surface, throwing a grenade. Or they swim toward the landing craft, pushing antiboat mines until they explode in contact with the oncoming craft. . . .

Many small depth-charge suicide boats intended for large-scale use in smashing Allied landing and supply operations in the Pacific were discovered in the Philippines and in the Ryukyu Islands. More than 300 of the boats and tons of explosives were captured in caves near the beaches in the Kerama Islands before the Japanese could use them. The boats, intended for attacking Allied convoys approaching a beach landing area, were to be manned by units composed of 100–150 young men with special physical, educational, and character qualifications.

Most recently the Japanese, in an effort to stimulate home front morale and also to frighten the Allies into a revision of the unconditional surrender formula, have been threatening a last-ditch civilian resistance in the home islands. Addressing the 87th Extraordinary Session of the Imperial Diet in June 1945, Premier Suzuki declared: "Judging from the trends within enemy countries and considering the developments in the international situation, I cannot help feel strongly that the only way for us to do is to fight to the last." Other Japanese spokesmen have described "the natural aptitude of the Japanese to die to the last man," and have pictured "an entire nation armed physically and spiritually to stamp out any attempt to defile Japan's sacred soil. . . ." The national song of the Civilian Volunteer Corps promised, "Our orders have come, O land of Japan: To death we fight, to our last man." If carried out, these threats would exploit to the final limit the Japanese capacity for suicide.[16]

The OSS analysts qualified their warning about the enemy's "suicide" tactics, adding that such expressions of determination might be nothing more than a propaganda maneuver. "Japanese success in exploiting suicide as a military device does not mean that national suicide is inevitable." The report concluded with this final thought:

> The Japanese soldier's willingness to sacrifice his individual life in his country's interest is based in part on his strong feeling on the continuity of Japan's national life. Regardless of the current propaganda, should the continued existence of Japan as a nation be threatened by the possibility of anything approaching the total extinction of its population, many Japanese soldiers and civilians might well come to prefer surrender to death.[17]

Whether or not this R&A thesis was valid was never put to the test. The first experimental atomic bomb was exploded at Alamogordo, New Mexico, on July 16, 1945. Meantime, a high-level debate as to whether to employ this destructive weapon was outweighed by the fear of suicide tactics by the Japanese in defense of their homeland. Both the JCS and Secretary of War Henry L. Stimson recommended that the bombs be dropped and that the shocking explosions and destruction would convince Japanese military leaders that it was fruitless to continue. Also, the very destructiveness of these weapons would present them with a valid excuse to surrender. The JCS feared that Japan's four million undefeated soldiers would continue fighting in China, Manchuria, and Southeast Asia and, assisted by civilians, would defend the home islands to the death, killing many thousands of Allied invasion troops even as the Japanese went down in defeat.

President Truman approved the use of two atomic weapons, and on August 6 Hiroshima, a city of 300,000, underwent the first atomic holocaust which killed 78,150, most of them outright, and wounded 70,000. Three days later Nagasaki became the second city to provide an example of Allied might. A seaport and industrial city of 230,000 people, the population was decreased by nearly 40,000 while 25,000 were injured. On that same day, the Soviet Union declared war on Japan, which the next day offered to surrender. On August 15, a cease-fire became effective and on September 2, aboard the battleship USS *Missouri* anchored in Tokyo Bay, General MacArthur, as Supreme Commander–Allied Powers, received the official surrender of Foreign Minister Mamoru Shigemetsu.

World War II had come to an end and the Office of Strategic Services, born of necessity and a creature of the global war in the shadows, had completed the mission for which it had been created.

23

I repeat that the United States can accept no
result save victory, final and complete.
—FRANKLIN D. ROOSEVELT to the American
people, December 9, 1941

In the midst of war, President Roosevelt wrote to General
Donovan on October 31, 1944, requesting that the OSS chief
give some thought to the establishment of a postwar intelligence agency. The prewar experience which led to the surprise
Pearl Harbor attack had convinced the President that if there
had been an active national intelligence center and the adequate machinery to disseminate sensitive and "hot" information, the United States would have been forearmed as well
as forewarned. Actually, the United States had been forewarned thanks to the decoding of Japanese diplomatic cables,
but the commanders at Pearl Harbor never received the information which would have warned them to go on a red
alert.

The OSS director replied on November 18 with a memorandum setting down his thoughts for the future and a basic
blueprint for the executive authority that could establish what
Donovan called a Central Intelligence Service. In his memorandum he pointed out that information important to the
national defense that was then collected by other Government
departments and agencies "is not being used to full advantage
in the war. Coordination at the strategy level would prevent
waste, and avoid the present confusion that leads to waste
and unnecessary duplication." General Donovan and OSS
had not resolved all of the earlier problems with other
Government agencies, and these hang-ups were still curtailing

some of the work of OSS. Then he closed his communication to the President by underscoring the availability of "trained and specialized personnel" to staff any postwar intelligence organization.[1]

His memorandum, classified SECRET and stamped TOP SECRET by JCS, to which he had directed a copy, was head-lined on February 9, 1945, in three newspapers—the Washington, D.C., *Times-Herald*, the Chicago *Tribune*, and the *Daily News* in New York City, all of conservative or isolationist bent. Donovan's memorandum found its way into the hands of officials of other Federal agencies and departments, and it appears that his arch-enemy, J. Edgar Hoover of the FBI, leaked the plan to the Chicago *Tribune* and the Washington *Times-Herald*. The plan represented a threat to Hoover's FBI, which had carved out a niche in the Americas during World War II. North America and Latin America had been designated the sole province of the FBI in all intelligence-gathering and security matters. Hoover wanted to retain this control after the war, and in leaking the Donovan memo, he knew a furor would be raised on Capitol Hill, forcing the President to table any plans for a postwar national intelligence organization.[2]

Aside from the political sniping, did the creation of OSS fill a national need? And did OSS function efficiently? Definitely not! claimed military historian Hanson Baldwin and *New York Times* military correspondent in World War II: "Much balderdash has been written about the 'brilliance' of the work of the OSS. Some of it was brilliant—particularly in Switzerland and some of the work in China and Southeast Asia—but much of it was inefficient, some of it was stupid, and for a considerable part of the war, we were dependent upon the British for much of our secret information."[3]

Be that as it may, OSS was organized by inexperienced amateurs who learned the intelligence business strictly by on-the-job-training. Errors in judgment were made; in such an organization perfection was the exception rather than the rule. But as time passed the scales soon balanced out in favor of perfection. At least 831 men and women were decorated for bravery by OSS, several with the nation's second highest military decoration for battlefield heroism, the Distinguished

Service Cross. Yet none of the OSS men or women ever were considered for the nation's highest military award, the Congressional Medal of Honor. But by any definition of bravery and self-sacrifice, including the decision not to escape but to remain in a Nazi cell and face possible torture or execution, T/5 Salvador Fabrega should have been nominated for the Medal of Honor; or Major Ortiz—and many others who were willing to give their lives deliberately.

Nor is there any statistical breakdown of how many OSS personnel were killed in action or wounded in action. And the number of men and women who served in OSS varies, with one source claiming 13,000 workers engaged in some kind of strategically important work; another estimates 22,000 and a third claims "more than 30 thousand men and women."[4] The Special Operations Division which supported the SO detachments sent some 1,600 operatives behind enemy lines[5] but there's no figure of how many fifteen-to-twenty-man OG units also worked behind the lines, or the number of SI agents who assumed specially prepared cover identities for "black" penetrations into German-occupied countries or areas occupied by the Japanese.* The hazards of operating behind enemy lines took its toll of the men and women who braved torture and execution to seek out intelligence information for the Allies. During the three years that SOE deployed more than five hundred liaison officers into northern Italy, it was estimated by General Sir Colin Gubbins, wartime director of the British agency, that the "useful life" of agents before "expenditure" was estimated at six months. The toll was high.[6]

Nor was OSS as an organization favorably accepted by the traditionalists in the armed forces. The *New York Times* military correspondent's view represented much of the attitude of the professionals in the Pentagon. They had been plagued during the war by citizens in uniform who had become officers only because they were in OSS, and it rankled Regular Army colonels and generals when they discovered

---

*Actually, the number of people who served in or with OSS should take into consideration those assigned full-time, those temporarily assigned, and those partisans and guerrillas around the world who were directly under the command of OSS officers. Thus, any accurate number is difficult to ascertain.

that an OSS colonel had received his eagles by direct appointment rather than from long service. And even more frustrating for the military professionals were the irreverent individualists in OSS who constantly flouted both authority and standard operating procedures.

That OSS had provided a valuable service to the armed forces during the war was quickly forgotten when the intelligence agency was disbanded on October 1, 1945, by Executive Order of President Harry S Truman, whose only link with General Donovan was that they both had served in France in the AEF in World War I. Where Donovan was a confidant of the late President Roosevelt, he was a relative stranger to President Truman who, burdened with an office and responsibilities for which he was ill prepared, had no concept of OSS as an organization nor what it represented for the future of American foreign-policy decision-making.

In an effort to obtain public recognition for the role of OSS in World War II, General Donovan in late August 1945 directed that some of the SO and OG files be sanitized, deleting sensitive and possibly embarrassing information, and then declassified and presented to the press through a new Reports Declassification Section established for this purpose. The new section, commanded by Commander John M. Shaheen, who had led the unsuccessful "MacGregor" Mission in Italy, among others, began producing material immediately. Along with Captain Roger Hall of Norso II and other OSS personnel who in civilian life had been journalists, authors, screenwriters, and photographers, the new section launched a tremendous effort to tell the OSS story by writing up the reports for clearance or permitting civilian newspaper and magazine journalists and free-lance writers to research their stories from the sanitized reports. For a few short weeks the lid was off America's first intelligence service. Then, as quickly as it had been lifted, the records were closed abruptly on October 1, the day that President Truman abolished OSS.[7]

But some of the files were too good to let go, and with this processed information in hand, many of the people who staffed the Reports Declassification Section managed to leave the OSS with these gems, most of which have since appeared in print in books, magazine articles, and embellished for the movies. These were the action and adventure stories that have been related time and again and are enhanced with each telling or by new versions. This was the OSS legacy to the American public.*

Its legacy to the Government was trained people and the massive files collected by R&A that ended up at the State Department, later to become part of that agency's Bureau of Intelligence and Research. The SI, X–2, and SO files, and whatever staff remained in these sections, went to the Army's newly established Strategic Services Unit headed by the very capable Colonel William Quinn, who was Seventh Army G–2 from Operation ANVIL-DRAGOON, the invasion of Southern France on August 15, 1944, all the way through the march into Germany.[8]

As quickly as the armed forces disbanded after V-J Day, so, too, did the OSS Staff leave their posts overseas and in Washington. Within a matter of weeks the huge R&A organization was nothing more than a shell and a handful of people. The men and women in R&A were later described by Mc-George Bundy as the first great center of area studies in the United States "not located in any university." Bundy emphasized that in very large measure "the area study programs developed in American universities in the years after the war were manned, directed, or stimulated by graduates of the OSS—a remarkable institution, half cops-and-robbers and half faculty meeting." The core of OSS—Research and Analysis —has since had a great impact on Government policy-making and proved that scholarly research and analysis could produce information unavailable by espionage.[9]

For several thousand Americans and foreign nationals, the "great game" of wartime espionage had come to an end, but for a small percentage of OSS alumni it would continue with the CIA. Behind were the unforgettable memories: Fact-finding in libraries and interviewing people from far-away places with strange-sounding names; translating aged and crumbling publications and studying photographs old and new under magnifying lenses that wearied the eyes and

---

*Many of the books and magazine articles about the adventures of OSS people published in the U.S. during 1945 to 1948 are the fruits of those who labored in the Reports Declassification Section. See the Bibliography for a partial list.

brought forth throbbing migraines; physical conditioning, techniques training, and studying how-to manuals to insure survival in a hostile environment; infiltrating front lines in the midst of combat or parachuting behind enemy lines to a hopefully friendly reception; raising hell in enemy territory and deliberately destroying structures and people necessary to the other side; or playing a strange role in the guise of a "dead" identity temporarily revived where a single slip or a run of bad luck could result in an L-pill suicide, or the agony of torture meted out by experts, or a firing squad or hangman's noose.

This was the wartime Office of Strategic Services, a onetime happening in the nation's recent history. There was nothing like it before and there will not be the likes of it again. It had its place in the events of our time and OSS left its imprint, rather than a recognizable trail.

Its intelligence-collection methods have been replaced by refinements in science and technology, and many of its alumni have passed on, returned to their former careers, or entered new careers after the war. A generation from now the great majority of those who served in OSS will be gone along with their memories of adventures past.

OSS? It was one hell of an organization staffed by geniuses, screwballs, misfits, and just plain people, who somehow managed a sense of cohesion and accomplishment. And there are many stories yet to be told.

The midsummer Mediterranean moon lurked behind billowing black clouds as the four-engine RAF Halifax bomber, on a course from Algiers to southern France, peeled off and left behind a flight of American B-24 Liberators on their way to bomb German supply lines along the French coast. It was late July 1944.

Aboard the bomber, converted for dropping secret agents and supplies and equipped for other secret missions behind enemy lines, were three men clad in carefully selected civilian clothing worn beneath their jumpsuits. They carried forged identification papers that would pass all but the closest scrutiny. Two of the agents were Americans who carried quick-acting poison pills in the event of capture and torture by the Gestapo.

One of the two Americans, Captain Geoffrey M. T. Jones, also was privy to the biggest Allied secret of that time. He knew most of the plans and the proposed date for Operation Dragoon, the code name for the invasion of southern France in mid-August.[1]

The second American aboard the black-painted Special Missions aircraft of 624 Squadron of the RAF was a radio operator, and the third agent was "Alain," a French naval officer and aviator, and the oldest member of the trio. The two Americans and their French colleague were in a race against time. It was the third attempt for their mission, code-named Lougre, to penetrate occupied France behind enemy lines. On their first attempt a few nights earlier, the Halifax had joined up with a flight of B-17 Flying Fortresses on a mission to bomb Wehrmacht coastal artillery positions. As the flight of bombers neared their target, the Halifax would pull away while enemy radar and antiaircraft was focused on the B-17s. But this ruse didn't work. Luftwaffe night fighters rose to meet the formation of bombers, and the Halifax was inadvertently caught in a flak barrage, forcing the RAF pilot to scrub the mission and head back to await another opportunity.

The Halifax touched down at Blida, the Allied air base outside of Algiers, and taxied to a corner of the field shared with a U.S. Army Air Force Special Operations squadron of black-painted B-24s and B-17s.[2] Another attempt would have to be scheduled as quickly as possible as events were unfolding quickly. It was critical that Captain Jones and his radio operator parachute into France. The U.S. Fifth Army in Italy had broken out of the Anzio beachhead at the end of May, and American troops entered Rome on June 4. Two days later, on D-Day in Normandy, the Allies breached Hitler's Fortress Europe on the Western Front. General Eisenhower's grand strategy was to follow up with an invasion of southern France in August or September 1944. This would prevent German troops in that part of France from reinforcing the Wehrmacht armies opposing Allied forces battling their way east—toward Germany.

This strategy required all-out support from the intelligence organizations of Britain, France, and the U.S. In France, the plan called for using the *maquis,* the generic term for the many local resistance forces that, though oftentimes divided politically, were united in their determination to rid their country of the hated Wehrmacht.

Jones was given the mission to parachute into southern France and organize the French resistants in the areas where the seaborne landings of Allied troops would be made; lead and direct the destruction of the sole radar station in the area; and supervise the clearing and securing of the key airborne drop zones and glider landing areas that would be used by paratroopers and glider troops of the U.S. and British airborne units. These airborne elements would form a defensive screen to protect the landings on the beaches against any enemy counterattack.

The mission of "Alain," the French naval officer, was to make contact with key officers of the French fleet based in Toulon and talk them into joining the Allies or remain neutral by not opposing the invasion forces.

It was against this backdrop of rapidly unfolding events on

other military fronts in Western Europe that Jones and his two colleagues made a second attempt to parachute into France a few days later. By the time their Halifax appeared over the drop zone, weather conditions had obliterated most of the coast. There was heavy turbulence over the drop zone, Mont de Malay, the last big mountain in the chain that stretches north to south into the Basses-Alpes, and it forced the RAF pilot to turn back.

The two "Joes," as the American agents were called, were especially unhappy to again show up at OSS headquarters, where they faced a good-natured razzing from their colleagues who accused them of lacking the proper moral fiber when they reached the drop zone. This kind of camaraderie was often displayed in an effort to take the edge off the dangers that accompany the business of spying during wartime.

It was now their third try. The Halifax had finally reached the drop-zone area. The pilot had been told that this was a critical mission, and there was no time to wait for a flight of bombers to provide cover against radar or patroling Luftwaffe night fighters. The amber ready light in the Halifax came on, and the French naval officer moved into the "hole" through which he would drop when the green light flashed on. Jones followed behind Alain after both men had nodded their determination to make their jump no matter what.

But the pilot and copilot observed vehicle headlights in the darkness below. They were unable to spot the signal fires on the plateau that had been set up at the Mission Lougre drop zone, the nautical name for a "lugger," a small sailing vessel. The pilot switched off the amber light. Alain, determined not be thwarted a third time, stepped through the hole followed by Jones. The RAF handlers grabbed the radio operator to prevent him from following Jones, as the pilot, not wishing to jeopardize the three agents, banked into a turn for the return flight to Blida.

As Jones and Alain dropped through the darkness beneath the black canopy spread over each man, they quickly picked out the vehicle lights below. But they were unable to spot the signal fires. Alain missed the plateau and smashed against a rock outcropping on one side of Mont de Malay, painfully injuring himself. Jones dropped onto the other side of the mountain below the plateau, but his chute caught on a rock outcropping that saved him from slamming into the mountainside and suffering injury similar to Alain's.

Jones gathered up his chute and shed his jumpsuit to hide both from any unfriendly eyes when he heard what sounded like the heel of a heavy jackboot on rock. He cursed himself for not carrying a gun instead of the penknife hidden in the lining of his jacket. He moved away from his position just in case it was the sound of an enemy patrol looking for the two parachutists. Wherever he moved, he heard the sound of boots thudding against rocks.

Jones was wearing an old blue suit, the kind that ordinary French workers wore in factories or in the fields. His hair was unkempt and his features were graced with a four-week-old mustache that he had grown in an effort to help change his Anglo-Saxon look. His ID noted that he was a mute, a disability that kept him from military service or working in a factory. His "cover" relegated him to working in the fields helping farmers. Captain Geoffrey M. T. Jones looked every bit the part of an itinerant French laborer.

As he moved away from the sounds of what he thought might be an enemy patrol, Jones came across several goats. In the summer night beneath the moon's pale light, he suddenly realized that the goats were wearing wooden bells with the clappers removed; each time a goat bent down to chew some grass, the bell would strike an occasional rock. These goats made up the enemy patrol. He decided to remain close to the goats so that when someone came to fetch the animals he could ask for directions; then he could locate the resistance group that was supposed to be waiting for Mission Lougre.

He had much to think about during those hours of darkness. His parachute jump into southern France was a homecoming of sorts and, in microcosm, he was an example of how the OSS recruited many of its agents for secret intelligence missions and special operations behind enemy lines or deep inside enemy territory.

In his youth, Jones had lived in France many years, specifically in the Provence region, where his family owned a home not too far from where the Allied invasion was scheduled to land. Having grown up with the language, he spoke French fluently. There were many pleasant memories that came to mind as he waited out the darkness. He followed the course of World War II carefully since September 1, 1939, when Hitler invaded Poland and later defeated France. He graduated from Princeton in

June 1942, and along with his diploma he received an ROTC commission in the U.S. Army with an immediate assignment to Fort Bragg's Artillery Replacement Center. When he heard about the formation of new airborne divisions, he volunteered for this special training. Meanwhile the military planners were trying to figure out how artillery elements would fit into airborne operations.

He was assigned to an artillery battery that used the 75-mm, mule-carried howitzers left over from World War I, and he worked on the plans to parachute this weapon in parts for reassembly on the ground and subsequent use in battle. After graduating from the first parachute artillery class at Fort Benning, Jones was assigned to the newly formed 11th Airborne Division, where he found himself one of the few officers in the division's artillery unit who was a college graduate. His Princeton diploma got him the assignment of assistant G-2 at division headquarters.

This was followed by his selection as aide-de-camp to Major General Joseph Swing, the 11th Airborne's commanding general. This assignment also included a stint at the U.S. Army Command and General Staff College at Fort Leavenworth, a posting usually given to majors and lieutenant colonels. Unbeknownst to Jones at the time, his military-training schools and diverse experiences and duties were preparing him for future adventures in France.

It was while he was General Swing's aide that Jones learned with dismay that the 11th Airborne was scheduled for deployment to the Pacific Theater of Operations. But the young lieutenant had other visions, one of which was to help free France from Nazi domination. His boyhood years attending school in Cannes and growing up in the family villa in Mrujes, near St. Tropez, were part of the mystique of wanting to fight in France and help liberate Paris.

Shortly after learning about the 11th Airborne's Pacific destination, Jones heard about a new, supersecret intelligence organization called the Office of Strategic Services. The OSS, he was told, was seeking recruits who spoke foreign languages and had lived or traveled abroad before the war and were not averse to volunteering for "dangerous and hazardous duty." He applied for and was accepted by the OSS. He passed the rigorous recruitment tests and training before receiving what he later called his "cloak and dagger." Within a week, after passing his OSS training course, he was on a plane bound for Casablanca by way of Brazil and Dakar in West Africa.

His assignment included moving about the Moroccan city wearing his uniform that bore the 11th Airborne Division shoulder patch, which enemy spies would be certain to report along with his presence. This intelligence ploy was designed to lead the enemy into thinking that Jones was a member of an advance party from the new airborne division. It was one of several elaborate disinformation schemes to confuse the Nazi high command.

But by the time that Jones arrived in Africa, the original mission for which he had been recruited had been scrubbed. At the time he joined the OSS in 1943, the French resistance was quite active in the Vercors area, so much so that it was believed an airborne artillery officer and his heavy weapons like the 75-mm howitzer could be dropped to the underground fighters, who could put such weapons to good use once they were trained in their deployment. After he arrived in Africa, the *maquis* at Vercors suffered a devastating defeat at the hands of German airborne troops. Jones's artillery and military operations staff experience was tabled for a future time.

From Casablanca he was assigned to OSS headquarters at Maison Blanche, a white-painted building on the outskirts of Algiers. The only Command and General Staff College graduate on the OSS staff at this headquarters, Lieutenant Jones was assigned to the Special Projects Operation Center (SPOC), the inter-Allied group responsible for all secret operations in southern France and Italy. His initial assignment: to begin the training of and working with agents who were preparing to return to their homelands.

The five-week course at Club des Pines, the OSS special training center in the mountains outside of Algiers, provided eager students with instruction in military tactics, map reading, demolitions with the new C-3 explosive the French had dubbed *plastique*, and other field training needed by agents who would parachute into their occupied homeland or be landed by submarine or fast boat. Jones often accompanied his "students" on their one-way flights to France. The majority spoke no English, and he felt he could be helpful to RAF flight crews of the modified Halifax and Sterling bombers of the 624 Special Operations Squadron by interpreting for both parties.

After several months at Maison Blanche, Jones had the distinction of being one of the lowest-ranking OSS officers in charge of developing operational plans and one of the very few Americans privy to the sensitive and highly secret Allied military plans for the Mediterranean Theater of Operations (MTO). The OSS role had spread throughout the MTO as secret operations were launched simultaneously in occupied Greece, Yugoslavia, Albania, and northern Italy, along with France. These operations were designed to support the big picture, as well as provide the kind of on-the-ground intelligence information that the Allied general staff required.

Jones also realized that he would never be allowed to go on an OSS mission to France because of his operations and training role. The risk of capture was too great.

Jones was aware that the resistance forces in France were limited in numbers of active *marquisards*. The French, men and women, especially those who lived in the countryside and in smaller cities and towns, historically were galvanized into action when a major change was about to occur. Under the Nazi occupation, the majority of French citizens held their own counsel and remained unobtrusive under the eyes of the ever-watchful enemy and their Vichy government collaborators. OSS agents sent into France had to be especially careful under these circumstances.

By early July 1944 the timetable for Operation Dragoon was set in motion for the Allied invasion of southern France in mid-August. Jones had an important part in planning the OSS role. He knew that Jean D'Errecalde, code name "D" for "Donal," an experienced American operative of French parentage, had parachuted into France in early June. His mission: to organize the resistance forces to support the Allied invasion by sabotage, hit-and-run raids against vital enemy installations, and the collection of up-to-date vital information to be passed back to the intelligence and military operations planners for inclusion in the master plan. SPOC had passed the word up the chain of command that a top-notch agent had been successfully infiltrated into the invasion area and would take charge of that part of the invasion plan calling for operations behind enemy lines.

D'Errecalde's instructions were to gather information about the number of enemy troops in the designated landing areas;

obtain unit designations for the Order of Battle information that
Allied field commanders would need; sabotage key communications centers; and destroy the vital Luftwaffe radar installation
at Fayence at least six hours before the Allied airborne units
landed by parachute and gliders. His mission also included
clearing the vital glider landing and parachute drop zones of
Rommelspargel, or Rommel's asparagus. Named after the
Wehrmacht's wily "Desert Fox," *Rommelspargel* were tall,
sharpened stakes that had been planted and strung with mines
and barbed wire in most clearings and open areas that could be
used by the Allied airborne forces. Jones was quite aware that
the *Rommelspargel* would tear the balls off parachutists or rip
the flimsy canvas and plywood gliders to ribbons if the traps
were not removed.[3]

But D'Errecalde was unlucky. Shortly after his arrival, he was
arrested by the Gestapo. That was all that the OSS in Algiers
could learn. Fortunately, the hapless agent was not aware of the
invasion date. Nor was it known if he had broken under torture.
This unlucky agent knew only what he was supposed to know,
no more and no less.

Meanwhile, the planning for Dragoon continued at Allied
Force Headquarters (AFHQ) at Caserta, Italy. The plans continued to be formulated under the assumption that intelligence
agents would be organizing the local resistance forces and carrying out the various D-Day-minus plans. The senior OSS staff at
Maison Blanche had not forwarded the information to AFHQ
that their key agent had been lost. Should an admission be made
that the mission was blown? What to do? Who else could be sent
in to replace D'Errecalde?

The Wehrmacht's *Abwehr* intelligence arm expected an Allied invasion of southern France, and the enemy counterintelligence was alert to any influx of Allied agents into the various
departments of southern France. The enemy left nothing to
chance. Patrols in the air, along the coast, and along the highways were alert to the possibility that Allied agents were in
southern France in force.

Colonel Ellery Huntington, senior OSS officer in Algiers, ago-
nized over this turn of events. There was no one on his staff who
could replace the agent in Gestapo custody. The staff officers
had no agent training. They were older men. Jones, among the

youngest officers, initially was ruled out. He knew too much about the invasion plans and the entire OSS operation at Maison Blanche and the SPOC operation at Blida air base.

But Jones, recently promoted to captain, had quickly sized up the problem facing his superiors. For two days after word came in of D'Errecalde's arrest, Jones pressed his superiors that he should replace the arrested agent. He had the training; he spoke French; he knew the area of operations; and he had helped develop the OSS and French resistance plan. He also reminded his superiors that he was a trained paratrooper. In effect, he was not only the best qualified person to send into France, but he was the only person that the Algiers headquarters had available. It was that or inform AFHQ of the failure to organize behind-the-lines support of the Allied airborne force.

Time was short. Colonel Huntington finally gave Jones the green light, warning the entire staff to keep the substitution of Jones top secret. SPOC coordinated Jones's infiltration with that of the French naval officer Alain and his Lougre mission. To assist Jones in his mission, General DeGaulle's official Force Français de l'Intérieur (FFI), the resistance fighters who took their orders from the Free French Provisional Government in London, appointed the American captain a Délégué Militaire of the Alpes Maritime Department so that he could carry more weight with the leaders of the *maquis.*

It was now first light when his thoughts returned to his present predicament. Where the hell is our reception committee?, he kept asking. But the first people he met were the goatherders, who were surprised to find a stranger among their animals. They put him in touch with resistance fighters. It was then that he learned the extent of the French agent's injuries. Morphine was the only treatment available to ease his pain. Accompanied by Jones, Alain was finally moved by mule to another location in the mountains that was made up of *maquis* who were communists. They had been trained by Loyalists who had fought against Franco during the Spanish Civil War, and after their defeat had crossed over the Pyrenees Mountains into France to bide their time.

The group had no radio, and getting one was the OSS agent's first priority. He had to get word back to Algiers that he was alive and functioning. There were those at Maison Blanche and at SPOC who would be chewing their nails at what they considered yet another unfortunate turn of events when the Halifax had returned to Blida with the radio operator.

Finally, Jones made contact with a "radio," as the location and unknown operator were referred to in the local glossary of resistance terminology. SPOC received the coded message that Jones was safely on the ground and would immediately organize for the big event. The 150 resistance fighters, known as the Maquis de Mons (after a nearby town), were impressed with the American captain's Délégué title and attached great importance to his presence. But he observed over the course of a few short days that they were not trained to carry out any real military operations against the Germans. It also had taken them more than two days to put him in touch with the "radio."

And the clock was ticking. The 10,000 men of the First Airborne Task Force (FABTF) were readying for their nighttime drop and glider landings.[4] In Naples, U.S. troops who had been a part of the American Fifth Army were assembling in preparation for the boarding of the invasion fleet. Axis Sally, one of the Nazi propaganda voices of Radio Berlin, warned these American troops that there would be a hot reception committee awaiting their arrival when they charged ashore in southern France. Among the troops were the First Special Service Force, the tough and ferocious U.S. and Canadian troops who were called "The Devil's Brigade" by the Wehrmacht, and the highly decorated GIs of the 442nd Infantry Regiment, made up of Japanese-Americans (Nisei) who fought admirably on Italy's bloody battlefields.

Jones had only a few days to organize his own forces. He assembled all of the resistance leaders in his area and briefed them on their missions when Operation Dragoon started. He had the radio and operator moved to the Mont de Malay command post. From there he could view the entire coast north to San Remo in Italy and west as far as Toulon and Marseille.

The radio operator monitored the BBC, which regularly broadcast coded signals and messages to the anti-Nazi underground, while Jones ventured into the nearby small towns to collect firsthand information. He also learned that the local *gendarmerie* were strong anti-Nazis and fervently against the Vichy, the puppet French government established by the German conquerors of France. These seven *gendarmes* were not only willing to share information with Jones, but they agreed to become his eyes and ears in the landing area, where they were sworn to represent law and order and keep the peace.

Luckily, the local authorities and the Wehrmacht permitted the *gendarmes* to move about freely. Jones took advantage of this and traveled with them in what had become safe and swift movement in a region dotted with roadblocks and other inspection stops. With his uniformed police "agents" in place, and requests among the citizens for information, vital intelligence began flowing in Jones's direction. The strength and unit designations of the Wehrmacht troops in the area were radioed back to OSS headquarters in Algiers. He was able to ascertain the kind of military support the *maquis* groups could provide to the invasion forces. Nothing was being left to chance.

The enemy had used local workers to erect the *Rommelspargel*. Jones discovered that the laborers had not embedded the stakes too deeply. A strong push would knock down the stakes; then the barbed wire could be pulled off, leaving the fields clear for the paratroopers and subsequent glider landings.

Five days before D-Day, information from Jones and other agents in southern France produced a final Order of Battle detailing the enemy's troop strength and deployments. FABTF, the airborne invasion force, would be matched against the Wehrmacht's Nineteenth Army, which had nine divisions in southern France. In the Le Muy area, where the main air drop was planned, the enemy had 1,000 officer candidates at an antiaircraft school, 500 labor troops, an infantry battalion, an armored tank battalion, and several assault-gun units.[5]

In order to keep the Nazi high command off balance, the OSS used Jones and other agents to leak misleading intelligence information that would be certain to be picked up by the enemy's counterintelligence organization. These leaks told of an Allied landing at sites that varied from along the coast between Marseille and Toulon to as far away from France as Genoa, Italy, where partisans and OSS OG units were active. For days prior to D-Day, Jones's "radio" was transmitting reports almost hourly.

Meanwhile, the BBC's radio transmissions to Allied intelligence agents in southern France increased. On the afternoon of August 14, the BBC transmitted the coded signal that Operation Anvil-Dragoon would commence in the early hours of the following day. The operations plan called for the *maquis* to go into action. Jones quickly assembled the resistance leaders in his operational area along with his friendly *gendarmes* and began issuing final instructions. It was imperative that the operation go off like clockwork.

Among the supplies that had been dropped for his personal use were pearl-handled revolvers. He handed them to leaders of the *maquis,* who preferred these status symbols to the U.S. military .45-caliber pistol. Jones had also requested additional arms and munitions for his "troops." Included were special containers made of lightweight disposable cardboard that could fire off two high-explosive mortar shells.

He handed out these mortars to the *maquis* group slated to attack the enemy's radar station at Fayence. His plan also called for *maquis* units to fire on any enemy patrols near the landing sites being cleared, to distract them away from the invasion.

With only hours remaining before the air assault would begin, Jones, some of the resistants, and the seven *gendarmes* climbed into the back of a dilapidated old truck and headed for the main landing zone. A German-speaking *gendarme* sat beside the French driver, proceeding with headlights on, as the Germans did in their own vehicles. They passed one checkpoint after another under the guise of *gendarmes* transporting prisoners who were assigned to road repair work. What they didn't anticipate were Allied invasion aircraft attacking every target of opportunity—*including all vehicles with their headlights on.*

One American pilot spotted the headlights of the truck transporting Jones and his party. It swooped down and dropped one bomb that exploded twenty yards behind the truck, wounding several of the *maquisards* with shrapnel, but none seriously. Jones's group drove through small towns and villages, keeping off the main roads. On one occasion they passed a tavern where off-duty German soldiers, encamped nearby, were drinking and carousing.

When they reached the main landing zone, Jones deployed the *maquis* and the *gendarmes,* ordering them to wait for further instructions. He removed his civilian clothing, under which he was wearing regulation U.S. Army summer khaki shirt and pants, which he hoped would help him pass through the Allied lines and link up with the FABTF command post. A head-and-shoulders photo of Jones, taken in Algiers before this mission, was circulated to the airborne units; he would be easily identified as an American agent when he surfaced during the first hours of the invasion.

But the best laid plans, especially in wartime, often are thwarted by unforeseen factors. At 0300 hours, Allied aircraft disgorged paratroopers spread out over a forty-kilometer area. As they came in contact with the enemy, firefights, exploding mortar and artillery shells, and falling flares started fires in the highly prized vineyards. A thick ground fog was rising where Jones and his men were waiting to make contact with friendly troops.

At first light Jones moved carefully through the gray morning mist. There were jittery American paratroopers out there. At one point, where the fog had cleared momentarily, Jones could spot them. He was startled to see that they were clad in O.D. (olive drab) uniforms instead of the summer tans that he was wearing. He later learned that the order had gone out to the invasion force to wear heavier clothing. They were expected to move north to link up with Allied troops who had moved out of Normandy and were approaching Paris. But the strategy behind Anvil-Dragoon also included the protection of the Allied southern flank, where U.S., British, and Canadian troops fanned out after breaking out of Brittany.

On his first attempt to make contact, Jones, in his pun tans, appeared out of the mist looking more like a Wehrmacht Afrika Corps officer than a member of the U.S. Army. Due to a navigation error that had spread the paratroopers over a wider area, they were naturally cautious. Nor did the chilly ground fog help matters. Jones heard random firing closeby, though there were no enemy troops near the landing zone. After escaping several encounters with nervous paratroopers, Jones finally called out to one GI. Hands held high, Jones slowly approached, speaking calmly and identifying himself to a very suspicious sergeant of the 517th Parachute Infantry Regiment. It was the battalion Jones had originally joined in 1942. He had helped it develop the 75-mm mountain howitzer for airborne use, and a stripped-down air-transportable jeep that also could be parachuted.

Jones began to name some of the officers with whom he had worked at Fort Bragg two years earlier, and the sergeant loosened up at mention of familiar names and places. The sergeant, still careful, brought Jones to a small group of battalion officers who immediately identified their former colleague as an American. He was immediately escorted to the regimental command post and began to provide the unit's commander with firsthand knowledge of enemy deployment and strength in the area. He told the CO that *maquisards* were available to help collect the "forcemen," as the FABTF paratroopers and glider troops were called, and that he also had seven *gendarmes* who could serve as guides.

As the day progressed, Jones sent *gendarmes* and *maquis* to the nearby Chateau de St. Roseline, which he had earmarked for his OSS headquarters. French civilians began to appear during the day, some of them owners of the vineyards requesting help from the GIs in putting out fires that were destroying the grapevines. Although it was not an important military maneuver while small battles were raging in the region, Jones did manage to secure the assistance of troops to help extinguish these fires.

By late morning, FABTF had established its key CP, and about an hour later a tall sandy-haired man in his midtwenties, clad in rumpled khakis, was brought into the Force headquarters. "Since the war, he is mentioned 'for security reasons' in various memoirs of the period as 'Captain Sanders' or 'Geoffrey Stanley' but [it] was actually Geoffrey Jones, the OSS agent who had parachuted into this part of France two weeks before."[6]

"When I finally met up with Bob Frederick (Major General Robert Frederick, FABTF commanding general), I said to him, 'What do you want to know?' I could say this with assurance because between my *gendarmes* and myself, we knew where everybody was, the conditions of the roads and bridges, the location of the electric power lines, and just about everything else he had to be sure of that night.

"Then I flopped into a hayloft and had my first real sleep in three or four days. It was a good feeling to know that there were Americans all around me."[7]

Geoffrey Jones slept with the knowledge that he had successfully completed his mission and also had contributed to one of the most triumphant airborne operations of World War II.

25

"For exceptionally meritorious conduct . . ." The recently
retired Major General William J. Donovan began reading before
the small group of former OSS associates gathered in the New
York City law offices of Donovan Leisure Irvine to honor Major
Hans V. Tofte, the handsome sandy-haired Dane who had
risked his life during the war to join the U.S. Army.[1] These
former comrades-in-arms, who had fought a secret war, were
there to witness the belated presentation of the Legion of Merit
to Tofte. The award was for conceiving and developing a plan
that set a record for establishing a gunrunning and supply operation between Italy and Marshal Tito's partisans in enemy-
occupied Yugoslavia. This plan was a dangerous sea lift that
began at a crucial time in late 1943 when the Allies needed
to step up the pressure on Hitler. It created another front destined to become a quagmire in the Balkans to bog down the
Wehrmacht.

"Under the direction of Major Tofte," General Donovan continued, "an operations base was established at Bari and a constant flow of vital supplies of arms, ammunition, and medical
supplies, as well as thousands of gallons of diesel oil, kerosene,
gasoline, and lubricating oil, was maintained in Yugoslavia despite increasing enemy activity during the months of November
and December. In addition, a brigade of more than 2,000 troops,
recruited among Yugoslavs in internment camps in Italy, was
transported across the Adriatic to join the fighting Partisans.
Thousands of refugees were evacuated to Italy and over 800
wounded Partisans were shipped to Italy for hospitalization.

"In November 1943, when the Germans initiated a drive to
destroy the shipping operation, Major Tofte reconnoitered the

Yugoslav coast, determined Partisan needs to stave off the attack, and personally directed the shipment of these supplies. Due to the timely arrival of the supplies, every landing beach on Vis Island, which was to have been the focal point of the German attack, was heavily fortified . . . The initiative, perseverance, ingenuity, and personal courage displayed by Major Tofte . . . were responsible for the successful supply of thousands of Partisan forces thus enabling them to divert strong German divisions from the Western Front thereby facilitating the rapid advance of the Allied Armies."

The group that was assembled in General Donovan's Wall Street office included Allen Dulles, OSS chief in Berne during the war, and a recently discharged Navy officer, Lieutenant Commander William J. Casey, about to return to his interrupted legal practice. All were aware of Tofte's unique career.

In 1936, Tofte already had been in China for several years working for a Danish shipping company that had sent him to Asia with specific instructions. He was told to learn everything he could about China and its people, including how to read, write, and speak Mandarin and any other dialects he could master. He also had to learn how to operate a shipping company with its own fleet of freighters and passenger vessels.[2]

Born in Copenhagen in 1911, Tofte was a twenty-five-year-old business executive in the mid-1930s with several years of China service and travels elsewhere in Asia under his belt. As a young businessman on the go, he bore witness to the history of that era in China. It was the period that included the incursion into that vast and politically weakened country by Imperial Japan's armed forces. He saw some of the destruction firsthand and wondered about the future of China and the rest of Asia as an industrialized Japan grew stronger militarily and politically.

He was in Denmark in September 1939 continuing his career with the shipping firm when Hitler invaded Poland. The country fell before the Wehrmacht onslaught from the west and the Soviet incursion from the east. The war clouds darkened over Europe, and in April 1940, Hitler's armies invaded and occupied Norway and Denmark. France and the Low Countries soon fell beneath the invincible Wehrmacht. Soon the dreaded Gestapo descended on the countries to maintain the Nazi version of law and order in the occupied territories.

During his years in the shipping business, Tofte had made friends around the world, including many Americans. He was determined to leave Denmark and reach the U.S., where he believed, mistakenly, that he could join the army to fight in the war that he was convinced would spread and involve the United States. To reach freedom, he had to plan his escape from Denmark carefully.

The route he followed took him through Nazi Germany, where his light Nordic features fit in with the so-called blond Aryans of the super race that Hitler wanted to create. Tofte made his way into occupied France, passed through Vichy France to the south, crossed the Pyrenees Mountains into Spain, and continued on to Lisbon. There he boarded a Pan-American "Clipper" flying boat in May 1941. His trip ended in New York, where he was met by American friends. Now a "refugee" like thousands of other Europeans who had managed to reach the U.S., Tofte learned that he could not join the American army or navy because he wasn't a citizen; his "refugee" classification obstructed his effort to enlist.

Meanwhile, British intelligence operatives were active in the U.S., and it wasn't long before they took note of Tofte's presence, along with his China background. Britain, at war and beleaguered on many fronts, was preparing for the conflict to spread to Asia. Singapore and Hong Kong had to be protected along with Burma and Siam. A mission to China was in the works. Tofte was introduced to William Stephenson, England's famed secret agent, "Intrepid," and subsequently was offered a commission in His Majesty's Royal Army. Within a few short weeks, Major Hans V. Tofte, RA, was on his way to Singapore as a member of the SOE assigned as second in command of the China Commando Group (CCG), an organization of volunteers from neutral and occupied countries who would lead Chinese guerrilla forces.

By the time December 7, 1941, had become a red-letter day for the U.S., Tofte had completed his commando training in Singapore. He began operating a supply network using the trail that ran from Burma across the mountains into China and would become the Burma Road. Tofte was one step ahead of the Japanese when Singapore fell in early 1942; he had flown to Burma to relocate the China Commando Group. After the Japanese army moved into Burma, Tofte's group took to the hills.

Itching to see more action, Tofte was frustrated by the indecision of the British military officers and diplomats in China, whose habits, he recalled, were "procrastination and muddling through."

Even the Nationalist Chinese, not known for their political acumen or military expertise, wearied of the British military mission that forever seemed to remain on square one. The SOE's mission was kicked out, including Tofte, whose China experience was a key factor in the CCG's operational plans but whose British uniform miligated against him personally. He had friends in high places in the Kuomintang, but he, along with his British colleagues, was *persona non grata* as long as he wore His Majesty's uniform.

It was time, Tofte decided, to return to the U.S., which was now at war with the Axis. He knew that he could get into the U.S. Army—to fight. He resigned his Royal Army commission and was flown back to the U.S. via the Middle East. Once back in New York City and about ready to take off his British uniform, he was summoned to the OSS headquarters in Washington. General Donovan had learned of Tofte's experiences in Burma. He wanted to target them to launch an operation against Japanese forces that later became Detachment 101's operational area.

Tofte was introduced to Donovan and his staff by Colonel Carl Eifler, later assigned to head up the OSS Burma operation. He was asked to brief the group on what could be expected in that part of Southeast Asia. The questions flew thick and fast. Tofte responded. Donovan was obviously impressed, and when the briefing was over he asked the Dane where he would be assigned next. When Donovan learned that Tofte had resigned his commission to join the U.S. Army, he set the wheels in motion for a direct commission, U.S. citizenship, and an assignment to OSS. In four days he became Captain Hans V. Tofte, 0-525313, Army of the United States.

General Donovan's new organization was growing fast, but seasoned trainers with Royal Army or Royal Marines Commando experience were next to impossible to find. In Tofte not only had the OSS gained an experienced officer with Commando training, but he came along with SOE operations background. Captain Tofte was made second-in-command of the OSS training school housed in the exclusive Congressional Country Club.

During the four months that he was there, he wrote the original OSS training manual, incorporating some of the hugger-mugger skills he had learned in Commando School in Singapore and in the SOE.

The Allied invasion of North Africa in November 1942, along with the defeat of the Afrika Korps at El Alamein by the British Eighth Army, started the rollback of the Wehrmacht. But Tofte had still seen no action with OSS. One of the groups he trained were Albanians about to return to their country with a senior British SOE officer. Aware of Tofte's British military experience, they asked that he also be assigned to their mission. But the mission and the country were, in Tofte's estimation, "too small and unimportant." This was at a time in the development of the OSS when personnel could refuse an assignment for whatever reason.

Administratively, the OSS wasn't the most efficiently managed organization. Many of its personnel were entrepreneurs in uniform trying to sell their own ideas about how to win their secret war. In August 1943, Tofte found himself assigned to OSS headquarters in Cairo. Nobody there knew why he had been sent to Egypt, where Allied Force Headquarters for the entire Mediterranean Theater of Operations was located.

Tofte looked at a map. Operation Avalanche, the invasion of Italy and Salerno, would come off in early September. Captain Melvin Benson, a former SOE officer, was the first agent to parachute into Yugoslavia and make contact with the Partisans. He had come out and reported that Tito's army needed guns and supplies and would fight the Germans anywhere in their country. Tofte knew Benson by reputation, and if this is what he reported then the Dane could make it happen. His entrepreneurial instincts, sharpened by almost a decade of shipping experience, spurred Tofte to develop a plan. It was a sea lift of arms and supplies to Yugoslavia from Allied-held Italian territory on the Adriatic. The sea lift could be extended to supply Partisans in Albania and Greece.

As luck would have it, General Donovan was in Cairo, where plans were being made for the OSS to support Avalanche, scheduled for September 9. The Allies' strategy also called for putting more pressure on the Wehrmacht divisions in the Balkans by increasing the number of OSS and British SOE operations against the common enemy. Tofte gained the OSS chief's attention and presented his plan.

"Go to it, Captain!" he ordered. The plan was predicated on the availability of Yugoslav vessels that could be found in many of the war-torn peninsula's Adriatic ports. Tofte was the only person in the OSS who knew how to run an ocean freight line. The operation would be managed like a commercial shipping line, with complete documentation for the cargo right down to the basic bills of lading.

A letter from General Eisenhower, Supreme Commander, authorized this temporary "confiscation" of ships for the war effort. As the British Eighth Army battled its way up the Adriatic coast, Tofte would follow with a visit to each of the small seaports looking for coastal steamers and schooners with Yugoslav names. Accompanied by an English-speaking Partisan liaison officer, Tofte would introduce himself to the vessel's skipper and show him an important-looking letter signed by General Eisenhower, authorizing the temporary seizure of the boat. He would ceremoniously take possession and sign his and General Eisenhower's name to the receipt. He would then order the boat's captain to take the vessel and crew and set sail immediately for Bari, where the OSS had established headquarters. It would later become the intelligence organization's Strategic Balkan Services.

In one of Tofte's early trips to Yugoslavia, he stopped at the island of Hvar, a major Partisan headquarters. It later became one of the key unloading centers for the sea lift. There he learned that Captain Benson had just completed a two-hundred-mile trek through German-occupied territory after parachuting into the mountains to make his second OSS contact with Marshal Tito.

"Benny," as the tall Minnesotan of Swedish descent was known to his buddies, had been a Pinkerton detective and a private eye operating his own agency before the war.

His military experience coincided with Tofte's, although they had never met. Benson had been recruited for the SOE operation in China in late 1941 and was aboard a ship en route to Singapore shortly after the attack on Pearl Harbor. But Singapore and Rangoon fell to the Japanese forces. Benson, aboard a small freighter trying to dodge the Japanese navy and aircraft, finally made it to Java, where he jumped ship. After a number of close shaves, Benson made it to Australia. The British ordered him on to Egypt via Capetown, South Africa, where he went through the commando training course.

With the U.S. now fully committed to the Axis defeat, Benson decided it was time to head back to America and join the army. He volunteered for the OSS and, like Tofte, was accepted without having to undergo specialized training. Now, nearly two years and thousands of miles later, they were about to meet.

As the boat carrying Tofte pulled up to the dock, he saw a tall American officer who he surmised must be Captain Benson.

In Tofte's eyes the lean figure and weathered features made the former SOE officer a dead ringer for the movie image of a Western lawman.

After the introductions, they settled down for some serious talk about the mission that Benson had just completed. Winding up his debriefing, the Minnesotan allowed how nice it was to finally meet the man who would have been his boss in China.

As Tofte's new "shipping line" grew in size, the Partisan base outside of Bari expanded. A large rear-echelon military compound was built by the Partisans to collect some two thousand Yugoslavs from different internment camps in Italy. They were given basic training and then shipped back to Yugoslavia to join Tito's forces. By the end of 1943, the OSS sea lift had collected forty-four coastal ships, schooners, and a large freighter. The German naval blockade was penetrated seventy-five times, and the OSS fleet delivered 28,932 rifles, 5,458 machine guns, 2,000 81-mm trench mortars with 9,513 cases of mortar ordnance, 12,511 cases of land mines, 5 tons of medical supplies, and 10 tons of biscuits. In addition, 5,032 bales of winter clothing and shoes, 2,338 drums of olive oil, and 10,281 cases of preserved meat were welcomed by the Partisans.

Tofte's small group of Americans included movie actor Sterling Hayden, alias Captain John Hamilton, USMC, who was an experienced sailor married to the famous British actress and comedienne Madeleine Carroll. The blonde film star had joined the American Red Cross and had been assigned to one of the U.S. Army Air Corps bomber wings in the Foggia area. Periodically, she and her husband would spend time together in a small villa on the Adriatic coast halfway between Bari and Foggia.

Although the ships of this OSS sea lift sailed virtually every night with their precious cargoes, there was nothing haphazard about the routes taken to reach islands like Vis and Hvar. The gunrunning vessels, filled and lying low in the water, would clear the harbor entrance at Bari, or Monopoli thirty miles south, late in the day and put out to sea on what often became a perilous voyage for so short a distance.[3]

The ships would sail north along the Italian coast, hugging the Adriatic shoreline under the protection of patroling Allied aircraft until they arrived off Manfredonia in the crook of Testa del Gargano, the Italian spur. Steaming at a slow 3 to 5 knots, they would usually pass the spur about noon the day after departure.

Though none of the ships carried radios, it was possible for the crews to receive messages from the shore via semaphore and flags. Once beyond the spur, they would continue past the small port of Vieste, where they could be reached in an emergency before the final dash to Vis or another island off Yugoslavia. Once the gunrunners were on the way, they were on their own. There was no way of warning the vessels about Allied naval activities on the night gunrunning was planned, or alerting them of a sudden destroyer sweep with orders to sink anything afloat. And there was always the possibility of enemy air activity. To prevent any tragic confrontations between the British Royal Navy's patrol craft in the Adriatic and the OSS sea lift, Tofte would regularly visit "Navy House" in Bari to report on the movement of the OSS fleet to the British navy officer-in-charge.

About twenty-four hours after putting to sea, usually at about 1700 hours, a small freighter would swing out from Vieste in the gathering dusk and pass through a "safety channel" into what the ships' crews called "the twilight zone." As darkness fell, the ship would turn straight north and start the run for Vis Island at full speed ahead, showing no navigation lights along the carefully plotted route.

With any luck, the vessels steaming at 7 knots would arrive at the mouth of Vis Bay no later than 0400 hours, well before first light. Partisans from the Yugoslav Naval Command on Hvar would be waiting with a harbor pilot to board the blockade runner. The ship would creep toward the harbor under the eyes of the Partisan shore batteries and be directed to a hiding place in one of the rugged coves. Partisan work gangs would carefully hide the vessel with trees, bushes, fresh green foliage, and camouflage nets.

By sunrise, the gunrunning vessel had blended into the land-scape, where it would lie at anchor throughout the day, well hidden from German Luftwaffe air patrols. Partisan work gangs of men, women, and children would swarm over the gunrunner in the dark and unload the cargo into smaller boats to carry the loads to shore.

Soon after dark on the second night in the island harbor, the blockade runner would begin the return journey back to Italy. A normal round-trip without enemy interference would take a minimum of four days and nights. The Germans continued to patrol the Dalmatian Islands. Their aircraft and roving E-Boats controlled the Adriatic and the straits among the islands during daylight hours.

The German navy and Luftwaffe had sown minefields throughout the Adriatic and kept well away from shore, fearful of their own mines. The Partisans often knew where the mines were and moved them around to create safe passages in the minefields for the OSS vessels.

Occasionally, the German mines created havoc for ships of all sizes as they tried to sail into the harbor at Bari. There would be a sudden loud blast, and a pall of smoke would hang over the patch of sea where an unlucky vessel had sunk. Once in a while, there were survivors; at other times, none. Frequently, Luftwaffe ME-109s would attack freighters spotted during daylight hours. The OSS sea lift was forced to become a total night operation.

"Early one afternoon a terrific detonation rocked the port," Tofte wrote in his wartime diary.[4] "German planes had just dropped a number of mines in the waters outside Bari forcing the harbor to close except for some British naval vessels and minesweepers. They were busy from dawn to dusk sweeping the waters outside Bari when an explosion centered on a British destroyer that had just struck a mine. I could see H.M.S. *Hebe* settling in the water, her stern ripped open.

"Stipanovic saw it from the *Makaraska* and jumped into a launch with a crew of Partizans and made for the harbor entrance. The RAF crash boats roared out at top speed fol-lowed by several powerful craft from the base ship H.M.S. *Vienna*. Forty men were in the mess having tea when the mine exploded."

" 'It was the most God awful sight I've seen for a long time,'

Jack said afterward. 'The wardroom mess half-full of water and forty blokes blasted to smithereens drifting about in a mess of saltwater, blood and oil and all sorts of filth and stink!'

"Meanwhile, Stipanovic returned with a grisly load of 12 dead and wounded Englishmen. The docks were again filled with ambulances. The destroyer was towed into port. Then it happened again a few days later. This time to one of our fleet. We were having a conference with Giles in *Makaraska's* cabin when Randic barged in reporting that the *Jela* was outside the harbor and on the way in. Here was a ship we had been waiting for, a 400-ton schooner.

"We ran up on deck and saw the big ship still a few cable lengths outside but nicely silhouetted between the breakwaters. At that moment a sheet of flame shot a hundred feet into the air from the *Jela* followed by a resounding explosion. The schooner split in two and the front half immediately disappeared while the after section floated for a few short minutes before sinking. Ten minutes later only a dark patch of smoke floating above the sea where the explosion had occurred was the only sign left of the schooner."

As the OSS sea lift expanded during the final months of 1943, the Allies maintained a firm grip on the Italian peninsula in a slugging match with Hitler's entrenched legions. The grand strategy was to keep the enemy in Italy pinned down and unavailable to reinforce Hitler's other armies guarding "Fortress Europe" against the expected Allied invasion. Bari, a major Italian port on the Adriatic, was filled with destroyers and Liberty ships on December 2. Tofte had wisely split the OSS fleet by anchoring half of his ships at Monopoli to the south. He also had dispersed his fleet beyond the breakwater because he feared an enemy air attack against so tempting a target.

His fears became reality at about 1900 hours on December 2, a date referred to by military historians as "Little Pearl Harbor." In a low-level attack out of the darkness, a flight of Luftwaffe medium bombers struck at the mass of ships at anchor. Most of the ships carried cargo to support the British Eighth Army and the American air units of the Fifteenth Air Force located a few miles inland along the Adriatic coast. Freighters were loaded with 500- and 1,000-pound bombs. Tankers were low in the water with hundreds of thousands of gallons of the

100-octane aircraft gasoline that they carried. Tofte was in the harbor aboard his "flagship."

Radar had failed to pick up the low-flying aircraft. There was no warning. One moment Tofte's flagship was riding at anchor, and suddenly huge explosions reverberated across the water. The flagship rocked violently as the crew and Tofte clambered to the deck. Tracer from the machine guns and 40-mm antiaircraft pom-poms laced across the sky in the glow of burning aviation fuel that cast a red-orange hue across the harbor. Explosions added to the turmoil in the Port of Bari.

At first light the next morning, the masts and occasional superstructure of seventeen freighters, tankers, and British navy destroyers could be seen poking from the now placid waters as small boats cruised the area searching for survivors and floating bodies. The OSS sea lift was lucky that night. Not a single one of Tofte's vessels had been destroyed or damaged.

Despite Tofte's successful efforts in support of the Partisans, he was caught in a bind that was little appreciated at Allied headquarters or by the OSS. Originally, the SOE was to provide the logistics effort for Tito. But there were conditions unacceptable to Tito. He turned to the OSS, which imposed no real conditions, political or otherwise. The British Foreign Office had already recognized the Yugoslav government-in-exile, and young King Peter was residing in London. The Partisans did not recognize King Peter's government or accept him as ruler. This clash of politics between Whitehall and Tito was further carried out by SOE representatives who were sent to Yugoslavia as liaison officers and to keep an eye on things. The British, observed Tofte, were envious of the sea lift that he had established and of his rapport with the Partisans.

But OSS headquarters in Cairo, concerned with other issues, failed to appreciate Tofte's efforts. Cairo, a British center of political intrigue since Queen Victoria's reign, was a strange new battlefield for the OSS staff. It did not recognize the political nuances behind Winston Churchill's push for a major Allied effort against what he called "the soft underbelly of Europe." Although the OSS had sent Captain Walter Mansfield into Yugoslavia to contact the Chetniks, the British, who were in charge of the Allied Military Mission to that country, pushed for total operational control of the OSS effort in the Balkans.

Tofte, ever independent, believed strongly that the British

would muck up as they had in China when he wore their uniform. He also felt that Colonel Toulmin, the OSS chief in Cairo, was too much the conservative Boston banker. He had displayed his colors in previous meetings with Tofte, and preferred to go along with the British because "they knew the Balkans better than OSS."

"It was definitely a struggle to keep the shipping operation under exclusive American control," Tofte wrote in his diary while under house arrest in Cairo awaiting courtmartial on charges that he had left his post in wartime.[5]

"It was obvious to anyone that whoever controlled the ships, and thus the actual delivery of supplies to the Partizans, also had a unique opportunity to maintain a singularly close liaison with Tito's representative. I had adopted a strict adherence to facts and the paragraphs of the initial agreement later verified in Cairo and set forth in a directive, stated that the operation of the supply line across the Adriatic was exclusively an American responsibility—in fact, an OSS/SO responsibility.

"It was a rather nervewracking daily ordeal with fencing and parrying in a highly cordial diplomatic way at these meetings where representatives of all parties interested in Yugoslavia were present in the palatial office of 'Special Force' where Lord Harcourt and the kindhearted, amiable but shrewd Brigadier Miles resided."

Randolph Churchill, the British wartime leader's son, and Brigadier Fitzroy Maclean had parachuted into Yugoslavia to begin their mission on behalf of the Allies. When Maclean tried to take control of the OSS sea lift, Tofte fought him every inch of the way until the SOE officer's own views finally prevailed. It was Maclean's protests to OSS Cairo that set up the dereliction of duty charges against Tofte. The Dane's headquarters were in Bari, but he often boarded his ships for the dangerous voyage to the Dalmatian Islands. From there, more often than not, he would set out with a Partisan patrol into the interior of Yugoslavia to observe firsthand how the supplies were being handled. These absences from his Bari headquarters prompted the courtmartial charges.

The OSS sea lift, with only Captain Tofte and five junior officers, employed more than two thousand Partisans. The logistics chain included the seagoing crews, administrators ashore, and the people who loaded and unloaded the ships and transported the supplies from the islands off Yugoslavia's coast to the mainland. Brigadier Maclean, of higher rank, commanded far less. This professional jealousy was the root of Tofte's problem with his superiors in Cairo.

It was extremely difficult to keep the OSS sea lift secret. Enemy agents were everywhere in Italy. Photos of Tofte, taken secretly by an enemy agent on one of the Dalmatian Islands, surfaced later. His many trips to the islands and into Yugoslavia during the seven months he commanded the OSS sea lift also turned Tofte into a popular figure.[6] But, he acknowledged in his wartime diary, the U.S. Army officers who commanded the depots in southern Italy never raised an eyebrow when the OSS sea lift commander presented them with a list of supplies, weapons, and ammunition that the Partisans needed to fight the common enemy.

General Donovan immediately countermanded the courtmartial charges and ordered Tofte back to the U.S. for his next assignment, which included a promotion to major and thirty days leave.[7] When he departed Cairo, Tofte had left behind a successful OSS operation that would soon grow into a larger fleet of more than sixty ships, the newer additions skippered and crewed by Greek sailors in their own vessels.

Epilogue

> Those who cannot remember the past are condemned to repeat it.
> —GEORGE SANTAYANA:
> *The Life of Reason*, 1906

The death of OSS was temporary. Like the mythological phoenix, the World War II intelligence agency rose from the ashes, but in another form and bearing another name. Reconstitued by necessity on January 22, 1946, the new image of OSS R&A was called the Central Intelligence Group and operated under the supervision of the National Intelligence Authority, an Executive Branch council composed of the Secretaries of State, War, and Navy and President Truman's personal representative, Admiral William D. Leahy. Rear Admiral Sidney W. Souers was named the first director of CIG.

President Truman's personal prejudices against a national cloak-and-dagger agency changed within months after V-J Day. The Soviet Union, America's World War II ally, had turned a cold shoulder on the "spirit at the Elbe" where GIs and Soviet troops linked up amid warm declarations of lasting friendship at the river where they met during the Allied march through defeated Nazi Germany. The Cold War which was proclaimed formally by Winston Churchill in his famous speech at Westminster College, in Fulton, Missouri, thirteen months after V-E Day when he warned that "From Stettin in the Baltic to Trieste in the Adriatic, an iron curtain has descended across the continent."

Following World War II, global changes of great magnitude began to shake old political assumptions. In Asia, the colonies

371

were in turmoil; England, France, and the Netherlands were faced with revolution in their respective areas of interest. China, America's World War II ally, was in the throes of a massive civil war. There were revolutionary stirrings in Greece, and in France and Italy the powerful Communist parties launched their campaigns to win political power at the polls—using some tried and true techniques perfected in the Comintern *agitprop* office. The Arab states in the Middle East were at odds with the western powers over Jewish immigration to Palestine and, in terms of oil, unhappy with their share of the profits. Behind many of these problems was Stalin's hand; by 1948 the USSR would control all of Eastern Europe.

There was more than traditional diplomacy going on around the world. Communist secret agents were behind some of the regional flare-ups; the Cold War would require activities in kind. Their Germans against our Germans; their Italians versus our Italians; their Chinese fighting our Chinese or Koreans or Indochinese or whatever the nationality or race or part of the world. Too much had been happening too fast since the prewar age of innocence came to an end on September 1, 1939.

Because there was no adequate national intelligence organization, President Truman was quick to use the National Security Act of 1947, which not only launched the Defense Department, but on July 26 established the Central Intelligence Agency with a charter to collect information and channel it to the proper Government agencies. A few years would pass before CIA would engage in secret political and para-military action abroad.

It was during this period in the late forties that CIA, despite growing pains, recruited a number of former members of OSS, some for important operational positions. A portion of the wartime OSS R&A files found their way into CIA hands along with the Army's SSU files. However, the original CIA of 1947, styled after OSS R&A and CIG with whatever other postwar refinements had been instituted in the intelligence-gathering processes, closely resembled its World War II forebear. That is, without the covert huggermugger. Clandestine operations would, however, soon become part and parcel of the CIA role as the United States assumed the role of protector of the weak and world policeman, a new role that kept pace with and then expanded with the events of the times.

Events in Asia were coming to a boil. In China the Communist armies overwhelmed their Nationalist enemies, and by 1949 Mao Tse-tung had become the leader of the new China. In Indochina on the southeast rim of the Asian continent, the French colonial forces supported by the Foreign Legion were battling the Viet Minh, losing the colony mile by mile with each passing day and guerrilla ambush. Information from this part of the world was sparse in Washington. Three years earlier the leaders of these very same Viet Minh nationalist forces had held the United States and its OSS representatives in the highest esteem.

Also during the critical postwar year of 1948, there was alarm in Washington at the Communist takeover of Czechoslovakia and the forthcoming Italian elections in the fall. Secretary of Defense James Forrestal, alarmed by the rising Communist Party strength in Italy began a fund-raising campaign among his wealthy friends for the purpose of establishing a clandestine operation that would support anti-Communist candidates and turn the tide against the Reds. Whatever he may have understood to be clandestine operations, there was no definite plan for using this money. Among the men with whom Forrestal had discussed his Italian project was Allen Dulles, former chief of OSS in Switzerland. Dulles had returned to his law practice, and other than offering his services to the government as a consultant on intelligence matters, he had no official connection with CIA in 1948. However, he, too, was alarmed by events in Europe and felt that the Italian problem could best be handled by the U.S. government's use of an official covert organization, not a private organization for private use. There was no covert operations section in CIA, which was then one year old, nor was there any provision in the 1947 National Security Act for covert activities. In the summer of 1948 the National Security Council authorized covert activities, or, as it was called, "special operations." There were two important considerations: CIA huggermugger must be kept secret and, if the flap hit the fan, any official denial would have to stand up under the scrutiny of the simple peoples of the world.[1]

When the Central Intelligence Agency Act was passed in

1949, it exempted CIA from disclosing the "functions, names, official titles, salaries, or numbers of people employed by the Agency." The director of CIA, again without having to answer to the laws of these United States, was given a blank check for which he was accountable to no one outside of the Executive Branch. Taking a page from OSS, the 1949 CIA Act also allowed the CIA director to bring in one hundred aliens secretly and outside the immigration laws and, for "services rendered," they could expeditiously be granted American citizenship.[2]

To head up these secret political operations, CIA brought Frank G. Wisner from State Department. Wisner had served OSS in Istanbul and Bucharest in World War II. In 1950 Allen Dulles took six weeks' leave from his law practice to assist CIA officials. He was to remain in Washington for eleven years. In 1951 he was made deputy director and appointed director by President Eisenhower in 1953.

One of the first attempts at strategic services on a wartime footing was launched in January 1951 during the Korean War, when Eighth Army headquarters organized the catch-all Miscellaneous Group 8086 Army Unit, later called the United Nations Partisan Forces Korea, for behind-the-lines operations similar to those of OSS in World War II. Only there were no OSS veterans at the beginning when the unit was organized by Colonel John H. McGee, who had fought as a guerrilla in the Philippines in World War II. One of the first OSS veterans to be assigned to UNPFK was Lieutenant André Bouchardon. Later there were a handful of other OSS veterans along with a CIA contingent which immediately tried to insinuate itself into what originally had started out as an all-military show designed to support and control guerrilla operations deep inside North Korea. Although a failure for several reasons, UNPFK infiltrated agents and teams sixty miles up the Yalu River, and elsewhere in North Korea. It took British Army Major Ellery Anderson, with World War II SOE experience, to prove that occidentals could operate behind the lines in an Oriental environment. He parachuted behind enemy lines with four American sergeants and for some weeks they called in airstrikes and naval artillery fires while trying to organize local guerrillas. The lessons of OSS

Detachment 101 in Burma had been forgotten only six years after World War II.[3]

There was even a "dirty tricks" department whose plans for raising hell behind enemy lines were denied time and again, even when the opportunity presented itself to poison the entire North Korean general staff. This special operations unit had infiltrated four female agents into the enemy's headquarters kitchen. On another occasion several tons of counterfeit North Korean currency was printed but the distribution plan came to naught.

However, the anti-Communist guerrillas of UNPFK did kidnap fishermen from their small craft at sea for questioning about conditions on the Communist mainland. And UNPFK partisans did blow up bridges, highways, and railroad tracks and tunnels; and "black" propaganda broadcasts to the north were transmitted from mobile radio stations set up on the offshore islands.[4]

Ten years after strategic-services military operations had been launched behind enemy lines in North Korea, an operation of similar magnitude was begun—the "secret" invasion of Cuba. It was not much of a secret, and it came a cropper in mid-April 1961: the Bay of Pigs invasion. Dulles, then director of CIA, denied there was any intelligence "estimate that a spontaneous uprising of the unarmed population of Cuba would be touched off by the landing" of 1,400 anti-Castro Cubans.[5] The invasion was a failure; the causes of the failure verged on outright ineptness on the part of the CIA and Pentagon planners. Still unexplained is why CIA and the military insisted on the type of operation that was launched when the U.S. Army at the time was touting its own brand of special-forces operations—the Green Berets, some of whom already had seen action in covert operations in Southeast Asia.

Beginning in the sixties, the heavy use of electronic surveillance techniques from ships at sea, high-flying SR–71 Mach 3 (three times the speed of sound) aircraft, and orbiting spy-in-the-sky satellites, all tied into powerful high-speed data processing systems, brought to intelligence gathering a new dimension and style. At CIA installations in the

United States and abroad the emphasis was—and still is—on scientific and technological expertise covering the full spectrum of the physical and chemical sciences. And in the jungles of Southeast Asia, Americans were pitted against Viet Cong guerrillas in counterinsurgency operations that for many reasons would fail to halt the advance of the Communist forces from North Vietnam. The Vietnam experience had its parallel in the Korean special operations efforts.

As early as May 11, 1961, President John F. Kennedy approved a series of covert warfare operations recommended by his administration's Vietnam Task Force. During President Eisenhower's tenure in office, secret operations had been launched, but on a lesser scale. Unfortunately, the civilian and military members of this planning group in 1961 were nothing more or less than theoreticians who fancied themselves experts in clandestine warfare.

Setting the scene in perspective, it was an era when the Green Berets flourished under President Kennedy's aegis, and the glamorous aura of special warfare operations was the name of the game. Guerrilla forces had defeated the French in Indochina and later in Algeria; guerrillas had prevailed in Cyprus against British forces; and halfway across the world in Malaya, Chinese Communist insurgents had given the British a rough time for more than a decade. Finally, a scant ninety miles from Miami Beach, Cuban guerrillas were victorious thanks to their insurgent leader, Fidel Castro.

These experiences, along with those of many other nations that had fought counterinsurgency actions against guerrilla forces, had been studied to death by this handful of Vietnam Task Force theoreticians. Later, they farmed out additional studies to favored "think tanks." Nor was a study of the derring-do of covert OSS operations in World War II neglected.

However, these theoreticians had failed to learn their lessons thoroughly; they overlooked their own country's colossal failure in mounting covert warfare operations against North Korea during the Korean War years. Incredibly, the same errors of judgment and the same tactical mistakes that had been made a decade earlier were repeated again in Indochina beginning in 1961.

Most of the officers and enlisted men among the Americans

engaged in the Indochina special-operations effort were not
aware of the Korean experience. They had never heard of
the United Nations Partisan Forces Korea.[6]

During the Korean War there was little information available about the POW camps in North Korea which held thousands of captured troops—Americans, Koreans, British and
other Commonwealth forces, Turks, and a smattering of other
nationalities among the UN forces. In fact, none of the
UNPFK recon teams had ever gotten close enough to a prison
camp to effect the rescue of a single American POW. The
unsuccessful Son Tay raid in late 1971 to free American
POWs in North Vietnam had its own parallel in the Korean
War. Several months before the armistice was signed at Panmunjom in July 1953, a special force of UNPFK volunteers
had been organized. Their mission: to parachute into a POW
camp and rescue the prisoners.* The armistice canceled the
rescue operation.[7]

Examined from a strictly military standpoint the UNPFK
operations against enemy forces in North Korea succeeded in
one respect. It was estimated that nearly half a million Communist Chinese and North Korean troops were deployed to
guard the sea frontiers of the Communist half of the peninsula
against forays by UN partisan raiders whose landings might
have presaged an invasion by United States naval and marine
amphibious forces. But forcing the enemy to pin down a
half a million men was of no consequence, as military
tacticians of that era had learned from bitter experience. In
Asia there always will be too many of the enemy and never
enough of U.S. and allied forces. This was the first important
lesson overlooked by the American counterinsurgency theoreticians.

Their second failure was in not learning a lesson in basics
taken from the UNPFK experience. The many similarities of
geography were not considered. The Vietnam coastline is
similar to that of the Korean peninsula, and both areas are

---

*A special force of Rangers was created and a plan drawn
up for this group to parachute to a prison camp in North
Korea (the one nearest the Yellow Sea), forcibly enter the
camp, and move the prisoners out toward the sea, where
Navy craft would be standing by to evacuate the released
captives.

dotted with offshore islands. Both areas have a frontier that abuts mainland China, and the northern areas of each region are mountainous. Both areas have populations politically divided by artificially imposed frontiers and strong state security forces trained to hunt down armed enemies of the state. Finally, and most important, the peoples of Korea and those of Indochina are Asian in both psychology and tradition.

In each instance, during the Korean War and also during the Vietnam conflict, those who planned and carried out covert warfare activities knew little about the target nations when they decided to wage a very special kind of war.

It wasn't until after the Korean War that the U.S. Army hired a Washington "think tank" to analyze the UNPFK experience. Civilian researchers finally delivered a report that was strong in statistical measurements of cost and efficiency factors but lacking as a thorough and detailed practical analysis based on interviews with American, British and Korean participants. An Army historian visited the partisan-held islands at one time during the war, but his interviews lacked depth and were obviously hurried.[8]

Former Korean partisans, whose views had never been solicited, explained that many covert operations had failed because there was a heavy turnover of American leaders and that those assigned to UNPFK knew little about either the enemy or their partisan allies.

One high-ranking ROK Army general officer reluctantly admitted that when he was assigned to UNPFK he preferred not to work with American military intelligence operatives. In early 1951 Lieutenant Colonel Chae Myung Shin led a partisan band in North Korea clad in enemy uniforms. On this particular mission the partisans kidnapped a high-ranking Communist official and credited their success to their own talents. "When we operated freely, not the way the Americans wanted us to, we usually were successful," related the former partisan leader. "They [the Americans] never understood us or our country."[9]

American theoreticians who planned covert operations in Vietnam had never learned the lessons of history. Why should they succeed in Vietnam when a similarly planned operation had failed in another war? If the Vietnam planners, policy-makers, and the military and civilian officials of the U.S. Military Assistance Command Studies and Observation Group (or, correctly, Special Operations Group) in Saigon had profited from the Korean experience, perhaps covert warfare operations against North Vietnam might never have occurred.

Unfortunately, American military planners have always looked upon guerrilla warfare and counterinsurgency operations as falling within a particular "doctrine" or military strategy—or tactics or logic or whatever. The term, as used by the military, is one that smacks of intellectual containment. It circumscribes logic and initiative. There never has been a successful "doctrine" for guerrilla warfare nor should there have been a counterinsurgency "doctrine." The conduct of guerrilla warfare, by its very nature, is as broad in scope as man's imagination, and guerrillas throughout history have been most imaginative. In Vietnam, the counterinsurgency force likewise should have been free from the restrictions of military "doctrine."

Although the CIA is supposed to supervise all intelligence presentations to the President via the National Security Council, the director of CIA, "as the Government's principal intelligence officer," is also responsible for the "coordination and effective guidance of the total United States foreign intelligence effort."[10] But there's also the Defense Intelligence Agency, established August 1, 1961, to handle the vast amount of military intelligence which, at times, has duplicated the CIA output. However, there is a close inter-relationship between CIA and DIA. The CIA utilizes a large number of military personnel who are under "contract" for one, two, or three years or, in the case of Lieutenant Colonel Lucien Conein, U.S. Army (Ret.),* a longer period which became a singular career.[11]

Many of the "civilians" who were employed by CIA in

---

*Conein, a major in 1954, was then a member of the Saigon Military Mission, a cover for the CIA, which arrived on June 1 with Colonel (later Major General) Edward Lansdale, also former OSS, in charge. Mission: black propaganda and covert operations.

Laos to supervise training and operations of the friendly forces were faces familiar in Vietnam, where they had served as U.S. Army colonels at the Fifth Special Forces Group at Nha Trang. Even the former commander of OSS Detachment 101, Lieutenant General William R. Peers, spent a surreptitious tour with CIA in 1972, during which time he disappeared from the active military scene.*

And the present director of CIA, Richard Helms, is an OSS veteran, as were some of his major department heads: Ray S. Cline, now head of State Department Intelligence; William Colby who headed up the pacification program in South Vietnam; and Lawrence R. Houston, now the Agency's general counsel. But the roster of OSS alumni now in CIA grows thin with the passing years, as men reach retirement age or pass on.

Yet historians always refer to OSS when they comment about the origins and genealogy of the CIA and some of its covert as well as overt operations. America's first attempt at creating a national intelligence service began with a bumbling start in the summer of 1941 and took on new dimensions in the summer of 1942 with the creation of the Office of Strategic Services. Today, the Central Intelligence Agency has improved upon the operations of the wartime OSS. But no matter what the generation—past, present, or future—the "craft of intelligence," as the late Allen Dulles called Kipling's "great game," always will have its serious adherents and its adventure-loving fans—and its enemies, too, at home and abroad. And there always will be casualties left in the wake of some intelligence operations, for it is the nature of the business—especially that part of it conducted in the shadows.

As an OSS sergeant once told the author as they viewed the tortured remains of an agent in Yugoslavia: "Nobody said it wasn't a dirty business!" And an ancient Chinese sage observed that an army without secret agents is exactly like a man without eyes or ears.

The same holds true today for all nations as well as their

---

*General Peers trained Nationalist Chinese guerrillas for raids on the mainland and also was chief of covert training for CIA during this period in the early fifties.

respective armed forces. It took the OSS experience of World War II to alert the United States to the fact that sharp eyes and ears will go far to insure national survival in this dangerous age.

Glossary

AAF	Army Air Force (U.S. World War II designation)
AAMM	Anglo-American Military Mission (U.S.-British Mission in Yugoslavia attached to Marshal Tito's headquarters)
Abwehr	German military intelligence organization in WW II
ACRU	Air Crew Rescue Unit (U.S.) created to rescue airmen downed in enemy-occupied territory
AEF	American Expeditionary Force in World War I
AFHQ	Allied Force Headquarters, originally established in Algiers and then at Caserta, Italy after the invasion—a joint staff for the Italian campaign in WW II
Afrika Korps	The German military command and forces in North Africa
Allies	All belligerents in World War II who were at war with Germany, Italy, and Japan. Also, same designation in World War I for all belligerents at war with Imperial Germany
Alsos	A group of American scientists operating in the wake of Allied forces who searched out German scientific secrets. This group took its name from the Greek word *alsos* which means grove, as in

olive groves, as a compliment to General Leslie Groves, during World War II the chief of the Manhattan Project for the development of the atomic bomb

AMM — American Military Mission in Greece and other occupied countries

Andarte — Greek word for guerrilla

AO — Area of (military) operations

Axis — Popular designation for the three World War II enemy nations—Nazi Germany, Fascist Italy, and Imperial Japan

BAF — Balkan Air Force

BATS — Balkan Air Terminal Service, British organization created to maintain secret air strips in enemy-occupied areas

"Bennies" — American slang for Italian agents taken from the Italian phrase *"Va bene,"* "That's good." When GIs landed at Salerno local Italians answered every question with *Va bene*

Black Operations — Clandestine work by secret agents working under cover

CBI — Initials for China-Burma-India Military Theater of Operations

CCLN — Central Committee of National Liberation in Italy (also referred to as CLN), the leaders of the resistance

CCS — Combined Chiefs of Staff composed of U.S. and British military leaders, with liaison officers attached from all occupied nations or belligerents including France and the Soviet Union

CFI — Czechoslovak Forces of the Interior, the resistance

Chetniks	Serb guerrillas who fought in the resistance army commanded by Royal Yugoslav Army General Draza Mahailovic
Chindit	The British, Indian, and Burmese troops commanded by British Brigadier Orde Wingate
CIA	Central Intelligence Agency (U.S.)
COD	U.S. Navy designation for aircraft used for transport and administrative flight operations from land to aircraft carriers and from carrier to carrier
COI	Coordinator of Information, predecessor of OSS
Cover	Assumed name and false identity papers and personal history used by secret agents
Dakota	British Royal Air Force designation for U.S. twin-engine C–47 transport
DF	Direction Finder. DF-ing is using a direction finder to locate a hidden radio transmitter
DIA	Defense Intelligence Agency (U.S.)
DZ	Drop zone, an area used to parachute or air-drop supplies
EAM	In Greece the political arm of the Communist Popular Front
EDES	National Republican Greek League, a grouping of anti-Communist political parties of center-right
ELAS	The military arm of the Greek Popular Front, called the Greek Peoples Liberation Army, and often referred to as EAM/ELAS
FDR	President Franklin Delano Roosevelt

FFI	French Forces of the Interior, the organized resistance movement
FIS	Foreign Information Service, the U.S. organization (today using initals FBIS—the B for Broadcasting) charged with monitoring all foreign broadcasts and publications during World War II
FO	The British Foreign Office
Gestapo	Acronym for *Die Geheime Staatspolizei*, Nazi Germany's Secret State Police
GHQ	General Headquarters—designation for General Douglas MacArthur's headquarters in the Pacific through World War II and during his tenure in Japan after the war
Gooney Bird	Nickname for the U.S. C–47 twin-engine transport
Hump	Flying across the Himalaya Mountains was called flying over "the Hump"
Jane	Slang name for a female agent
Joe	Slang name for a male agent
JEDBURGH	Joint Allied effort to develop inter-allied teams of three men to parachute into France and the Low Countries and organize resistance forces
JCS	Joint Chiefs of Staff, the U.S. high command
Kachin	The hill tribes of Northern Burma
LZ	Landing zone
LO	Liaison officer
Line-Crosser	Agents who sneak across the lines to spy out the enemy's positions and collect battlefield or tactical intelligence for immediate use

Luftwaffe	The German Air Force in World War II
MAAF	Mediterannean Allied Air Force composed of USAF, RAF, and the air force units of other nations which even included two Russian squadrons
Maquis	Also known as *Maquisard,* French resistance fighters who took their name from the tough and thorny bush in Corsica
MTO	Mediterannean Theater of Operations
MI–6	The popular name for British Secret Intelligence Service (SIS)
Milorg	Acronym for the Norwegian resistance movement
Music Box	British intelligence slang expression for a radio transmitter
Naga	Burmese hill tribe along the frontier between India and Burma and sometime headhunters
Oflag	Acronym for German prisoner of war camp for officers
ONI	Office of Naval Intelligence (U.S.)
OSS	Office of Strategic Services
OSS/AOS	OSS Air Operations Section
OSS/FN	OSS Foreign Nationalities Section
OSS/MO	OSS Morale Operations Section which worked on "black propaganda" projects
OSS/MU	OSS Maritime Unit of fast patrol and torpedo boats for running enemy blockades and infiltrating agents through a sea cordon, and slower craft for supply
OSS/OG	OSS Operational Group, a detachment of fifteen to twenty men sent into enemy-

occupied territory to organize guerrilla operations and, when necessary, ambush, attack, and raid the enemy

OSS/R&A — OSS Research and Analysis Branch, the brain center of the organization, responsible for the collection and analysis of all intelligence openly or covertly acquired

OSS/SO — OSS Special Operations, teams of three to five men who joined guerrillas to train and lead them and to execute intelligence missions when necessary

OSS/SI — OSS Secret Intelligence, the division that trained and fielded spies for deep penetration missions into enemy areas

OSS/S&T — OSS Schools and Training was responsible for testing and training all recruits as spies and agents of various types

OSS/X–2 — OSS Counterintelligence arm to keep secure the organization and investigate suspects

OWI — Office of War Information responsible for all censorship of news and psychological warfare operations

Partisan — Resistance fighter, also called *partizan*. Term most popular in the Balkans, Northern Italy, and Central Europe and the Soviet Union

Pianist — British slang for a radio operator

PID — Political Intelligence Department (British)

PM — The Prime Minister, Winston Churchill

PT Boat — U.S. Navy Patrol-Torpedo Boat and extremely fast for infiltrating agents or supplies by sea and also exfiltrating men and women

PWE	British Psychological Warfare Executive similar to OSS/MO Division engaged in "black propaganda" operations
R&A	OSS Research and Analysis Division
RAF	Royal Air Force (British)
ROTC	Reserve Officers Training Corps in American universities for developing officers
SACO	Sino-American Cooperative Organization, a guerrilla organization organized in China by the U.S. Navy
SAS	Special Air Service, set up by the British to work similar to OSS/OG teams
SBS	Strategic Balkan Services, a section of the 2677 OSS Regiment (Provisional) with missions to the Balkans
SD	Initials of *Sicherheitdienst*, the Gestapo Security Police
SEC/NAV	Secretary of the Navy (U.S.)
SEC/WAR	Secretary of War (U.S.)
SF	Special Forces, British designation for joint OSS/SOE efforts in northern Italy
SFHQ	Joint OSS/SOE Special Forces Headquarters in London
SHAEF	Supreme Headquarters Allied Expeditionary Force, Allied Headquarters in London
Shan	Burmese hill tribe
SI	Secret Intelligence division of OSS for conducting black espionage operations
SIS	Secret Intelligence Service or MI–6 (British)
SO	Special Operations teams of three to five men in OSS

SOC	Special Operations Committee, an Allied group to approve missions behind the lines
SOE	Special Operations Executive, the OG and SO half of British Intelligence Service
Spook	American slang for spy
Stalag	German acronym for a prisoner-of-war camp
UNPFK	United Nations Partisan Forces Korea, a behind-the-lines organization that operated and raided in North Korea during the Korean War—similar to OSS
USMACV	United States Military Assistance Command in Vietnam
USMACSOG	United States Military Assistance Command Studies and Observation Group, a cover name for the joint military/CIA Special Operations Group engaged in covert operations in North Vietnam, Laos, and Cambodia during the Vietnam conflict
Ustashi	Croat Fascist organization which collaborated with German occupation forces in Yugoslavia during World War II, and were used as police troops by the Nazis
Vichy	The city of south-central France which was the seat of the defeated French Government headed by Marshal Henri Pétain and Pierre Laval
Wehrmacht	The German Army of World War II

Appendix

1: EXECUTIVE ORDER 8826
DESIGNATING A
COORDINATOR OF INFORMATION

By virtue of the authority vested in me as President of the United States and as Commander in Chief of the Army and Navy of the United States, it is ordered as follows:

1. There is hereby established the position of Coordinator of Information, with authority to collect and analyze all information and data, which may bear upon national security; to correlate such information and data, and to make such information and data available to the President and to such departments and officials of the Government as the President may determine; and to carry out, when requested by the President, such supplementary activities as may facilitate the securing of information important for national security not now available to the Government.

2. The several departments and agencies of the Government shall make available to the Coordinator of Information all and any such information and data relating to national security as the Coordinator, with the approval of the President, may from time to time request.

3. The Coordinator of Information may appoint such committees, consisting of appropriate representatives of the various departments and agencies of the Government, as he may deem necessary to assist him in the performance of his functions.

4. Nothing in the duties and responsibilities of the Coordinator of Information shall in any way interfere with or impair the duties and responsibilities of the regular military and naval advisers of the President as Commander-in-Chief of the Army and Navy.

5. Within the limits of such funds as may be allocated to the Coordinator of Information by the President, the Coordinator may employ necessary personnel and make provision for the necessary supplies, facilities, and services.

6. William J. Donovan is hereby designated as Coordinator of Information.

FRANKLIN D. ROOSEVELT

THE WHITE HOUSE

July 11, 1941.

2: MILITARY ORDER
OFFICE OF STRATEGIC SERVICES

By virtue of the authority vested in me as President of the United States and as Commander-in-Chief of the Army and Navy of the United States, it is ordered as follows:

1. The Office of the Coordinator of Information, established by Order of July 11, 1941, exclusive of the foreign information activities transferred to the Office of War Information by Executive Order of June 13, 1942, shall hereafter be known as the Office of Strategic Services, and is hereby transferred to the jurisdiction of the United States Joint Chiefs of Staff.

2. The Office of Strategic Services shall perform the following duties:

a. Collect and analyze such strategic information as may be required by the United States Joint Chiefs of Staff.

b. Plan and operate such special services as may be directed by the United States Joint Chiefs of Staff.

3. At the head of the Office of Strategic Services shall be a Director of Strategic Services who shall be appointed by the President and who shall perform his duties under the direction and supervision of the United States Joint Chiefs of Staff.

4. William J. Donovan is hereby appointed as Director of Strategic Services.

5. The Order of July 11, 1941, is hereby revoked.

FRANKLIN D. ROOSEVELT
Commander-in-Chief

THE WHITE HOUSE

June 13, 1942.

3: MEMORANDUM FOR THE PRESIDENT
SECRET

Pursuant to your note of 31 October 1944 I have given consideration to the organization of an intelligence service for the post-war period.

In the early days of the war, when the demands upon intelligence services were mainly in and for military operations, the OSS was placed under the direction of the JCS.

Once our enemies are defeated the demand will be equally pressing for information that will aid us in solving the problems of peace.

This will require two things:

1. That intelligence control be returned to the supervision of the President.

2. The establishment of a central authority reporting directly to you, with responsibility to frame intelligence objectives and to collect and coordinate the intelligence material required by the Executive Branch in planning and carrying out national policy and strategy.

I attach in the form of a draft directive (Tab A) the means by which I think this could be realized without difficulty or loss of time. You will note that coordination and centralization are placed at the policy level but operational intelligence (that pertaining primarily to Department action) remains within the existing agencies concerned. The creation of a central authority thus would not conflict with or limit necessary intelligence functions within the Army, Navy, Department of State and other agencies.

In accordance with your wish, this is set up as a permanent long-range plan. But you may want to consider whether this (or part of it) should be done now, by executive or legislative action. There are common-sense reasons why you may desire to lay the keel of the ship at once.

The immediate revision and coordination of our present intelligence system would effect substantial economies and aid in the more efficient and speedy termination of the war.

Information important to the national defense, being gathered now by certain Departments and agencies, is not being used to full advantage in the war. Coordination at the strategy level would prevent waste, and avoid the present confusion that leads to waste and unnecessary duplication.

Though in the midst of war, we are also in a period of

transition which, before we are aware, will take us into the
tumult of rehabilitation. An adequate and orderly intelligence.
system will contribute to informed decisions.

We have now in the Government the trained and specialized
personnel needed for the task. This talent should not be dispersed.

WILLIAM J. DONOVAN
DIRECTOR

November 18, 1944

4: "TAB A" CENTRAL INTELLIGENCE SERVICE
SECRET

In order to coordinate and centralize the policies and actions
of the Government relating to intelligence:

1. There is established in the Executive Office of the President a central intelligence service, to be known as the _____,
at the head of which shall be a Director appointed by the
President. The Director shall discharge and perform his functions and duties under the direction and supervision of the
President. Subject to the approval of the President, the Director
may exercise his powers, authorities and duties through such officials or agencies and in such manner as he may determine.

2. There is established in the _____ an Advisory Board
consisting of the Secretary of State, the Secretary of War, the
Secretary of the Navy, and such other members as the President may subsequently appoint. The Board shall advise and
assist the Director with respect to the formulation of basic
policies and plans of the _____.

3. Subject to the direction and control of the President, and
with any necessary advice and assistance from the other Departments and agencies of the Government, the _____ shall
perform the following functions and duties:

(a) Coordination of the functions of all intelligence agencies of the Government, and the establishment of such policies
and objectives as will assure the integration of national intelligence efforts;

(b) Collection either directly or through existing Government Departments and agencies, of pertinent information, including military, economic, political and scientific, concerning
the capabilities, intentions and activities of foreign nations, with
particular reference to the effect such matters may have upon
the national security, policies and interests of the United
States;

(c) Final evaluation, synthesis and dissemination within
the Government of the intelligence required to enable the

Government to determine policies with respect to national planning and security in peace and war, and the advancement of broad national policy;

(d) Procurement, training and supervision of its intelligence personnel;

(e) Subversive operations abroad;

(f) Determination of policies for and coordination of facilities essential to the collection of information under subparagraph "(b)" hereof; and

(g) Such other functions and duties relating to intelligence as the President from time to time may direct.

4. The _____ shall have no police or law-enforcement functions, either at home or abroad.

5. Subject to Paragraph 3 hereof, existing intelligence agencies within the Government shall collect, evaluate, synthesize and disseminate departmental operating intelligence, herein defined as intelligence required by such agencies in the actual performance of their functions and duties.

6. The Director shall be authorized to call upon Departments and agencies of the Government to furnish appropriate specialists for such supervisory and functional positions within the _____ as may be required.

7. All Government Departments and agencies shall make available to the Director such intelligence material as the Director, with the approval of the President, from time to time may request.

8. The _____ shall operate under an independent budget.

9. In time of war or unlimited national emergency, all programs of the _____ in areas of actual or projected military operations shall be coordinated with military plans and shall be subject to the approval of the Joint Chiefs of Staff. Parts of such programs which are to be executed in a theater of military operations shall be subject to the control of the Theater Commander.

10. Within the limits of such funds as may be made available to the _____, the Director may employ necessary personnel and make provision for necessary supplies, facilities and services. The Director shall be assigned, upon the approval of the President, such military and naval personnel as may be required in the performance of the functions and duties of the _____. The Director may provide for the internal organization and management of the _____ in such manner as he may determine.

5: EXECUTIVE ORDER 9621
TERMINATION OF THE OFFICE OF STRATEGIC SERVICES
AND DISPOSITION OF ITS FUNCTIONS

By virtue of the authority vested in me by the Constitution and Statutes, including Title I of the First War Powers Act, 1941, and as President of the United States and Commander in Chief of the Army and the Navy, it is hereby ordered as follows:

1. There are transferred to and consolidated in an Interim Research and Intelligence Service, which is hereby established in the Department of State, (a) the functions of the Research and Analysis Branch and of the Presentation Branch of the Office of Strategic Services (provided for by the Military Order of June 13, 1942), excluding such functions performed within the countries of Germany and Austria, and (b) those other functions of the Office of Strategic Services (hereinafter referred to as the Office) which relate to the functions of the said Branches transferred by this paragraph. The functions of the Director of Strategic Services and of the United States Joint Chiefs of Staff, relating to the functions transferred to the Service by this paragraph, are transferred to the Secretary of State. The personnel, property, and records of the said Branches, except such thereof as is located in Germany and Austria, and to much of the other personnel, property and records of the Office and of the funds of the Office as the Director of the Bureau of the Budget shall determine to relate primarily to the functions transferred by this paragraph, are transferred to the said Service. Military personnel now on duty in connection with the activities transferred by this paragraph may, subject to applicable law and to the extent mutually agreeable to the Secretary of State and to the Secretary of War or the Secretary of the Navy, as the case may be, continue on such duty in the Department of State.

2. The Interim Research and Intelligence Service shall be abolished as of the close of business December 31, 1945, and the Secretary of State shall provide for winding up its affairs. Pending such abolition, (a) the Secretary of State may transfer from the said Service to such agencies of the Department of State as he shall designate any function of the Service, (b) the Secretary may curtail the activities carried on by the Service, (c) the head of the Service, who shall be designated by the Secretary, shall be responsible to the Secretary or to such other officer of the Department of State as the Secretary shall direct,

and (d) the Service shall, except as otherwise provided in this order, be administered as an organizational entity in the Department of State.

3. All functions of the Office not transferred by paragraph 1 of this order, together with all personnel, records, property, and funds of the Office not so transferred, are transferred to the Department of War; and the Office, including the Office of the Director of Strategic Services, is terminated. The functions of the Director of Strategic Services and of the United States Joint Chiefs of Staff, relating to the functions transferred by this paragraph, are transferred to the Secretary of War. Naval personnel on duty with the Office in connection with the activities transferred by this paragraph may, subject to applicable law and to the extent mutually agreeable to the Secretary of War and the Secretary of the Navy, continue on such duty in the Department of War. The Secretary of War shall, whenever he deems it compatible with the national interest, discontinue any activity transferred by this paragraph and wind up all affairs relating thereto.

4. Such further measures and dispositions as may be determined by the Director of the Bureau of the Budget to be necessary to effectuate the transfer or redistribution of functions provided for in this order shall be carried out in such manner as the Director may direct and by such agencies as he may designate.

5. All provisions of prior orders of the President which are in conflict with this order are amended accordingly.

6. This order shall, except as otherwise specifically provided, be effective as of the opening of business October 1, 1945.

HARRY S TRUMAN

THE WHITE HOUSE
September 20, 1945.

Notes

PROLOGUE

1. Aldo Icardi, *Aldo Icardi: American Master Spy*. New York: University Books, Inc., 1956, pp. 54–57.
2. Ibid., pp. 219–220.
3. N.Y. *World Telegram & Sun*, August 16, 1951.

CHAPTER 1

1. Author's interview with Colonel Charles M. Sweeny, U.S. Army (Ret.), in 1960.
2. Ibid.
3. David Kahn, *The Code-Breakers*, p. 359.
4. Ibid., p. 360.
5. Ibid., p. 360.
6. Ibid., p. 361.
7. Ibid., p. 3.
8. Corey Ford, *Donovan of OSS*, p. 94.
9. H. Montgomery Hyde, *Room 3603*, p. 50.
10. Ibid., p. 51.
11. Ford, *op. cit.*, pp. 92, 93.
12. Hyde, *op. cit.*, p. 52.
13. Ford, *op. cit.*, p. 91.
14. Ibid., p. 94.

CHAPTER 2

1. Corey Ford, *Donovan of OSS*, p. 90.
2. Ibid., p. 98.
3. H. Montgomery Hyde, *Room 3603*, p. 59.
4. M.R.D. Foot, *SOE in France*, p. 31.
5. Hyde, *op. cit.*, p. 61.
6. Ford, *op. cit.*, p. 102.

7. Hyde, *op. cit.*, p. 61.
8. Ford, *op. cit.*, p. 105.
9. Ibid, p. 105.
10. David Kahn, *The Code-Breakers*, p. 24.
11. Executive Order Number, July 11, 1941.
12. Hyde, *op. cit.*, p. 174.
13. Ibid., p. 174.
14. Thomas Grandlin, "The Political Use of Radio," *Geneva Studies*, Vol. X, No. 3, August 1939.
15. Paul M. A. Linebarger, *Psychological Warfare*, p. 91.
16. Ford, *op. cit.*, p. 111.
17. Ibid., p. 111.
18. Ibid., p. 115.
19. Ford, *op. cit.*, p. 117.
20. Hyde, *op. cit.*, p. 177.

CHAPTER 3

1. Corey Ford, *Donovan of OSS*, p. 122.
2. Author's interview with Colonel Sweeny, 1960.
3. Edward Hymoff, "Halt—Or I'll Shoot You with My Broomstick!" *Saga*, April 1964.
4. *New York Times*, July 10, 1972, obituary of Thomas G. Cassady.
5. Stewart Alsop and Thomas Braden, *Sub Rosa: The OSS and American Espionage*, pp. 80, 81.
6. Ibid., p. 79.

CHAPTER 4

1. Vincent J. Esposito, ed., *West Point Atlas of American Wars*, Vol. II, map 82.
2. Stewart Alsop and Thomas Braden, *Sub Rosa*, p. 85.
3. Corey Ford, *Donovan of OSS*, p. 128.
4. Lyman B. Kirkpatrick, Jr., *The Real CIA*, p. 149.
5. Alsop and Braden, *op. cit.*, p. 85.
6. Ibid., p. 96.

CHAPTER 5

1. Stewart Alsop and Thomas Braden, *Sub Rosa*, p. 23.
2. Corey Ford, *Donovan of OSS*, p. 160.
3. Lyman B. Kirkpatrick, Jr., *The Real CIA*, p. 12.
4. Ibid., pp. 12, 18, 19.

5. OSS Assessment Staff, *Assessment of Men: Selection of Personnel for the OSS*, p. 4.
6. Ibid., p. 13.
7. Ibid., p. 12.
8. Ibid., pp. 58–202; Ch. 3 and 4.

CHAPTER 6

1. Charles A. Willoughby and John Chamberlain, *MacArthur 1941–1951*, p. 144.
2. Charles F. Delzell, *Mussolini's Enemies: The Italian Anti-Fascist Resistance*, p. 365.

CHAPTER 7

1. Author's interview with Ralph W. Donnelly, Washington, D.C. June, 1972.
2. OSS R&A Report No. 2229, June 15, 1944. *Burma: Enemy Shipping October 1943–April 1944.*
3. William R. Peers, and Dean Brelis, *Behind the Burma Road*, p. 26.
4. Author's interview with Turhan Celik, June, 1972, in Wilmington, Delaware. Celik, a pseudonym for a long-time friend of the author, preferred that his true identity not be used because the nature of his work for an American corporation requires much travel abroad.
5. To come.

CHAPTER 8

1. Andrew Molnar et al., *Undergrounds in Insurgent, Revolutionary and Resistance Warfare*, p. 201.
2. Otto Heilbrunn, *Partisan Warfare*, p. 164.
3. William R. Peers and Dean Brelis, *Behind the Burma Road*, p. 72.
4. D.M. Condit, *Case Study in Guerrilla War: Greece During World War II*, p. 29.
5. Ibid., p. 51.
6. Ibid., p. 44.
7. Francis Reid, *I Was in Noah's Ark*, p. 58.
8. Harris G. Warren, *Special Operations: AAF Aid to European Resistance Movements 1943–1945*, pp. 8, 9.

CHAPTER 9

1. Edgar McGinnis, *The War: Fourth Year*. London: 1944.
2. Harris G. Warren, *Special Operations: AAF Aid to European Resistance Movements 1943–1945*, p. 8.
3. Monro MacCloskey, *Secret Air Missions*, p. 13.
4. Warren, *op. cit.*, pp. 32–37.
5. MacCloskey, *op. cit.*, pp. 22–25.
6. Ibid., p. 27.
7. Ibid., p. 28.
8. Warren, *op. cit.*, pp. 22–26.
9. Ibid., p. 22.
10. Ibid., p. 166 n. 42.
11. Ibid., p. 166 n. 37.
12. Ibid., p. 167 n. 43.
13. MacCloskey, *op. cit.*, p. 29.
14. Ibid., p. 29.
15. Warren, *op. cit.* pp. 52–55.
16. Ibid., p. 194 n. 48.
17. Ibid., pp. 125, 126.
18. Vladimir, Dedijer, *Tito*, p. 217.
19. Warren, *op. cit.*, pp. 125, 126.

CHAPTER 10

1. John K. O'Doherty, "The Balkan Air Force." *The Airman*, November 1964.
2. Harris G. Warren, *Special Operations: AAF Aid to European Resistance Movements 1943–45*, pp. 124–126.
3. Ibid., p. 127.
4. O'Doherty, *op. cit.*
5. Warren, *op. cit.*, p. 23.
6. Vladimir Dedijer, *Tito*, pp. 214–216.
7. Ibid., p. 215.
8. Warren, *op. cit.*, p. 117, 118.
9. Ibid., p. 30.
10. D.M. Condit, *Case Study in Guerrilla War: Greece During World War II*, p. 86.
11. Ibid., p. 86.
12. Basil Davidson, *Partisan Picture*, p. 104n.
13. Dedijer, *op. cit.*, p. 202.
14. Author's 1944 observations.

CHAPTER 11

1. William R. Peers and Dean Brelis, *Behind the Burma Road*, p. 84.
2. Ibid., p. 123.
3. Ibid., p. 132.
4. Ibid., p. 173.
5. Lee Bowen, et al., *USAF Airborne Operations World War II–Korean War*, p. 34.
6. Ibid., p. 35.
7. 60th Troop Carrier Group, Balkan Air Force. Historical Narrative "Story of Resupply." 1945.
8. Stanley Lovell, *Of Spies & Stratagems*, p. 8.
9. Ibid., pp. 40, 41.
10. Samuel A. Goudsmit, *Alsos*, p. 11.
11. Ibid., p. 38.

CHAPTER 12

1. Norman Lewis, *The Honored Society*, p. 8.
2. D. M. Condit, *Case Study in Guerrilla War: Greece During World War II*, pp. 58, 59.
3. Lewis, *op. cit.*, pp. 10, 11.
4. Ibid.
5. Stanley Lovell, *Of Spies and Stratagems*, p. 114.
6. Charles F. Delzell, *Mussolini's Enemies*, p. 309, 310.
7. Ibid.
8. Howard Mc. Smythe, *United States Army in World War II: Sicily and the Surrender of Italy*, Ch. 7.
9. Delzell, *op. cit.*, p. 256.
10. Samuel Eliot Morison, *History of U.S. Naval Operations in World War II: Sicily-Salerno-Anzio*, p. 241.

CHAPTER 13

1. OSS R&A Report No. 2993, "The Contributions of the Italian Partisans to the Allied War Effort," March 31, 1945.
2. Stanley Lovell, *Of Spies and Stratagems*, p. 115.
3. Ibid., p. 120.
4. Peter Tompkins, *A Spy in Rome*, p. 7–14.
5. Ibid., p. 53.
6. Sanche de Gramont, *The Secret War*, p. 127.

7. David Kahn, *The Code-Breakers*, p. 508.
8. Florimond Duke, with Charles M. Swaart, *Name, Rank and Serial Number*, p. 3–5.
9. Ibid., p. 43.
10. Arthur S. Gould Lee, *Special Duties*, p. 240.

CHAPTER 14

1. Jozef Garlinski, *Poland, SOE and the Allies*.
2. Steve J. Catlos and Kenneth V. Dunlevy, "Operational History of the American Military Mission to the Czechoslovak Forces of the Interior," written by two of the five survivors of three OSS missions sent to Slovakia. May 1945. 46 pages.
3. Ibid. Also, author's subsequent interview with John Schwartz in 1965.
4. Catlos and Dunlevy, *op. cit.* Also, author's interviews with Catlos and Dunlevy, 1965.
5. Ibid.

CHAPTER 15

1. Steve J. Catlos and Kenneth V. Dunlevy, "Operational History of the American Military Mission to the Czechoslovak Forces of the Interior."

CHAPTER 16

1. Author's interview with John Schwartz in 1965.
2. Edward Hymoff, "The OSS Revolt that Failed." *Saga*, April 1965.
3. Ibid.
4. Richard M. Kelly, "Torture Preferred," *Bluebook*, June 1946.
5. Alfred C. Ulmer, Jr., "The Gulliver Mission," *Bluebook*, April 1946.
6. Ibid.

CHAPTER 17

1. OSS R&A Report No. 1999, "The Belgian Underground," August 19, 1944.
2. Ibid.

3. Gordon A. Harrison, *U.S. Army In World War II, European Theater of Operations: Cross Channel Attack,* p. 204.
4. Ibid., p. 204.
5. Ibid., p. 202.
6. E.H. Cookridge, *Set Europe Ablaze,* p. 98.
7. M.R.D. Foot, *SOE in France,* p. 222n.
8. Harrison, *op. cit.,* p. 202.
9. Ibid., p. 203.
10. Foot, *op. cit.,* p. 33.
11. Ibid., p. 357.
12. Arthur Widder, *Adventures in Black,* p. 101.
13. Stewart Alsop and Thomas Braden, *Sub Rosa,* p. 143.
14. Ibid., p. 148.
15. Roger Hall, *You're Stepping on My Cloak and Dagger,* pp. 165, 166.

CHAPTER 18

1. John H. Van Vliet, "The Massacre at Katyn," *Argosy,* December, 1962, written in collaboration with the author.
2. Ibid.
3. Winston S. Churchill, *The Second World War: Triumph and Tragedy,* vol. VI, pp. 129, 130.
4. Ibid.
5. U.S. Congress, House, Select Committee on Communist Aggression, Polish Documents Report, Appendix, December 31, 1954. Document No. 60, p. 88.
6. Churchill, op. cit., p. 130.
7. Jozef Garlinski, *Poland, SOE and the Allies,* p. 184.
8. Churchill, *op. cit.,* p. 130.
9. Garlinski, *op. cit.,* p. 188.
10. Churchill, *op. cit.,* p. 130. Prime Minister's cable to Stalin of August 4, 1944.
11. M.R.D. Foot, *SOE in France,* p. 400.
12. U.S. Congress, House, *op. cit.,* Document No. 67, p. 99.
13. Harris G. Warren, *Special Operations: AAF Aid to European Resistance Movements 1943–45,* pp. 76, 77.
14. Churchill, *op. cit.,* p. 145.
15. Arthur Campbell, *Guerrillas: A History and Analysis,* London: 1967, p. 113.
16. D.M. Condit, *Case Study in Guerrilla War: Greece During World War II,* p. 169.
17. Ibid., p. 4.
18. Campbell, *op. cit.,* p. 113.

19. W. Byford-Jones, *The Greek Trilogy: Resistance— Liberation—Revolution*, p. 93.
20. Ibid., p. 94.
21. Ibid., p. 95.
22. Condit, *op. cit.*, p. 177.
23. Author's conversations in Italy in 1944 with members of OSS OG teams that had returned from Greece.

CHAPTER 19

1. Norman Lewis, *The Honored Society*, p. 11.
2. William R. Peers and Dean Brelis, *Behind the Burma Road*, p. 69.
3. Harold S. Quigley, *Far Eastern War 1937–1941*, p. 192.
4. Nicol Smith and Blake Clark, *Into Siam, Underground Kingdom*, p. 91.
5. Ibid., p. 199.
6. Ibid., p. 228.
7. OSS R&A Current Intelligence Study No. 4, "Japanese Seizure of French Indochina," March 30, 1945.
8. Smith and Clark, *op. cit.*, p. 74.
9. R&A Intelligence Study No. 4, *op. cit.*
10. Chester L. Cooper, *The Lost Crusade*, 1970, p. 25.
11. Ibid., p. 525 n4.
12. Bernard B. Fall, *The Two Viet-Nams*, p. 100.
13. Denis Warner, *The Last Confucian*, p. 208.
14. Ibid., p. 47.
15. Robert Shaplen, *The Lost Revolution: Vietnam 1945–65*, p. 30.
16. Fall, *op. cit.*, p. 41n.
17. Cooper, *op. cit.*, p. 40.
18. Shaplen, *op. cit.*, p. 41.
19. Ellen J. Hammer, *The Struggle for Indochina*, p. 130n.
20. Cooper, *op. cit.*, p. 40.
21. Arthur J. Dommen, *Conflict in Laos*, p. 322.
22. Ibid., p. 26.
23. Hammer, *op. cit.*, p. 118, and Warner, *op. cit.*, p. 50.
24. New York *Herald Tribune*, April 3, 1961.
25. Ibid.
26. Fred Hoffman, Associated Press Report A87WX, April 4, 1961, from AP's Pentagon Correspondent.

CHAPTER 20

1. Andrew Molnar et al., *Undergrounds in Insurgent, Revolutionary and Resistance Warfare*, p. 214.
2. Ibid., p. 215.
3. Ibid., p. 63.
4. Jozef Garlinski, *Poland, SOE and the Allies*, p. 238.
5. Monro MacCloskey, *Secret Air Missions*, p. 117.
6. Florimond Duke, *Name, Rank and Serial Number*, p. 149.
7. Molnar, *op. cit.*, p. 241.
8. Ibid., p. 223.
9. Ibid., p. 227.
10. Walter R. Mansfield, "Marine With the Chetniks," *The Marine Corps Gazette*, February 1946. This was the second of two articles about Captain Mansfield's experiences with the Chetniks. He wrote a third article in MCG about his experiences in China.
11. Ibid.
12. Author's interview with Congressman Blatnik in Washington, D.C., September, 1965.
13. OSS R&A Study, "Development of German Pattern of Occupation," Report No. 1756, January 27, 1944.
14. Roger Hall, *You're Stepping on My Cloak and Dagger*, p. 193.
15. Ibid., p. 195.
16. Harris G. Warren, *Special Operations: AAF Aid to European Resistance Movements 1943–45*, p. 65.
17. E.H. Cookridge, *Set Europe Ablaze*, p. 346.
18. Stewart Alsop and Thomas Braden, *Sub Rosa*, p. 125; and Hall, *op. cit.*, p. 207.

CHAPTER 21

1. M.R.D. Foot, *SOE in France*, p. 260.
2. E.H. Cookridge, *Set Europe Ablaze*, p. 154.
3. Foot, *op. cit.*, p. 371.
4. Ibid., p. 73.
5. Ibid., p. 392.
6. Ibid., p. 393.
7. Ibid., p. 394.
8. Ibid., p. 390.
9. Roger Hall, *You're Stepping on My Cloak and Dagger*, p. 170.

10. Harris G. Warren, *Special Operations: AAF Aid to European Resistance Movements 1943–45*, p. 115.
11. Information about Brunner and Sweeny obtained from U.S. Marine Corps archives, Washington, D.C.
12. Benis M. Frank and Henry I. Shaw, Jr., *Victory and Occupation: History of U.S. Marine Corps Operations in World War II*, Vol. V, Historical Branch, G–3 Division, Headquarters, U.S. Marine Corps, Washington, D.C. 1968. p. 747.
13. Ibid. p. 747.
14. Ibid. p. 747n.
15. Ibid. p. 748.
16. Ibid. p. 749.
17. Allen W. Dulles, *The Secret Surrender*, pp. 24, 25.
18. Richard W. Rowan, with Robert G. Deindorfer, *Secret Service: 33 Centuries of Espionage*, p. 624.
19. Dulles, *op. cit.*, p. 68.
20. Ibid., pp. 120, 143, 144.
21. Ibid., pp. 190, 191.
22. Ibid., pp. 216, 217.
23. Charles F. Delzell, *Mussolini's Enemies*, pp. 536–538.
24. Ibid., pp. 540, 542, 542n.
25. OSS R&A Current Intelligence Study Number 18, "Political Results of the Liberation of Northern Italy," May 11, 1945.
26. OSS R&A "Concentration Camps in Germany," Report No. 1844, October 3, 1944.
27. Ibid.
28. John Toland, *The Last 100 Days*, p. 376.

CHAPTER 22

1. Allen W. Dulles, *The Secret Surrender*, pp. 23, 24.
2. OSS R&A "South Germany: An Analysis of the Political and Social Organization, the Communications, Economic Controls, Agriculture and Food Supply, Mineral Resources, Manufacturing and Transportation Facilities of South Germany," Report No. 232, September 22, 1944.
3. Ibid.
4. Rodney G. Minot, *The Fortress That Never Was*, p. 26.
5. Ibid., pp. 54, 55.
6. Ibid., p. 150.
7. Walter R. Mansfield, "Ambush in China," *Marine Corps Gazette*, December 1945.
8. Ibid.

9. Ibid.
10. Ibid.
11. Ibid.
12. Paul M.A. Linebarger, *Psychological Warfare,* pp. 187, 189.
13. OSS R&A Current Intelligence Study Number 19, "Japan: Winter 1944–1945," May 18, 1945.
14. OSS R&A Current Intelligence Study Number 31, "Japan's 'Secret' Weapon: Suicide," July 20, 1945.
15. Ibid.
16. Ibid.
17. Ibid.

CHAPTER 23

1. Corey Ford, *Donovan of OSS,* pp. 302, 340–342.
2. Ibid., p. 302.
3. Hanson Baldwin, *The Price of Power,* p. 205.
4. Harry Howe Ransom, *The Intelligence Establishment,* p. 70; Richard Kelly, "The Norso Mission," *Bluebook,* February, 1947; and Ford, *op. cit.,* respectively.
5. Ransom, *op. cit.,* p. 70.
6. Charles F. Delzell, *Mussolini's Enemies,* p. 306.
7. Roger Hall, *You're Stepping on My Cloak and Dagger,* p. 216.
8. Ransom, *op. cit.,* p. 78.
9. Ibid., p. 73.

CHAPTER 24

1. Interviews with Geoffrey M. T. Jones, President, Veterans of the OSS, in October 1985, and March and June 1986, New York City.
2. Monro MacCloskey, *Secret Air Missions,* p. 22.
3. Jones, personal memoir, "The Liberation of the French Riviera, The 'Champagne Campaign' of the First Airborne Task Force," May 1980.
4. *The Champagne Campaign,* p. 72.
5. Ibid, p. 131.
6. Ibid, p. 133.
7. Ibid, p. 146.

CHAPTER 25

1. U.S. Army Legion of Merit Citation, March 30, 1946, presentation ceremony of medal to Major Tofte by General Donovan.
2. Interviews with Tofte in October 1981 and June 1986, Gilbertsville, N.Y.
3. Tofte's unpublished memoirs, written in 1958.
4. Ibid.
5. Tofte diary written in Cairo, Egypt, April 1944, while awaiting courtmartial.
6. Tofte was awarded the Order of Merit to the People of Yugoslavia upon instructions from Marshal Tito. Letter Yugoslav Embassy, Washington, D.C. to Major Tofte from Dr. Sergije Makiedo, Chargé d'Affaires, February 4, 1946.

     In 1947, King Frederick IX of Denmark knighted Sir Hans V. Tofte for his military service in the SOE and OSS, and that same year King Haakon VII of Norway presented Tofte with the Norwegian Freedom Cross.
7. Tofte's last OSS assignment following the sea lift operation was a posting to OSS headquarters in London as second in command to George Pratt, a civilian OSS official who specialized in labor issues. Pratt's assignment, under Lieutenant Commander Casey, was to make contact with labor leaders in occupied territory as part of the plan to send in OSS agents to Europe and inside Germany. Tofte joined the CIA when it was created and had a distinguished career in many parts of the world, later becoming head of covert operations until his retirement.

EPILOGUE

1. David Wise and Thomas B. Ross, *The Invisible Government,* p. 95.
2. Ibid., p. 96.
3. Author's research in 1965 based upon observations and experiences with UNPFK during the Korean War.
4. Ibid.
5. Allen W. Dulles, *The Craft of Intelligence.*
6. Author's interviews with U.S. Military special operations (MACSOG) people in Vietnam and Thailand at different times during the period 1966–69.
7. Author's Korean War research and experience.
8. Military History Detachment. *UN Partisan Forces in the Korean Conflict 1951–1952.* Far East United

States Army Force, Eighth U.S. Army (EUSAK), 285 p., illustrations, supporting documents. Typescript unpublished manuscript. Classification SECRET. A study of the 8086 Army Unit and the characteristics and operations of partisan forces.

9. Author's interview with Lieut. General Chae Myung Shin, commanding general of all Republic of Korea forces in South Vietnam, at his headquarters in Saigon, June 13, 1968.

10. Lyman B. Kirkpatrick, Jr., *The Real CIA*, p. 237.

11. Neil Sheehan et al., *The Pentagon Papers*, Bantam Books, N.Y. 1971, p. 55.

Bibliography

BOOKS

Alsop, Stewart, and Braden, Thomas. *Sub Rosa: The OSS and American Espionage*. New York: Reynal and Hitchcock, 1946.

Baldwin, Hanson. *The Price of Power*. New York: Harper, 1947.

Bowen, Lee, et al. *USAF Airborne Operations: World War II and the Korean War*. Washington, D.C.: USAF Historical Division Liaison Office, 1962.

Byford-Jones, W. *The Greek Trilogy: Resistance—Liberation—Revolution*. London: Hutcheson & Company, Ltd., 1946.

Churchill, Winston S. *The Second World War: Triumph and Tragedy*. Vol. VI. Boston: Houghton Mifflin Company, 1953.

Condit, D.M. *Case Study in Guerrilla War: Greece During World War II*. Washington, D.C.: Special Operations Research Office (U.S. Army), American University, 1961.

Cookridge, E.H. *Set Europe Ablaze*. New York: Thomas Y. Crowell Company, 1966.

Cooper, Chester L. *The Lost Crusade*. New York: Dodd, Mead & Company, 1970.

Davidson, Basil. *Partisan Picture*. Bedford (England): Bedford Books, Ltd., 1946.

Dedijer, Vladimir. *Tito*. New York: Simon & Schuster, 1953.

de Gramont, Sanche. *The Secret War*. New York: G.P. Putnam's Sons, 1962.

Delzell, Charles F. *Mussolini's Enemies: The Italian Anti-*

Fascist Resistance. Princeton, N.J.: Princeton University Press, 1961.

Dommen, Arthur J. *Conflict in Laos.* New York: Praeger Publishers, 1971.

Duke, Florimond, with Charles M. Swaart. *Name, Rank and Serial Number.* New York: Meredith Press, 1969.

Dulles, Allen W. *The Craft of Intelligence.* New York: Harper & Row, 1963.

——*The Secret Surrender.* New York: Harper & Row, 1966.

Depuy, R. Ernest, and Dupuy, Trevor N. *The Encyclopedia of Military History.* New York: Harper & Row, 1970.

Esposito, Vincent J., ed. *The West Point Atlas of American Wars.* Vol. II. New York: Frederick A. Praeger, 1959.

Fall, Bernard B. *The Two Vietnams.* New York: Frederick A. Praeger, 1967.

Foot, M.R.D. *SOE in France.* London: Her Majesty's Stationery Office, 1966.

Ford, Corey. *Donovan of OSS.* Boston: Little, Brown & Company, 1970.

——and MacBain, Alastair. *Cloak and Dagger.* New York: Random House, 1945.

Goudsmit, Samuel A. *ALSOS.* New York: Henry Schuman, Inc., 1947.

Garlinski, Jozef. *Poland, SOE and the Allies.* London: George Allen and Unwin, Ltd., 1969.

Hall, Roger, *You're Stepping on My Cloak and Dagger.* New York: W.W. Norton & Company, 1957.

Hammer, Ellen J. *The Struggle for Indochina.* Stanford, Calif.: Stanford University Press, 1954.

Harrison, Gordon A. *U.S. Army in World War II, European Theater of Operations: Cross Channel Attack.* Washington, D.C.: Office of the Chief of Military History, U.S. Army, 1962.

Heilbrunn, Otto. *Partisan Warfare.* New York: Frederick A. Praeger, 1962.

Hyde, H. Montgomery. *Room 3606.* London: Mayflower-Dell Books, 1964.

Kahn, David. *The Code-Breakers.* New York: The Macmillan Company, 1963.

Kirkpatrick, Lyman B., Jr. *The Real CIA.* New York: The Macmillan Company, 1968.

Lee, Arthur S. Gould. *Special Duties*. London: Sampson Low, Marston Company, Ltd., 1946.

Lewis, Norman. *The Honored Society*. New York: G.P. Putnam's Sons, 1964.

Linebarger, Paul M.A. *Psychological Warfare*. Washington, D.C.: Infantry Journal Press, 1948.

Lovell, Stanley. *Of Spies and Stratagems*. Englewood Cliffs, N.J.: Prentice-Hall, Inc., 1963.

MacCloskey, Monro. *Secret Air Missions*. New York: Richards Rosen Press, 1966.

Minott, Rodney G. *The Fortress that Never Was*. New York: Holt, Rinehart & Winston, 1964.

Molnar, Andrew et al. *Undergrounds in Insurgent, Revolutionary and Resistance Warfare*. Washington, D.C.: Special Operations Research Office (U.S. Army), American University, 1963.

Morison, Samuel Eliot. *History of U.S. Naval Operations in World War II: Sicily-Salerno-Anzio*. Vol. IX. Boston: Little, Brown & Company, 1954.

OSS Assessment Staff. *Assessment of Men: Selections of Personnel for the OSS*. New York: Rinehart & Company, Inc., 1948.

Peers, William R., and Brelis, Dean. *Behind the Burma Road*. Boston: Little, Brown & Company, 1963.

Quigley, Harold S. *Far Eastern War 1937–41*. Boston: World Peace Foundation, 1943.

Shaplen, Robert. *The Lost Revolution: Vietnam 1945–65*. London: Andre Deutsch, 1966.

Sheehan, Neil, et al. *The Pentagon Papers*, New York: Bantam Books, 1971.

Smith, Nicol, and Clark, Blake. *Into Siam, Underground Kingdom*. Indianapolis: The Bobbs-Merrill Company, 1945.

Smythe, Howard Mc. *U.S. Army in World War II: Sicily and the Surrender of Italy*. Washington, D.C.: U.S. Government Printing Office, 1962.

Ransom, Harry Howe. *The Intelligence Establishment*. Cambridge, Mass.: Harvard University Press, 1970.

Reid, Francis. *I Was in Noah's Ark*. London: W. & R. Chambers, Ltd., 1957.

Rowan, Richard W., with Robert G. Diendorfer. *Secret Service: 33 Centuries of Espionage*. New York: Hawthorn Books, 1967.

Toland, John. *The Last 100 Days.* New York: Random House, 1965.

Tompkins, Peter. *A Spy in Rome.* New York: Simon & Schuster, 1962.

Warner, Denis. *The Last Confucian.* London: Angus & Robertson, 1964.

Widder, Arthur. *Adventures in Black.* New York: Harper & Row, 1962.

Willoughby, Charles A., and Chamberlain, John. *MacArthur 1941–1951.* New York: McGraw-Hill, 1954.

Wise, David, and Ross, Thomas B. *The Invisible Government,* New York: Random House, 1964.

DOCUMENTS

Obtained from the Rare Books Collection, Library of Congress, Washington, D.C.

U.S. Congress, House, Select Committee on Communist Aggression, Polish Documents Report. Appendix, December 31, 1954. Document No. 60, p. 88.

OSS R&A, Current Intelligence Study Number 4, *Japanese Seizure of French Indochina,* March 30, 1945.

——Current Intelligence Study Number 18, *Political Results of the Liberation of Northern Italy,* May 11, 1945.

——Current Intelligence Study Number 19, *Japan: Winter 1944–1945,* May 18, 1945.

——Current Intelligence Study Number 31, *Japan's 'Secret' Weapon: Suicide,* July 20, 1945.

——Report Number 232, September 22, 1944, *South Germany: An Analysis of the Political and Social Organization, the Communications, Economic Controls, Agriculture and Food Supply, Mineral Resources, Manufacturing and Transportation Facilities.*

——Report Number 1756, January 27, 1944, *Development of German Pattern of Occupation.*

——Report Number 1844, October 3, 1944, *Concentration Camps in Germany.*

——Report Number 1999, August 19, 1944, *The Belgian Underground.*

——Report Number 2229, June 15, 1944, *Burma: Enemy Shipping October 1943–April 1944.*

————Report Number 2993, March 31, 1945, *The Contributions of the Italian Partisans to the Allied War Effort.*

Warren, Harris G. *Special Operations: AAF Aid to European Resistance Movements 1943–45.* Washington, D.C.: USAAF Air Historical Office, 1947. Unpublished manuscript declassified from SECRET.

PERIODICALS AND JOURNALS

Grandlin, Thomas, "The Political Use of Radio," *Geneva Studies*, vol. X, No. 3, August 1939.

Grell, William F., "A Marine with OSS," *The Marine Corps Gazette*, December 1945.

Hymoff, Edward, "The OSS Revolt that Failed," *Saga*, April 1965.

Kelly, Richard M., "Behind the Enemy Lines," *Bluebook*, January 1946.

————"He Never Stopped Trying," *Bluebook*, September 1946.

————"JEDBURGH Mission Hamish," *Bluebook*, July 1946.

————"Mission to Greece," *Bluebook*, November 1946.

————"Operation Aztec," *Bluebook*, May 1946.

————"Secret Agents at Anzio," *Bluebook*, December 1948.

————"The Halyard Mission," *Bluebook*, August 1946.

————"The Norso Mission," *Bluebook*, February, 1947.

————"The Burma Mission," *Bluebook*, June 1947.

————"Torture Preferred," *Bluebook*, June 1946.

————"With the Greek Underground," *Bluebook*, July 1947.

Mansfield, Walter R., "Ambush in China," *The Marine Corps Gazette*, March 1946.

————"Marine with the Chetniks," *The Marine Corps Gazette*, January and February 1946.

O'Doherty, John K., "The Balkan Air Force," *The Airman*, November 1964.

Ulmer, Alfred C., Jr., "The Gulliver Mission," *Bluebook*, April 1946.

Van Vliet, John H., "The Massacre at Katyn," *Argosy*, December 1962.

Index